Agent-Oriented Software Engineering

Onn Shehory • Arnon Sturm
Editors

Agent-Oriented Software Engineering

Reflections on Architectures, Methodologies, Languages, and Frameworks

Editors
Onn Shehory
IBM Haifa Research Laboratory
Haifa
Israel

Arnon Sturm
Ben-Gurion University of the Negev
Beer-Sheva
Israel

ISBN 978-3-662-52279-0 ISBN 978-3-642-54432-3 (eBook)
DOI 10.1007/978-3-642-54432-3
Springer Berlin Heidelberg New York Dordrecht London

Printed on acid-free paper

Springer is part of Springer Science+Business Media (www.springer.com)

Foreword

In the late 1960s, computing practitioners began to realize that the rapid developments in computer hardware—making computers cheaper, faster, smaller, and more reliable—were not being matched by comparable developments in software. On the contrary, it was realized that developing correct, efficient, reliable software was *much* harder than had been generally anticipated. The situation was brought into crisp focus by a stream of high-profile (and highly expensive) software project failures. The term "software crisis" was coined to describe this dismal state of affairs, and thus was born the discipline of software engineering. Describing the software development process as "engineering" made plain the aspirations of the new discipline. The idea was that, ultimately, software development should be an engineering discipline as robust and well understood as other engineering disciplines. Thus, building a large software system should be no more challenging than a civil engineering project such as building a bridge: complex, certainly, but manageable and predictable nonetheless. Of course, things haven't quite turned out that way, or at least not yet. In the 45 years since the software crisis, we have, for sure, learned a huge amount about the nature of software and software development, and the everyday software applications we take for granted would surely be regarded as miraculous by the early software engineering pioneers. But this undoubted success masks a disappointing truth: software remains hard to develop, and software project failures are far from uncommon. Poorly designed, poorly implemented, and error-prone software is all too common. The discipline of software engineering thus remains as relevant and central to computer science as it was in 1970.

Contemporary software engineering encompasses a wide range of computational paradigms: procedural programming, object-oriented programming, service-oriented programming, aspect-oriented programming, functional programming, logic programming, and so on. Each different paradigm encourages us to think about computation in a different way, and each comes with its own collection of models and development techniques and its own design aesthetic. Logic programming, for example, promotes the idea of computation as automated deduction, while service-oriented computing adopts the idea of programs as service providers. The multi-agent systems research domain, which emerged largely as a subfield of artificial intelligence in the 1990s, is concerned with building computer systems that can effectively cooperate with each other, and in the 1990s, a number of researchers, myself included, began to think about agents as a software engineering paradigm. If the banner carried by the logic programming community carries the slogan "computation as deduction," then the banner carried by the multi-agent systems community might read "computation as cooperation," or perhaps "computation as interaction." Adopting an agent-oriented view of software engineering implies conceptualizing computer systems as consisting of collections of interacting (semi)autonomous agents: the agents are seen as acting independently in pursuit of goals delegated to them by users. The arguments in support of an agent-oriented software engineering viewpoint are well known, and I won't rehash them here: for me, the key point is that the most natural way of conceptualizing certain systems is as societies of interacting, semiautonomous agents. Indeed, in a system where control is inherently distributed over multiple stakeholders with potentially competing interests, it is hard to imagine any other reasonable conceptualization. If you accept this, then what follows is the paradigm of agent-oriented software engineering.

If we hope to put agent-oriented software engineering on a par with other software engineering paradigms, then there are a whole raft of issues we need to address. First, and most fundamentally, we need to develop the right conceptual toolkit: What are the key concepts in agent-oriented software engineering that we use in the analysis and design of systems? These concepts will then underpin methodologies for the analysis and design of multi-agent systems, programming languages and development platforms for building and deploying systems, and so on. There have been substantial developments in all of these areas since agent-oriented software engineering was first mooted in the 1990s.

The present volume is a state-of-the-art collection of chapters on agent-oriented software engineering. The chapters presented herein address all the issues that I mentioned above, from methodologies to programming languages and development platforms. While this volume does not mark the end of the story of agent-oriented software development, it does, I think, represent an important milestone in the history of the field and will surely prompt much future research and development.

Oxford, UK
Spring 2014

Michael Wooldridge

Preface

Agent-based systems have evolved significantly during the last two decades. The development of such systems involves, among others, artificial intelligence, distributed systems, and software engineering. In this book, we focus on the software engineering facet of agent-based systems, namely, Agent-Oriented Software Engineering (AOSE). In particular, the book consists of a collection of state-of-the-art studies in the AOSE domain. The chapters are organized in five parts: Part I introduces the AOSE domain; Part II refers to the general aspects of AOSE; Part III deals with AOSE methodologies; Part IV addresses agent-oriented programming languages; and finally Part V presents studies related to the implementation of agents and multi-agent systems.

Part I Introduction

This part includes Chaps. 1, 2, and 3 and introduces AOSE as detailed below.

Chapter 1 introduces the notion of software agents with an emphasis on core design and engineering aspects. It elaborates on agent properties and dimensions, emphasizing the novel concepts and abstractions introduced by agent-based systems to software systems' design and implementation.

In Chap. 2, we attempt at defining what AOSE is, make the case for its emergence, and review its evolution throughout the years. We also provide insights into the current status of the AOSE domain and point out future research directions.

Chapter 3, written by Jörg Müller and Klaus Fischer, examines the practical application of multi-agent systems and technologies. The examination is based on a comprehensive survey of MAS deployments and checks the maturity, ownership, application domains, programming languages, and platforms of these deployments. The chapter concludes that MAS applications have been successfully deployed in a significant number of applications and were found to be useful in various market sectors.

Part II Aspects of Agent-Oriented Software Engineering

This part includes Chaps. 4, 5, and 6 and discusses the general aspects of AOSE.

In Chap. 4, we discuss the notion of multi-agent architectures and address the merits of agents and multi-agent systems as a software architecture style.

Chapter 5, written by Joanna Juziuk, Danny Weyns, and Tom Holvoet, provides a review of the usage of design patterns that are related to MAS. Overall, the authors found that although many patterns exist, these are not well documented, organized, and linked. Thus, the authors provide guidelines for the required efforts in order to increase the usage of such patterns.

Chapter 6, written by Marc-Philippe Huget, overviews the landscape of MAS communication as a major means for applying MAS. In particular, the chapter discusses agent communication languages, ontologies, protocols, dialogue games, argumentation systems, and multiparty communication.

Part III Agent-Oriented Software Engineering Methodologies

This part includes Chaps. 7, 8, 9, and 10 and introduces AOSE methodologies.

In Chap. 7, we discuss agent-oriented methodologies, their desired characteristics, and the extent to which they address these properties. In addition, we review research efforts related to AOSE methodologies.

In Chap. 8, written by Lin Padgham, John Thangarajah, and Michael Winikoff, the authors discuss Prometheus, a well-established and widely used methodology. In particular, they stress the importance of testing within the development of MAS and the challenges that exist in this respect.

In Chap. 9, written by Scott DeLoach, the need for practical, industrial strength of agent-oriented methodologies is emphasized. In this respect, the chapter introduces a customizable methodology that can be adapted and extended for a wide variety of uses.

In Chap. 10, by Jorge Gomez-Sanz, the evolution of INGENIAS (a MAS methodology) is described. In particular, the chapter emphasizes the engineering aspect of designing the methodology and its supporting tools.

Part IV Agent-Oriented Programming Languages

This part includes Chaps. 11, 12, and 13 and presents agent-oriented programming languages.

In Chap. 11, by Mehdi Dastani, a survey of the multi-agent programming research field is presented. In particular, it defines the concepts and abstractions used in multi-agent systems and the way these are integrated into the agent programming languages and frameworks.

Chapter 12, by Koen Hindriks and Jürgen Dix, introduces a BDI-based MAS programming language that incorporates SE principles. The chapter also demonstrates the use of the language and its success within an exploration game.

Chapter 13, by Olivier Boissier, Rafael Bordini, Jomi Hübner, and Alessandro Ricci, introduces JaCaMo, a platform for multi-agent-oriented programming that incorporates abstractions related to agents, organizations, and environments, which are essential parts of MASs.

Part V Multi-agent Systems Implementation

This part includes Chaps. 14, 15, and 16 and focuses on multi-agent implementation.

In Chap. 14, we survey MAS platforms and frameworks that facilitate MAS implementation. We introduce the reader to a variety of tools and analyze their suitability for MAS implementation needs. The analysis reveals that although many tools were developed over the years, only a few of those are continually being used; it has also become apparent that the evaluations of these tools are rather limited.

Chapter 15, by Renato Levy and Goutam Satapathy, discusses design considerations of very large agent-based systems as applied to an energy distribution use case. They further explore the nuances of the implementation of this use case in CybelePro—an agent infrastructure—and stress the importance of verifying the properties of such systems.

Chapter 16, by Benny Lutati, Inna Gontmakher, Michael Lando, Arnon Netzer, Amnon Meisels, and Alon Grubshtein, introduces a framework for agent-oriented programming for distributed constraint reasoning. The framework facilitates the programming of such agents, the simulation of such systems, and the evaluation of the system's performance.

In this book, we aim to expose the reader to various facets of AOSE. We therefore provide a collection of state-of-the-art studies in this field. We believe that the studies in this book are of interest to researchers, practitioners, and students who are interested in exploring the agent paradigm for developing software systems. We note that although many research efforts have been made in this area, there are many open issues and challenges that need to be addressed and explored.

Beer-Sheva, Israel — Arnon Sturm
Haifa, Israel — Onn Shehory

Contents

Contributors

Olivier Boissier EMSE, St. Etienne, France

Rafael H. Bordini FACIN-PUCRS, Porto Alegre – RS, Brazil

Mehdi Dastani Institute of Information and Computing Sciences, Utrecht University, Utrecht, The Netherlands

Scott A. DeLoach Kansas State University, Manhattan, KS, USA

Jürgen Dix Clausthal University of Technology, Clausthal-Zellerfeld, Germany

Klaus Fischer DFKI GmbH, Saarbrücken, Germany

Jorge J. Gomez-Sanz Facultad de Informática, Universidad Complutense de Madrid, Madrid, Spain

Inna Gontmakher Department of Computer Science, Ben-Gurion University of the Negev, Beer-Sheva, Israel

Alon Grubshtein Department of Computer Science, Ben-Gurion University of the Negev, Beer-Sheva, Israel

Koen V. Hindriks Delft University of Technology, Delft, The Netherlands

Tom Holvoet Department of Computer Science, Katholieke Universiteit Leuven, Leuven, Belgium

Jomi F. Hübner DAS-UFSC, Florianópolis – SC, Brazil

Marc-Philippe Huget LISTIC/Polytech Annecy-Chambéry, Université de Savoie, Chambéry, France

Joanna Juziuk Department of Computer Science, Linnaeus University, Växjö, Sweden

Michael Lando Department of Computer Science, Ben-Gurion University of the Negev, Beer-Sheva, Israel

Renato Levy Intelligent Automation, Inc., Rockville, MD, USA

Benny Lutati Department of Computer Science, Ben-Gurion University of the Negev, Beer-Sheva, Israel

Amnon Meisels Department of Computer Science, Ben-Gurion University of the Negev, Beer-Sheva, Israel

Jörg P. Müller Department of Informatics, TU Clausthal, Clausthal-Zellerfeld, Germany

Arnon Netzer Department of Computer Science, Ben-Gurion University of the Negev, Beer-Sheva, Israel

Lin Padgham RMIT University, Melbourne, VIC, Australia

Alessandro Ricci University of Bologna, Cesena, Italy

Goutam Satapathy Intelligent Automation, Inc., Rockville, MD, USA

Onn Shehory IBM Haifa Research Lab, Haifa, Israel

Arnon Sturm Department of Information Systems Engineering, Ben-Gurion University of the Negev, Beer-Sheva, Israel

John Thangarajah RMIT University, Melbourne, VIC, Australia

Danny Weyns Department of Computer Science, Linnaeus University, Växjö, Sweden

Michael Winikoff University of Otago, Dunedin, New Zealand

Part I
Introduction

Chapter 1
A Brief Introduction to Agents

Onn Shehory and Arnon Sturm

Abstract Agents and multi-agent systems (MAS) are a branch of Artificial Intelligence (AI) that attempts to combine AI, distributed system, and software engineering in a single discipline. For more than three decades, agents and MAS have been studied, implemented, and evaluated. Significant research and practice efforts were invested in moving agents from science to engineering and from labs to the field. To facilitate engineering, the agent-oriented software engineering community has produced methods, methodologies, and tools in support of agent and MAS development. The Foundation for Intelligent Physical Agents (FIPA) organization has delivered specifications and standards. Agent programming languages have flourished. These are all vehicles that aim to facilitate development and deployment of agents and MAS in practice.

Agents and MAS introduce concepts and abstractions of which the combination provides a novel approach to software systems design and implementation. In this chapter, we introduce the fundamentals of agents.

Keywords Agent • Multi-agent system • Autonomy • Intelligence • Sociality • Mobility

O. Shehory (✉)
IBM—Haifa Research Lab, Haifa, Israel
e-mail: onn@il.ibm.com

A. Sturm
Department of Information Systems Engineering, Ben-Gurion University of the Negev, Beer-Sheva, Israel
e-mail: sturm@bgu.ac.il

O. Shehory and A. Sturm (eds.), *Agent-Oriented Software Engineering*, DOI 10.1007/978-3-642-54432-3_1, © Springer-Verlag Berlin Heidelberg 2014

1 Introduction

Computer programs commonly exhibit limited flexibility in their ability to handle unforeseen events and environmental conditions. That is, they can only act upon events and conditions they were designed for, and they do so only in the ways they were programmed to react upon those events. In many domains, such rigidity and program behavior address well the application requirements. For instance, a warehouse inventory management application needs to process only predefined inventory conditions and events. However, there are application domains in which rigidity of this type may negatively affect system behavior and even deem the system impractical. For example, an unmanned vehicle may face a variety of unanticipated conditions, e.g., changes in road shape and obstacle distribution. These may require new maneuvers and planning for which the vehicle was not pre-programmed. In light of the growing need for computer systems that can cope with dynamic, unpredictable environments, and to cope with ever more networked and distributed computing environments, agent-based systems have evolved, comprising software agents of various types and designs. In this chapter, we introduce such agents and agent-based systems.

A software agent is a software entity that performs tasks on behalf of another entity, be it a software, a hardware, or a human entity. This is a widely agreed-upon interpretation of the term agent in the context of software systems. This however leaves much freedom for further classification of agents. Common dimensions according to which such classification may be performed are autonomy and intelligence. That is, one may examine whether an agent is autonomous in its activity and whether its computation and actions exhibit intelligence.

With such dimensions in mind, an agent in its basic form is neither autonomous nor intelligent. For example, it may perform pre-defined tasks such as data collection and transmission as in the case of Simple Network Management Protocol (SNMP) agents [11] (which are used for network management). The fact that the tasks are pre-defined leaves little freedom of action; hence, the agent's autonomy is rather limited. The fact that the agent merely collects and transmits data leaves no room for intelligent manipulation; hence, the agent needs no intelligence.

Following these dimensions, more sophisticated agents may exhibit either autonomy or intelligence, or both. For example, Belief, Desire, Intention (BDI) agents [2] are agents that are equipped with software layers specifically designed for intelligent reasoning and action. They maintain and manipulate plans and plan-relevant data and then execute their preferred plans to meet their goals. Such intelligent behavior is based on concepts such as belief, desire, intention, and goal, all of which are implemented as software artifacts within the agents. Thus, BDI agents exhibit both intelligence and autonomy.

Another important dimension of agenthood is sociality. Sociality refers to the ability of an agent to engage in meaningful interaction and collaboration with other agents and non-agent entities. For instance, an agent may need to execute a task that can be performed only in a collaborative manner. To collaborate, an agent must be able to communicate with, and understand, other agents. It may also need to negotiate, coordinate, and share resources. In some cases, agents may need to take part in a larger system comprised of multiple agents, referred to as a multi-agent system.

To facilitate the development of agents that exhibit such dimensions (and others), it is necessary to specify the dimensions, the underlying concepts, and the software constructs needed. In this chapter, we aim to briefly introduce these.

2 Dimensions of Agenthood

There are many dimensions of agenthood. Yet, there is no single set of dimensions that is widely agreed upon as the fundamental set for defining agents. Nevertheless, we refer here to a core set that we find central to the definition and the development of software agents. These include autonomy, intelligence, sociality, and mobility, on which we elaborate in the following.

2.1 Autonomy

Autonomy appears among the most important and distinctive agent properties. Autonomy refers to the ability of an agent to perform unsupervised computation and action and to pursue its goals without being explicitly programmed or instructed for doing so. Autonomy further refers to the encapsulation of data and functionality within the agent. This aspect of autonomy is however also present in objects as defined in object-oriented paradigms and is therefore not unique to agents. An autonomous agent is assumed to have full control of its internal state and its behaviors. To enable such autonomy, an agent's blueprint should consist of components that support autonomy.

An important autonomy-enabling component is an *internal state* module. Such an internal state usually holds and maintains the state of the agent in its environment as perceived and interpreted by the agent itself. For example, an agent may believe that its physical location is at some (x, y) coordinate in a plane. Regardless of this being its true location, its internal state should hold that information and update it as the agent finds suit. An internal state of this sort facilitates autonomy as it allows the agent to act upon its state without being in need for external supervision. An internal state is also important for implementing artificial intelligence capabilities within the agent, as we discuss later in this chapter.

Agents additionally exhibit autonomy by implementing *behaviors*. A behavior is usually an activity which is comprised of more than one elementary action. It is commonly assumed to be initiated and controlled by the agent itself, without external instruction. Some behaviors may be iterative or continuous, while others are exercised in a one-shot fashion. Regardless, behaviors allow an agent to pursue its goals in an autonomous manner.

In many cases, autonomy is also associated with pro-activeness. An agent may react upon internal and external states and events—in which case it is reactive. However, it may also initiate actions, e.g., in anticipation of states and events. In the latter case, it is proactive. Re-activeness and pro-activeness may co-exist in the same agent. Both may be present in an autonomous agent. Yet, pro-activeness is more commonly associated with autonomy because it exhibits agent behavior, which is seen as independent of direct external triggers. As such, pro-activeness indeed suggests a higher level of agent autonomy.

Other agent autonomy enablers and indicators exist too; however, one can build an autonomous agent based on the properties referred to above. To do so, the architectural properties of the agent should include an internal state, behaviors, and means for pro-activeness. Agent architectures indeed include such constructs.

2.2 Intelligence

Software agents need not be intelligent; however, intelligence and agenthood are frequently associated with one another. Indeed, the notion of intelligent agents is used not only in agent-based systems but in general artificial intelligence as well. The motivation for associating agenthood and intelligence likely originates from the agent having to act on behalf of another. In many cases, such action necessitates intelligence. Therefore, commonly, intelligent agents are those that reason about serving others and act accordingly.

Intelligence was never simple to define, and the task does not become easier when moving to artificial intelligence. This chapter has no intention to define these notions; however, it aims to present some of the major elements associated with, and enabling, the incorporation of intelligent reasoning and behavior into software agents. Such elements in turn entail architectural and engineering requirements that are of much interest to this book.

Agent intelligence may require capabilities such as learning, reasoning, planning, and decision making. These should in turn allow an agent to make educated decisions and to behave rationally. These should also allow it to be goal-oriented. That is, an agent can have abstract goals for whose achievement it may make plans, reason about its plan alternatives, decide rationally upon the best one, and act accordingly. The results of its action can serve as feedback for learning, to improve future reasoning and action and to better meet its goals.

To facilitate such capabilities, an agent may need some specialized software constructs. Several architectural approaches have been devised in support of agent intelligence. The BDI approach, mentioned earlier, includes a beliefs component that holds facts that are believed to be true by the agent. It also includes plans that

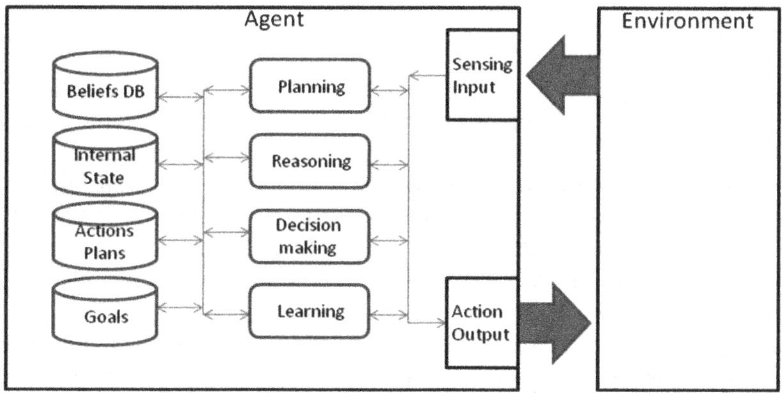

Fig. 1.1 Intelligence-enabling software constructs within an agent architecture

the agent builds and can manipulate (referred to as desires in the BDI approach). For this, plan segments and planning facility are required. It further requires a mechanism for plan selection. This is typically a filtering, refinement, and eventually decision-making mechanism, which allows the agent to select a single, preferred plan of action (which is referred to as an intention). BDI is merely an example out of a flora of goal-based, intelligent agents.

From an architectural viewpoint, goal-based agents commonly implement an architecture similar to the one in Fig. 1.1. As shown in that figure, the agent interacts with the environment by receiving sensor (or other) input and acting on the environment via actuators. The inputs are stored in a persistent internal data store, e.g., a beliefs database (DB), which includes facts about the environment. The agent may hold a set of actions or plan fragments from which it can construct plans. It commonly also implements some reasoning component which is used for making decisions about preferred plans and actions and for updating the facts in the beliefs DB. Reasoning may rely on, e.g., a rule base, an inference system, a decision tree, and many other alternatives. A goal-based agent usually implements an internal state module (see also autonomy, above). This is a data store, which may be part of the facts (or beliefs) DB. Goals are usually also stored and serve for planning and decision making. In some intelligent agents, a learning component is also present.

Note that the specific details of each component and the interaction among the components need further architectural refinement, which may have significant effect on the functionality and efficiency of the agent. Details of specific internal agent architectures are widely present in the art, including textbooks such as [3, 4].

Further note that intelligent and goal-based agents commonly reside in a multi-agent environment, where they need to interact intelligently to meet their goals. In Fig. 1.1 we have not included software constructs that explicitly support such interaction.

2.3 Sociality

In many cases, an agent is situated in a multi-agent environment. To meet its goals, the agent may need to interact with other agents and coordinate, collaborate, or compete with them. For instance, an agent may need to form a team to perform a rescue task in a disaster recovery mission. To facilitate such capabilities, the architecture of the agent should include sociality-supporting constructs. At the infrastructural level, communication is required. A communication component should allow message sending, receiving, and processing. It should also support specific communication languages, message formats, and protocols (e.g., FIPA ACL and protocols [5]). Message parsing and understanding is also a fundamental need for any meaningful communication. Chapter 6 provides more details on agent communication.

In addition to communication, meaningful interaction with other agents commonly necessitates that an agent maintain models of other agents or at least hold some data regarding them, e.g., their contact information, capabilities, and possibly logs of past interaction with them. That is, the architecture of the agent should include models of both self and other agents. The reasoning component should include means for reasoning about others and about the interaction with them. Similar extensions are also needed to the planning, decision-making, and learning modules. That is, shared plans [6], joint decision making, and multi-agent adaptation and learning [7] should be supported.

Further capabilities may be required to facilitate social behaviors. For instance, mechanisms for collaboration, for team and coalition formation [8, 9], and for strategic behavior in competitive scenarios all enable sociality. An example of a need for such a mechanism is the case where an agent needs to buy some goods on behalf of a human user and a discount schedule is available, which is based on the number of items purchased. In such a case, it may be beneficial for the agent to form a buyers' group to obtain a discount. To this end, a proper mechanism, and strategies to behave given that mechanism, are needed. Software constructs that support comprehension of, and participation in, such mechanisms are needed as part of a socially capable agent.

Agents that interact with others in a competitive environment may need to negotiate and possibly use strategies and argumentation as part of this negotiation. Hence, they should be equipped with negotiation and argumentation modules to facilitate such capabilities. There are myriad ways to implement such modules and the details are out of the scope of this chapter. A prominent reference to agent negotiation and interaction is the book *Rules of Encounter* [10].

2.4 Mobility

Some agents and multi-agent systems exhibit mobility. That is, agents may be able to change their logical or physical location. One way of mobility manifestation is for the agent to move from its current execution environment (the host on which it runs) to another execution environment. Another incarnation of mobility is found in cases where agents reside on mobile devices such as smartphones. In such cases, even if the agent never leaves its host, the hosting device itself may roam, thus changing location and environmental conditions. As a result, the agent that executes on the device roams and changes its environmental conditions as well. Both types of mobility require that agents be designed for mobility and be equipped with the proper software artifacts to manage it.

Mobility in which agents move from one execution environment to another typically requires more infrastructure than other types of agent mobility. We therefore discuss it (briefly) here. An agent that moves to another host (either physical or logical) needs to record its state before moving, generate a copy of itself on the target host, stop its execution on the source host, and resume execution on the target. A special set of mobility behaviors should hence be incorporated in an agent that needs to execute mobility. Yet, it is not sufficient that the agent itself is equipped with mobility constructs. There is a need for the hosts on which mobile agents can execute to have some mobility-supporting infrastructure such as a docking station. The latter is an execution environment that provides the mobile agent with the resources it needs for execution, yet guards the target host from overexploitation and attacks.

Additional aspects of agent mobility are discussed in Chap. 4 of this book.

2.5 Other Dimensions

There are plenty of other agent properties that affect their engineering. As stated earlier, we have no intention to cover all of them. An important property of some agents is their ability to adapt to changes in goals and in environmental conditions. Adaptation is indeed considered a dimension of agenthood; however, in many cases, it does not necessitate a special adaptation module. For instance, adaptation may be addressed by learning, planning, and reasoning capabilities.

Another aspect of agenthood is the interaction of agents with human users. Since in many cases agents perform tasks on behalf of human users, the quality of the interaction with the human is of much importance. This interaction must be supported by human–computer interaction components, and indeed many agents implement such components. Human–computer interaction is a broad field of research and practice that spans beyond agents, multi-agent systems, and AI. We leave this for the reader to explore.

Agents can have a physical body, such as in the case of robots. The physical properties of agents introduce an array of requirements that are not present in software agents. These are well addressed in the field of robotics. Again, we refer the reader to that field for further details.

Some other aspects such as agent emotions [1] and self-awareness, agent security, agent resource and quality management, and others introduce yet another set of software components that can be incorporated into agents. It is important to note however that seldom agent designers and developers incorporate all, or even a large portion, of all of the dimensions introduced here, let alone those which were not presented in this chapter.

3 Concluding Notes

As presented in this chapter, there are many dimensions that characterize agents and affect agent design, implementation, and engineering in general. One may have noticed that across our discussion we incorporated very little details on the engineering needs of multi-agent systems. This comes for a reason. In Chap. 4 of this book, we introduce agent architectures. In that chapter, we focus on architectures of multi-agent systems. To facilitate the discussion there, multiple aspects of MAS are presented and elaborated upon. We believe that via those details we cover well all major MAS dimensions needed for engineering such systems. In fact, we include virtually no discussion of single-agent architectures in Chap. 4. Again, this is done because in the current chapter we put much focus on single agents and their engineering needs.

As discussed here, the core dimensions of agenthood are autonomy, intelligence, and sociality, while other aspects, though important, are not those defining agents and distinguishing them from other software entities. We however stress that full-fledged software agents should inevitably include software constructs that support multiple agent dimensions to address well both functional and non-functional requirements commonly set for intelligent software agents.

References

1. Dastani M, Meyer JJC (2006) Programming agents with emotions. In: Proceedings of ECAI 2006, pp 215–219
2. Rao AS, Georgeff MP (1995) BDI-agents: from theory to practice. In: Proceeding of the first international conference on multiagent systaems (ICMAS'95), pp 312–319
3. Weiss G (ed) (2013) Multiagent systems, 2nd edn. MIT Press, Cambridge, MA
4. Jennings NR, Wooldridge MJ (eds) (1998) Agent technology: foundations, applications and markets. Springer, Heidelberg
5. FIPA (2005) FIPA specification, http://www.fipa.org/specifications/index.html (last access January 2014)
6. Grosz BJ, Kraus S (1996) Collaborative plans for complex group action. Art Intel 86(2):269–357
7. Panait L, Luke S (2005) Cooperative multiagent learning: the state of the art. Auton Agents MultiAgent Syst 11(3):387–434
8. Shehory O, Kraus S (1998) Methods for task allocation via agent coalition formation. Art Intel 101(1–2):165–200

9. Tambe M (1997) Agent architectures for flexible, practical teamwork. In: Proceedings of the 14th national conference on artificial intelligence (AAAI-97), pp 22–28
10. Rosenschein JS, Zlotkin G (1994) Rules of encounter. MIT Press, Cambridge, MA
11. Harrington D, Presuhn R, Wijnen B (2002) An architecture for describing simple network management protocol (SNMP) management frameworks http://tools.ietf.org/html/rfc3411

Chapter 2
Agent-Oriented Software Engineering: Revisiting the State of the Art

Arnon Sturm and Onn Shehory

Abstract The field of Agent-Oriented Software Engineering (AOSE), which has evolved during the last two decades, attempts at introducing artificial intelligence concepts into the practice of software engineering. Despite considerable progress, it seems that the challenges the field encountered at its early days still hold. In particular, the adoption of AOSE principles in the academia, and even more so in the industry, is limited. This chapter aims to specify what AOSE is, to determine the related research areas, to examine historical perspectives of AOSE evolution, and to analyze its progress and point out challenges and future research directions.

Keywords Multi-agent systems • Agent-oriented software engineering • Survey • Adoption

1 Introduction

Agent-oriented software engineering (AOSE) entails the application of software engineering and artificial intelligence principles to the analysis, design, and implementation of software systems. Among the founders of the AOSE field are Nick Jennings and Mike Wooldridge who, via a series of seminal papers [1–5], introduced concepts and foundations for the domain. The intention at that time was to recruit Artificial Intelligence (AI) for the purpose of Software Engineering (SE), and in particular for building distributed complex systems.

A. Sturm (✉)
Department of Information Systems Engineering, Ben-Gurion University of the Negev, Beer-Sheva, Israel
e-mail: sturm@bgu.ac.il

O. Shehory
IBM—Haifa Research Lab, Haifa, Israel
e-mail: onn@il.ibm.com

O. Shehory and A. Sturm (eds.), *Agent-Oriented Software Engineering*,
DOI 10.1007/978-3-642-54432-3_2,

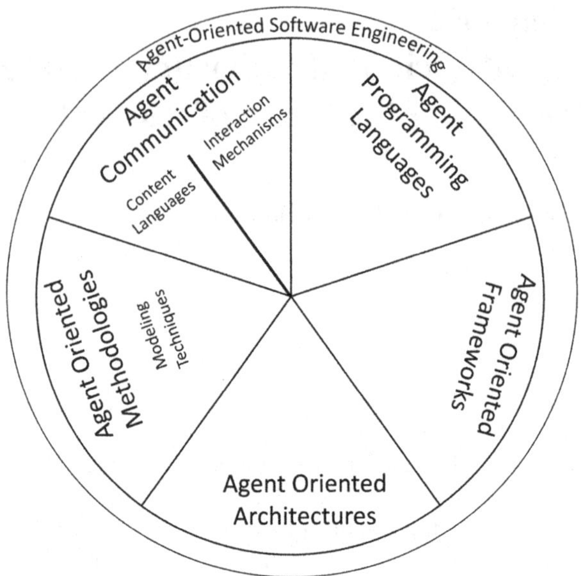

Fig. 2.1 Agent-oriented software engineering thematic map

Agent-based systems focus on dynamically interacting components. Each of these components has its own thread of control, and is engaged in complex coordination protocols. The emphasis is on the *interaction* of the components more than on the internals of the components themselves [1]. Agent-oriented software engineering is interpreted in two different ways. The first aims to support the development of agent-based system, whereas the second is more revolutionary and aims to support the development of complex systems where the notion of agent is being used. While it appears that the AOSE community made considerable progress towards the first, the second has not advanced much. This is stressed by Ricci and Santi [6] as well.

During the last two decades, the AOSE field has evolved to address many subjects. At present, the field includes the following high-level themes: methodologies, modeling techniques, framework implementations, agent-programming languages, and agent communication. The field's thematic map is depicted in Fig. 2.1.

This book provides a comprehensive view of the AOSE field and of the themes it comprises. This chapter merely aims to provide an overview of the research areas within the AOSE domain, focusing on progress and on challenges to be met. It also takes a historical perspective, examining the academic evolution of AOSE and pointing at future research. In the next section, we elaborate on the themes covered by the domain. Following, we take a historical viewpoint: we analyze surveys and overview papers discussing the AOSE domain to better understand its evolution. Finally, we conclude and point at voids and research challenges.

2 AOSE Themes

In this section, we elaborate on the aforementioned AOSE themes. This should facilitate the introduction of research questions and challenges the AOSE domain aims to address. We do not aim at providing a comprehensive list of topics, rather to reflect the type of research and development involved in the domain.

The AOSE paradigm is relatively new. As such, its establishment requires further considerations as we discuss below.

- A crisp definition of the agent notion and its most important properties is not yet fully agreed upon. There is much agreement on agent properties such as autonomy, dependability, and robustness; however, several other properties are not at consensus. Thus, the determination of the core set of agenthood properties is clearly a challenge.
- To promote AOSE adoption, there is a need to clarify how agent-based solutions facilitate complexity management in software engineering. The context and trade-offs of using the AOSE technology and paradigm require further deliberations.
- As a new discipline, the organizational implication of using AOSE should be carefully examined. In this respect, studies may take various viewpoints including technological, psychological, organizational, etc.
- Through its evolution, many alternative AOSE technologies were developed. To facilitate industrial adoption of AOSE, standardization is required. Indeed, standardization efforts of multi-agent systems are ongoing within working groups in FIPA, IEEE, and OMG. Nevertheless, these are progressing in low pace.
- There is a need to explore ways to integrate multi-agent and mainstream technologies to further increase agent technology usability and adoption.

2.1 Applications

There is an ongoing search for the types of applications for which agents are an adequate, valuable development approach. Below we list fields for which the agent-oriented paradigm was studied or examined, or is considered promising. We split the list into agent-oriented sub-list, which refers to the way in which agent technology is weaved in with other technologies and domain-oriented sub-list, which refers to application domains in which agents were found useful.

The agent-oriented fields consist of the following:

- Agent-based grid computing
- Agents and services—alignment of agents with service-oriented software development
- Agents for self-adaptive systems

- Integration of agent-oriented software into existing business processes and implications on business process reengineering
- Integration of agents with legacy systems
- Multi-agent-based simulation

The domain-oriented fields consist of the following:

- Self-organizing systems
- Social engineering
- Electronic commerce
- Tourism services
- Games

The chapter 3 of this book refers to applications and their impact on the agent technology.

2.2 *Agent-Oriented Architectures*

Multi-agent systems (MAS) can be considered as a new architecture style. Such architectures may offer diverse ways for developing MAS applications and frameworks. They may also suggest new ways for developing other types of large, complex software systems. The subfield of agent-oriented architecture studies, and likely needs to further explore, the following topics:

- New and adjusted software architectures for multi-agent systems
- The desired properties for such architectures, and the trade-offs among the architectures
- Reuse of agent-based systems design knowledge, patterns, and reference architectures

The chapter 4 of this book elaborates on issues related to software architectures of agents and MAS.

2.3 *Agent Communication*

An important aspect of agents is their ability to communicate. Communication can be exercised in many different ways. In the art, agent communication has been addressed from various viewpoints such as performance, scalability, reliability, security, and privacy. Various levels of abstraction also affect the focus of communication studies. As a result, multiple topics related to agent communication are found in research and practice, including the following:

- Agent Communication Languages (ACLs) including semantics and pragmatics
- Argumentation

- Commitments in communication
- Communication infrastructure
- Conversation
- Conversational agents
- Coordination and cooperation
- Dialogue games
- Human-agent communication
- Integration of interaction protocols within agents
- Interoperability
- Multiparty conversations
- Natural language processing application to communication
- Negotiation
- Ontologies and communication
- Reuse in communication

The chapter 6 further elaborates on agent communication.

2.4 Agent-Oriented Methodologies

Agent-oriented methodologies are a main research theme within the field of AOSE. It focuses on the development processes of multi-agent systems as well as the techniques to be applied in that context. It mainly covers the analysis and design stages within the development life cycle. Clearly, there is a need to further study other stages, including requirements, implementation, and testing. Topics related to agent-oriented methodologies are:

- Agent-oriented modeling techniques of various types (such as goal-oriented, BDI, etc.)
- Agents and model-driven approaches
- CASE tools to support agent-oriented software development in practice
- Evaluation and comparison of modeling techniques and methodologies

Part III of this book further elaborates on these issues.

2.5 Agent Programming Languages

Agent programming languages were an important step towards the adoption of the agent abstraction for software development [7]. One of the main ideas of agent programming languages is to introduce the notion of mentality (of agents) into the programming environment. Following this idea, research in the area addresses various topics including:

- Type of programming languages:
  - (Constraint) logic programming approaches to agent systems
  - Declarative approaches to engineering agent-based systems
  - Domain/purpose specific languages
- Applications of multi-agent programming languages including: legacy systems, pervasive applications, multi-robot systems, autonomous software (e.g., UAVs), (Semantic) Web and Grid-based applications, and deployed (industrial-strength) multi-agent systems
- Benchmarks and test-beds for comparing multi-agent programming languages and tools
- Evaluation of agent programming approaches including experiments and industrial experiences
- Verification of agent-based software
- Modal and epistemic logics for agent modeling
- Model checking agents and multi-agent systems

Part IV of the book further elaborates on these aspects.

2.6 Agent-Oriented Frameworks

Over the years, as agent technology evolved, there was a need to develop software tools and frameworks to accommodate the execution and development of such systems. Some software tools include frameworks to develop individual agents whereas others aim at MAS development. Many of these tools are open source in the sense that they are freely available to use and allow extensions. The majority of these frameworks was developed by the academia, and only a few were devised by the industry. This opens a new venue for applied research. Research questions addressed in this domain include the following:

- What should be the services included in agent-oriented frameworks?
- What are the required building blocks?
- How can such frameworks benefit from other evolving technologies?

The chapter 14 further elaborates on these agent-oriented frameworks, infrastructure, and platforms.

3 AOSE Surveys Analysis

Having explored major topics within the AOSE domain, in this section we review AOSE surveys performed over the years. From these, we extract (our subjective) observations of the domain and its evolution and perform a chronological review to demonstrate the evolution of the field over time. Note that the observations we mention in this chapter are only those which are relevant to AOSE.

3.1 Agent-Oriented Software Engineering: The State of the Art (2001) [8]

In this study, the authors refer to AOSE as a means for managing software complexity, and examine the developed techniques. They focus on two issues: agent-oriented analysis and design and formal methods. In the context of agent-oriented analysis and design, they explore AOSE methodologies and have the following observations:

- AOSE methodologies can be classified as either Object-Oriented or Knowledge Engineering approaches. They suggest that the object-oriented approach dominates the area by either extending or adapting object-oriented methodologies.
- Following that observation they claim that the object-oriented approach is lacking in capturing most of the agent characteristics such as proactiveness and dynamic reaction. This led them to require further clarification regarding the relationship between objects and agents. In addition, they make an analogy to the object-oriented paradigm in which (according to an extreme approach) everything is an object and raise the question of whether everything should be an agent.

In the context of formal methods they assert the following challenges:

- Being used for specification, formal methods (such as BDI logic [9]) lack in their semantics. They assume that agents are perfect reasoners—which is not the case for real agents. Hence, their mapping of BDI elements into computational entities does not fully meet the capabilities of real agents.
- The survey refers to three implementation alternatives: (1) manual implementation through refinement; this is error-prone and a complex task; (2) a direct execution approach (such as Metatem [10]); this requires following a specific way of implementation; and (3) translation/compilation approach (such as in [11]), in which the code is automatically created from the specification language.
- The survey has identified two verification approaches: (1) the axiomatic approach in which one could take a specific program and systematically derive a logical theory (such an approach could be found in Hoare logic [12]); and (2) Model checking, which is more effective, yet hinders the problem of converting a program into a BDI logic.

In general, the issues that still need to be addressed by formal logic are complexity, decidability, and semantics.

In that survey, the authors also state challenges to be addressed. These include the following:

- The understanding of relationships to other paradigms
- The need for devising appropriate methodologies
- The need to address engineering for open systems
- The need to address engineering for scalability

3.2 A Manifesto for Agent Technology: Towards Next Generation Computing (2004) [13]

As part of their leadership of the AgentLink network of excellence [14], Luck et al. [13] published a comprehensive manifesto for agent technology. In that paper, they address various aspects of agents among which is the domain of AOSE. In the following, we summarize their observations at that time (2004) and their estimations and long-term vision of the field:

- Within the area of AOSE, the authors claim that the main focus in on analysis and design and on programming languages. They stress that the development of these methods is at the prototype stage and evaluations of these have been done in an ad hoc manner rather than in a systematic way.
- The authors assert that agent architectures focus on reactive and deliberative ones, and suggest that, at that time, agent-based solutions were tailor-made and not general ones based on generic architectures.
- When referring to communication language, the authors refer to KQML [15] and FIPA ACL [16] as the two main major languages. They suggest that, although both are well-developed, they do not address human and organization communication.
- Discussing applications, the authors mentioned many domains in which agents are being used. However, the use of AOSE within the development of these applications is neglected (both by the survey and the related publications).
- Referring to industrial interest, the authors report on many companies that employ agent-based research and development activities.
- The survey suggests several future AOSE challenges as follows:
  - Further develop AOSE methodologies
  - Provide developers with libraries of agent models
  - Improve tool support
  - Integrate existing and emerging technologies into agent development
  - Further develop the notion of open systems

3.3 *Challenges and Research Directions in Agent-Oriented Software Engineering (2004) [17]*

Zambonelli and Omicini [17] present AOSE as a new software engineering paradigm, which may contribute to various types of system engineering:

- First, they introduce AOSE as a novel approach to software engineering, which relies on the concept of an agent as its main new abstraction, encompassing properties such as autonomy, situatedness, and sociality. They consider the environment to be an important part of designing the system. They also make the distinction between objects and agents, where objects are statically connected and agents dynamically interact. They make the observation that other technologies such as components and active objects do progress towards agenthood.
- Second, they stress that agent properties address well-distributed systems' engineering needs.
- Third, they indicate the potential of using AOSE to promote artificial intelligence research from theory to practice.

Since AOSE is a new paradigm, Zambonelli and Omicini suggested that mainstream research should continue with the direction of agent modeling, MAS architectures, MAS methodologies, notation techniques, and MAS infrastructure, in order to increase the acceptance and the usability of AOSE. They divided the (other) research directions into three scales of observation: micro, macro, and meso, which differ in system size. In the following we summarize their observations:

- At the micro scale, there is a need
  - To assess the advantages of agents in software engineering
  - To explore nonstandard and extreme development processes
  - For novel modeling techniques (to address agent abstractions and needs)
  - For further exploration of formal methods
  - To further stress the interweaving of AI into AOSE
- At the macro scale, there is a need
  - To look for measurements for MAS in the macro scale, e.g., entropy [18] and coordination [19]
  - For general-purpose techniques to understand and control macro-level behavior
  - To devise a common model for different types of natural systems, to allow the comparison of such mechanisms
- At the meso scale, there is a need
  - To find ways of defining system boundaries
  - To find ways to formalize nonformalized phenomena
  - To adopt trust mechanisms

– To identify ways to empower social intelligence, as intelligence cannot be understood from a single agent or system

3.4 Moving Multi-agent systems from Research to Practice (2009) [20]

DeLoach [20] identified three main obstacles in adopting MAS for practical development:

- The lack of common interpretations of MAS concepts. This relates to two aspects: (1) no agreement on the concepts that constitute MAS and their interrelations; thus, DeLoach calls for reaching an agreement on these. (2) some of these concepts are too complex. For instance, some concepts are based on the BDI approach, which is more complex than the object-oriented approach. DeLoach further suggests to focus on the usefulness of AOSE and not on its agenthood properties.
- The lack of common notation and models. In that sense DeLoach calls for adopting common notation and models to allow for easy comparison among methods. He, however, suggests to avoiding formal standardization at this stage, as the AOSE community may need more time for its technologies to mature.
- The lack of industry acceptance of AOSE methodologies. DeLoach explains it by the lack of flexibility the AOSE methodologies introduce. Thus, he suggests to adopt the method engineering approach.

3.5 Future Directions for Agent-Based Software Engineering (2009) [21]

Winikoff [21] stated that there is a limited number of well-developed methodologies which have tool support and are used in various case studies. Nevertheless, their usefulness has not been proven yet, and there is a need for quantitative proofs rather high-level and abstract arguments. Thus, he suggested to act in various directions:

- Identifying the "value-added" of adopting agent technology
- Documenting case-studies
- Making other scientific communities such as service-oriented commuting, the grid, and autonomic computing, aware of the achievement made within the AOSE domain
- Developing useful tools to support the real users
- Understanding the problems in real settings

From the research point of view, Winikoff suggests to explore the following:

- From the foundation point of view, to examine the notion of goals and to further weave it with other important concepts such as interaction and organization
- From the engineering point of view, to further understand and develop the validation and verification aspects

3.6 Challenges and Directions for Engineering Multi-agent systems (2012) [22]

Later on, Winikoff [22] revised his observations, suggesting that there are many areas in which the agent paradigm was implemented and that some quantitative results were produced too. He also stressed that educational resources (e.g., books and tools) have become available as well. Having analyzed the industry involvement and adoption of agent technology, he found out that industrial interest in agent technology has declined. Thus, he suggested to reengage with the industry. Following the analysis performed by Dignum and Dignum [23] indicating that in agent-based projects AOSE techniques were used to a limited extent, he suggested to stop designing programming languages and methodologies, but rather to look at techniques that weave the micro and the macro aspects of such systems. In addition, he suggested to develop the thread of MAS assurance.

3.7 Engineering Multi-agent systems (2012) [24]

In 2012, a Dagstuhl seminar on the engineering of multi-agent systems was held [24]. The seminar's goal was to establish a roadmap for the AOSE domain. Thirty-seven leading researchers, mostly from the academia, participated and contributed. The seminar covered many aspects of agent-oriented software engineering. The observations produced in that seminar can be found in [25]. Following, we present the most relevant ones within the context of this book:

- With respect to verification of MAS, Natasha Alechina sets the following challenges: (1) Addressing scalability issues in model checking; (2) Addressing human agents; (3) Specifying systems at the right level of abstraction for the purpose of model checking; and (4) Dealing with undecidable situations.
- Rem Collier, based on his experience in developing an agent-based framework and in teaching MAS courses, stated that the agent community does not provide enough resources in order to support MAS development, and there is no good evidence that demonstrates the supremacy of agent technology. Thus, there is a need to develop better tools for debugging and testing as well as metrics

for evaluating the technology (and alternatives). These observations were also supported by Jeremy Baxter.

- Birna Van Riemsdijk suggested that there is a lack in evaluating various techniques and there is a need to employ empirical approaches that are based on data to demonstrate the usability of agent-based approaches. This was also reinforced by Tom Holvoet who concluded that there is a need for thorough evaluation and guarantees.
- Many of the participants agreed that the advances made within the domain of AOSE had a limited effect on communities other than the AOSE community. Tom Holvoet pointed out that the reason for low impact is that AOSE is 90 % software engineering and only 10 % MAS. As such, it is preferable that AOSE results are communicated to other relevant communities. Another important aspect that he referred to was real-world applications. He asserted that we need to further collaborate with the industry on this, as also mentioned by Jörg P. Müller and Amal El Fallah Seghrouchni. Christian Guttmann furthered that direction and stressed that there is a need to clearly point out the advantages of agent technology in order for the industry to adopt the agent notion.

In the following, we attempt to summarize the surveys discussed above and other publications made in that area. First, it seems that agent communication has gained much attention and has evolved continuously. This evolution includes various research directions, such as protocols, dialogs, and conversation mechanisms. The area of agent-oriented methodologies and programming languages received major attention in the early days of the AOSE field. In recent years, the pace of progress was much slower. This may suggest that there is a need to further explore this area. The same holds for the area of frameworks and architectures: in early AOSE times many frameworks, platforms, and architectures were devised; later on many of these became obsolete; nowadays only a few are active. From the research point of view, little innovation has been proposed in that area in recent years, although support tools and improved interfaces were provided. The area of AOSE adoption has advanced rather little over the years. It seems that the notion of agent-oriented software engineering is not well accepted within the industry. Although, various organizations, companies, and applications use the term agent, it is aimed at its weak notion of independent components, neglecting the strong notion of agenthood that includes autonomy, proactiveness, etc. Moreover, the engineering aspect is also hardly adopted by the industry, and AOSE methodologies and programming languages are rarely used.

4 Concluding Remarks

Agent-Oriented Software Engineering exists for almost 20 years. Its main purpose was to introduce Artificial Intelligence to Software Engineering and to suggest a new abstraction level in which agents play a major role. The domain has evolved to encompass a wide range topics including formal specification and validation, programming languages, development methodologies, software engineering techniques, architectures and infrastructure, communications, and applications as well.

Despite the depth and breadth of research in the field, it seems that agent-based systems, and in particular AOSE, did not find their way to the industry. One of the main reasons for this is that the benefits of multi-agent systems have not been demonstrated, needless to say proved. We can say that instead of introducing AI to SE, SE was introduced to AI, and enabled its refreshment by establishing ways for implementing various theoretical AI approaches.

To address AOSE challenges and in particular the acceptance and adoption challenge, there is a need to clearly state for what purposes and under what conditions is the agent abstraction is better than alternative software engineering approaches. To this end, it could be useful to develop or adopt a set of metrics to measure the contribution of a specific approach to the industry. These metrics may include technical aspects, organizational aspects, financial aspects, and so on. Using the metrics, a comprehensive study should be performed to allow evaluation of AOSE comparison with other SE alternatives. Such evaluation and comparison can foster the AOSE research as they may reveal new improvement and innovation opportunities.

References

1. Jennings NR (2000) On agent-based software engineering. Art Intel 117(2):277–296
2. Wooldridge M, Jennings NR (1995) Intelligent agents: theory and practice. Knowledge Eng Rev 10(2):115–152
3. Wooldridge M, Jennings NR (1998) Pitfalls of agent-oriented development. In: Proceedings of the 2nd international conference on autonomous agents. Minneapolis/St. Paul, MN, pp 385–391
4. Wooldridge M, Jennings NR (1999) Software engineering with agents: pitfalls and pratfalls. IEEE Internet Comput 3(3):20–27
5. Wooldridge M (1997) Agent-based software engineering. Proc IEE Software Eng 144(1):26–37
6. Ricci A, Santi A (2012) Agent-oriented computing: agents as a paradigm for computer programming and software development. Int J Adv Software 5(1 & 2):36–52
7. Shoham Y (1993) Agent oriented programming. J Art Intel 60:51–92
8. Wooldridge M, Ciancarini P (2001) Agent-oriented software engineering: the state of the art. In: Proceedings of the first international workshop on agent-oriented software engineering. Springer, New York
9. Wooldridge M (2000) Reasoning about rational agents. MIT Press, Cambridge, MA
10. Fisher M (1994) A survey of concurrent METATEM — the language and its applications. In: Gabbay DM, Ohlbach HJ (eds) Temporal logic — proceedings of the first international conference (LNAI volume 827). Springer, Berlin, pp 480–505
11. Rosenschein SJ, Kaelbling LP (1996) A situated view of representation and control. In: Agre PE, Rosenschein SJ (eds) Computational theories of interaction and agency. MIT Press, Cambridge, MA, pp 515–540
12. Hoare CAR (1969) An axiomatic basis for computer programming. Commun ACM 12(10):576–583

13. Luck M, McBurney P, Preist C (2004) A manifesto for agent technology: towards next generation computing. Auton Agents Multi-Agent Syst 9(3):203–252
14. AgentLink: http://www.agentlink.org. Last accessed August 2013
15. Finin T, Labrou Y, Mayfield J (1997) KQML as an agent communication language. In: Bradshaw J (ed) Software agents. MIT Press, Cambridge, MA, pp 291–316
16. FIPA: Agent Communication (2013) http://www.fipa.org/repository/aclspecs.html. Last accessed August 2013
17. Zambonelli F, Omicini A (2004) Challenges and research directions in agent-oriented software engineering. Auton Agents Multi-Agent Syst 9(3):253–283
18. Parunak HVD, Brueckner S (2001) Entropy and self-organization, in multi-agent systems. In: Proceedings of the 5th international conference on autonomous agents. ACM Press, Montreal (CA), pp 124–130
19. Roli A, Mamei M, Zambonelli F (2003) What can cellular automata tell us about the behaviour of large-scale agent systems. In: Proceedings of software engineering for large scale agent systems, LNCS 2603. Springer, Heidelberg, pp 216–231
20. DeLoach SA (2009) Moving multi-agent systems from research to practice. Int J Agent-Orient Software Eng 3(4):378–382
21. Winikoff M (2008) Future directions for agent-based software engineering. Int J Agent-Oriented Software Engineering 3(4):402–410
22. Winikoff M (2012) Challenges and directions for engineering multi-agent Systems. CoRRabs/1209.1428
23. Dignum V, Dignum F (2010) Designing agent systems: state of the practice. Int J Agent-Orient Software Eng 4(3):224–243
24. Dix J, Hindriks KV, Logan B, Wobcke W (2012) Engineering multi-agent systems. Dagstuhl Report 2(8):74–98
25. Dix J, Hindriks KV, Logan B, Wobcke W (2013) Engineering multi-agent systems, seminar 12342, http://www.dagstuhl.de/mat/index.en.phtml?12342. Last accessed August 2013

Chapter 3
Application Impact of Multi-agent Systems and Technologies: A Survey

Jörg P. Müller and Klaus Fischer

Abstract While there is ample evidence that Multi-agent Systems and Technologies (MAS&T) are vigorous as a research area, it is unclear what practical application impact this research area has accomplished to date. In this chapter, we describe methods and results of a survey aiming at a comprehensive and up-to-date overview of deployed examples of MAS&T. We collected and analyzed 152 applications, covering important perspectives, such as ownership, maturity, vertical sectors, and usage of programming languages and agent platforms. We conclude that MAS&T have been successfully deployed in a significant number of applications, though mostly in what could be called niche markets. Off the spotlights of mass markets and current funding buzzwords, it appears that MAS&T is useful for various sectors.

Keywords Application impact • Applications of agents and multi-agent systems

1 Introduction

Since its inception in the 1980s, multi-agent systems and technologies (MAS&T) research has established itself as a recognized field within Computer Science, reaching out into other areas including economics, sociology, and psychology. With successful conferences such as AAMAS [3], IAT [17], MATES [23], and PAAMS [29], and with journals such as JAAMAS[19], AAAI [1], AAIJ [2], and KER [20], there appears to be a stable community built around the questions

J.P. Müller (✉)
Department of Informatics, TU Clausthal, Clausthal-Zellerfeld, Germany
e-mail: joerg.mueller@tu-clausthal.de

K. Fischer
DFKI GmbH, Saarbrücken, Germany
e-mail: klaus.fischer@dfki.de

O. Shehory and A. Sturm (eds.), *Agent-Oriented Software Engineering*,
DOI 10.1007/978-3-642-54432-3_3, © Springer-Verlag Berlin Heidelberg 2014

of understanding and constructing large-scale open decentralized systems that consist of autonomous components or systems, endowed with properties such as proactiveness, reactiveness, and the ability of flexible social action to achieve their design goals.

In the period from the mid-1990s until the early 2000s, the MAS&T research field went through (we could also say: benefitted, or suffered from…) a phase of hype, characterized by glossy conferences with heavy involvement from companies ranging from Pixar and Disney to Siemens, Daimler, Motorola, and British Telecom, and by ample public funding both in America (most notably the DARPA programmes in agent communication (leading to KQML) and CoABS (Control of Agent Based System)) and in Europe (exemplified by the AgentLink network[1]) in Europe. In particular, AgentLink acted as an important dissemination channel toward industry, pushing the perception of *application impact* through the Agent Technology Conference series (held annually from 2002 until 2005) and through the AgentLink case studies featuring "real" applications of MAS&T.

However, since the mid-2000s, public perception of our research community appears to have become less prominent: Information and Communication Technologies (ICT) funding programmes were focusing on other labels, such as Service-Oriented Computing, Grid Computing, Autonomic Computing, or The Cloud; success stories in the software business, be it Apple, Facebook, Google, or SAP, have not been associated with MAS&T—at least not in the public perception.

Before this background, recently a perception among some MAS&T researchers appears to have formed—a perception that the field is lacking practical impact outside our own research community. The question driving this research activity has been to gain information and insights as to the extent to which this is true or not. We wish to study the application-oriented impact our research area has reached today.

There are some studies investigating agent applications, but we did not find any up-to-date work on the application *impact* of MAS&T, that is, the force of impression in the sense of being routinely and productively used in industrial, commercial, or public contexts. An obvious starting point for related work are the AgentLink case studies [4, 6]. While they did investigate a good selection of promising applications, they came too early to produce results related to impact—indeed, by the time of publication, the case studies were still prototypes or at the beginning of commercial use. After the end of AgentLink, the further impact of the applications described in the case studies was not systematically followed up.

In a study carried out in 2008 [9], Dignum and Dignum have collected and systematically analyzed agent applications. Their survey revealed a rather limited coverage in terms of replies, with very little industry participation. The focus of their study was on the characteristics of the applications rather than on their impact. [21] present a collection of industrial (manufacturing, logistics) applications; they do not aim at a systematic discussion or comparison of impact.

[1] www.agentlink.org.

In a recent paper [5], Balke et al. analyze how implementations of software systems employing agent technology are represented in research-oriented publications, both at conferences (AAMAS, PAAMS, ICAART [18], MATES) and in journals (e.g., JAAMAS, AAIJ, KER). Their focus is on the impact of applications-related work in general on scientific publication venues. The focus is neither on practical application impact nor on specific applications. Their paper does not investigate the outreach of agent technology beyond the agents/AI community.

Looking at related studies done for other, similar studies, we came across an assessment project done by the Software Engineering research community: In [28], Osterweil et al. establish a scholarly assessment of the impact that research in software engineering has had so far on the practice in software engineering. In Sect. 2, we will discuss commonalities and differences of their approach and results when compared with our work.

In essence, the absence of systematic studies on the application impact of MAS&T has been the motivation for us to produce the work reported in this chapter. We describe the methods and results of a survey aiming at a comprehensive and up-to-date overview of deployed examples of MAS&T.

In Sect. 2, we define our notion of application impact and review approaches to describing and measuring it. Section 3 underlines method and settings of the survey. Results are described in Sect. 4. In Sect. 5, we provide an analysis of the most important vertical sectors (according to our survey) where MAS&T have developed impact. We discuss our findings and draw conclusions in Sect. 6.

2 Defining Application Impact

Merriam-Webster Online Dictionary [25] defines impact as *the force of impression of one thing on another*, or as *a significant or major effect*. In our work, we are interested in the application impact of MAS&T, that is, the force of impression/the significant effect that MAS&T have had on applications. Capturing this requires us to study related work on impact of ICT. Most literature definitions roughly classify impact into economic, social, and sometimes also environmental impact. *Economic impact* entails decreasing cost or increasing turnover/profits. *Social impact* includes aspects such as supporting human work to make it more satisfying and productive, changing the manner in which human users interact and cooperate, or making work environments safer or healthier. *Environmental impact* means decreasing environmental pollution or increasing sustainability of economic activities.

A prominent approach to defining and measuring ICT impact has been put forward by the Organization of Economic Cooperation and Development (OECD) in [27]; it has been adopted and extended by the United Nations Conference on Trade and Development (UNCTAD) in [24]. The model indicates the web of relationships between impact areas, and with the broader economy, society, and environment. Impacts of ICT arise through ICT supply and ICT demand and are likely to be influenced by the following factors (at a level of individual countries):

1. The existing ICT infrastructure which enables an ICT critical mass that can amplify impacts.
2. The country level of education, skills, and income, which influences both supply and demand.
3. The Government ICT policy and regulation, and the level of e-government.

With respect to measuring ICT impact, the OECD model identifies a number of interrelated segments, including (1) ICT demand (users and usage), (2) ICT supply (being the players of the ICT sector), (3) the level of/investment in the ICT infrastructure, (4) ICT products, information, and electronic content, and (5) ICT in a wider social and political context. The model proposes different types of impacts that address different (positive or negative) impact factors from the perspectives of these segments. These measurable factors appear to be very broad and diverse in terms of intensity, directness, scope, stage, timeframe, and characterization (e.g., economic/social/environmental impact, positive/negative impact, intended/unintended impact, subjective/objective impact).

While the OECD/UNCTAD approach can help us form an understanding of the general nature of ICT impact and its influence factors, we found it to be of limited use for addressing the particular problem of identifying and measuring the impact of the particular ICT research field of multi-agent systems. Firstly, OECD investigates impact by country, whereas we are interested in obtaining results involving a global but still relatively small research community. Secondly, while OECD can build on elaborated statistical data collected from countries and international bodies, no such statistics are available for MAS&T. Third, while (or because) the OECD model is very broad, it is not operational under the limited resources available for this study. Fourth (and maybe most importantly), OECD starts from sectoral and demand sides (e.g., studies the impact of ICT in healthcare, or the impact of ICT to specific user groups), whereas our interest is to measure the impact of a specific bag of models, methods, technologies and tools over a range of sectors and users.

Indeed, the application impact of a research area is hard to capture. While there is a considerable body of work on measuring effects and impact of science and technology [8, 14, 24], they are mostly either domain-specific (e.g., ICT impact for law enforcement [15]) or technology-specific (e.g., RFID technologies [32]). For most relevant MAS applications, a mixture of both domain-specific and technology-specific consideration is required: On the one hand, MAS have been applied in a large number of application domains. On the other hand, the notion of agents and MAS has been very broadly interpreted, making it difficult to subsume the applications under one technology-specific perspective. Also, when MAS researchers talk about impact, they often talk about two very different things: We (as a community) know our academic/scientific impact (measured in citation indices, scientific awards, or acquired research funds) quite well. However, what we know much less well is our *application-related* (i.e., economic, social, environmental) impact.

The aforementioned study by Osterweil et al. [28] (further referred to as *SE study*) investigated determining the impact of Software Engineering research on practice. This study was performed by leading players of the Software Engineering research area in a funded project, involving different subgroups being responsible for different subareas (such as software configuration management, middleware, or programming languages). The SE study was performed in

> the form of a series of studies and briefings, each involving literature searches and, where possible, personal interviews [28, p. 39].

While there are similarities between the SE study and our domain, there are some important differences, too. First, software engineering has a much longer history than MAS&T. A key finding of the above study has been that

> [e]xperience, both in software engineering and diverse other disciplinary areas, has indicated that the impact of [...] prototypes might take 20 years to manifest [28, p. 41]

and that

> [i]t typically takes at least 10 to 20 years for a good idea to move from initial research to final widespread practice.

Acknowledging that first concepts and prototypes featuring MAS&T are dating back 20 years or less (as opposed to almost 50 years in the case of software engineering), we must also acknowledge that our field is much less mature than software engineering. Second, the perception of the importance of software engineering to industry is very much different from the perception of MAS&T: Software engineering promises to address an urging problem faced by virtually every enterprise in the world, that is, to build robust, safe, efficient, scalable, and sustainable software systems. While we strongly argue that MAS&T can play a similarly important role in supporting future *software-intensive societies* by enabling cooperation, coordination, and evolution of large-scale mixed human-machine systems, our research community has so far been much less successful in attracting funding for a study like the one at hand. This leads to the third difference: Our study is a pure volunteer effort which fully relies on help from within the community. Hence, its scope is limited compared to the SE study. What we can hope for is to take a first step toward better understanding the current level of diffusion of MAS&T in practical applications.

Despite some above-mentioned valuable work done within our community, in studying the application impact of MAS&T we very much start on greenfield, especially concerning the work that has been done from 2004 onwards (i.e., after the end of the AgentLink network activity). While a reasonable number of application-related papers have been published in venues such as the AAMAS industry track, the PAAMS and IAT conferences, many of them are research prototypes, and so far, there have been no systematic efforts to monitor their development over time. Also, apparently there are companies that have been successfully building and improving their businesses using agent (or agent-like) technologies and systems. However, data on and insights into these applications [which are often "non-agent agent systems" (a marvelous phrase coined by Les Gasser in [34])] are often difficult to get from the owners of these applications, as also reported by Dignum and Dignum in their study [9]. These observations lead us to set up the comprehensive study described in this chapter. Our methodology is described in the following section.

3 Survey Methodology

As stated above, the overall objective of this activity is to gain information and insights of the application-oriented impact of MAS&T, and to provide a comprehensive and up-to-date overview of deployed MAS. To this end, we carried out a survey of deployed applications that use/are based on MAS&T, starting from year 2000 onwards. Rather than just providing a list of applications, our approach was to:

1. Classify the systems with respect to their maturity based on a set of indicators. As a baseline for our maturity classification, we use the NASA Technology Readiness Levels (TRL), which are a widely accepted standard [22]. We map the original set of nine TRL levels into the three categories: TRL1 to TRL4 correspond to Maturity Level C (lowest), TRL5 to TRL7 correspond to Maturity Level B, and TRL8/TRL9 correspond to Maturity Level A. We refer to Sect. 4.2 for further information.
2. Provide an at least qualitative characterization of the application impact based on a set of criteria, and identify particularly high-impact application.
3. In particular, follow up the development and impact of previously published application-oriented work (e.g., the AgentLink case studies as well as work presented in the AAMAS industry tracks).

To achieve these goals, we pursued the following activities:

1. An open call for nominations of deployed MAS&T using a web-based online system. This aimed at academic and industrial members of the broad MAS community.
2. A mail-based survey directed toward the authors of papers presented at the AAMAS2005 to AAMAS2012 Industry/Innovative Applications.
3. Direct/personal mails directed to dedicated (industrial but also key academic) players, which would be unlikely to respond to 1 or 2.

In the course of the study, we have been collecting different sets of information: In the first round (web-based survey), we were asking researchers to nominate real-world applications that were deployed in the year 2000 or later, in a corporate, administrative, or public environment. In particular, we were requiring that these applications should have considerably and positively contributed to corporate or administrative value creation, to public/social welfare, or to application-oriented grand technology challenges (such as e.g. RoboCup). To restrict the survey to MAS&T, we further imposed the requirement that the application uses research results (models, methods, architecture, algorithms, technologies and platforms, tools) in the realm of MAS&T at its core—no matter whether the label of MAS&T is actually used or not. In parallel, we carried out a literature research to identify prospective deployed applications based on work published in the AAMAS Industry/Innovative Applications Tracks 2005–2012. Metadata and deployment information was collected from these papers and a consolidated list of candidate applications was created containing the applications from the survey plus the applications identified from the AAMAS industry track papers. In the second round, a fact sheet form was created and mailed to the developer/owner of each of the applications gathered previously. The objective of this second round was to validate the deployment status based on first-hand, up-to-date information, and to obtain a common level of information for comparing and uniformly presenting the results of the survey, regarding development/deployment timeline, resources spent, and benefits achieved for the different applications.

4 Survey Results

Based on the goals and method of the survey laid out in the previous section, this section reports our results. Advertised using the major agent-related mailing lists, the online survey was performed from July to early October 2012. People were invited to propose either own applications or nominate applications they know about and give a contact person for reference. One hundred and three applications were nominated using the online survey. In parallel, 99 applications were identified as the result of a literature research in the proceedings of the AAMAS Industry and Innovative Applications tracks from 2005 to 2012. The two sets were merged, duplicates and irrelevant entries (e.g., work finished before year 2000, just overview or white paper but no application) were removed. The result was a list of 152 applications, which form the basis of the results presented in this chapter.

For each of the 152 applications, we identified a contact person we approached in order to obtain additional information about the applications. We did so by designing a simple fact sheet template, which we asked the contact person to fill in. We received factsheet information for 89 applications, corresponding to 59 % of all applications. While this appears to be an excellent return, the completeness of input to the different factsheet questions varies. For instance, while over 80 % of the returned factsheet provide information regarding the agent platform used, only 55 % provide information regarding the development resources. Thus, while the fact sheets have fulfilled the purpose to verify the deployment status (maturity) of the applications, they have only to a smaller extent allowed us to gather information about timelines, resources, usage numbers, and quantitative benefits (such as revenue) created through agents and multi-agent systems.

4.1 Distribution of Applications Across Partner Types

Based on information collected from the survey, the fact sheets, and additional resources (publications and web pages related to the applications), we classified the applications according to the partner characteristics, making a distinction between applications developed (and owned) by industrial or governmental organizations, applications that were developed in industry-academic cooperations, and applications developed/owned solely by academic partners. Forty-seven applications (corresponding to 31 %) were exclusively developed and owned by industrial or governmental players, whereas 43 applications (28 %) were built by academic partners, and 62 applications (41 %) were created in industry-academic cooperation. Thus, academic partners were involved in 69 % of the applications. This ratio can be partly explained by the high level of participation of academics compared to industrials in the survey: 61 % of the applications were proposed by academic participants, in 39 % of the cases industrial or governmental players were proposers or otherwise involved in providing the information.

An interesting question is whether there is a correlation between the developer/owner category and the maturity of the applications. One would expect that in general, applications developed by academic partners have lower maturity than applications developed by industrial or governmental organizations. But how about industry-academia co-productions? For this purpose, in the next subsection, we consider the maturity of applications.

4.2 *Maturity of Applications*

Based on information collected from the survey, the fact sheets, and additional resources (publications and web pages related to the applications), we classified the 152 applications in the following three maturity classes (see also Sect. 3):

- Systems that are or have been in operational use in a commercial or public environment (Maturity Level A, corresponds to TRL 8 to 9)
- Industry validated research prototypes (i.e., prototypes that are being validated/piloted in an industrial or public environment with online industrial data under live conditions) (Maturity Level B, corresponds to TRL 5 to 7)
- Research prototypes validated with offline real-world data or in an offline environment (Maturity Level C, corresponds to TRL 1 to 4)

A fourth category contains systems or activities that are not applications in a strict sense, but that have (or have had) some indirect impact via technology challenges, benchmarking activities, or standardization efforts (such as e.g., IEEE-FIPA). Figure 3.1 shows the distribution of the applications in the survey according to their maturity levels. Forty-six applications (31 %) out of those classified as A, B, or C are (or have been) in operational industrial or public deployment. Further 55 applications (37 %) have been validated/piloted in an industrial or public environment with online industrial data under live conditions, whereas other 46 (31 %) are research prototypes that were never (or not yet) deployed. The latter category mainly comprises applications that were described in AAMAS Industry Track papers. We decided to include them in our survey but clearly mark them with respect to their maturity. Using the fact sheets, we tried to confirm the maturity status of all applications in the survey with their developers or owners. We were able to confirm 76 % of maturity class A applications, 59 % of class B, and 44 % of class C. In the remaining cases where no confirmed information about the maturity

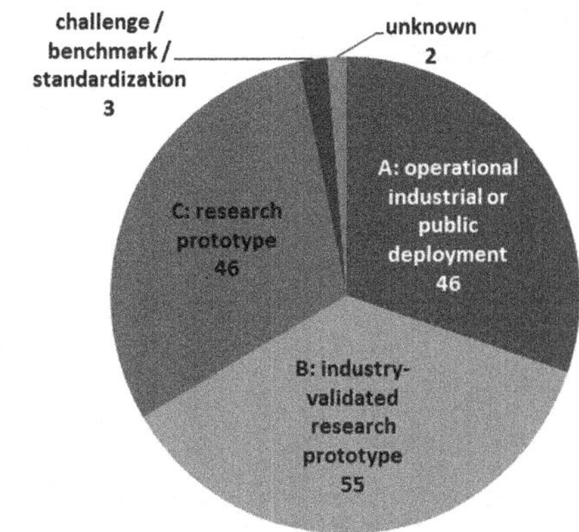

Fig. 3.1 Maturity levels of applications

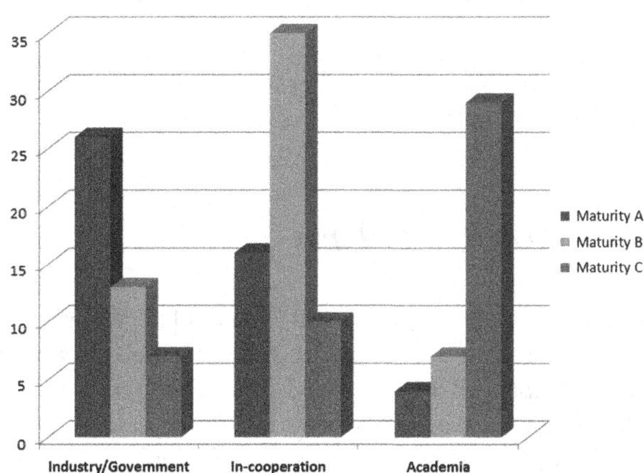

Fig. 3.2 Maturity levels of applications by partner types (y-axis shows absolute numbers of applications)

status was available, we perform the classification based on available information such as publications, product/project websites, and personal communication.

Next let us revisit the correlation between partner types (Sect. 4.1) and maturity of the applications. Figure 3.2 shows the maturity levels of the applications grouped by different partner types. Not surprisingly, applications owned and developed by industrial and governmental players have a considerably higher maturity (26 maturity class A applications, and only 7 maturity class C applications) than applications developed by academics (only 4 maturity A, but 29 maturity C). An interesting result is, however, that applications developed in cooperations of academic institutions with industry or public bodies are performing remarkably well in terms of maturity. This result goes in line with the observation made by [28, p. 41], for software engineering research that

> [t]echnology transition is most effective and best expedited when research and commercialization maintain a close synergy over an extended period.

It will be interesting to see how many of the in-cooperation applications currently in maturity level B will ultimately migrate to level A. Our subjective impression

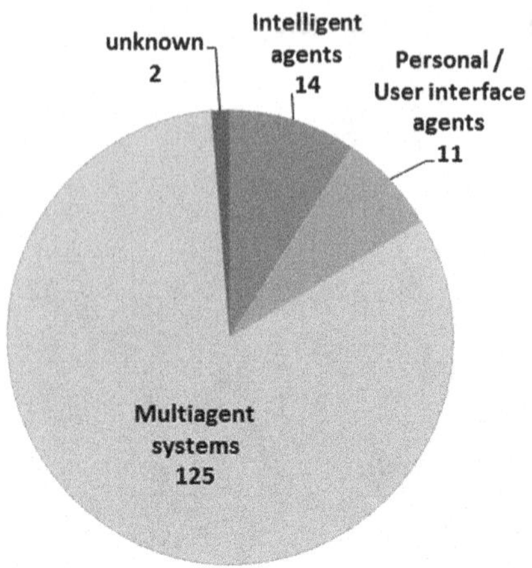

Fig. 3.3 Applications by agent system types (figures are absolute numbers)

based on feedback from the fact sheets is that there are quite a few new and emerging applications "in the pipeline."

4.3 Agent System Types

It is not only since Franklin and Graesser [12] that we are aware of the heterogeneity of the notion of agents and its interpretation. It would be surprising if a survey on the impact of MAS&T did not reflect this heterogeneity. We have classified the applications in our survey into three categories according to the most well known system types: (1) multi-agent systems focusing on interaction, cooperation, and coordination; (2) intelligent agents focusing on single-agent aspects such as planning or learning; and (3) personal/UI agent focusing on agent-human interaction and assistance. Figure 3.3 shows the distribution of the applications considered in the survey. The large number of applications in the multi-agent systems category certainly reflects the focus towards multi-agent topics in the call for participation rather than a lack of intelligent agent or personal/UI agent applications. Also note that the three categories considered are, while being helpful, not orthogonal and of limited discriminatory power: In many multi-agent systems, single-agent local aspects play an important role. Also, human-agent interaction can be viewed as multi-agent interaction as well depending on the perspective. Also, UI agents should often reveal intelligent behavior. Yet, in most cases, some focus can be observed, which is why we decided to keep these three categories.

4.4 Applications by Country

Next, we consider the distribution of the creators of the 152 applications covered in the survey by country. As a general rule, in the case where an agent's company

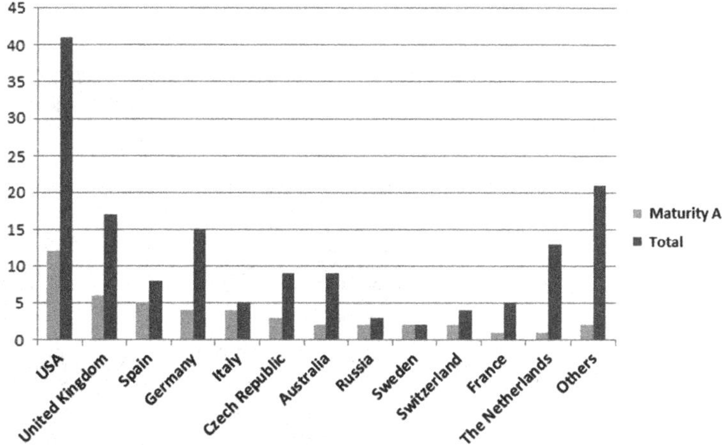

Fig. 3.4 Applications by countries (absolute numbers, total and maturity A only)

located in country A has created an application for a customer located in country B, we allocate this application to country A. In case of a company with multiple locations we use the country of the responsible location in case we know it (e.g., in the case of IBM, two applications were collected from the Haifa Lab, so they count for Israel); otherwise, we count the application for the country where the company headquarter is located. Figure 3.4 illustrates the distribution of applications by the countries of their creators. The 152 applications covered by the survey were created by parties from 21 countries. The USA is by far the country creating the largest number (41, corresponding to 27 %) of MAS&T applications, followed by the UK, Germany, the Netherlands, the Czech Republic, and Australia. Also when considering Maturity A applications only, USA takes the clear lead (12, corresponding to 26 %), with runners-up being the UK, Spain, Germany, Italy, and the Czech Republic. The strong presence of Spain and Italy for highly mature applications is due to the strong industrial players Telefonica T+D and Telecom Italia.

4.5 Applications by Vertical Sectors

The pie chart in Fig. 3.5 shows the distribution of applications across vertical sectors. Within the 152 applications, 22 sectors are represented. It is noticeable here that eleven sectors cover 86 % of all applications, whereas the top six sectors (logistics and manufacturing, aerospace, energy, defense, security and surveillance, and telecommunications) still represent 59 % of the applications. The picture changes considerably if we do not only consider the number but also the maturity of the applications in the different sectors. Figure 3.6 illustrates the number of

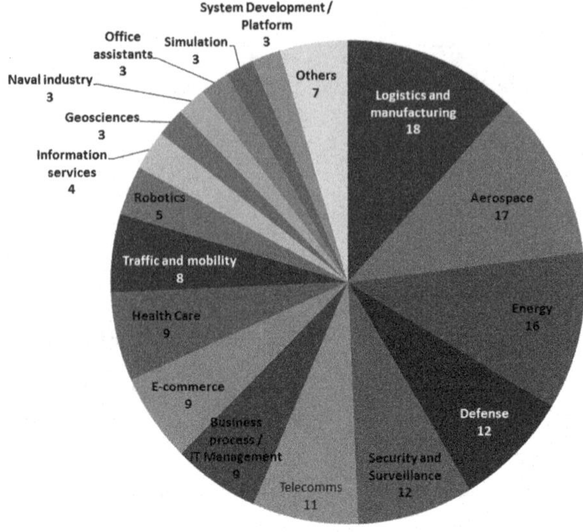

Fig. 3.5 Number of applications by vertical sectors

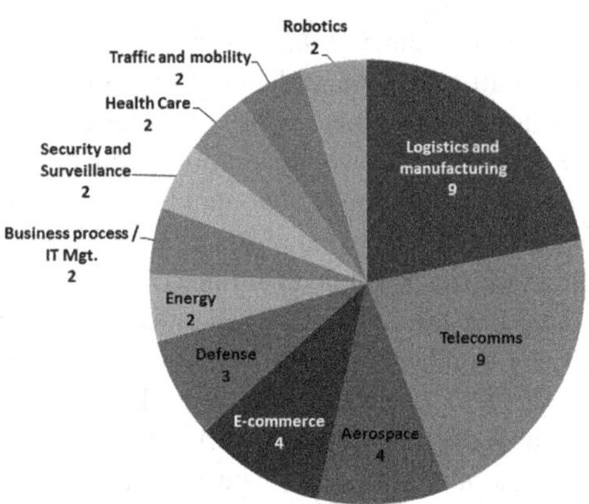

Fig. 3.6 Number of applications by vertical sectors (maturity class A only)

applications with maturity level A by vertical sector. It only displays the sectors for which five or more applications have been recorded. From this view, we see that logistics and manufacturing and telecommunications are the domains with the overall highest number of mature agent applications, whereas energy, security and surveillance, and defense appear to be emergent applications with yet little impact. However, especially in the defense domain, it is well possible that confidentiality issues may distort the picture—we may just not be aware of some successful applications of MAS&T in this domain.

A final consideration reflects on the vertical sectors with a particular high percentage of high-maturity applications. For this, we consider again the vertical sectors for which at least five applications were listed and calculate the percentage of maturity class A applications amongst all applications recorded for this sector. The results are illustrated in Fig. 3.7. We observe that the Telecommunications

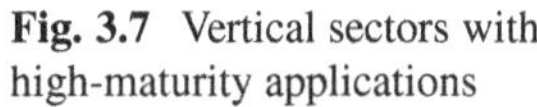

Fig. 3.7 Vertical sectors with high-maturity applications

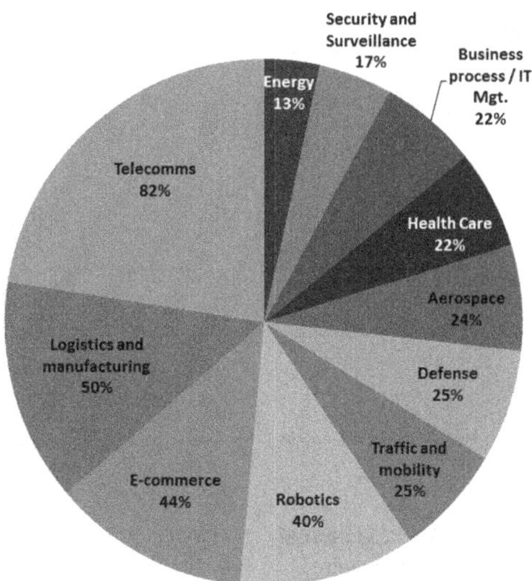

sector is very mature in terms of agent-based solutions, reflecting the historical development with early involvement of telecommunications companies, such as Telecom Italia, Telefonica I+D, British Telecom, Siemens, and Motorola. Logistics and manufacturing, e-Commerce, and robotics follow with 50 % to 40 % share of maturity A applications. At the lower end of the spectrum in terms of relative maturity, security and surveillance as well as energy sectors feature a large number of applications, but most of them are (still?) of low maturity. Note that the figure for the defense sector are associated with a high degree of uncertainty due to the confidentiality requirements in this domain.

In Sect. 5, we shall review and discuss in more detail the most prominent vertical domains emerging from our survey.

4.6 Programming Languages and Agent Platforms

Seventy-three out of 87 submitted factsheets provide information about the programming languages used in application development. Since we were particularly interested in the usage of dedicated agent platforms and tools, we asked for that information separately. Seventy-five factsheets provide information about agent platforms and tools used (including the rather frequent answer "None"). Java has been by far the most popular programming language, used in 53 applications. It is followed by C/C++/C# (used in 15 applications, including but not restricted to embedded or real-time applications), PHP (seven applications), and Python (four applications). These four groups were used in 75 % of the applications for which information was available to us. Note that some applications have used more than one programming language. Figure 3.8 illustrates the coverage of dedicated agent platforms in the applications.

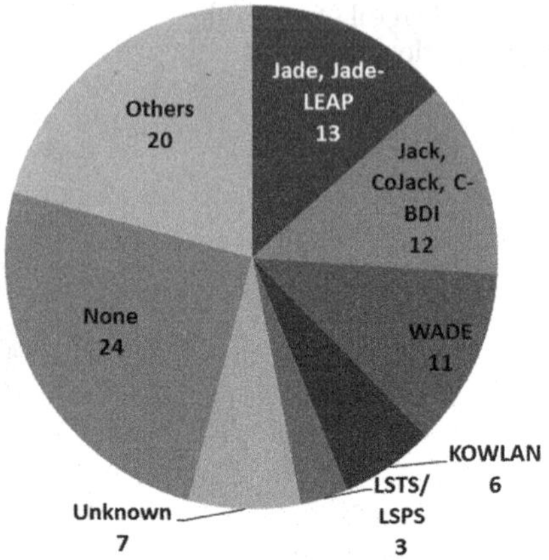

Fig. 3.8 Usage of agent platforms in applications (figures are absolute numbers)

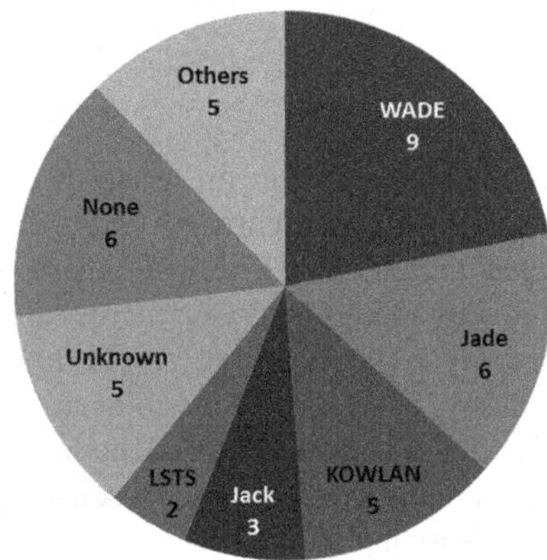

Fig. 3.9 Agent platforms used for highly mature applications (figures are absolute numbers)

We can draw a couple of observations from this chart. First, a large majority of applications (24, corresponding to 32 %) has not used any dedicated agent platform or tool. Second, the most commonly used platforms are JADE (13 applications, $\approx$ 15 %), AOS's Jack, CoJack, and C-BDI product family (12, $\approx$ 16 %) as well as WADE (11, $\approx$ 14 %). Taking into account that WADE is a JADE extension, JADE can be regarded the overall most-used agent platform. These are followed in respectful distance by KOWLAN, and Whitestein's Living Systems platforms (LSTS and LSPS). Third, there is a high fragmentation in the agent platforms landscape in that 20 different platforms and tools were used in a single application only. This fragmentation was already observed in the study by [9].

At the end of this subsection, we shall investigate the question whether the distribution of agent platforms shown in Fig. 3.8 will change if we only consider applications with maturity level A, that is, in operational use. Figure 3.9 shows the absolute usage numbers of agent platforms in these applications. This information was extracted from 30 fact sheets submitted for maturity level A applications, which have provided information about the agent platforms used. What is striking when comparing it to the numbers over all applications considered in the survey is that the ratio of applications that do NOT use dedicated agent platforms is significantly lower in the case of maturity A applications: only six out of 30 maturity A applications that provide information about agent platforms have NOT used an agent platform, compared to 24 out of 75 applications in total. On the one hand, this reflects the strong role of players such as Telecom Italia, Telefonica I+D, AOS, and Whitestein, who have been applying their agent platforms (JADE/WADE, KOWLAN, JACK/CoJACK, LSTS/LSPS) to build a number of successful deployed applications. On the other hand, we might conclude from this that dedicated agent platforms actually can make a difference regarding business success.

A further interesting observation in this context is that the agent platform landscape is much less fragmented for highly mature applications: While 20 out of 75 applications in our survey are based on proprietary platforms which are not used by any other application, in the case of maturity A applications, only five out of 30 applications are based on "singular" platforms.

For maturity A applications, WADE and JADE are again the most frequently used platforms, followed by KOWLAN, Jack, and the Living Systems Technology Suite (LSTS). Apparently, mature applications, which often have a longer development history, tend to be based on mature platforms; more recent platforms such as CoJack, C-BDI, or Whitesteins Living Systems Process Suite may take some more time to mature with the applications constructed with them.

4.7 AgentLink Case Studies Revisited

Running from 1998 until 2006, The European AgentLink Coordination Action for Agent-Based Computing has gathered important application-oriented work in its case studies. Elaborated in 2004/2005, eight prominent MAS&T applications were described and analyzed [6]. The case studies are still available on the AgentLink website [4]. Eight years after the case studies were written, we have reexamined these eight applications, trying to gather up-to-date information with respect to their further development. Table 3.1 summarizes the key information we were able to obtain. The table provides the maturity level (see Sect. 4.2 above) reached by the systems described in the case studies as well as the information whether the systems are still maintained.

It reveals that, according to our findings, four out of eight case studies (the ones by AOS, Whitestein, Magenta, and Almende) are still maintained and in operational use (maturity A). Three are confirmed to be no longer used, of which only one (EuroBIOS / SCA) had reached maturity A status at some point in time. Combined Systems was a research project, the use case was not taken up after its end. Also, the Chilled Water System Automation case study (Rockwell, CTU Prague) developed a research prototype and was not commercialized. For one case study (Acklin B.V.), no information was available to us.

Beyond the operational status (and connected revenue generation for their owners) reached by specific AgentLink case studies, an important positive effect we can

Table 3.1 What happened to the AgentLink case studies?

App id	Title	Partners	Maturity level	Still maintained?
64	Living Systems/Adaptive Transportation Networks	Whitestein Technologies	A	Yes
69	HV-CGF: Intelligent Human Variability in Computer Generated Forces	AOS, UK Ministry of Defense	A	Yes
71	Agent-based Factory Modelling	EuroBios, SCA Packaging	A	No
73	Intelligent Scheduling of Cargo Fleets	Magenta Technology, Tankers International	A	Yes
75	Software Agents for International vehicle Traffic Insurance	Acklin B.V.	No info	No info
84	Chilled Water System Automation	Rockwell, CTU Prague	B	No
87	Combined Systems	D-CIS, Thales	C	No
88	Agents for Intelligent Communications Systems / Self-organizing systems	Almende, ASK CS	A	Yes

observe from the AgentLink case studies is that these applications have sustainably fertilized products and businesses of the companies involved. For example, the main result of the HV-CGF project was the CoJack reactive architecture, which AOS has been using in further deployed applications. As another example, Whitestein Technologies has not only created additional business in the area of logistics based on the LS/ATN reference application, it has also used the experience with LS/ATN to develop development and execution platforms (in particular, the LSTS and the Living Systems Process Suite, which have been the basis for generating additional business. Also, even if the Chilled Water System Automation case study was not commercialized, results from that project have initiated and driven further successful applications reported by the CTU team.

In summary, we regard the fact that 8–10 years after publication, four out of eight applications are still operational and (apparently) thriving, a positive rather than negative news, given that according to [13], from ten venture-backed startups, three to four fail completely and only two produce substantial returns. To us, this demonstrates that beyond past hype and disillusionment, successful and sustainable businesses can be built on the grounds of MAS&T.

4.8 Agent Companies

A major indication of impact of a specific technology is the number of companies which successfully build business from selling products or services based on this technology. In the following, we give examples of companies whose business is known to build on agent technologies. Our list is exemplary and by no means meant to be exhaustive. It is difficult (and was not in the scope of this survey) to find out details of the business models of individual companies.

We start with a list of companies which successfully managed to establish themselves in the market[2]:

Whitestein Technologies[3] offers agent-based solutions for business process management and execution in the areas of financial services, manufacturing, telecommunications, or logistics. Additionally Whitestein offers solutions for logistics management, optimization, and control.

Agent-Oriented Software (AOS)[4] claims to be the leading company for providing autonomous and semi-autonomous systems. AOS provides platforms and development tools for the design of agent-based systems (most noticeably Jack and CoJack, the latter of which was a result of the HV-CGF project reported as an AgentLink case study, see above) as well as solutions for dedicated application domains like for example assisting surveillance and intelligence agencies as well as for Oil and Gas industry.

Real Thing[5] is a rather young company. It is not purely specialized on agent technologies but also offers Apps for smart phones. However, toy robots for kids are clearly agent-related. From the information available in open source, it is difficult to decide which concrete technologies the products of this company build on.

In addition to the above-listed success stories, there are also unavoidably examples of startups who did not manage to establish themselves in the market:

xaitment was a startup founded by members of the multi-agent system group at the German Research Center for Artificial Intelligence (DFKI) GmbH. The company specialized on middleware for the development of computer games. xaitment recently merged with iOPENER.[6]

Agentis Software was a startup founded by members of the Australian Artificial Intelligence Institute (AAII). The main objective of Agentis Software was to apply the concepts of BDI agents to business process management and execution.

[2]Note we have not included players such as Telecom Italia or Telefonica I+D in this list because, while they are using agent technology in their operations, their business does not build on it.

[3]http://www.whitestein.com/.

[4]http://aosgrp.com/.

[5]http://aosgrp.com/.

[6]http://www.iopenermedia.com/.

Nevertheless, the positive examples are a clear indication that it is possible to successfully build business models around agent technologies.

5 Vertical Sector Analysis

In Sect. 4.5, we have identified the vertical domains that, following the results of our survey, appear to be most relevant for agent-related research and application development. In this section, we provide a brief characterization of these sectors.

Aerospace is a very diverse application area with a large number of applications in commerce, industry, and military. Early work in distributed artificial intelligence (DAI) investigated the use of agent and multi-agent system technology for robots designed for exploring the surface of remote planets. The majority of applications collected in our survey investigates agent technologies for unmanned aerial vehicles (UAVs). Additional applications are involved with the support of pilots in military situations.

Defense To identify research on military applications is not really easy because researchers working on such applications are at least sometimes not allowed to publish their results with a direct pointer to the military context. Sometimes a completely artificial application domain is chosen to obfuscate the real application. Nevertheless, our study could identify a significant body of work in this area. An obvious application of agent technologies in a military application is the simulation of a human engaged in a military mission. Simulation of human to human and human to environment interaction are investigated. Simulation of unmanned vehicles or other intelligent and autonomous devices, as well as the use of game-theoretical models for decision support are other relevant MAS&T topics within deployed defense applications.

E-commerce Although online shopping was already invented in the late 1970s, it became in broader use only after the advent of the World Wide Web and its commercialization in the late 1990s. Online shopping forms a major part of e-commerce but any kind of business interactions using the Internet falls into this application area. With this broad scope it has a significant overlap with supply chain management and manufacturing & logistics. The settings e-commerce are inherently multiparty and geographically distributed, see [26].

Energy is a vibrant sector following an important societal theme, which has been providing ample funding opportunities for research over the past few years. Unsurprisingly, it has recently become attractive for agent-related research. With the global change to produce energy (especially electricity) from fossil or nuclear sources to sustainable sources, the control of electricity networks became an even more demanding task than it already used to be. It is very likely that in the near future completely decentralized control mechanisms need to be put in place because individual households are likely to be at the same time source and drain of flow of electricity. Even small electronic devices will get into the position to buy and sell energy when it is economical in a given market situation. It is therefore not astonishing that agent research tries to adopt well-understood negotiation and market mechanisms for this application domain. Other applications support the retrieval of energy sources [e.g. iWD™ (intelligent Watchdog)].

Health Care Similar to energy, health care is an application area with great importance especially when the demographic change in the western world is taken into account. Related to health care is the application area of ambient assisted living (AAL). With the increase in networking of devices on a wireless basis in the general public or in the users' homes, there is a huge potential of innovative applications for agent technologies in this area. The applications include monitoring of a person's health status, selection of candidates for transplant surgeries, resource management in hospitals, or the supervision and support of people with health problems in their homes.

Manufacturing & Logistics has been an interesting application area for agent-related research from the very beginning in the early to mid-1980s DAI research. Already in the first DAI book by Huhns [16], manufacturing was listed as a major application domain by Parunak [30]. In logistics, early work on transportation scheduling was reported by Sandholm [31] and Fischer and colleagues [11]. Indeed, references collected for this survey reach over the whole period back till 2000, which we used as a cut of year for collecting data. The different applications in the survey collection cover a broad spectrum of topics. Production planning and control, task allocation, product memories, negotiation, and simulation were topics the applications in the survey collection dealt with. Commercialization driven by companies such as Whitestein Technologies and Magenta Technologies are active in this application area.

Robotics A relatively small but notable and successful part of the applications in our survey deal with robotics, and, in particular, multirobot systems. Robotics has always been a natural application area for AI, and such have multirobot systems been a natural application domain for MAS&T. An autonomous robot is a prototype of an autonomous agent which has a physical body. At the same time, coordination and cooperation processes in multirobot systems can be efficiently modeled and implemented using MAS&T, as examples such as Kiva or CogniTAO on the commercial side, and Robocup [33] on the research side show. Robotics itself is a huge application area in which other disciplines (especially engineering) meet with research on pure agent technologies. The Autonomous Agents (AA) conference in 1997 was the first international conference where the two research areas of pure agent technologies and physical robots met in a major international scientific event. Later on the AA, ATAL, and ICMAS conference joined forces to form the AAMAS conference as we know it today.

Security and Surveillance Security is important for basically every application domains. The Internet makes the need for security more than clear to all participants. Agent research offers very interesting settings in which theoretical solutions can be deployed and prove their strength. Surveillance puts the idea of security to another level. In our networked society where wireless networks spread out in an extremely fast manner, surveillance is getting more and more widely used which in some cases does increase security but also raises issues with respect to privacy. Because the application domain is naturally distributed, it is an ideal setting for the application agent technologies.

Telecommunications Telecommunication companies have been interested and involved in agent-related research from an early stage on. Although the absolute number of applications in our survey was not that high, as already noted, the maturity of the applications has been outstanding (see Fig. 3.7), notably driven by companies such as Telecom Italia and Telefonica I+D, which continue to be active innovators. In present days, where smart phones take over mobile telephony market, mobile devices are ubiquitous which can easily run a MAS application and interact with similar applications running on other devices. It is therefore very likely that there will be a boost of such applications in the near future.

6 Discussion, Conclusion, and Outlook

When we started out with preparations for this survey in Spring 2012, we did so with a certain degree of skepticism and with rather modest expectations. Our (subjective) observation of the multi-agent systems research field as that it was fairly healthy as a research field, but its track record in terms of application impact did not seem to be prominent. Industry participation at conferences (most notably AAMAS) had been considerably decreasing over the past years (see also the analysis by [5]), project funding for research performed under the MAS&T label has become more difficult to obtain, and agent companies and products are rarely a topic in daily technology news. The agent application survey done by Dignum and Dignum in 2008 and published in 2010 [9] enforced our skepticism. They noted that they

> were surprised by the small number of responses and by the dominance of academic respondents ([9, p. 231])

and conjectured that

> [a]lthough the reasons may be partially related to the announcement medium (the agents mailing lists are mostly used within the academic world), this small number may be an indication that there are indeed not many real applications of MAS around.

Almost 1 year later, at the time of writing this concluding section, we feel we can be somewhat more confident and more optimistic regarding the current and future impact of our research field. Supported by a large number of agent researchers and practitioners (see Acknowledgements), we identified and analyzed 152 applications of MAS&T, out of which 31 % are deployed applications, while additional 38 % were validated/piloted in industrial or public environments with online industrial data under live conditions. So indeed, there are a considerable number of "real applications of MAS around." Also, an investigation of the destinies of the applications known as the *AgentLink case studies* revealed that half of these are still operational 8–10 years after their inception.

Looking closer at the results of this survey, we can summarize our main conclusions. The main players bringing about significant successful deployed applications over a longer period in time, appear to be (more or less surprisingly) Telecom Italia, Telefonica I+D, Agent-Oriented Software and Whitestein Technologies. On the academic side, various research groups, for example, at CMU (Sandholm), Czech Technical University (Pěchouček), DFKI and, most recently, USC (Tambe) have repeatedly and successfully crossed the prototype-to-deployed-application chasm.

Looking at the main industry players that have been traditionally associated with agent technology (beyond those already mentioned above), some of them seem to have disappeared from the multi-agent business (e.g., Siemens, Motorola); some others market their "agenty" solutions under different labels (IBM, Daimler, NASA, Google), some (e.g., British Telecom) keep on developing their successful agent technologies in the rather small scale, some are developing agent technologies for their business using prototypes (e.g., Aerogility, Thales).

Yet, MAS&T seem to thrive best in what we could call niche markets. For instance:

- Multi-agent architecture and distributed management have been successfully applied in telecommunications network management.
- Flexible control, scheduling, planning, and optimization solutions have been successfully applied in manufacturing and logistics.
- Agent-based simulation has become a respectable and respected microsimulation approach for modeling large-scale systems consisting of autonomous entities, so far in specific domains, including crowd, pedestrian, and traffic simulation.
- Applied game theory has grown into an very attractive application area, in particular for security, surveillance, and defense applications.
- Very interesting work is being done in (multi-)robotics by relatively small players (e.g., Kiva Systems, Cognitao).

So one could argue that we have not seen success stories of MAS&T—neither in the large mass markets (such as consumer products) nor in the societal priority areas such as energy and health care yet. Trying to contradict to this argument, in the survey we noted a substantial number of research prototypes in these areas (in particular: energy). As the field matures, many of them may turn into deployed applications.

A second observation we made regarding success stories while doing this survey is somewhat anecdotal. In fact, two applications were proposed, which at first sight beyond doubt qualify for the *success story* predicate: One is the use of proxy bidding agents [10] in Google's AdWords product, which is allegedly Google's main source of income.[7] This work has been nominated by numerous researchers for consideration in the survey. In his nomination, David Parkes wrote:

> Google (and other search engines) use a multi-agent architecture to provide automated bidding for their advertisers. An advertiser expresses a high level goal (e.g., maximize my number of clicks without spending more than US$1,000 a day) and they try to meet that

[7] According to http://en.wikipedia.org/wiki/AdWords.

> on behalf of the advertiser using an agent that represents the advertiser. This is one of my favorite examples of MAS thinking and a truly agent-based market system.

The second relevant application has been PTIME [7], an application developed by SRI as part of the DARPA-funded CALO research project, an effort to build an adaptive cognitive assistant situated in the office environment. A PTIME agent is an autonomous entity that works with its user, other PTIME agents, and other users, to schedule meetings and commitments in its user's calendar. Indeed, some results developed in CALO were acquired by Apple and formed the technological basis for the Siri assistant today available in Apple mobile phones.

What both high-impact applications seem to have in common is that the owners of these applications do not seem to consider them as applications of MAS&T: Despite numerous attempts, we could not obtain a response from the responsible technical people at Google. When asked about the deployment of results from CALO, we received an email response from a senior scientist at SRI stating that

> The [CALO] system as a whole was never deployed externally although several parts of it were deployed in fielded government systems or used as seed technology for startup companies. In none of these cases, however, would I describe the deployed components as multi-agent systems.

In summary, however, we can state that off the spotlights of ICT wonderland, MAS&T has been successfully used in a significant number of applications, and continues to be an increasingly useful and impacting technology in various sectors. Yet, there is no reason for over-enthusiasm: Coming back to the comparison to the Software Engineering study already discussed in Sect. 2, one finding of that study has been that

> [c]ontinued support for sustaining a vigorous research community is required ([28, p. 45]).

In our research community, there seems to be selective, but no broad continuous support (public or industrial) over the past few years (in Europe, there has not been much after AgentLink), which is definitely problematic.

In this chapter, we have provided the main results of the impact survey, covering some important perspectives, such as maturity, vertical sectors, and usage of programming languages and platforms. For other aspects, such as the analysis of the system complexity, development effort, timescale, and economic performance of MAS&T, our current data basis for now is insufficient to derive significant results. Therefore, we have not included these aspects in this paper. In future work, we shall attempt to complete our data collection with respect to these aspects, to be able to carry out further analyses.

Additional Information

The following table (Table 3.2) lists the 46 applications contained in the survey, which were classified as maturity level A (TRL 8/9).

Table 3.2 List of maturity A applications contained in the survey

App id	Application name	Sector	Owner/developer
1	Generalized combinatorial multi-attribute auctions/CombineNet for Sourcing	Logistics and manufacturing	CombineNet, CMU, US
2	Live-donor (US-wide) kidney exchange	Health Care	T. Sandholm, CMU, US
3	Poker	Entertainment	T. Sandholm, CMU, US
5	cdmNet	Health Care	Precedence Healthcare, AU
10	GlacsWeb	Geosciences	Southampton University, UK
15	Global package tracking, tracing, recovery	Logistics and manufacturing	DHL, Agentis, US
20	Debatescape	E-commerce	British Telecom, UK
21	Kiva systems	Robotics	Kiva Systems, Peter Wurman, US
23	Proxy bidding agents at Google	E-commerce	Google, US
26	PROTECT	Security and Surveillance	USC Teamcore, US
27	ARMOR	Security and Surveillance	USC Teamcore, US
28	IRIS	Defense	USC Teamcore, US
36	CAST Terminal	Aerospace	Airport Research Center GmbH, DE
38	Catalogue manager and price checker/setter	E-commerce	The Book Depository, UK
51	Wizard	Business process/IT Management	Telecom Italia S.p.A., IT
52	WANTS-Delivery (aka Network Neutral Element Manager)	Telecommunications	Telecom Italia S.p.A., IT
53	WANTS-Assurance	Telecommunications	Telecom Italia S.p.A., IT
54	WeFlow	Telecommunications	Telecom Italia S.p.A., IT
56	Legion	Traffic and mobility	Legion Ltd., UK
57	Steps	Traffic and mobility	Mott McDonald, UK
64	Living Systems/Adaptive Transportation Networks	Logistics and manufacturing	Whitestein Technologies, CH
65	LS/AMC	Logistics and manufacturing	Whitestein Technologies, CH
67	MasDISPO_xt	Logistics and manufacturing	Saarstahl AG, DFKI, DE

(continued)

Table 3.2 (continued)

App id	Application name	Sector	Owner/developer
69	HV-CGF: Intelligent Human Variability in Computer Generated Forces	Defense	Agent-Oriented Software Ltd., UK MoD, AU
71	Agent-based Factory Modelling	Logistics and manufacturing	EuroBIOS, SCA Packaging, SE
73	Intelligent Scheduling of Cargo Fleets	Logistics and manufacturing	Magenta Technology, Tankers International, RU
77	AgentFly	Aerospace	AgentFly Technologies and Agent Technology Center, Czech Technical University, CZ
80	ExPlanTech PPS system	Logistics and manufacturing	Modelarna Liaz, SkodaAuto, CZ
82	Ad-hoc networking in disruptive environments	Defense	CTU Prague, CZ
88	Agents for Intelligent Communications Systems/Self-organizing systems	Telecommunications	Almende, ASK CS, NL
96	DHS Control	Energy	NODA Intelligent Systems AB, SE
99	SUPREMA	E-government	Knowledge Genesis, RU
102	MAS-Dispo	Logistics and manufacturing	Saarstahl AG/DFKI, DE
112	KOWLAN MACROLAN	Telecommunications	Telefónica España (MACROLAN), ES
115	CORMAS	Simulation	Francois Bousquet, FR
116	INNSIST	E-commerce	Grupo TCA. Monterrey, MX
123	ASE (Autonomous Sciencecraft Experiment)	Aerospace	NASA, US
126	OCA Management System (OCAMS)	Aerospace	The Work Systems Design & Evaluation group at NASA Ames Research Center, US
131	CogniTAO (Think As One)	Robotics	Cogniteam, Ltd., IL
133	EV2G (Electric Vehicles to Grid)	Energy	Willett Kempton, University of Delaware, US

(continued)

Table 3.2 (continued)

App id	Application name	Sector	Owner/developer
139	Living Systems Process Suite (LSPS)	Business process/IT Management	Whitestein AG, CH
142	Tacsim	Defense	AOS, Australian Defence Department, AU
150	KOWLAN CZ IP Connect	Telecommunications	Telefónica España (MACROLAN), ES
151	KOWLAN Digital probes	Telecommunications	Telefónica España, ES
152	KOWLAN Iberbanda	Telecommunications	Telefónica España, ES
153	KOWLAN BA	Telecommunications	Telefónica España, ES

Acknowledgements Numerous people, agent researchers and practitioners alike, have contributed to this work by participating in the online survey, thus pointing us to a large number of interesting applications, by providing information about applications they have been involved in, by email and in some cases via phone interviews. We are indebted to Amal El Fallah Seghrouchni, Ana Bazzan, Ladislau Bölöni, Francois Bousquet, Jeff Bradshaw, Jean-Pierre Briot, Birgit Burmeister, Stefan Bussmann, Giovanni Caire, Jiri Chabera, David Clarke, Juan Manuel Corchado, Paul Davidsson, Keith Decker, Frank Dignum, Virginia Dignum, Klaus Dorer, Emad Eldeen Elakehal, Yehuda Elmaliah, Javier Garcia Algarra, Mike Georgeff, Maria Gini, Andrey Glaschenko, Jorge J. Gomez-Sanz, Amineh Gorbani, Danilo Gotta, Dominic Greenwood, Hiromitsu Hattori, Axel Hessler, Koen Hindriks, Benjamin Hirsch, Tom Holvoet, Michael Huhns, Nick Jennings, Catholijn Jonker, Olaf Junker, Gal Kaminka, Jan Keiser, Victor Lesser, Renato Levy, Andrew Lucas, Mike Luck, Philippe Mathieu, Peter McBurney, Felipe Meneguzzi, Tim Miller, Tsunenori Mine, Anabel Montero, Prabhu Natarajan, Bernhard Nebel, Pablo Noriega, Ingrid Nunes, James Odell, Steve Osborn, Julian Padget, Lin Padgham, David Parkes, Michal Pěchouček, Raymont Perrault, Valentin Robu, Alex Rogers, Tuomas Sandholm, Paul Scerri, Glenn Semmel, Alexei Sharpanskykh, Onn Shehory, Maarten Sierhuis, David Sislak, Petr Skobelev, Nikolaos Spanoudakis, Patrick Storms, Milind Tambe, Simon Thompson, Pavel Tichy, Luca Trione, Wim van Betsbrugge, M. Birna van Riemsdijk, Ondrej Vanek, Giuseppe Vizzari, Pavel Vrba, Michael Wellman, Danny Weyns, Michael Winikoff, and Peter Wurman.

References

1. AAAI conference on artificial intelligence (2013) Association for the advancement of artificial intelligence. http://www.aaai.org/Conferences/AAAI/. Last accessed 20 March 2013
2. AAIJ: Applied Artificial Intelligence Journal (2013) Taylor and Francis. http://www.tandfonline.com/toc/uaai20/current. Last accessed 20 March 2013
3. AAMAS: international joint conference on autonomous agents and multiagent systems. International foundation for autonomous agents and multiagent systems. http://ifaamas.org. Last accessed 20 March 2013
4. Agentlink case studies. AgentLink website. http://www.agentlink.org/resources/casestudies.html. Last accessed 11 April 2013
5. Balke T, Hirsch B, Lützenberger M (2013) Assessing agent applications: r&D vs. R&d. In: Ganzha M, Jain LC (eds) Multiagent systems and applications, vol 1, practice and experience. Springer, Berlin, pp 1–20

6. Belecheanu R, Munroe S, Luck M, Payne T, Miller T, Pechoucek M, McBurney P (2006) Commercial applications of agents: lessons, experiences and challenges. In: Proceedings of industrial track, fifth international joint conference on autonomous agents and multi-agent systems (AAMAS 2006), ACM, Hakodate
7. Berry P, Peintner B, Conley K, Gervasio M, Uribe T, Yorke-Smith N (2006) Deploying a personalized time management agent. In: Proceedings of the fifth international joint conference on autonomous agents and multiagent systems (AAMAS'2006), ACM, New York, pp 1564–1571
8. Bubela T, Strotmann S (2008) Toward a new era of intellectual property: from confrontation to negotiation. In: Designing metrics to assess the impacts and social benefits of publicly funded research in health and agricultural biotechnology. The international expert group on innovation and intellectual property, Toronto
9. Dignum F, Dignum V (2010) Designing agent systems: state of the practice. Agent Oriented Software Eng 4(3):224–243
10. Edelman B, Ostrovsky M, Schwarz M (2007) Internet advertising and the generalized second-price auction: selling billions of dollars worth of keywords. Am Econ Rev 97(1):242–259
11. Fischer K, Kuhn N, Müller JP (1994) Distributed, knowledge-based, reactive scheduling in the transportation domain. In: Proceedings of the tenth IEEE conference on artificial intelligence for applications, San Antonio, March 1994, pp 47–53
12. Franklin S, Graesser A (1996) Is it an agent, or just a program?: a taxonomy for autonomous agents. In: Müller JP, Jennings NR, Wooldridge MJ (eds) Intelligent agents III: agent theories, architectures, and languages. Lecture notes in artificial intelligence, vol 1193. Springer, Berlin, pp 21–35
13. Gage D (2012) The venture capital secret: 3 out of 4 start-ups fail. The Wall Street Journal, (September 2012). http://online.wsj.com/article/SB10000872396390443720204578004980476429190.html. Last accessed 20 March 2012
14. Godin B, Doré C (2012) Measuring the impacts of science: beyond the economic dimension, inrs urbanisation, culture et société. In: Proceedings of international conference "science impact - rethinking the impact of basic research on society and the economy", Vienna, May 2007. The Austrian Science Fund (FWF) and the European Science Foundation (ESF). http://www.csiic.ca/PDF/Godin_Dore_Impacts.pdf. Last accessed 20 March 2012
15. Groff E, McEwen T (2012) Identifying and measuring the effects of information technologies on law enforcement agencies. US Department of Justice and Institute for Law and Justice, Alexandria. http://www.cops.usdoj.gov/Publications/e08084156-IT.pdf. Last accessed 20 March 2012
16. Huhns MN (1987) Distributed artificial intelligence. Pitman/Morgan Kaufmann, San Mateo
17. IAT (2013) International conference on intelligent agent technology. http://cs.gsu.edu/wic2013/iat (URL for the 2013 conference, no series website available). Last accessed 20 March 2013
18. ICAART (2013) International conference on agents and artificial intelligence. http://icaart.org. Last accessed 20 March 2013
19. JAAMAS (2013) Autonomous agents and multiagent systems. Springer, New York. http://link.springer.com/journal/10458. Last accessed 20 March 2013
20. KER (2013) The knowledge engineering review. Cambridge Journals. http://journals.cambridge.org/action/displayJournal?jid=ker. Last accessed 20 March 2013
21. Leitao P, Vrba P (2011) Recent developments and future trends of industrial agents. In: Marik V, Vrba P, Leitao P (eds) Holonic and multi-agent systems for manufacturing (HoloMAS 2011). Lecture notes in computer science, vol 6867. Springer, Berlin
22. Mankins JC (1995) Technology readiness levels: a white paper. NASA Office of Space Access and Technology. http://decadal.gsfc.nasa.gov/PACE-IDL/Final_Report/Additional_Docs/Technology_Readiness_Levels-expanded.pdf. Last accessed 20 March 2012
23. MATES (2013) German conference on multiagent technologies. http://www-ags.dfki.uni-sb.de/~klusch/mates-series/index.html. Last accessed 20 March 2013

24. Measuring the impact of information and communication technology for development. United notations conference on trade and development, 2011. http://unctad.org/en/docs/dtlstict2011d1_en.pdf. Last accessed 20 March 2012
25. Merriam-Webster Online Dictionary (2013) Merriam-Webster. http://www.merriam-webster.com. Last accessed 2 April 2013
26. Müller JP, Bauer B, Friese T, Roser S, Zimmermann R (2006) Software agents for electronic business: opportunities and challenges (2005 re-mix). In: Chaib-Draa B, Müller JP (eds) Multi-agent-based supply chain management. Studies in computational intelligence. Springer, Berlin, pp 63–102
27. OECD guide to measuring the information society 2011. The OECD's working party on indicators for the information society, 2009. http://www.oecd.org/sti/measuring-infoeconomy/guide. Last accessed 20 March 2012
28. Osterweil LJ, Ghezzi C, Kramer J, Wolf A (2008) Determining the impact of software engineering research on practice. Computer 41(3):39–49
29. PAAMS (2013) International conference on practical applications of agents and multi-agent systems. http://www.paams.net. Last accessed 20 March 2013
30. Parunak HVD (1987) Manufacturing experience with the contract net. In: Huhns MN (ed) Distributed artificial intelligence. Morgan Kaufmann Publishers, San Mateo, pp 285–310
31. Sandholm T (1993) An implementation of the contract net protocol based on marginal cost calculations. In: Proceedings of the eleventh national conference on artificial intelligence (AAAI). AAAI Press, 1993
32. Subirana B, Eckes C, Herman G, Sarma S, Barrett M (2003) Measuring the impact of information technology on value and productivity using a process-based approach: the case for RFID technologies. Technical report 4450-03.CCS 223, MIT Sloan
33. Veloso M, Stone P, Han K (1998) The CMUnited-97 robotic soccer team: perception and multiagent control. In: Proceedings of the second international conference on autonomous agents, ACM, pp 78–85
34. Wagner T, Gasser L, Luck M, Odell J, Carrico T (2005) Impact for agents. In: 4th international joint conference on autonomous agents and multi-agent systems (industry track), ACM, pp 93–99

Part II
Aspects of Agent-Oriented Software Engineering

Chapter 4
Multi-agent Systems: A Software Architecture Viewpoint

Onn Shehory and Arnon Sturm

Abstract Studies in agent-oriented software engineering address the merit of agents and multi-agent systems as a *software architecture* style, though only in part. MAS software architecture styles are of interest to both the MAS and the software engineering communities. This chapter provides an introduction to these software architectures. As we demonstrate, MAS implementations spanning across decades have several common architectural characteristics, despite different design and implementation details.

An important question associated with MAS development is whether MAS constitute an appropriate solution for a computational problem at hand, and if so, what type of MAS should be preferred for that solution? Preferably, this question better be answered early on, to prevent the use of MAS as a solution approach where simpler, more efficient solutions apply. MAS should be considered among an array of alternative solution approaches. To assist system designers in their assessment of MAS as a solution approach to their problem, we present architectural properties of MAS and we demonstrate these properties by example.

Keywords Software architecture • Agent-oriented software engineering • Architectural styles • MAS design

O. Shehory (✉)
IBM—Haifa Research Lab, Haifa, Israel
e-mail: onn@il.ibm.com

A. Sturm
Department of Information Systems Engineering, Ben-Gurion University of the Negev, Beer-Sheva, Israel
e-mail: sturm@bgu.ac.il

O. Shehory and A. Sturm (eds.), *Agent-Oriented Software Engineering*,
DOI 10.1007/978-3-642-54432-3_4,

1 Introduction

The field of Multi-agent Systems (MAS) focuses on solutions to decentralized problems in dynamic, open computational domains. It discusses issues of intelligence which include, among others, learning [1], negotiation [2, 3], strategic behavior [4, 5], social behaviors and norms [6–8], cognitive activities, and mental states (reasoning [9], beliefs, desires, intentions [10], emotions [11]). Thus, MAS combine research from several fields, and in particular from the fields of Distributed Artificial Intelligence (DAI) and Software Engineering (SE). The latter two constitute the subfield of Agent-Oriented Software Engineering (AOSE), which complements MAS research with practical means for developing multi-agent systems that implement the desired intelligence properties.

A major focus of AOSE, as reflected in this book, is placed on methods, methodologies, and tools for life cycle support of agents and MAS. Methodologies commonly address a wide range of problem domains and types. Yet, when attempting to address a specific problem, system developers frequently need to develop software components and architectures which may already be present in other solutions. In such cases, blueprints of agents and MAS—i.e., their software architectures (SAs)—should be most valuable and facilitate reuse. The focus of this chapter is on such architectures. To a large extent, the chapter is based on earlier work by the authors [12].

Studies in software engineering have identified an array of architectures and patterns and introduced blueprints to facilitate software architecture reuse (for an elaborate discussion of software architecture refer to the seminal book by Garlan and Shaw [13]). MAS research has introduced a variety of architectures to support intelligent behaviors, however seldom in the form of software architecture. Indeed, one aspect of AOSE which is only partly addressed in the art is the merit of agents and multi-agent systems as a *software architecture*. This chapter provides a brief introduction to MAS software architectures. As we demonstrate, MAS implementations spanning across decades have several common architectural characteristics, despite different design and implementation details. Several studies have compared among MAS architectures (e.g., [14]). Work that extends the MAS architecture line of thought, with emphasis on MAS design and implementation based on architecture, is presented by Weyns [15].

MAS studies commonly address questions such as:

- Can a MAS serve as a solution to a given computational problem?
- How should such a solution be built?
- What is the class of problems that a given MAS solves?

AOSE studies commonly address questions such as:

- Can one devise a generic specification language or a protocol for MAS design and specification?
- If this is possible, can one develop a tool to translate the specification into code?
- What is the process to be followed from conception to a working system?

While the questions above are well-addressed in the MAS art (see, e.g., classical resources such as [16–18]), some questions are not always well answered, e.g.:

- Do MAS constitute an *appropriate* solution for a computational problem at hand? (That is, it is not sufficient for MAS to provide a solution—it should be an appropriate one, where MAS are the preferred solution.)
- If so, what type of MAS should be preferred for that solution?

Preferably, these questions better be answered early on, to prevent the use of MAS as a solution approach where simpler, more efficient solutions apply. MAS should be considered among an array of alternative solution approaches. To assist system designers in their assessment of MAS as a solution approach to their problem, we present architectural properties of MAS, we demonstrate these properties by example, and analyze advantages and drawbacks of the architectures.

The rest of this chapter is organized as follows. First, we provide a brief introduction to software architecture (Sect. 1.1) and to MAS (Sect. 1.2). Then, in Sect. 1.3, we introduce some MAS terminology. Following, in Sect. 2, we present properties of multi-agent systems relevant to software architecture, and assess the advantages and disadvantages of different styles of MAS. We proceed in Sect. 3, where we present specific multi-agent infrastructures and analyze them in light of the properties discussed in Sect. 2. Finally, in Sect. 4, we conclude and point at open questions and future directions.

1.1 Introduction to Software Architecture

Software architecture (SA) is an important software engineering discipline. As a result of the increase in size and complexity of software systems, specification and design of the overall structure of such systems has become an increasingly dominant part of their development. At the abstract level, SA involves the description of components of which systems are comprised, the interaction among these components, and the patterns according to which the components are combined to form the whole system. At the practical level, SA refers to the design and specification of issues such as component decomposition and organization, communication protocols, control and data flow and structure, synchronization and access to data, and so forth. Note that in contrast to methodologies, architectures focus on specific problem types or solution types. Hence, they complement methodologies: once a specific architecture was identified for solving a problem at hand, methodologies and tools can be used to develop the solution. The identification of the preferred architecture is commonly part of the analysis and possibly an early part of the design of the target system.

When solving a computational problem, solution designers usually analyze the problem, its characteristics, and typical patterns. These are matched against similar patterns of problems encountered in the past and common software architectures. Applying the most appropriate architecture should reduce development time and increase the efficiency and adequacy of the resulting computational solution.

To differentiate among architectural styles, software architecture usually employs a common framework. The framework adopted in this chapter is based on treating a system as a collection of components and a set of interactions between these components (which is practically a MAS framework). The framework determines what the components that construct instances of the architectural style and what the constraints on the ways in which these components can be combined and interact are. These may include, among others, constraints on the topology of the system (for instance, can an agent be subsumed by another agent), or constraints on the semantics of execution. Once the framework is used to describe styles and systems, one can have a better understanding of the underlying computational model. This can be used to sort out the essentials of the style. It also supports comparison between styles and between systems within the style, thus evaluating advantages and disadvantages of the style.

To utilize this approach, we need to distinguish unique components, interactions, and constraints of different MAS, thus facilitating assessment of advantages and drawbacks of different styles and substyles.

1.2 Software Architectural Aspects of Multi-agent Systems

We attempt to examine MAS mainly with respect to their software architecture styles and attributes stemming from these styles, such as robustness, flexibility and adaptability, code reusability, throughput, and other architectural properties. An analysis of MAS at the architectural level is not common in the art. The AOSE literature, including this book, analyzes attributes as suggested here. However, that analysis is typically done at the methodology level, which is at a higher level of abstraction. Methodologies which support domain engineering can focus on specific architectures, but this is not commonly done, in particular not for MAS. We find it necessary to analyze the relationship between the software architecture of a MAS and its functionality. This analysis should provide system designers and engineers with information upon which they can decide both whether a MAS is an appropriate computational solution to a problem at hand, and if so, what type of MAS provides the most appropriate solution for this problem.

Viewing them as a software architecture style, MAS are systems comprising components called agents. The agents are usually designed to be autonomous, where autonomy refers to a component not depending on the properties or the states of other components for its functionality.

MAS components are usually capable of interaction, typically by message passing in a predefined protocol (agent communication languages, e.g., FIPA-ACL [19] and KQML [20]). In contrast to distributed object architectures (CORBA [21]), it is commonly assumed that no direct function call or implicit event invocation between components (that is, the agents) are allowed. In particular, the autonomy of an agent **a** means that although others can request a service **S** which is provided by **a**, it has the sole control over the activation of its service **S** and may refuse to provide it, or ask for a (monetary) compensation for its service.[1] In this respect, Service-Oriented Architectures (SOA) [22] exhibit similar attributes.

Several architectural styles have been recognized and described in the general SE literature; however, agents and MAS architectures which are well-documented (see, e.g., [23]) are not widely recognized by practitioners. With the increase in the number of MAS industrial solutions, it is necessary to increase the visibility and the accessibility of agent and MAS architectures. Due to their unique suitability to several classes of computational problems, it is important to characterize MAS as a software architecture style and to provide the architectural specifications of such systems. Some effort in this direction was made by [15]. Such specifications should equip system designers with a family of appropriate solutions for highly distributed problems in open, heterogeneous, dynamic, and information-rich environments.

1.3 MAS Terminology

During more than two decades of multi-agent research and practice [24], many terms describing agents and MAS have been introduced [25–27]. While some terms are widely agreed upon, not all have a single widely accepted definition. Nevertheless, to discuss architectural properties, one needs to remove ambiguity in the terminology describing systems, components, and the relationships between them. Below, we define some agents and MAS terms to be used in this chapter:

- *Agent architecture* describes the modules from which a single agent is comprised, the relationships between, and the interactions among these modules. For example, agents (in the context of MAS) usually have a communication module to facilitate communication with other. Some types of agents have internal AI modules such as a reasoning module or a planning module. Incoming messages received by the communication module may affect reasoning and planning (e.g., reason to understand the effects of the message and plan to address these effects). The internal AI modules may create outgoing messages to be processed and sent out by the communication module.
- *MAS organization* describes the way in which a collection of agents is organized to form a MAS. Relationships and interactions among the agents and specific agents' roles within the organization are the focus of MAS organization. The agent architecture is not part of the MAS organization (although interrelations between the two may exist). For instance, the agents may be organized in a rigid hierarchy in which the interrelations are predefined. This may reduce the need to locate other agents and reason about them, and the amount of communication necessary for the system to function well.

[1]In object-based systems, a request for a service **s** from a service provider **a** would be performed by calling a method of **a**'s. Also, a public method of an object o_1 can be activated by another object o_2, and o_1 is not assumed to have control over this activation.

- *Multi-agent services* include services aimed to support a variety of MAS needs. The service types listed below are examples of multi-agent services:
  - Dynamic organizational activity facilitation, notably agent location and coordination mechanisms (possibly implemented by means of middleware or middle agents)
  - Increased system efficiency and resource utilization (e.g., technologies for network sensing, mobility facilitation, dynamic resource allocation and load balancing)
  - Agent and MAS activation, interfacing and testing tools (possibly delivered as part of agent frameworks)
  - Security infrastructure and services (for protecting the agents, information they hold and transactions they perform)

  Multi-agent services are usually associated with the MAS infrastructure.
- *Multi-agent infrastructure* combines *agent architecture*, *MAS organization*, and *multi-agent services*. It also describes dependencies between these when present, thus providing an infrastructure that enables constructing a domain-specific MAS. Commonly, the infrastructure is associated with services which facilitate MAS activity and organization (e.g., agent naming service, agent directory service, agent execution platform, etc.).

The terms above are elaborated upon in the following sections to facilitate the discussion of agent architectures.

2 Agents and MAS Organization

In this section, we present architectural properties of agents and MAS. These properties and their evaluation should facilitate comparison between, and assessment of, different MAS infrastructures. The attributes discussed in this section are later illustrated by examples.

2.1 Agent Internal Architecture

Over the years, a large variety of agent internal architectures were introduced by agent researchers and practitioners. In this chapter we only briefly discuss them, while keeping the major focus on MAS architectures. It is important to note that the incorporation of an agent architecture in a MAS may in times be difficult or not possible at all. This is because, for agents to be incorporated into MAS, it is necessary to equip them with components that facilitate interaction with other agents and users (e.g., communication and cooperation components). Additionally, being part of a MAS imposes restrictions on the admissible interactions among the agents.

Agents, either stand-alone or as part of a MAS, must be able to exhibit behaviors, perform tasks, or provide services, regardless of their internal architecture. In similarity to the information hiding provided via encapsulation in object-oriented programming, agent designers and developers typically prefer that the details of an agent's internal architecture be hidden from other agents and users. This should allow entities with which the agent interacts to assume some capability of the agent's and some interaction protocols (and maybe additional qualitative assumptions), but will prevent the need that they know what methods and components are employed by the agent to behave, perform its tasks, and provide its services.

In practice, although information hiding is a desired architectural property, it is not always present in agent implementations. Often, agents that take part in a MAS do assume some type and structure with respect to the agents with which they interact. Nonetheless, MAS interoperability is facilitated, to a large extent, via standard protocols (e.g., FIPA protocols), public ontologies (e.g., OpenCyc [28]), and communication languages. Another aspect of internal agent architecture is its influence on the overall MAS behavior and the ability of the MAS to efficiently perform its tasks. Although such influence seems an inevitable property of MAS, no extensive software engineering research was performed to investigate this issue.

2.2 *MAS Organization*

Generally speaking, MAS are organized in one of the following ways: hierarchical organization, flat organization (in times referred to as democracy), subsumption organization, and modular organization. Hybrids of these and dynamic changes from one organization style to another are also possible, though not very common in implemented MAS (probably due to the complexity of implementing dynamic reorganization and the limited merit stemming from it). We summarize below the properties of these MAS organizational models.

2.2.1 Hierarchical MAS Organization

Hierarchical MAS (e.g., federated MAS) are organized such that agents can only interact (and in times only communicate) subject to a hierarchical structure. A prominent advantage of the hierarchical structure in MAS is the significant reduction in complexity, and therefore in communication, in the system. Another advantage of a hierarchical MAS is that there is no need for a mechanism for agent registry and location, which are commonly part of MAS infrastructure. For example, in Sect. 4.4, where we present a federated MAS, the components in the upper level of the hierarchy, the facilitators, are in charge of locating agents. The disadvantage of the hierarchical organization is the rigid structure, which does not allow agents to dynamically organize themselves to best fit varying needs and specific tasks. Further, typically the hierarchy implies that the lower-level agents depend on the higher-level agents (e.g., in OAA [29]), and higher-level agents may even be in partial or full control of the lower-level agents. This may contrast requirements for agent autonomy and for agent self-interest.

A hierarchical organization may also imply, to some extent, a centralized control, which is undesirable in systems which are comprised of components that belong to different organizations, and may be geographically distributed as well. An example of a hierarchical MAS organization is presented in Sect. 4.4.

2.2.2 Flat MAS Organization

A flat organization of a MAS implies that each agent can directly contact any of the other agents. No fixed structure is imposed on the system; however, agents may dynamically form structures to perform specific tasks. In addition, no control of one agent by another agent is assumed. Such an organization requires that either the system is closed in the sense that each agent knows all of the others ahead of time, or (when the system is open) an agent location mechanism must be provided as part of the infrastructure. A flat organization is advantageous since it fully supports autonomy and self-interest of agents as well as distribution and openness of the MAS. It also allows for dynamic adjustments of the MAS organization to changes in tasks and the environment. However, openness and dynamism come at a cost: they impose communication overheads, a need for agent location mechanisms, and a need for mechanisms for dynamic MAS reorganization.

Additionally, the amount of reasoning an agent performs with regard to other agents (and consequently the local computational overhead of an agent) increases significantly in a flat organization. An example of a flat MAS organization is presented in Sect. 4.1. MAS based on the Jade platform [30] are another example of a flat organization (although other organizations can be implemented using Jade).

2.2.3 Subsumption MAS Organization

There are MAS where some agents are components of other agents. These agents are subsumed by the container agents, which in turn may be components of larger container agents. The subsumption model, which takes its roots in robotics [31], however, applies well to distributed AI and MAS in general. It has some similarity with the hierarchical model; however, it takes it to the extreme by requiring that the subsumed agents completely surrender to the control of the container agent. From a software architectural viewpoint, such architecture resembles an inclusion of objects within a larger object, except for the (important) difference in the control methods. That is, while objects are usually controlled and activated by (possibly remote) procedure call or by event invocation, agents are activated by high-level communication, i.e., message transmission. The strict control relationships in the subsumption organization, which result in efficient task execution and low communication overhead, however, restrict the system to address a well-defined set of tasks, with limited flexibility and adaptability. It is also not simple to modify a subsumption MAS (e.g., add a new component) in the face of long-term changes in tasks and the environment of the system. An example of a MAS with a subsumption organization is presented in Sect. 4.2.

2.2.4 Modular MAS Organization

A MAS exhibits a modular organization when it is comprised of several modules, where each of these modules can be perceived as a virtually stand-alone MAS. Typically, the partition of the system into modules is done along dimensions such as geographical vicinity or a need for intense interaction among agents and services within the same module. Often, the system is comprised of such parts as a result of its development process, during which new modules were gradually added to an already existing system.

Modularity increases efficiency of MAS task execution and reduces communication overhead. Also, in similarity to a flat organization, each module exhibits internal high flexibility. On the other hand, cross-module reorganization is rather complex, hence in this dimension flexibility is limited. In addition, modularity implies constraints on inter-module communication. For instance, while intra-module communication is usually connection-oriented, inter-module communication may be connectionless, which prohibits the execution of tasks that require inter-modular concurrency. The OSACA [32] system provides an example of a modular MAS architecture.

3 MAS Architectural Properties

MAS organization constitutes an essential element of its architecture. Other architectural properties such as communication structures and protocols, system openness level, flexibility, infrastructure services, and robustness, also take part in MAS architecture. These are referred to here as they are also commonly referred to in general software architectures [13].

3.1 Communication

In the early days of MAS, a common practice was for MAS to implement a specially designed communication protocol that best fits their agent architecture, MAS organization, and the typical tasks of these systems (e.g., ARCHON [8] or OAA [29], which uses an agent communication language (ACL) developed specifically for OAA agents). In recent years, MAS increasingly rely on standard communication languages and protocols (typically FIPA[2] ACL and protocols), although proprietary languages and protocols are still in use. The advantage of proprietary protocols is in their efficiency: the agents are implemented using the same communication infrastructure and transmit only the information necessary with very little overhead and message packaging and parsing.

The major disadvantage is the difficulty to facilitate conversations with agents that are not part of the proprietary communication environment, as it is most unlikely that other agents will have those specialized communication protocols implemented in them.

To overcome this limitation, some MAS platforms implement both a proprietary and standard communication languages. Several other agent platforms do not implement proprietary communication infrastructure and focus on standard communication protocols (e.g., Jade [30], FIPA-OS [33]). Contemporary MAS typically support agent communication languages (ACLs) such as FIPA-ACL (and in times KQML, which is older than FIPA-ACL). This, however, does not mean that two agents from different systems that support the same ACL are able to understand each another. Interoperability requires a common ontology as well. To date, this issue is only partly resolved: standard ontologies do exist and are available online; however, they are either not used, extended and modified by their users, or leave ambiguities even when used with no change. Nevertheless, communication modules that are generic in nature were developed and some are available publicly (e.g., in Jade [30], RETSINA [34] and D'Agents [35]).

Distributed computational systems implement several standard communication protocols. We distinguish three main attributes of such protocols, which are relevant to MAS and to their architecture:

1. *Symmetry*: In many systems, client/server protocols are used for communication. Since client/server protocols are well-supported and documented as part of operating systems and programming languages, such implementations are simple and efficient. The drawback of client/server protocols is that they imply asymmetry between the communicating entities: one is in control of the communication, whereas the other party can only respond upon request and cannot initiate communication. In some MAS—in particular, those implementing proprietary communication—agent communication is implemented as a client/server architecture. Designers of MAS, especially open MAS with a flat organization, have realized that the asymmetry associated with such architecture is inappropriate for these systems and have implemented symmetric means of communication. This, however, increases protocol complexity and may affect communication speed.
2. *Message Recipients*: Messages in a network may be sent to a single addressee, to multiple ones (multicast), and to all (broadcast). In an open system, broadcast is

[2]FIPA stands for Foundation for Intelligent Physical Agents [23]. FIPA provides a specification for agent-based applications including, among other specifications, an ACL called FIPA-ACL and interaction protocols.

impractical, since an agent does not know all of the other agents. Therefore, open MAS usually implement peer-to-peer or multicast communication. In closed MAS, however, broadcast is commonly used (see examples in Sect. 4.1). The advantage of the latter is in the simplicity of the protocol. The disadvantage is that all of the agents receive the message, even when it is completely irrelevant for them, thus increasing network congestion.

3. *Connection Type*: Connection-oriented and connectionless communication are both implemented in MAS. The advantages and drawbacks of these are not unique to MAS, and can be found in standard networks' textbooks (e.g., [36]). Typically, MAS implement connection-oriented communication; however, in some cases connectionless protocols are supported as well. Connection-oriented communication is preferred when dependent tasks are performed concurrently by multiple agents, and close coordination is necessary during execution. In such situations, connectionless communication may prohibit coordination and proper task performance. In MAS where task execution is loosely coordinated and where concurrency is of minor importance, connectionless communication is sufficient.

3.2 System Openness

The openness of a MAS refers to the ability of introducing additional agents into the system in excess to the agents that comprise it initially, and the capability of agents to leave the system and of the system to cope with such departures. While some MAS architectures do not allow the addition of agents (at all), others may be more open, allowing to add agents with different styles of addition. In its basic level, MAS openness refers to the OSI (Open Systems Interconnection [37]) definition of system openness. However, in MAS, additional properties are considered. One can classify MAS openness into three broad categories:

1. *Dynamic Openness*: In MAS, the level of dynamism allowed for adding and removing agents has a significant effect on the properties of the system. MAS that allow agents to leave or join the system dynamically, during run time, without any explicit message to all of the other agents in the system, are the most open ones. The advantage of such openness is in the ability of the system to dynamically adjust itself to changes in the environment, tasks, and availability of resources. Dynamic openness facilitates online addition of third-party agents, which in turn enables dynamic introduction of new capabilities and resources. This type of dynamism is necessary when MAS are deployed in environments with high levels of uncertainty, unstable connectivity, and rapid changes in tasks. A prominent disadvantage of dynamic openness is the additional services and computation required to facilitate it. When agents can unpredictably appear and disappear, a robust agent location mechanism is essential. Also, agents must be provided with methods to alternate their tasks execution and planning, since availability

of necessary capabilities and resources varies over time as the agent population changes.

2. *Static Openness*: Less dynamic, yet considered open, is the case where agents can be added to the system without restarting it, but either all of the agents are notified on such an addition, or they all hold in advance a list of prospective additional agents. This type of openness eliminates the need for a complex agent location mechanism, and reduces the complexity of contingent execution and planning computation (although these are not eliminated). On the other hand, the flexibility of the system and its ability to adjust itself to dynamic changes is restricted. Such openness is insufficient for environments with high levels of uncertainty. It can better fit cases in which changes are more gradual and predictable. Online addition of third-party agents is not supported by this architecture, which in turn limits adaptability of MAS to changing conditions and tasks.
3. *Offline Openness*: The most restricted type of openness is the one that allows the addition of new agents only offline, by halting the system, adding agents, updating some connection information, and restarting the system. This approach allows for changes in the system over time; however, dynamic changes are not supported. While this restricts flexibility, it eliminates the need for infrastructure services and for additional computation to handle dynamic changes in the system. Hence, such systems perform more efficiently in cases of well-defined, predictable, and relatively static problem domains.

The classes of MAS openness listed above are part of a wide spectrum of openness levels and styles. Modifications of these classes and hybrids thereof allow gaining some advantages and compromising others.

3.3 Infrastructure Services

In some MAS infrastructure services are inseparable from the system, whereas in others they are optional or even unnecessary. We provide details of some of these services:

1. *Agent Naming*: An open MAS must be provided with an agent naming service, so that no two agents will have identical names, and the consequent confusion be avoided. Close systems or slightly open systems, where all of the agents (or the possible ones—in the latter systems) are known in advance do not need a naming service.
2. *Agent Location*: Another type of service necessary in open MAS is an agent location service (e.g., brokering or matchmaking [38]). When the existence and availability of agents are not common knowledge, this service is a precondition to the ability of a MAS to perform its tasks. An agent location service is sometimes implemented in a centralized manner, which may be simpler to implement and maintain, however more vulnerable, and creates a single point of failure of the MAS. In contrast, distributed location mechanisms (see, e.g., [39]) are more

complicated to design, implement, and maintain, and increase communication and computation overheads; however, they can provide a reliable, robust service.

3. *Security, Privacy, and Trust*: Security, privacy, and trust are optional services which can be very useful in open MAS. In such systems, an agent may be uncertain with regards to the true identity and the trustworthiness of other agents. Security mechanisms can reduce the risks that stem from this uncertainty. Security infrastructure is not commonly provided as part of MAS infrastructure; however, some support to agent trust [40] and secure transactions among agents can be found [41]. For MAS in which such services are absent, the addition of such services may require introducing trusted third parties such as electronic Certification Authorities as well as implementing protocols to be followed by the agents [42]. This, inevitably, increases computation (e.g., for encryption and decryption) and communication (e.g., for reputation management) overheads, and may create bottlenecks at the third parties.
4. *Mobility*: There is a unique family of MAS—those that allow for agent mobility (e.g., Agent Tcl [43], D'Agents [35], Aglets [44], Jade [30]), where an infrastructure service that supports mobility may be required. The most common way to provide this service is via mobility servers, sometimes called agent docks. Agent docks are servers which are running on machines where mobile agents are allowed to arrive. The mobile agent "docks" at the dock, and the dock provides interface and access to resources on that machine subject to the restrictions applicable to the arriving agent. Mobility servers increase computation overheads on the machines they run. On the other hand, they provide an essential service in case that mobility is necessary.

Other system services may be present as well (e.g., shared storage, dynamic resource management). We have presented above only those few which we have identified as more commonly used and required.

3.4 System Robustness

One of the advantages of MAS is the distribution of execution, which allows for an increase in overall performance. In addition, failure of one agent does not necessarily imply a failure of the whole system. The robustness provided by MAS is further increased by replicated capabilities. This replication is enabled by having multiple agents with the same or similar capabilities in the system. In such cases, when an agent that has some capability becomes unavailable, another agent with a similar capability may be approached. Replicated capabilities are more natural (and useful) in open MAS; however, they can support robustness in close MAS as well. The disadvantage of this replication is in the resulting redundancy, which in times is merely a waste of resources. The robustness of a MAS depends also on the type of services it uses and the way in which these are implemented, as mentioned above.

Other software architectural properties, although important, are of lesser significance for the design of multi-agent systems and therefore not included in the discussion above.

4 Illustrative Examples

In this section we present MAS examples and illustrate their architectural properties concentrating on the multi-agent infrastructure attributes of these systems. We analyze their properties along several dimensions, emphasizing the MAS organization. We discuss the advantages and drawbacks of different MAS infrastructures in light of MAS architectural properties presented in Sects. 2 and 3.

4.1 Early MAS Infrastructure

Among the earlier MAS infrastructures one may find Archon [8], which provides a system organization as well as agent internal architecture. In similarity with other early MAS infrastructures, Archon was developed at the time where no agents' standards and no common agent communication languages were available. The major goal of Archon was to reduce the complexity of control in large, complex (usually preexisting) computational systems. This was achieved via distribution of execution and control. A set of existing domain-specific applications which solve specific problems are assumed. The whole system is comprised of these component systems, and the MAS infrastructure provided by Archon facilitates this.

To implement cooperation among the component systems, Archon provides a layered organization, somewhat similar to the OSI [37] layered communication protocol. A session layer delivers interconnection services between agents. An Archon layer component is attached to each application to provide two interfaces: one to the underlying application and one to the rest of the agent community via the session layer. Each Archon layer component controls itself, its application system, and its interaction with other agents. In the Archon approach, an agent is the combined entity that includes the application system and its attached Archon layer. The application systems implement domain-specific functionality, and the Archon layer serves only for coordination and cooperation among domain-specific components.

The Archon architecture was aimed to be an open architecture. That is, applications may be added to the whole system by attaching an Archon layer component to the added domain-specific application. Although Archon openness complies with the OSI approach to openness, it is somewhat confined. First, the addition (or removal) of components cannot be done dynamically. Agents can locate (and communicate with) other agents using two complementing methods: (1) Hardwired addresses in the local address list of each agent; (2) Agents broadcast their availability to a single matching services agent, well known to all agents, which serves as a blackboard-like mechanism. The latter constitutes a centralized mechanism which results in a single point of failure, whereas the former limits the openness of the system, since only predefined agents can be added to it, or at least all of the addresses of agents that may potentially join the system must be known in advance. This

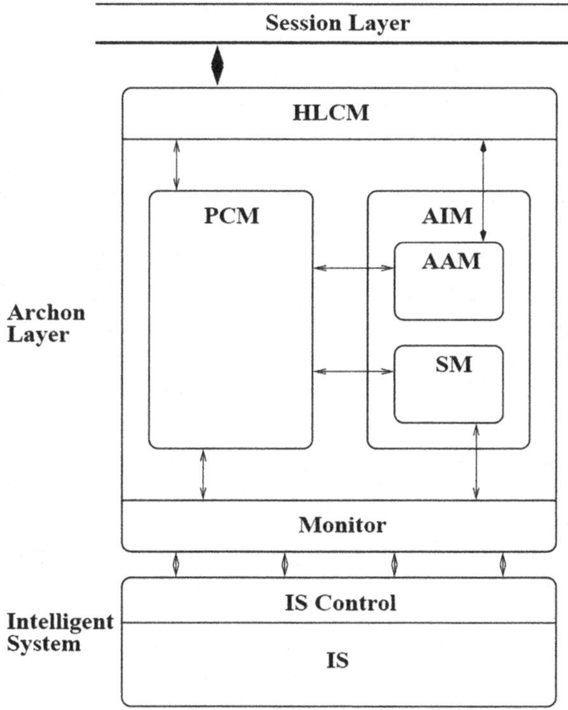

Fig. 4.1 The Archon agent architecture

means that new agents that appear dynamically cannot add themselves or be added to the system. In the case of dynamic multi-agent systems, such an organization is somewhat closed. Additionally, even when agents are known in advance, their ability to join the system depends on their ability to appear as Archon agents. That is, an agent can be connected to an Archon-based MAS only by using the Archon session layer, which requires following its communication protocols. Note that this confining attribute is typical to many early multi-agent infrastructures, mainly because of the lack of standard protocols for agent communication.

Note again that the Archon MAS infrastructure is brought here only by example. Other early MAS infrastructures deliver similar though not identical properties. For instance, OSACA, an Open System for Asynchronous Cognitive Agents [32], is a general multi-agent infrastructure which exhibits similar properties, although it is somewhat more open in its ability to add new agents dynamically. In addition to its MAS organization, Archon supports agent architecture as well. An Archon agent architecture is comprised of two components: the Archon layer and the Intelligent System (IS), which the Archon layer interfaces with, and monitors. The IS is usually a preexisting, separately designed, developed, and implemented component, which does not follow a dictated Archon architecture. The internal architecture of an Archon layer consists of modules as follows (see Fig. 4.1).

The *information management module* (AIM) provides a model and a language for information manipulation, for local and remote access and update. It subsumes two internal modules, the *self model* (SM) and *agent acquaintance module* (AAM). The SM holds a model of the IS and reasons about its state. The AAM contains models of other agents in the community. The *monitor module* monitors and manages the IS by checking the states of its tasks, starting and stopping tasks, and supplying data from external sources. The *planning and coordination module* (PCM) assesses interactional situations and plans and monitors cooperation with other agents. The *high-level communication module* (HLCM) is defined as the layer between the session layer and other Archon modules (collectively referred to as the Archon layer). The HLCM provides the other modules with three key services: intelligent addressing, and message filtering and scheduling.

To summarize, following the architectural terms defined in earlier sections, Archon is a multi-agent infrastructure with a flat organization and static openness. It allows for cooperation between previously existing specialized systems. It supports distributed control of these systems as well as high-level communication and information exchange among them. In addition, Archon enables adding new specialized subsystems to the system without recompiling the system. This addition is limited to previously known names and addresses of the components to be added. Archon was designed as a layered architecture. Conceptually, each layer may be replaced by a component that complies with the interface requirements of the adjacent layers. Issues such as security, privacy, and trust are not explicitly addressed in Archon, and mobility is not supported.

4.2 Agent-Agency Infrastructure

ADEPT (Advanced Decision Environment for Process Tasks) [45] is another example of an early multi-agent infrastructure. It was aimed at facilitating collaboration among autonomous units of organizations. ADEPT suggests a subsumption MAS organization: the MAS is comprised of agencies, where each agency may either be a single agent or, recursively, a collection of several agencies. Communication and cooperative task execution are performed either within an agency, among its members, or between agencies, however not directly between members of an agency and agents or agencies outside this agency. Each agency is represented by a single responsible agent. Consequently, ADEPT can support both hierarchical and flat organizational structures, and combinations thereof; however, the specific organization style must be set in advance and cannot be altered dynamically. While this organization is more flexible than the ones provided in Archon and OSACA, the partition into agencies limits dynamic changes in organizational structure.

The ADEPT system organization is depicted in Fig. 4.2. Agents and agencies can only communicate and (directly) cooperate with agents and agencies within their encapsulating agency. For example, agencies 5 and 8, which are subagencies of agency 4, cannot directly communicate with agencies 1 and 3. They can use

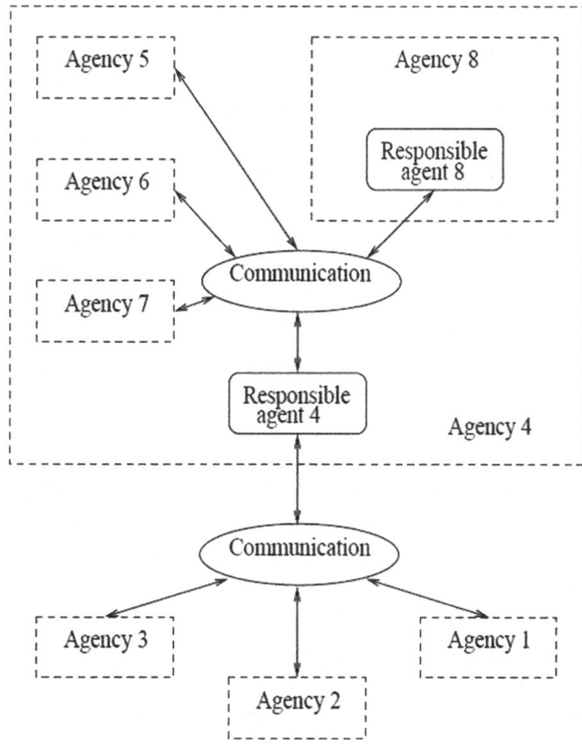

Fig. 4.2 The ADEPT MAS organization

the responsible agent 4 to contact entities external to agency 4 (however, they are not assumed to know these entities). In ADEPT, communication requires that agents, agencies, and tasks, which are all objects, register themselves with an Object Request Broker (ORB) as defined in the CORBA specifications [21]. The ADEPT internal agent architecture is similar to the one provided by Archon.

In summary, ADEPT supports a more flexible organization than other early MAS infrastructures do. Yet, dynamic organizational changes are not supported. An interesting property of ADEPT is of tasks being autonomous entities. This allows mobility of tasks among agents and agencies and thus may support dynamic mobility and load balancing. Issues of openness are not explicitly addressed in ADEPT, and it seems to allow a rather close openness level.

4.3 *Flexible MAS Organization*

Examples presented thus far show specific MAS organizations such as hierarchy, flat organization, and subsumption. Clearly, flexibility in MAS design is necessary. DESIRE is a framework for DEsign and Specification of Interacting REasoning components [46] which facilitates such flexibility. It was used for developing reusable multi-agent applications. Using logic, DESIRE enables specification of generic multi-agent models. DESIRE specifications are based on compositional, hierarchical architecture. In similarity to object-oriented design, each component has its input and output interfaces specifications defined and known to other components, whereas the internal structure is hidden from the rest of the system. This allows for reuse.

DESIRE classifies agent types including reflective, reactive, cognitive, social and BDI (believe, desire, intend) agents. This classification, although important for multi-agent research, has a limited significance when software architecture properties are examined. While reactive and proactive activity of agents can be referred to as software architecture issues, cognitive and social behaviors are not so. Nevertheless, the compositional approach of DESIRE presents interesting architectural properties. Some such properties can be found, e.g., in the *weak agent* type [10].

Following its compositional approach, the DESIRE framework does not dictate a specific agent organization. It allows for a variety of organizational styles, each designed to fit the properties of a specific problem domain. This results in flexibility in the design stage of MAS based on DESIRE; however, once such a system is implemented its organization is no longer flexible or dynamically adaptable. Similarly, agent mobility is not supported, although it can be implemented using an agent factory (thus providing generative agent migration). Issues such as security, privacy, and trust are not explicitly addressed either. Communication follows standard inter-object communication architectures.

4.4 Federated MAS

A different approach to constructing multi-agent systems is presented by Genesereth and Ketchpel [47], in which they introduce a system organization which consists of agents and *facilitators* as a means for interoperability. Facilitators and agents are organized into a federated system (see Fig. 4.3). An example of a federated system is OAA [29]. The federated organization suggests that agents communicate via facilitators. This way, each group of agents who are facilitated by a single facilitator is a *federation* in which an agent surrenders some of its autonomy to the facilitator. In this organization, the facilitator's role is to translate messages and direct them to agents that can handle them. In a federated MAS organization, agents can dynamically connect and disconnect from a facilitator, thus exhibiting dynamic openness. Upon connection to a facilitator, an agent specifies its capabilities and needs in an agent communication language (ACL). The federated organization facilitates application interoperability, however, compromises agent autonomy. Flexible interoperability can be supported by other types of middle agents [48]

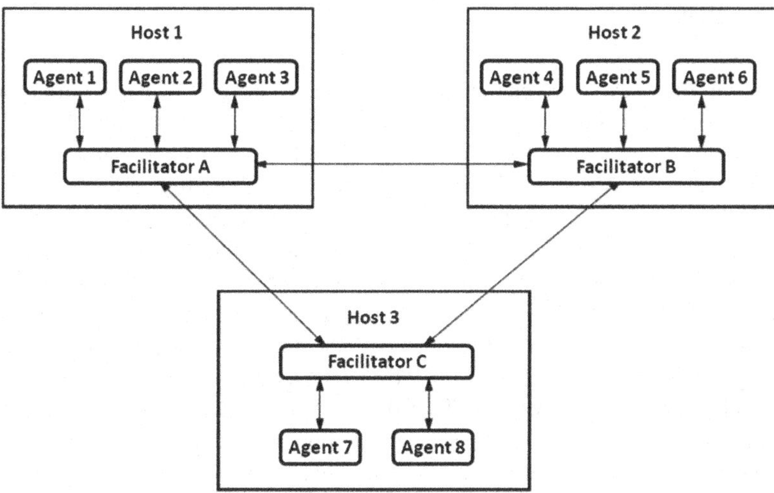

Fig. 4.3 Federated MAS organization

(e.g., matchmakers in [34, 49]). Issues such as security, privacy and trust are not explicitly addressed either but are partly supported by facilitators.

4.5 FIPA Specifications

FIPA, the Foundation for Intelligent Physical Agents [23], has produced a set of specifications for various aspects of agent architectures. These focus mainly on the communication and the agent location aspects of the architecture, e.g., agent communication language and agent interaction protocols, among others. Yet, FIPA does not provide specifications for MAS organization. Implicitly, the communication and agent location as specified by FIPA facilitate a variety of MAS organizations. Indeed, specific implementation of FIPA specifications in agent frameworks (e.g., Jade [30]) suggest several different MAS organizations. Dynamic openness is well-supported by FIPA specification and its implementations. Agents from various FIPA-compliant frameworks can interoperate, and can join MAS dynamically. FIPA also has security and mobility specifications.

Note also that examples presented in this section are in large part rather old MAS and agent systems and frameworks. There are several reasons for this choice. First, older architectures were usually the first ones to introduce the architectures we discuss. Second, older architectures tend to be simpler and thus more comprehensible than newer ones. Third, and most importantly, they indeed exemplify well some fundamental concept of MAS and agent architectures.

5 Conclusion

Software architecture involves the structure and organization of a software system as well as nonstructural properties associated with the system. In this chapter, we have discussed software architecture styles of multi-agent systems and illustrated these via examples. Many architectural properties presented here are not unique to MAS. However, when combined in a single system they typically constitute a MAS, establishing a unique architectural style. This combination and style facilitate the suitability of MAS for solving problems where information, location, and control are distributed, where heterogeneous autonomous (i.e., self-controlled) components comprise the system, where the system is open, the environment is dynamically changing, and uncertainty is present. In some cases, only a subset of these problem domain characteristics is present. This does not mean that MAS are no longer relevant as an architecture and as a solution approach. Yet, in such cases it may be advisable to consider architectures other than MAS as a solution approach. One should bear in mind that the high complexity of MAS and the amount of code replication in such systems may result in excessive, unnecessary efforts in the development and maintenance phases as well as inefficient solution and poor system performance.

There is a large variety of agent systems, frameworks, and architectures, many of which could serve as good examples of MAS software architectures too. We leave their examination as exercise to the reader or as subject for future studies on agent architecture. Indeed, there is a need to further study agents and MAS software architecture styles. To facilitate reuse, one needs to know what MAS styles are available and what the advantages and the drawbacks of each are. Additionally, accurate, formal specification of architectural styles is required. Further, methods and tools for applying agents and MAS architectures should assist in realizing architectural styles in practical software projects. Methods and tools are widely discussed in this book, but their association with agents and MAS architectural styles is yet to be explored in future research.

References

1. Haynes T, Sen S (1998) Learning cases to resolve conflicts and improve group behavior. International Journal of Human Computer Studies (IJHCS) 48:31–49
2. Kraus S, Wilkenfeld J, Zlotkin G (1995) Multi-agent negotiation under time constraints. Art Intel 75(2):297–345
3. Rosenschein JS, Zlotkin G (1994) Rules of encounter: designing conventions for automated negotiation among computers. MIT Press, Boston
4. Sandholm TW, Lesser VR (1997) Coalitions among computationally bounded agents. Art Intel 94:99–137
5. Shehory O, Kraus S (1996) A kernel-oriented model for coalition formation in general environments: implementation and results. In: Proceedings of AAAI'96. Portland, OR, USA, pp 134–140

6. Castelfranchi C (1990) Social power. In: Demazeau Y, Muller JP (eds) Decentralized AI. Elsevier Science Publishers, New York, NY, pp 49–62
7. Shoham Y, Tennenholtz M (1992) On the synthesis of useful social laws for artificial agent societies. In: Proceedings of AAAI'92, CA, USA, pp 276–281
8. Wittig T (ed) (1992) ARCHON: an architecture for multi-agent systems. Ellis Horwood, Chichester
9. Halpern JY (1994) A theory of knowledge and ignorance for many agents. Technical Report RJ 9894, IBM Research Division
10. Rao AS, Georgeff MP (1995) BDI agents: from theory to practice. In: Lesser V (ed), Proceedings of the first international conference on multi-agent systems. MIT Press, San Francisco, CA, pp 312–319
11. Bates J (1994) The role of emotion in believable agents. Commun ACM 37(7):122–125
12. Shehory O (2000) Software architecture attributes of multi-agent systems. In: Proceedings of AOSE'00, pp 77–90
13. Shaw M, Garlan D (1996) Software architecture: perspectives on an emerging discipline. Prentice Hall, New Jersey
14. Sloman A, Scheutz M (2002) A framework for comparing agent architectures. In: Proceedings UKCI'02: UK Workshop on Computational Intelligence
15. Weyns D (2010) Architecture-based design of multi-agent systems. Springer, Heidelberg
16. Huhns M, Singh M (eds) (1998) Readings in agents. Morgan Kaufmann, California
17. Jennings NR, Wooldridge M (eds) (1998) Agent technology. Springer, Heidelberg
18. Nwana H, Azarmi N (eds) (1997) Lecture notes in AI Vol. 1198 Software agents and soft computing. Springer, Heidelberg
19. FIPA Communicative Act Library Specification. TR XC00037 and others
20. Finin T, Fritzon R, McKay D, McEntire R (1994) KQML – a language and protocol for knowledge and information exchange. In: Proceedings of the 13th international workshop on distributed AI, Seatle, WA, July 1994. Lecture Notes in AI, vol 890. Springer, Heidelberg, pp 126–136
21. Mowbray TJ, Ruh WA (1997) Inside CORBA distributed object standards and applications. Addison Wesley, Boston, MA
22. Erl T (2005) Service-oriented architecture: concepts, technology, and design. Prentice Hall, New Jersey
23. http://www.fipa.org/
24. Weiss G (ed) (2013) Multiagent systems, 2013th edn. MIT Press, Cambridge, MA
25. Davidsson P, Wernstedt F (2004) A framework for evaluation of multi-agent system approaches to logistics network management. In: Multiagent systems, artificial societies, and simulated organizations, vol 10. Springer, Berlin, pp 27–29
26. Sturm A, Shehory O (2001) Evaluation of modeling techniques for agent-based systems. AGENTS'01. February 11–13, 2001, Montréal, Quebec, Canada, pp 624–631
27. Wooldridge M, Jennings N, Kinny D (1999) A methodology for agent oriented analysis and design. AGENTS'99. Seattle, WA, USA, pp 69–76
28. http://www.cyc.com/platform/opencyc
29. Martin DL, Cheyer AJ, Moran DB (1999) The open agent architecture: a framework for building distributed software systems. Appl Art Intel 13(1–2):91–128
30. http://jade.tilab.com/
31. Brooks RA (1991) How to build complete creatures rather than isolated cognitive simulators. In: VanLehn K (ed) Architectures for intelligence. Lawrence Erlbaum Associates, Hillsdale, NJ, pp 225–239
32. Scalabrin E, Barthes JP (1993) Osaca: une architecture ouverte d'agents cognitifs independants. In: Actes de la Journee "Systemes multiagents", Montpellier, France
33. Buckle P, Moore T, Robertshaw S, Treadway A, Tarkoma S, Poslad S (2002) Scalability in multi-agent systems: the FIPA-OS perspective. In: Foundations and applications of multi-agent systems. LNCS vol 2403. Springer, Berlin, pp 110–130

34. Sycara K, Decker K, Pannu A, Williamson M, Zeng D (1996) Distributed intelligent agents. IEEE Expert Intel Syst Appl 11(6):36–45
35. Gray RS, Kotz D, Cybenko G, Rus D (1998) D'agents: security in a multiple language, mobile agent system. In: Vigna G (ed), Mobile agent security, Lecture Notes in Computer Science. Springer, Heidelberg
36. Tanenbaum AS (1988) Computer networks. Prentice Hall, New Jersey
37. http://www.iso.org/iso/iso_catalogue/catalogue_tc/catalogue_detail.htm?csnumber=20269
38. Sycara KP, Widoff S, Klusch M, Lu J (2002) Larks: dynamic matchmaking among heterogeneous software agents in cyberspace. Auto Agents Multi-Agent Syst 5(2):173–203
39. Jha S, Chalasani P, Shehory O, Sycara K (1998) A formal treatment of distributed matchmaking. In: Proceeding of Agents'98, pp. 457–458, Minneapolis, Minnesota
40. Ramchurn SD, Huynh TD, Jennings NR (2004) Trust in multi-agent systems. Know Eng Rev 19(1):1–25
41. Chi Wong H, Sycara KP (2000) Adding security and trust to multiagent systems. Appl Art Intel 14(9):927–941
42. Mass Y (2000) Onn Shehory: distributed trust in open multi-agent systems. Trust Cyber-Soc 2000:159–174
43. Gray RS, Kotz D, Nog S, Rus D, Cybenko G (1996) Mobile agents for mobile computing. Technical report PCSTR96285. Dartmouth College, Computer Science, Hanover, NH
44. http://aglets.sourceforge.net/
45. Norman T, Jennings N, Faratin P, Mamdani E (1996) Designing and implementing a multiagent architecture for business process management. In: Muller J, Jennings N, Wooldridge M (eds) Intelligent agents 3. Lecture Notes in AI, vol 1193. Springer, Heidelberg, pp 261–275
46. Brazier F, Dunin Keplicz B, Jennings NR, Treur J (1995) Formal specification of multi-agent systems: a real world case. In: Victor L (ed), Proceedings of the first international conference on multi-agent systems. MIT Press, San Francisco, CA, pp 25–32
47. Genesereth MR, Ketchpel SP (1994) Software agents. Commun ACM 37(7):48–53
48. Decker K, Sycara K, Williamson M (1997) Middleagents for the internet. In: Proceedings of IJCAI97. Nagoya, Japan, pp 578–583
49. Kuokka D, Harada L (1995) On using KQML for matchmaking. In: Proceedings of the first international conference on multi-agent systems. AAAI Press, San Francisco, pp 239–245

Chapter 5
Design Patterns for Multi-agent Systems: A Systematic Literature Review

Joanna Juziuk, Danny Weyns, and Tom Holvoet

Abstract Design patterns document a field's systematic knowledge derived from experiences. Despite the vast body of work in the field of multi-agent systems (MAS), design patterns for MAS are not popular among software practitioners. As MAS have features that are widely considered as key to engineering complex distributed applications, it is important to provide a clear overview of existing patterns to make this knowledge accessible. To that end, we performed a systematic literature review (SLR) covering the main publication venues of the field since 1998, resulting in 206 patterns. The study shows that (1) there is a lack of a standard template for documenting design patterns for MAS, which hampers the use of patterns by practitioners, (2) associations between patterns are poorly described, which results in a lack of overview of the pattern space, (3) patterns for MAS have been used for a variety of application domains, which underpins their high potential for practitioners, and (4) classifications of design patterns for MAS are bounded to specific pattern catalogs, a more holistic view on the pattern space is missing. From our study, we outline a number of guidelines that are important for future work on design patterns for MAS and their adoption in practice.

Keywords Design patterns • Multi-agent systems • Systematic literature review

J. Juziuk • D. Weyns (✉)
Department of Computer Science, Linnaeus University, 35195 Växjö, Sweden
e-mail: jjuziuk@gmail.com; danny.weyns@gmail.com

T. Holvoet
Department of Computer Science, Katholieke Universiteit Leuven, Celestijnenlaan 200A, 3000 Leuven, Belgium
e-mail: tom.holvoet@cs.kuleuven.be

O. Shehory and A. Sturm (eds.), *Agent-Oriented Software Engineering*,
DOI 10.1007/978-3-642-54432-3_5,

1 Introduction

Capturing design knowledge in the form of patterns is a common practice in mainstream software engineering [2, 18, 19, 51]. Design patterns allow reuse of best practices and avoiding worst. The usefulness of patterns has been proven empirically [42, 47]. Design patterns improve software's quality properties, like maintainability and reusability, and speed up the development time. These factors are crucial in practice, especially for project managers, since improving them reduces costs.

During the last decade, the multi-agent system (MAS) community has put significant efforts in documenting design patterns. Despite the substantial body of work, design patterns for MAS have not received the attention they deserve, neither in the agent-oriented software community nor among software practitioners [59,62]. In [11], the authors state that:

> One of the main reasons why mainstream software developers do not benefit from MAS patterns is that they simply do not know them.

As MAS have features that are widely considered as key to engineering complex distributed applications [35, 63], it is important to provide a clear overview of existing patterns to make this knowledge accessible to practitioners. To that end, we performed a systematic literature review (SLR) covering the main publication venues of the field since 1998. From the 815 studies considered, 39 were included in the study, resulting in 206 patterns. In this chapter, we report the results of this literature review, and from our findings, we outline a number of guidelines that, in our opinion, are important for future work on design patterns for MAS and their adoption in practice.

2 Background

> To understand is to perceive patterns - Issaiah Berlin

The concept of *design pattern* was introduced in building architecture by Christopher Alexander in the 1970s [1]. According to Alexander, building structures and town planning should be supported by design patterns. These patterns consist of three layers as shown in Fig. 5.1.

Design patterns have been adopted in many disciplines, for example, psychology and social sciences. In the context of software engineering, patterns support better design decisions, improve communication among stakeholders, and save time by reusing proven solutions. Gabriel, as cited in [2], defines a design pattern as:

> [...] a three-part rule, which expresses a relation between a certain context, a certain system of forces which occurs repeatedly in that context, and a certain software configuration which allows these forces to resolve themselves.

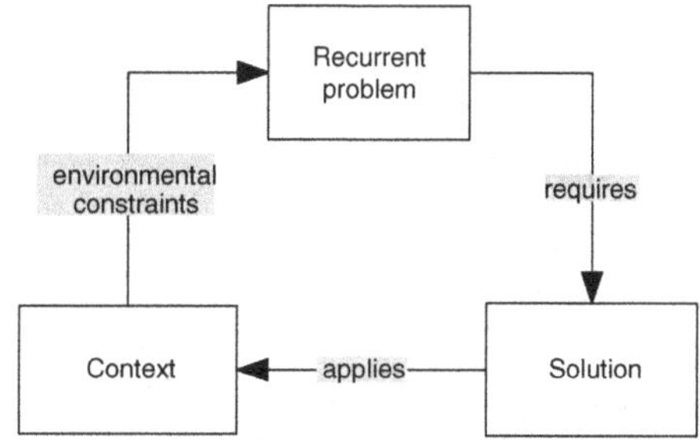

Fig. 5.1 Pattern anatomy [1]. The first layer embodies a recurring problem. A problem arises in a situation known as a context—i.e., the second layer. The third layer is the solution, i.e., a well-known and proven solution to a problem in a context

Design patterns are meant to be generic, so their application and implementation may vary. Furthermore, design patterns are pragmatic, yet tested solutions, as they are derived from experience with building real, concrete systems.

Design patterns are often classified and grouped in a form of a catalog. A catalog serves as a library of expertise of successful solutions, hence it is an effective tool for learning and teaching. The Gang of Four (GoF) proposed the first classification of software design patterns [19]. This pattern catalog uses a two dimensional classification based on scope and purpose. The catalog contains 23 design patterns that were previously undocumented. Buschman's classification [5] is another well-known organization of software design patterns. This catalog promotes functionality and structural principles and uses also a classification along two dimensions: granularity and purpose. Other popular catalogs are Fowler's pattern catalog [18], J2EE blueprints [2] for large scale enterprise applications, and Schmidt's catalog [50] that documents design patterns for concurrency.

In conclusion, design patterns are considered particularly useful assets in engineering complex systems, and various pattern catalogs have been documented.

3 Research Method

The research method used in this study is a SLR. An SLR is a well-defined approach to identify, evaluate and interpret all relevant studies regarding a particular research question, topic area or phenomenon of interest [31].

The study aims to provide an overview of documented design patterns for MAS. In particular, we aim to identify how the patterns are documented, whether and how the patterns are related, and for what applications the patterns have been applied. From our study, we aim to outline guidelines for future work on design patterns for MAS and in particular their popularization in practice. The main benefit of applying an SLR is that it decreases the likelihood that the results of our study will be biased. The material of the review is available online via http://homepage.lnu.se/staff/daweaa/SLR-MASpatterns.htm.

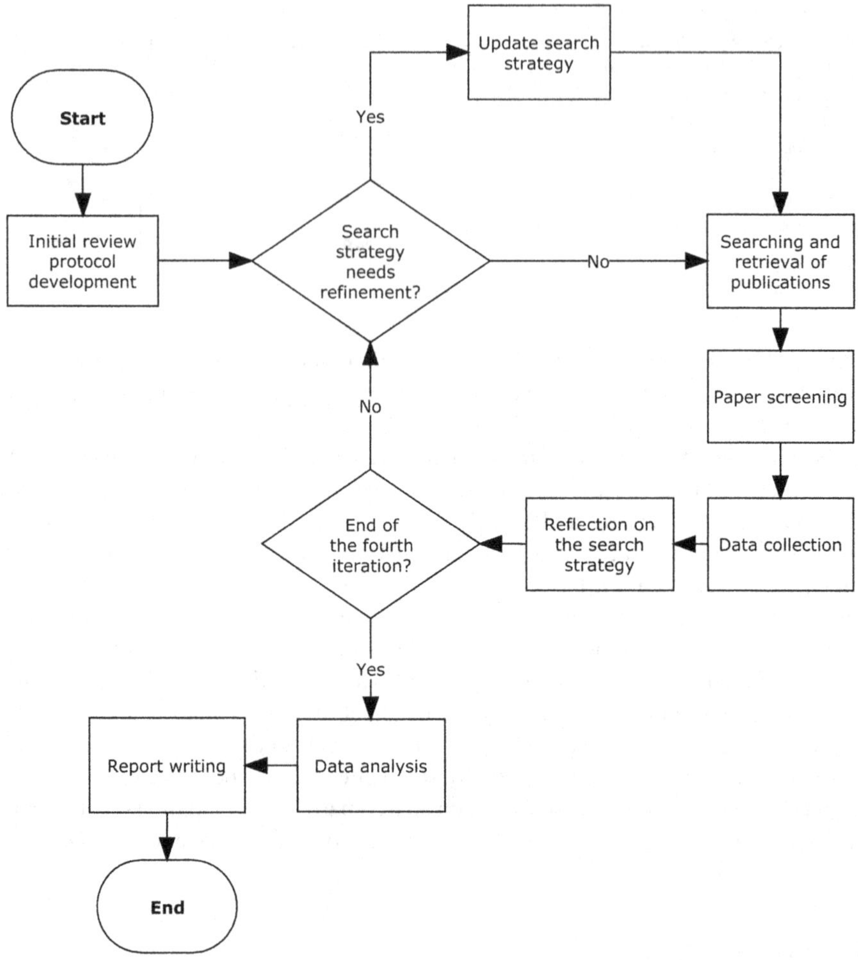

Fig. 5.2 SLR process used in our study

3.1 SLR Process

Figure 5.2 shows an overview of the SLR process we have followed. The study started with defining an initial review protocol, followed by retrieving and selecting publications, data analysis, and report writing. We organized the harvesting of the publications in four iterations. This approach was inspired by methodologies for Agile system development as their core principles are adaptive planning, time-boxed iterations, and rapid/flexible response to change [37]. We deviated from a single harvesting step of a regular SLR [31] as we wanted to learn from each iteration and adapt the search strategy accordingly.

The review was performed by three researchers. Two reviewers defined the initial protocol. The actual harvesting process was performed by one reviewer, while the three reviewers evaluated the results of the subsequent harvesting steps and adapted the search strategy in consultation. One reviewer extracted the data from the selected studies. Finally, two reviewers synthesized and analyzed the data and wrote the review report. These final steps were crosschecked by the third reviewer.

3.2 Research Questions

The following research questions are defined:

RQ1: How are the patterns documented and what pattern templates are used?
RQ2: How are the design patterns interconnected?
RQ3: For what types of systems have the design patterns been applied?
RQ4: How can the design patterns be classified?

As simplicity and overview of a template are crucial factors for the usability of patterns for practitioners, the motivation behind RQ1 is to study how pattern templates are used, identify whether there is any (need for) standardization to describe design patterns for MAS, and what may constitute as a common vocabulary for a future pattern language. We formulated RQ2 to understand the relationships between patterns. Visualizing associations between patterns will benefit users' learnability and help orientation in the space of design patterns for MAS. RQ3 aims to identify for which type of systems or application domains design patterns have been applied in practice. The answer may reveal potential domains for future application of design patterns for MAS. Finally, with RQ4 we aim to identify dimensions to classify design patterns. Such classification can serve as a roadmap to search for particular patterns. The coverage for the various dimensions can help in identifying areas that deserve attention in future work on patterns for MAS.

3.3 Review Protocol

A review protocol is essential to any SLR [31]. Driven by the research questions, the protocol defines inclusion/exclusion criteria to select primary studies, a search strategy, the data items that will be collected to answer the research questions, and finally the approach that will be used for data analysis. In the following sections, we explain in more detail how we have applied the different steps of the protocol.

3.3.1 Inclusion and Exclusion Criteria

A study was included if it fulfilled all the inclusion criteria, that is:

IC1: The study concerns design patterns for MAS
IC2: It is published between 1998 and 2012
IC3: The abstract and content are written in English

A study was excluded if it fulfilled one of the exclusion criteria, that is:

EC1: The patterns are not described in detail, or a structured template is lacking
EC2: A newer study exists that documents the same patterns
EC3: The paper concerns a review or evaluation of existing patterns for MAS

3.3.2 Search Strategy

As explained above, we followed an iterative approach to search studies. In the subsequent iterations we adopted a mixed search strategy to incorporate new search results. The first iteration included a manual search of the *International Journal of Agent-Oriented Software Engineering* (IJAOSE) and an automatic search based on a list of keywords in the electronic databases: ACM Digital Library, Science Direct and Lib Hub. The following Boolean search strings were used:

- (Multi-agent OR multi-agent OR MAS OR "multi-agent system" OR "multi-agent systems" OR "multi-agent system" OR "multi-agent systems") AND ("design pattern" OR pattern OR patterns OR "design patterns")
- (Agent-based OR agent-oriented OR agent) AND ("design pattern" OR pattern OR patterns OR "design patterns")

In the second iteration, the automatic search was extended to other databases: IEEE Xplore, SpringerLink and GoogleScholar. In the third iteration, after initial selection and creation of a preliminary list with patterns, other search techniques were incorporated. In particular, we searched the reference lists of the selected studies to find related missing articles and other publications of the same authors to exclude doubles of the same patterns, mainly using CiteSeerX. In the fourth iteration, we performed additional searches in three primary journals of the field: *The Knowledge Engineering Review* (KER) was searched automatically, *Transactions on Autonomous and Adaptive Systems* (TAAS) and *Journal of Autonomous Agents and Multi-Agent Systems* (JAAMAS) were searched manually.

3.3.3 Data Collection

Table 5.1 shows data items that were collected for each paper. Data items F1–F7 were used for documentation purposes, and include authors, year, title, venue, keywords, and design pattern name/alias. Catalog pattern categories (F8) refers

Table 5.1 Data collection form

Item id	Field	Concern
F1	Author(s)	Documentation
F2	Year	Documentation
F3	Title	Documentation
F4	Venue	Documentation
F5	Keywords	Documentation
F6	Design pattern name	RQ2
F7	Design pattern alias	RQ2
F8	Catalog pattern categories	RQ4
F9	Short pattern description	RQ3, RQ4
F10	Pattern application domains	RQ3
F11	Pattern associations	RQ2
F12	Pattern template details	RQ1

to different categories of patterns. We have built up a list of categories during data collection. A number of authors explicitly define categories of their patterns, such as Architectural, Mobility, Organizational, Mediation etc. Other categories were inferred from the publications' titles, descriptions of the patterns, such as Self-organizing, Large-scale, Bio-inspired, Social etc. F8 helps determining a pattern classification, answering RQ4. Short pattern description (F9) provides a brief overview of a pattern, which helps identifying pattern relations (RQ2) and supports pattern classification (RQ4). Pattern application domains (F10) refers to specific type of systems or domains where the patterns are initially applied, and is used to answer RQ3. This item includes the options domain-independent, industrial applications (process control and manufacturing, air traffic control, traffic and transportation), robotics, entertainment (games, etc.), and simulation. These options were derived from a number of papers and books that comment on practical MAS applications, including [15, 22, 28, 61, 64]. Pattern associations (F11) refers to explicitly documented relations with other patterns. This information can be found in template's paragraphs such as "See also" or "Related patterns." This data supports answering RQ2. Finally, pattern template details (F12) refers to the template paragraphs used to document the patterns (containing both textual and graphical data), which helps to answer RQ1.

3.3.4 Data Analysis

The process of synthesizing and analyzing the collected data included the following steps:

1. Listing of design patterns and articles
2. Analysis of the data
3. Answering research questions
4. Interpretation of the results

We used three different methods to perform data analysis: meta analysis to answer RQ1 and RQ3, cluster analysis based on a graph model to answer RQ2, and data classification to answer RQ4. During meta analysis we defined qualitative coding schema for different topics of interest with binary parameters. For RQ1, we marked a pattern with 1 if it was documented with a structured template, and 0 otherwise. Furthermore, we systematically listed the various template paragraphs. If a pattern template contained a paragraph we marked it 1, or 0 otherwise. We applied the same approach for the documented application domains of the patterns. The collected data was further analyzed using descriptive statistics. We used a graph-based model for cluster analysis aiming to identify groups of related patterns. The objective of topical classification of the patterns was to get a clear view on the pattern space. However, the results of this method may be biased as it relies on subjective categorization.

4 Data Collection and Results

In total, 815 papers were considered for the study: 526 journal articles and 289 papers derived from digital databases. From this set, 39 were included after applying exclusion criteria. Figure 5.3 shows the distribution of included studies from academic databases and search engines.

From the 39 articles, 206 patterns were identified written by 95 researchers. Table 5.2 lists the patterns in chronological order. Ninety-three percentage of the patterns have unique names which indicates that some existing patterns where rewritten.

Figure 5.4 shows the distribution of documented design patterns over the years. We notice three peaks around the years: 1998, 2004, and 2010. We could not identify clear arguments for these waves of publications over time. The Additional Information in Sect. 7 gives an overview of the publication venues.

4.1 How Are the Patterns Documented and What Pattern Templates Are Used? (RQ1)

The huge number of existing patterns indicates the need for a standard approach to document patterns (F12). Overall, 69 % of the patterns are described using a structured templates, which contains on average seven paragraphs. From the pattern with a structured template, 53 % contains some graphical descriptions. Seventy-three percentage of these graphical descriptions are modeled using UML.

In total, we identified 102 unique paragraphs. This huge number clearly indicates that there is no consensus about a pattern template. However, some of

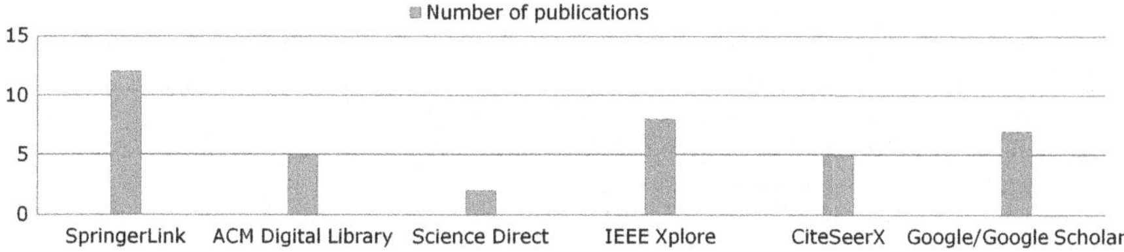

Fig. 5.3 Included studies from digital databases/search engines

Table 5.2 Design patterns for MAS (chronological order)

Patterns	Ref.	Year
Itinerary, Master-Slave, Meeting, Plan, Ticket, Facilitator, Forwarding, Organized group, Locker, Messenger	[3]	1998
The Layered Agent, Reactive Agent, Deliberative Agent, Opportunistic Agent, Interface Agent, Intention, Prioritizer, Adaptable Active Object, Message Forwarder, Plan as Command, Plan and Intention Factory, Conversation, Facilitator, Agent Proxy, Protocol, Emergent Society, Clone, Remote Configurator, Broker, Migration Thread Factory, Agent Builder, Layer Linker	[29]	
Basic Mobility, Itinerary, Star-shaped Movement, Branching, Contract net protocol, Cooperation Protocol Pattern, Direct Interaction, Mediation, Dispatching	[55]	1999
Broker, Embassy, Mediator, Monitor, Wrapper	[25]	
Metamorphic Architecture Pattern, Mediator, Task Decomposition Pattern, Virtual Clustering Pattern, The Partial Cloning Pattern, The Prototyping Pattern	[52]	
Direct Coupling Pattern, Proxy Agent Pattern, Communication Sessions Pattern, Badges, Event Dispatcher	[13]	
Sentinel Agent Behavior Pattern	[7]	2000
Receptionist, Session Pattern, Secretary, Mobile Session, Antenna, Private Session, Meeting with Moderator	[53]	
Blackboard, Market Maker, Meeting, Master-Slave, Negotiating Agents	[14]	2001
Synchronizer, Environment Mediated Communication, Updating shared state, Behavior-based Decision	[49]	2002
InteRRaP, Contract net protocol	[36]	
Agency Guard, Agent Authenticator, Sandbox, Access Controller	[39]	2003
Role Agent Pattern	[6]	
Monitor, Broker, Matchmaker, Mediator, Embassy, Booking, Call-For-Proposal, Bidding	[33]	
Reflective Blackboard	[54]	
Organisation schemes, Protocols, Marks, Influences, BDI architecture, Vertical architecture, Horizontal architecture, Recursive architecture, Iniquity, Discretisation, Physical entity	[48]	2004

(continued)

Table 5.2 (continued)

Patterns	Ref.	Year
Hybrid Recogniser, Sense-and-Infer, Assisted Sense and Infer, Ecological Recogniser, Assisted Ecological Recogniser, Clairvoyant	[26]	
Market-organiser, Agent-side comparison-shopping, Server-side comparison-shopping pattern, Itinerary-balancing pattern	[43]	
Pipeline	[23]	
Agent Society, Agent as Delegate, Agent as Mediator, Common Vocabulary, User Agent, Task Agent, Resource Agent	[58]	
Multi-agent layer pattern, Web usage mining pattern for adaptive multi-agent systems, WUMA-Interface, WUMA-UserM, WUMA-Acquirer, WUMA-Miner	[21]	2005
Rule Composer, Decision Tree	[57]	
Service Client Pattern, Service Representative	[41]	
Initiator, Observer	[38]	2006
Structure-in-5, Pyramid, Chain of values, The matrix, Bidding, Joint venture, Arm's-length, Hierarchical contracting, Co-optation	[34]	
Define Actors, Refine Actor Goals, Means-End Analysis, Contribution Analysis, AND/OR Decomposition, Ask for Help, Refine Models, System-to-Be	[40]	
Replication, Collective Sort, Evaporation, Aggregation, Diffusion	[20]	2007
Behaviour Helper Pattern	[8]	
Gradient Fields, Market-Based Control	[12]	
Agent Interface, SCADA control sequence agent, Agent optimization, Agent NET-MAP pattern	[16]	
Virtual Environment, Situated Agent, Selective Perception, Roles & Situated Commitments, Protocol-based Communication	[60]	2009
Perception Memory Pattern, Exponential Growth Pattern	[32]	
Disciplined flood, Propertinerary, Smart message, Delegate ant MAS, Delegate MAS	[27]	2010
Planner, VFHPlanner Pattern, A*Planner, Persistence agent, Memento agent, Social agent, Explorer, Sequential-resource share , Parallel resource share, Query, Inform, Request, Secure Query, Secure Request, Secure Inform, Contract net protocol, Publish-subscribe, Information agent, Holonic society, Supply chain	[10]	
Selection of Relevant Source Material	[9]	
Policy-based	[24]	2011
Scheduler Scramble, Context and Projection Hierarchy, Diffuser, Strategy, Logo World, Learning, Model-View-Controller, Double Buffer	[44]	
Aggregation, Spreading, Gossip	[17]	
Composite DelegateMAS	[11]	

the paragraphs are semantically more or less equivalent and can be grouped. For example paragraphs such as Related patterns, Associated patterns, See also, References, all refer to related patterns. For many other paragraphs it is difficult to identify semantic relations, and as such grouping them is not obvious, for example, Context/Applicability, Problem/Intent/Purpose, Examples/Known Uses or Participants/Entities.

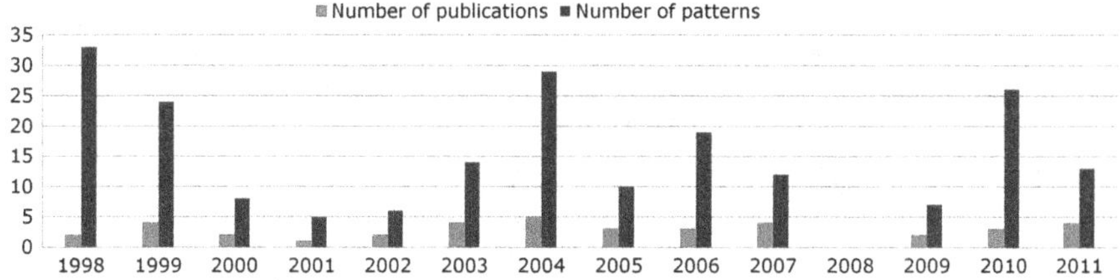

	Publications	Patterns
Mean	2,79	14,71
Median	3	12,50
Variance	1,57	98,37
Maximum	5	32
Total	39	206

Fig. 5.4 Publications and patterns per year

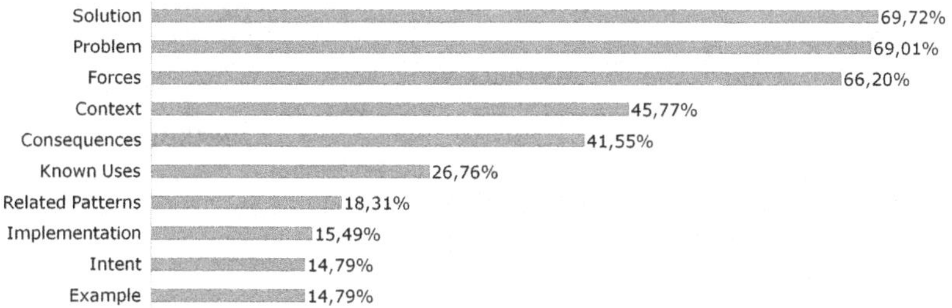

Fig. 5.5 Popular paragraphs in pattern templates

The most popular paragraphs are illustrated in Fig. 5.5. Several of these paragraphs are generally considered as essential for documenting design patterns, especially Problem, Context, and Solution. Other paragraphs are rare and rather unusual, for example, Technical Issues, Reasoning capabilities, Temporal context, and Configuration.

4.2 How Are the Design Patterns Interconnected? (RQ2)

To answer this question, we created a graph based on data extracted from data items: Pattern associations (F11), Design pattern alias (F7) and Design pattern name (F6). Figure 5.6 shows the directed graph (114 nodes, 130 edges, modularity: 0.762) with associations between the patterns. Three main clusters can be distinguished.

A first cluster contains patterns that are inspired by object-oriented pattern catalogs, such as the GoF catalog [19] (Proxy, Mediator), and by the concurrency patterns of [50] (Broker, Active Object). Those patterns are mainly concerned

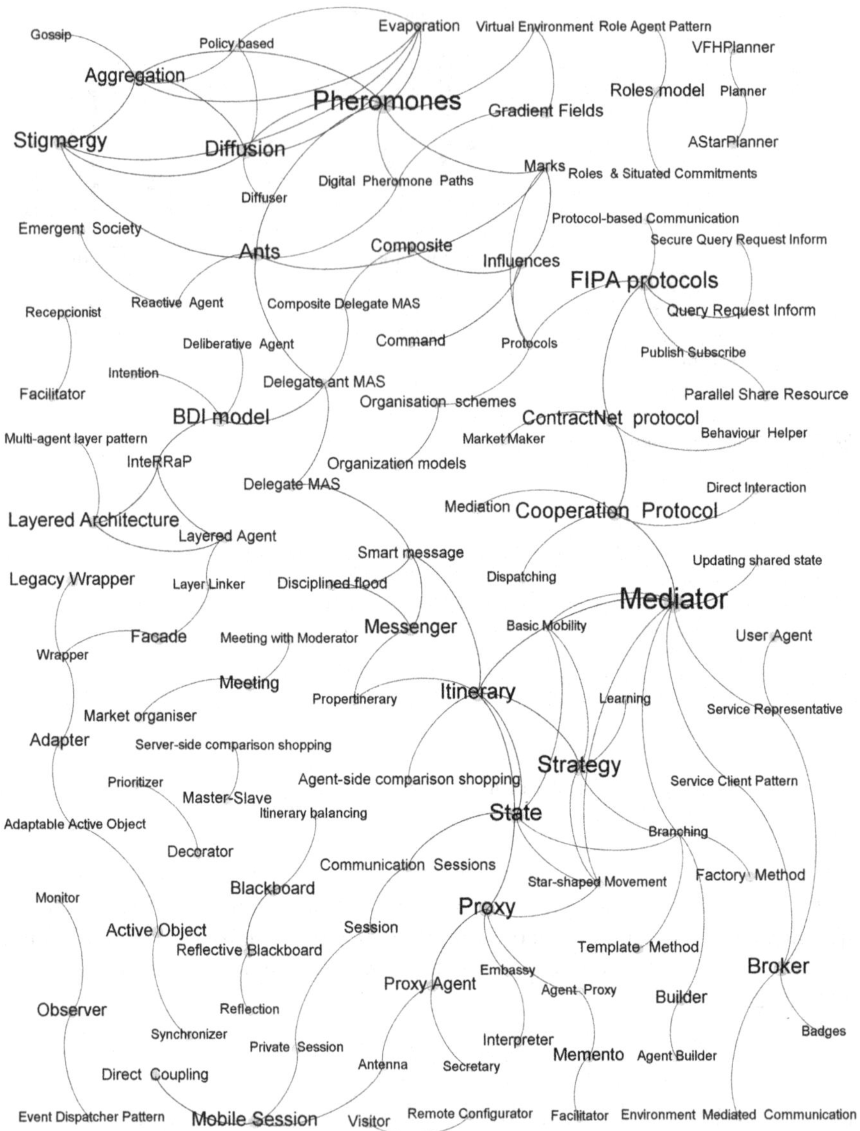

Fig. 5.6 Pattern space

with low-level design and implementation issues and are found in early papers: [25, 29, 49, 55].

A second cluster is built around bio-inspired concepts such as pheromones, ants, and stigmergy. This cluster includes recent patterns related to self-organization and adaptive behavior: [11, 12, 17, 20, 24, 27, 48].

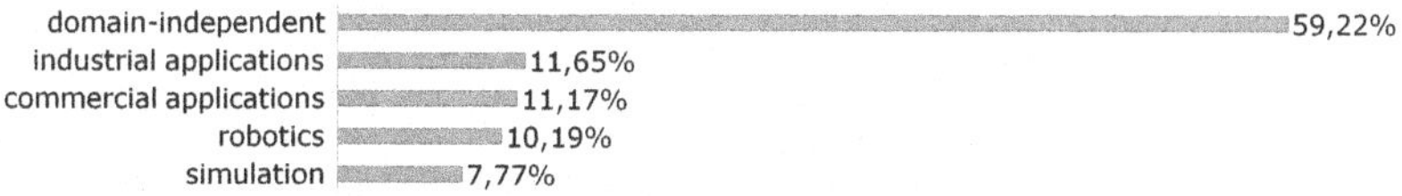

domain-independent 59,22%
industrial applications 11,65%
commercial applications 11,17%
robotics 10,19%
simulation 7,77%

Fig. 5.7 Pattern application domains

A third cluster groups patterns that are related to the mobile agents and Aglets patterns [3]. This group contains patterns from: [14, 27, 43, 53].

Another cluster groups protocols related to FIPA protocols [10, 36, 55]. Several closed clusters can be identified that typically include patterns from a single catalog and as such only contains relationships within the catalog. Several of these closed clusters contain domain specific patterns, for example, patterns for military simulations, e-commerce, intelligent manufacturing, and security [16, 26, 39, 43, 52].

4.3 For What Types of Systems Have the Design Patterns Been Applied? (RQ3)

To answer this research question, we derived data from Short pattern description (F9) and Pattern application domain (F10). Overall, there is not a dominant type of system for which MAS design patterns have been used. Figure 5.7 shows that 59 % of the patterns are domain-independent, while 41 % of the patterns focus on more specific uses.

For industrial applications, the main reported subdomains are process control and manufacturing (6 %) and traffic and transportation (5 %). For commercial applications, we identified information management (4 %) and electronic commerce (3 %). We found no patterns applied in the entertainment domain. Nevertheless, we observe that the design patterns for MAS have been used for a diversity of application domains, which reveals their high potential for software practitioners.

4.4 How Can the Design Patterns Be Classified? (RQ4)

The objective of classifying design patterns for MAS is to provide an intellectual graspable overview of the huge space of existing patterns. The classification offers engineers a general picture of the pattern space of MAS, and helps those who are not familiar with the domain to get an easy jump-start to understand the pattern space. Several researchers have proposed classifications of design patterns for MAS, but these classifications are either bound to a specific catalog of patterns, or to an development methodology [3, 10, 29, 45, 49, 55]. The classification presented in this paper covers the full space of patterns for MAS as document at the time of writing.

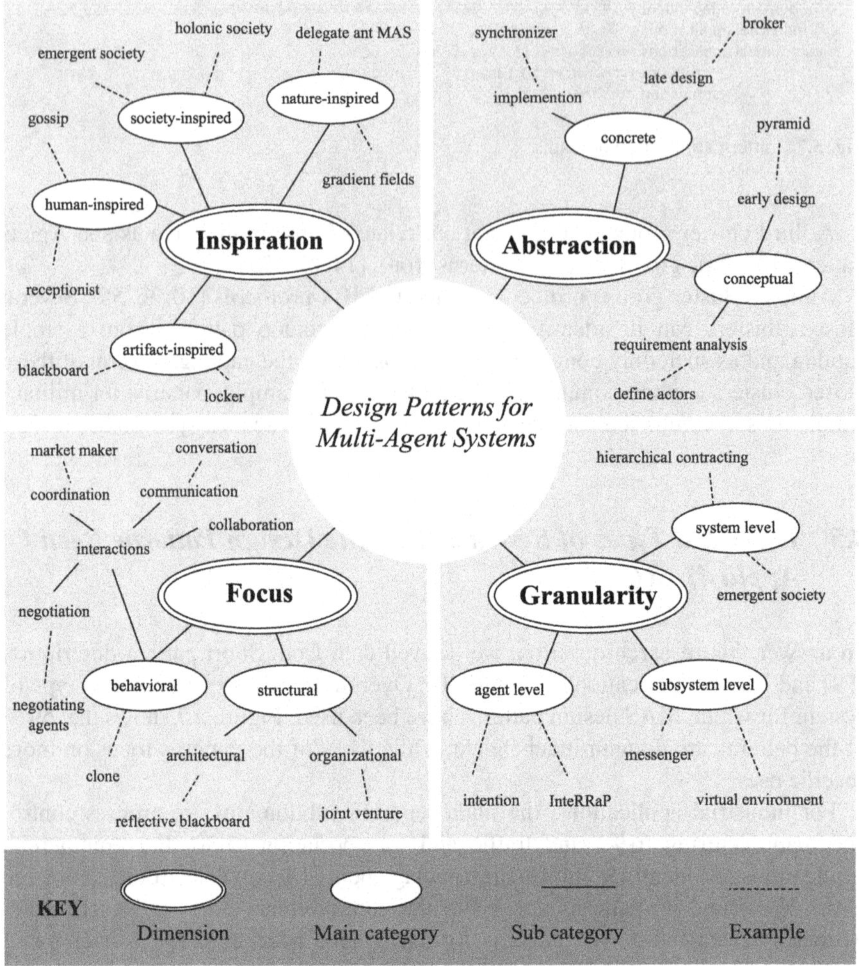

Fig. 5.8 Classification of patterns for multi-agent systems with example patterns

We derived the data for the classification resulted from Catalog pattern categories (F8) and Short pattern description (F9). Based on the analysis of the data, we identified four dimensions of patterns for MAS: inspiration, abstraction, focus, and granularity. Figure 5.8 shows a graphical overview of the dimensions, illustrated with example patterns.

4.4.1 Inspiration

Metaphors and analogies help in understanding complex systems. The *inspiration* dimension has four categories that provide intuitive domains from which patterns are derived. Examples of nature-inspired patterns are gradient fields [12] that is inspired by the fields in nature, and delegate ant MAS [27] that is inspired by behavior of social insects. Examples of society-inspired patterns are emergent society [29] and holonic society [10] that get their inspiration from the way societies emerge and structure themselves. Examples of human-inspired patterns are receptionist [53] and gossip [17]. Finally, locker [3] and blackboard [13] are example of patterns that get there inspiration from artifacts in our environment.

4.4.2 Abstraction

The *abstraction* dimension classifies patterns either as conceptual or concrete. Both these main categories are further refined in subcategories that refer to stages in the software life cycle where the patterns can be used. Define actors [40] and pyramid [34] are examples of patterns that are useful in early phases in the life cycle, while broker [25] and synchronizer [49] can be applied in detailed design and the implementation phase.

4.4.3 Focus

The *focus* dimension has two categories: structural and behavioral. Structural patterns are useful to deal with the decomposition of a system, while behavior patterns are useful to deal with interaction aspects. Examples of structural patterns are reflective blackboard [54] and joint venture [34], the former focusing a particular coordination structure for an agent system, the latter focusing on the way a community of agents is organized. Examples of behavioral patterns are market maker [13], negotiating agents [13], and conversation [29]. These patterns provide different approaches to support interactions among agents.

4.4.4 Granularity

Finally, the *granularity* dimension refers to the scope of the patterns, that is, the system or parts of the system. Hierarchical contracting [34] and emergent society [29] are examples of patterns that apply to a MAS as a whole. Messenger [3] and virtual environment [60] are patterns that apply to parts of a MAS. Intention [29] and InteRRaP [36] are patterns that support the design of individual agents.

5 Threats to Validity

The main threat to validity of the study is a potential lack of accuracy of search results due to the search strategy. To anticipate missing papers during automatic search, we performed pilot searches to tune the search criteria. Furthermore, we performed manual searches for the journal articles. We omitted theses and technical reports as we assumed that the patterns would eventually be published in journals or conference proceedings. We limited the time frame of searching to the period 1998–2011. This is motivated by the fact that the Agents conference started around 1998. Before that, we could not find documented design patterns for MAS. Finally, the data was collected by a single reviewer, which may result in a bias. To anticipate this threat to validity, we used various strategies, including:

- triangulation of data,
- crosschecking data from multiply sources,
- member checking,
- using rich and graphical descriptions to convey the findings,
- peer examination and reviewing.

6 Conclusions and Recommendations

The objective of this literature study was to summarize existing design patterns for MAS, to make this knowledge accessible to practitioners. To that end, we performed a SLR aiming to answer four research questions.

The first research question was concerned with the templates used to document the patterns. Analysis of the collected data shows that there are currently no agreed pattern templates to document design patterns for MAS. In addition, we observed that many patterns are documented without structured templates. This observation hampers the accessibility of the patterns for practitioners as well as students. Hence, there is a need for standard templates to document patterns for MAS. Such template should clearly define the semantics of the different paragraphs. We suggest to start from a state of the art pattern template and include at least the following paragraphs: Name, Problem, Solution, Context, Forces, Consequences, and Related Patterns. The first four paragraphs are essential as any design pattern should document a solution to recurring problem in a given context. Context and forces should be also included as these aspects are essential for software engineers to select proper design patterns and it also supports learning of the patterns. Documenting consequences is crucial to understand the design trade-offs implied by patterns. Finally, related patterns enable to connect patterns and build up pattern languages.

The goal of the second research question was to investigate how the design patterns for MAS are interconnected. We observed a strong coupling between patterns from the same catalog. However, more effort should be put in documenting associations between patterns. Moreover, duplicated efforts in describing the same patterns should be avoided.

The third research question identified the type of systems and application domains for which design patterns for MAS have been used. The collected data shows that the patterns have a wide range of applications. Nevertheless, although MAS are suggested to be primary candidates to design emerging domains such as cloud computing and smart grids, no applications of patterns for these systems are reported. Empirical evidence is required that demonstrates the usefulness of design patterns for MAS in these areas.

Finally, the fourth question was concerned with classifying design patterns for MAS. The data collected to answer this question shows that the space of design patterns for MAS is huge and very diverse. Patterns are related to a variety of disciplines, including Systems and Organization Theory, Social Sciences, Biology, Psychology, or Ecology. To bring order in this huge space, we identified four dimensions that enable classification of the patterns. This classification allows engineers to better browse the pattern space and helps those who are new to the field to better find their way through the myriad of patterns.

We conclude with some ideas for future work in the area of patterns for MAS:

1. Formalization and standardization of patterns (and pattern templates) will contribute to improve the quality of pattern documentation and eliminate ambiguity.
2. Empirical evaluation of the patterns is required to demonstrate the added value of the patterns (as well as their tradeoffs).
3. Creating catalogs and pattern languages will help to better interconnect patterns, and enhance their combined use.

Other opportunities for future research are identification and documentation of anti-patterns for MAS, that is, design patterns that have proven to be unsuccessful [4], evaluation of patterns using standard frameworks for evaluating design patterns [46], and development of CASE tools to support engineers with applying patterns during system development [10, 30, 56].

7 Additional Information

Year	Ref.	Venue
1998	[3, 29]	AGENTS'98: The 2nd International Conference on Autonomous Agents
1999	[55]	ICSE'99: The 21st International Conference on Software Engineering
	[25]	AGENTS'99: The 3rd International Conference on Autonomous Agents
	[13]	IC-AI'99: The International Conference on Artificial Intelligence
	[52]	The 2nd International Workshop on Intelligent Manufacturing Systems
2000	[53]	EuroPloP'2000: The 5th European Conference on Pattern Languages of Programs
2002	[49]	OOPSLA'02: Workshop on Agent-Oriented Methodologies
	[36]	AOSE'02: The 3rd International Conference on Agent-oriented Software Engineering

(continued)

Year	Ref.	Venue
2003	[33]	SEKE'03:The 15th International Conference on Software Engineering and Knowledge Engineering
	[39]	EuroPLoP'03: The 8h European Conference on Pattern Languages of Program
	[6]	IEEE SMC'03: IEEE International Conference on Systems, Man and Cybernetics
2004	[23]	AOSE'04: The 5th International Workshop on Agent-Oriented Software Engineering
	[43]	AusWeb04: The 10th Australian World Wide Web Conference
	[48]	MICAI'04: The 3rd Mexican International Conference on Artificial Intelligence
2005	[57]	QSIC 2005: The 5th International Conference on Quality Software
2006	[38]	ACS/IEEE International Conference on Computer Systems and Applications
2007	[8]	The 4th International Conference on Innovations in Information Technology
	[16]	ACM-SE 45: The 45th annual ACM southeast regional conference
	[20]	CEEMAS'07: 5th International Central and Eastern European Conference on Multi-Agent Systems
2009	[60]	WICSA/ECSA'09: Joint Working IEEE/IFIP Conference on Software Architecture & European Conference on Software Architecture
	[32]	MATES'09: The 7th German Conference on Multi-Agent System Technologies
2010	[27]	EuroPLoP'10: The 15th European Conference on Pattern Languages of Programs
	[9]	PRIMA'10: The 13th international conference on Principles and Practice of Multi-Agent Systems
2011	[11]	AGERE!: Programming Systems, Languages, and Applications based on Actors, Agents, and Decentralized Control
	[17]	EASe: The 8th IEEE International Conference and Workshops on Engineering of Autonomic and Autonomous Systems
	[24]	TrustCom'11: The 10th International Conference on Trust, Security and Privacy in Computing and Communications
	[44]	WSC'11: Winter Simulation Conference

References

1. Alexander C (1979) The timeless way of building. Oxford University Press, New York
2. Alur D, Crupi J, Malks D (2003) Core J2EE patterns: best practices and design strategies, 2nd edn. Prentice-Hall PTR, Upper Saddle River
3. Aridor Y, Lange DB (1998) Agent design patterns: elements of agent application design. In: Proceedings of the 2nd international conference on autonomous agents. ACM, New York, pp 108–115
4. Brown WJ, Malveau RC, McCormick HW, Mowbray TJ (1998) AntiPatterns: refactoring software, architectures, and projects in crisis. Wiley, New York
5. Buschmann F, Meunier R, Rohnert H, Sommerlad P, Stal M (1996) Pattern-oriented software architecture. A system of patterns, vol 1. Wiley, Chichester

6. Cabri G, Ferrari L, Leonardi L (2003) Role agent pattern: a developer guideline. In: IEEE international conference on systems, man and cybernetics, vol 5, pp 4114–4119
7. Chacon D, Mccormick J, Mcgrath S, Stoneking C (2000) Rapid application development using agent itinerary patterns. Technical Report 01, Lockheed Martin Advanced Technology Laboratories
8. Charan Ojha A, Kumar Pradhan S, Ranjan Patra M (2007) Pattern-based design for intelligent mobile agents. In: Proceedings of the 4th international conference on innovations in information technology, pp 501–505
9. Cheah W, Sterling L, Taveter K (2010) Task knowledge patterns reuse in multi-agent systems development. In: Proceedings of the 13th international conference on principles and practice of multi-agent systems, PRIMA'10. Springer, Berlin, pp 459–474
10. Chella A, Cossentino M, Gaglio S, Sabatucci L, Seidita V (2010) Agent-oriented software patterns for rapid and affordable robot programming. J Syst Software 83:557–573
11. Cruz Torres M, Van Beers T, Holvoet T (2011) (No) more design patterns for multi-agent systems. In: Proceedings of the compilation of the co-located workshops on DSM'11, TMC'11, AGERE!'11, AOOPES'11, NEAT'11, VMIL'11, SPLASH '11 workshops. ACM, New York, pp 213–220
12. De Wolf T, Holvoet T (2007) Design patterns for decentralised coordination in self-organising emergent systems. In: Engineering self-organising systems. Lecture notes in computer science, vol 4335. Springer, Berlin, pp 28–49
13. Deugo D, Oppacher F, Kuester J, Otte IV (1999) Patterns as a means for intelligent software engineering. In: Proceedings of the 1999 conference on artificial intelligence, pp 605–611
14. Deugo D, Weiss M, Kendall E (2001) Resuable patterns for agent coordination. In: Coordination of internet agents. Resuable patterns for agent coordination, Springer, London, pp 347–368
15. Dignum V, Dignum F (2010) Designing agent systems: state of the practice. Int J Agent-Oriented Software Eng 4(3):224–243
16. Eichelkraut C, Etzkorn L (2007) Describing agent based real-time distributed systems using design patterns. In: Proceedings of the 45th annual southeast regional conference, ACM-SE 45. ACM, New York, pp 156–161
17. Fernandez-Marquez JL, Arcos JL, Di Marzo Serugendo G, Casadei M (2011) Description and composition of bio-inspired design patterns: the gossip case. In: Engineering of Autonomic and Autonomous Systems (EASe), 2011 8th IEEE international conference and workshops on, pp 87–96
18. Fowler M (2003) Patterns of enterprise application architecture. Addison-Wesley, Boston
19. Gamma E, Helm R, Johnson R, Vlissides J (1995) Design patterns: elements of reusable object-oriented software. Addison-Wesley, Reading
20. Gardelli L, Viroli M, Omicini A (2007) Design patterns for self-organising systems. In: Burkhard HD, Lindemann G, Verbrugge R, Varga LZ (eds) Multi-agent systems and applications V, LNCS (LNAI), vol 4696. Springer, Berlin, pp 123–132
21. Girardi R, Marinho LB, de Oliveira IR (2005) A system of agent-based software patterns for user modeling based on usage mining. Interact Comput 17(5):567–591
22. Glass RL, Vessey I (2011) Naivete squared: in search of two taxonomies and a mapping between them. IEEE Software 28(5):14–15
23. Gonzalez-Palacios J, Luck M (2004) A framework for patterns in gaia: a case-study with organisations. In: Proceedings of the 5th international workshop on agent-oriented software engineering
24. Guo Y, Mao X, Hu C (2011) Design pattern for self-organization multi-agent systems based on policy. In: Proceedings of the 10th international conference on trust, security and privacy in computing and communications (TrustCom), pp 1572–1577
25. Hayden SC, Carrick C, Yang Q (1999) Architectural design patterns for multiagent coordination. In: Proceedings of the 3rd international conference on autonomous agents
26. Heinze C (2004) Modelling intention recognition for intelligent agent systems. Research Report DSTO-RR-0286, Air Operations Division Systems Sciences Laboratory

27. Holvoet T, Weyns D, Valckenaers P (2010) Delegate MAS patterns for large-scale distributed coordination and control applications. In: Proceedings of the 15th European Conference on Pattern Languages of Programs. ACM, New York
28. Jennings N, Wooldridge M (1998) Agent technology: foundations, applications, and markets. Springer, Berlin
29. Kendall EA, Murali Krishna PV, Pathak CV, Suresh CB (1998) Patterns of intelligent and mobile agents. In: Proceedings of the 2nd international conference on autonomous agents. ACM, pp 92–99
30. Khwaja S, Alshayeb M (2011) Towards design pattern definition language. Software Pract Exper, 43:747–757
31. Kitchenham B (2004) Procedures for performing systematic reviews. Technical Report TR/SE-0401, Department of Computer Science, Keele University, Department of Computer Science, Keele University, UK
32. Klügl F, Karlsson L (2009) Towards pattern-oriented design of agent-based simulation models. In: Proceedings of the 7th German conference on multiagent system technologies, MATES'09. Springer, Berlin, pp 41–53
33. Kolp M, Do TT, Pirotte A (2003) Social patterns for designing multiagent systems. In: Proceedings of the 15th International Conference on Software Engineering & Knowledge Engineering (SEKE'2003), pp 103–110
34. Kolp M, Giorgini P, Mylopoulos J (2006) Multi-agent architectures as organizational structures. Auton Agents Multi-Agent Syst 13:3–25
35. Kramer J, Magee J (2007) Self-managed systems: an architectural challenge. In: FOSE '07: Future of Software Engineering. IEEE Computer Society
36. Lind J (2003) Patterns in agent-oriented software engineering. In: Proceedings of the 3rd international conference on Agent-oriented software engineering III, AOSE'02. Springer, Berlin, pp 47–58
37. Martin R (2003) Agile software development : principles, patterns, and practices. Prentice-Hall, Upper Saddle River
38. Mohamad R, Deris S, Ammar HH (2006) Agent design patterns framework for MaSE/POAD methodology. In: Proceedings of the ACS/IEEE International Conference on Computer Systems and Applications, AICCSA '06. IEEE Computer Society, Washington, DC, pp 521–528
39. Mouratidis H, Giorgini P, Schumacher M (2003) Security patterns for agent systems. In: Proceedings of the 8th European Conference on Pattern Languages of Programs
40. Mouratidis H, Weiss M (2006) Patterns for modelling agent systems with tropos. In: Garcia A, Choren R, Lucena C, Giorgini P, Holvoet T, Romanovsky A (eds) Software engineering for multi-agent systems IV. Lecture notes in computer science, vol 3914. Springer, pp 207–223
41. Muller I, Braun P, Kowalczyk R (2005) Design patterns for agent-based service composition in the web. In: Proceedings of the International Conference on Quality Software (QSIC 2005), pp 425–430
42. Ng TH, Cheung SC, Chan WK, Yu YT (2006) Work experience versus refactoring to design patterns: a controlled experiment. In: Proceedings of the 14th ACM SIGSOFT international symposium on Foundations of software engineering, SIGSOFT '06/FSE-14. ACM, New York, pp 12–22
43. Nguyen A, Yang X (2004) Design patterns for mobile agent-mediated e-business. In: Proceedings of the 10th Australian World Wide Web Conference
44. North MJ, Macal CM (2011) Product design patterns for agent-based modeling. In: Proceedings of the 2011 Winter Simulation Conference (WSC), pp 3082–3093
45. Oluyomi A (2006) Patterns and protocols for agent oriented software development. Ph.D, The University of Melbourne
46. Petter S, Khazanchi D, Murphy JD (2010) A design science based evaluation framework for patterns. SIGMIS Database 41(3):9–26

47. Prechelt L, Unger-Lamprecht B, Philippsen M, Tichy WF (2002) Two controlled experiments assessing the usefulness of design pattern documentation in program maintenance. IEEE Trans Software Eng 28(6):595–606
48. Sauvage S (2004) Design patterns for multiagent systems design. In: MICAI 2004: advances in artificial intelligence. Lecture notes in computer science, vol 2972. Springer, Berlin/Heidelberg, pp 352–361
49. Schelfthout K, Coninx T, Helleboogh A, Holvoet T, Steegmans E, Weyns D (2002) Agent implementation patterns. In: Proceedings of the OOPSLA 2002 workshop on agent-oriented methodologies, pp 119–130
50. Schmidt DC, Stal M, Rohnert H, Buschmann F (2000) Pattern-oriented software architecture. Patterns for concurrent and networked objects, vol 2. Wiley, Chichester
51. Shaw M, Clements P (2006) The golden age of software architecture. IEEE Software 23(2): 31–39
52. Shu S, Norrie DH (1999) Patterns for adaptive multi-agent systems in intelligent manufacturing. In: Proceedings of the 2nd international workshop on intelligent manufacturing systems, pp 67–74
53. Silva IC, da Silva AR, Meira N (2000) A set of agent patterns for a more expressive approach. In: Proceedings of the EuroPLOP 2000, pp 331–346
54. Silva O, Garcia A, Lucena C (2003) The reflective blackboard pattern: architecting large multi-agent systems. In: Garcia A, Lucena C, Zambonelli F, Omicini A, Castro J (eds) Software engineering for large-scale multi-agent systems. Lecture notes in computer science, vol 2603. Springer, Berlin, pp 73–93
55. Tahara Y, Ohsuga A, Honiden S (1999) Agent system development method based on agent patterns. In: Proceedings of the 21st International Conference on Software Engineering, ICSE '99. ACM, New York, pp 356–367
56. Taibi T, Check Ling Ngo D (2003) Formal specification of design patterns - a balanced approach. J Object Technol 2(4):127–140
57. Taylor PR, Evans-Greenwood P, Odell J (2005) The genesis of a pattern language for agent-based enterprise systems. In: Proceedings of the 5th International Conference on Quality Software, QSIC '05. IEEE Computer Society, Washington, DC, pp 395–400
58. Weiss M (2004) A pattern language for motivating the use of agents. In: Giorgini P, Henderson-Sellers B, Winikoff M (eds) Agent-oriented information systems. Lecture notes in computer science, vol 3030. Springer, Berlin/Heidelberg, pp 142–157
59. Weyns D (2006) An architecture-centric approach for software engineering with situated multi-agent systems. Ph.D. Dissertation, Katholieke Universiteit Leuven
60. Weyns D (2009) A pattern language for multi-agent systems. In: Proceedings of Joint Working IEEE/IFIP European Conference on Software Architecture, pp 191–200
61. Weyns D (2010) Architecture-based design of multi-agent systems. Springer, Heidelberg
62. Weyns D, Helleboogh A, Holvoet T (2009) How to get multi-agent systems accepted in industry? Int J Agent-Oriented Softw Eng 3:383–390
63. Weyns D, Schmerl B, Grassi V, Malek S, Mirandola R, Prehofer C, Wuttke J, Andersson J, Giese H, Goschka K (2012) On patterns for decentralized control in self-adaptive systems. Lecture notes in computer science, vol 7475. Springer, Berlin
64. Wooldridge MJ (2009) An introduction to multiagent systems, 2nd edn. Wiley, Chichester

Chapter 6
Agent Communication

Marc-Philippe Huget

Abstract Traditional one-to-one communication à la Shannon as proposed in distributed systems is no longer the best means for communication between agents. Agents are interacting in the sense that they are communicating and expect some reactions from their messages. Agent communication, preferably named agent interaction, requires higher-level communication means such as an agent communication language and dialogue games to name a few. In this chapter, we present the different tools available for agent communication: agent communication languages, protocols, dialogue games, argumentation systems, and multi-party communication.

Keywords ACL • Protocols • Direct communication • Indirect communication • Dialog • Ontology

1 Introduction

Agent communication is essential for realizing the agent-oriented paradigm, as it facilitates cooperation, coordination, and other aspects of agent interaction. Two major approaches to agent communication exist: direct communication [1] and indirect communication [2]. Early work on agent communication focused on direct communication via protocols (see the seminal work by Davis and Smith on the Contract Net Protocol [3]). This approach was motivated by the need to have a reliable way to represent communication between agents without requiring excessive resources to interpret communication. Protocols are efficient means for information exchange and coordination; however, they restrict agents' autonomy; agents have to strictly follow the admissible sequence of messages imposed by the protocol.

M.-P. Huget (✉)
LISTIC/Polytech Annecy-Chambéry, Université de Savoie, Chambéry, France
e-mail: Marc-Philippe.Huget@univ-savoie.fr

O. Shehory and A. Sturm (eds.), *Agent-Oriented Software Engineering*,
DOI 10.1007/978-3-642-54432-3_6, © Springer-Verlag Berlin Heidelberg 2014

The dialogue games and the argumentation systems presented in this chapter are two examples of communication support that restore agent autonomy.

Protocols, dialogue games, and argumentation systems are specialized in communication between cognitive agents. Cognitive agents have a representation of themselves, of other agents, and of the world, and reason about their courses of action. Another kind of agent communication concerns reactive agents. Such reactive agents do not have a representation of themselves, of other agents, and of the world. They use a perception-action cycle, that is, they react to stimuli from the environment via actions without deciding which course of action is best fitted. For this kind of agents, it is necessary to define another way to communicate. For example, communication can be done through (metaphorical) pheromones as used in biological entities such as ants or termites. An agent releases specific kinds of pheromones in the environment to communicate. Agents sufficiently close to these pheromones can perceive them and properly react to them.

In this chapter, we use the term "direct communication" in reference to communication between cognitive agents and the term "indirect communication" in reference to communication between reactive agents. In cognitive agent communication, the recipient is formally defined, and therefore communication is direct. In contrast, in reactive agent communication such as pheromone-based communication, the pheromone is released in the environment and can be caught by any agent that perceives it. Thus, communication is indirect.

Communication in multi-agent systems follows Shannon's communication with a sender and a receiver. Even protocols dedicated to one-to-many communication such as the Contract Net protocol [3] are actually several concurrent one-to-one communications. In this chapter, we will cover the recent work on one-to-many and many-to-many communications that reinstate the notion of several parties in the communication. This one/many-to-many communication is called multi-party communication.

The chapter is structured as follows: In Sect. 2, we present direct agent communication with agent communication languages such as Knowledge Query and Manipulation Language (KQML) and FIPA Agent Communication Language (ACL), how ontologies are used to define terms employed in message content, and finally the communication support for direct communication. In Sect. 3, we describe indirect agent communication as used in biological examples such as ants and bees. Section 4 presents how direct communication is structured via protocols, dialogue games, and argument systems. Section 5 considers the novel approach of multi-party communication. Finally, Sect. 6 summarizes the chapter and sketches current effort on agent communication.

2 Direct Communication

Communication between cognitive agents (direct communication) has roots in distributed systems communication and Shannon's ideas: Communication is the action of sending data from a sender to a recipient over a channel [1]. In agent communication, the intent to communicate is to produce an effect on the recipients (crystallized by [4]): Message recipients will possibly act to provide an answer to the sender.

Several elements require attention when considering direct communication: an agent communication language, ontologies, and communication support. In the following we elaborate on these.

2.1 Agent Communication Languages

Communicating requires that the entities have the same language (for human conversations, we speak about English, for instance) to understand each other. Currently, there exist two main agent communication languages: KQML (Knowledge Query and Manipulation Language) [5] and FIPA ACL [6]. The first aim of KQML defined in the context of the Knowledge Sharing Effort was to allow data exchange between distributed knowledge bases. KQML is composed of 7 performatives for conversation management (sorry, error, etc.), 17 performatives for the conversation (ask-if, tell, etc.), and finally 11 performatives for conversation sending (forward, broker-all, etc.). KQML is the older of the two agent communication languages and is gradually replaced by FIPA ACL for several reasons: (1) There was a need for clear semantics for the language; (2) it was recommended to have a smaller set of communicative acts, while keeping the autonomy of agents; (3) FIPA ACL has implementation of various protocols; and (4) FIPA ACL supports communication at various levels.

The first point is certainly the one that makes the difference between KQML and FIPA ACL since it is important to have a rigorous definition of each communicative act. In this chapter, we only describe FIPA ACL.

Agent communication is based on human conversations. That is, a message contains a verb (called performative or communicative act in speech act theory [4, 7]) and a content. Formally speaking, a message is written as F(P), where F corresponds to the illocutionary force and P is the message content. For instance, inform(it rains) is such an example where inform is the illocutionary force and it rains is the content. The illocutionary force corresponds to the performative verb. Several types of speech acts exist in human conversations as shown by Austin [4]:

- *Representatives,* which give information
- *Directives,* which require something from the recipient
- *Commissives,* which commit the sender to do something in the future
- *Expressives,* which describe the mental states of the sender
- *Declarations,* which process an act just by saying it

Agents do not use all the types of verbs present in a natural language but a smaller subset thereof (the representative and directive speech acts). Agent communication languages do not offer a rich set of communicative acts as natural languages do; the latter require too much interpretation from agents.

Table 6.1 FIPA ACL performatives

Performative	Passing info	Requesting info	Negotiation	Performing actions	Error handling
Accept-proposal			√		
Agree				√	
Cancel		√		√	
Cfp			√		
Confirm	√				
Disconfirm	√				
Failure					√
Inform	√				
Inform-if	√				
Inform-ref	√				
Not-understood					√
Propose			√		
Query-if		√			
Query-ref		√			
Refuse				√	
Reject-proposal			√		
Request				√	
Request-when				√	
Request-whenever				√	
Subscribe		√			

Table 6.2 FIPA inform and request semantics

<i, inform(j, φ)>feasibility preconditionrational effect	$B_i\ \varphi \wedge \neg B_i(Bif_j\ \varphi \vee Uif_j\ \varphi) B_j\ \varphi$
<i, request(j, φ)>feasibility preconditionrational effect	$B_i Agent(j, \varphi) \wedge \neg B_i I_j Done(\varphi) Done(\varphi)$

Performatives in FIPA ACL are arranged into five categories: (1) passing information, (2) requesting information, (3) negotiation, (4) performing actions, and (5) error handling. Table 6.1 summarizes the different performatives and their categories.

The *inform* and *request* performatives are the primitive performatives in FIPA ACL; other performatives can be built on these. The *inform* performative means that an agent informs recipients about something it believes and it believes recipients do not yet believe it. The *request* performative requests that recipients perform actions. Moreover, the sender believes recipients are able to perform them. The main issue in KQML is the lack of semantics associated with the performative, and FIPA ACL addresses this issue via two parts: the *feasible preconditions* and the *rational effect*. The feasible preconditions correspond to the preconditions that have to be evaluated to true to execute the performative. The rational effect expresses what the sender hopes to bring about. Semantics are expressed via FIPA SL [8]. The semantics associated with the *inform* and *request* performatives are given in Table 6.2.

In the table, $B_i\ \varphi$ means that i believes φ. $Bif_j\ \varphi$ means that i has a definite opinion whether φ is true or false. $Uif_j\ \varphi$ means that j is uncertain about φ.

The feasibility precondition for the *inform* communicative act means that the sender i believes φ and i does not believe the recipient j has a definite opinion about φ or it is uncertain about φ.

The semantics for FIPA ACL are based on mentalistic modalities for both sender and recipient (their beliefs, desires, and intentions). It implies that both should adopt a Belief-Desire-Intention architecture [9, 66] as demonstrated by Guerin [10] and Singh [11]. An alternative to this semantics is the work on social semantics [12] and intentional semantics [13] based on, respectively, the commitments agents take and the intentions they have [67].

2.2 *Ontologies*

Discussing buying a car is not the same as discussing buying a book: Terms may have different meanings and one does not use the same terms in both domains. Moreover, it is possible that two agents speak about the same concept but not with the same term: using the terms "painter" and "artist," for instance. In order to avoid these differences, it is important to use a common vocabulary also called an ontology [14]. In [14], the following definition of an ontology is given:

> An ontology defines the basic terms and relations comprising the vocabulary of a topic area as well as the rules for combining terms and relations to define extensions to the vocabulary.

Below we present an example of an ontology—part of a computer science department ontology available on SHOE.[1] This part of the ontology describes the *is a* hierarchy that denotes the different terms used in the computer science department. Terms in square brackets refer to categories defined elsewhere. Terms in curly brackets refer to additional super categories used in multiple inheritance.

The relationships between the terms are presented in Table 6.3.

Ontologies are represented within a FIPA ACL message via the field:ontology. We let readers consult [14] to find examples of ontologies and their application to agent communication.

2.3 *Communication Support*

Communicating requires a communication support, which is a mechanism that stores, retrieves, and directs messages to the agents. Communication support is present in agent platforms such as JADE [15]. Another example is MadKit [16], where it is possible to send messages to (1) agents, (2) the roles they play in a group, or (3) a group.

---

[1] http://www.cs.umd.edu/projects/plus/SHOE/cs.html

- *[base.Entity]*
  - *[base.SHOEEntity]*
    - *Person*
      - *Worker*
        - *Faculty*
          - *Professor*
            - *AssistantProfessor*
              - *AssociateProfessor*
              - *FullProfessor*
              - *VisitingProfessor*
          - *Lecturer*
          - *PostDoc*
        - *Assistant*
          - *ResearchAssistant*
          - *TeachingAssistant*
        - *AdministrativeStaff*
          - *Director*
          - *Chair {Professor}*
          - *Dean {Professor}*
          - *ClericalStaff*
          - *SystemsStaff*
        - *Student*
          - *UndergraduateStudent*
          - *GraduateStudent*
    - *Organization*
      - *Department*
      - *School*
      - *University*
      - *Program*
      - *ResearchGroup*
      - *Institute*
    - *Publication*
      - *Article*
        - *TechnicalReport*
        - *JournalArticle*
        - *ConferencePaper*
      - *UnofficialPublication*
      - *Book*
      - *Software*
        - *Manual*
        - *Specification*
    - *Work*
      - *Course*
      - *Research*
    - *Schedule*

3 Indirect Communication

Direct communication is the most widely used means of communication and multi-agent systems, and accordingly we have elaborated on it. Indirect communication corresponds to communication where the message is released in the environment. Any agent sufficiently close to it can perceive it. Commonly, indirect communication is used by reactive agents. Indirect communication can only be used for

Table 6.3 Relationships in the computer science department ontology

Relation	Argument 1	Argument 2
publicationAuthor	Publication	Person
publicationDate	Publication	.DATE
publicationResearch	Publication	Research
softwareVersion	Software	.STRING
softwareDocumentation	Software	Publication
teacherOf	Faculty	Course
teachingAssistantOf	TeachingAssistant	Course
takesCourse	Student	Course
age	Person	.NUMBER
emailAddress	Person	.STRING
head	Organization	Person
undergraduateDegreeFrom	Person	University
mastersDegreeFrom	Person	University
doctoralDegreeFrom	Person	University
advisor	Student	Professor
subOrganization	Organization	Organization
affiliatedOrganization	Organization	Organization
member	Organization	Person
alumnus	Organization	Person
affiliateOf	Organization	Person
orgPublication	Organization	Publication
researchInterest	Person	Research
researchProject	ResearchGroup	Research
listedCourse	Schedule	Course
tenured	Professor	.TRUTH

limited coordination, since it is not possible to represent a wide range of messages. Examples of indirect communication include pheromones and forces. Such an example of indirect communication via pheromones is the MANTA project [2]. Ants and larva produce pheromones. There exist several kinds of pheromones; each one has a different meaning. For instance, a larva can produce a pheromone when it needs food. Pheromones can be used as well to highlight a path to goal states (e.g., food in insect societies).

Indirect communication via forces has seen several incarnations in AI, robotics, and multi-agent systems, e.g., [17]. For example, it has an interesting use in cartographic generalization. That is, generating a map is based on constraints such as (1) the elements to write on maps (tourist maps versus military maps, for instance), (2) the different constraints associated to each element (a building cannot go beyond its position and crosses roads), and (3) the final dimension of the map [18]. Each element (or part of it) on the map is a reactive agent that has attraction/repulsion forces. The force is computed based on the size of the element and its importance in the map. The system is stable when agents (or a portion of them) have found their stable position. Communication is ensured here via attraction and repulsion forces.

4 Structuring Communication

Three main different approaches exist to structure direct communication: (1) protocols, which are the most widely used, (2) dialogue games, and (3) argumentation systems.

Protocols are the main approach to represent communication in multi-agent systems. A protocol represents the way to structure communication in a rigid manner. A finite set of performatives is allowed for a particular state of the interaction. Dialogue games are based on work in philosophy and computational linguistics. Its aim is to offer more flexibility in communication in comparison with protocols. The communicative acts are paired, for instance, a question is paired with an answer [19]. Moreover, it is possible to embed dialogue games into other dialogue games. Finally, argumentation systems are a specific kind of communication system where agents can challenge the content of each message and as a consequence, agents have to justify their message content via arguments [20]. Argumentation is frequently used in negotiation-based systems [11].

4.1 Protocols

In multi-agent systems, we prefer using the term "interaction protocols" instead of "communication protocols" for two reasons:

1. Receiving messages implies that agents may be updating their state and reacting upon the messages based on the communicative acts used: This entails interaction.
2. Communication in multi-agent systems is more complex than in distributed systems: Agents are autonomous and use richer communication via communicative acts. Communicative acts and messages have semantics.

Research on protocols in multi-agent systems share work with communication protocol engineering [21] and interaction protocol engineering [22]. The latter is composed of several phases from analysis to execution:

Analysis This phase describes informally the protocol. That is, the admissible sequence of messages, the message content, and the different requirements the protocol should follow. This description is gathered within a document generally written in natural language [23]. This document is important since it conditions the success of the protocol design. If the document is too inaccurate, the protocol will be incomplete. Designers can also use chronograms and algorithms to describe the protocol.

Formal Description The previous phase gives an informal document. As Holzmann pointed it out in [21], it is necessary to have a formal description so as to avoid misunderstandings and to ease validation. Several formal description techniques are available for interaction protocol designers—some are coming from distributed systems and some are specific to agent systems:

1. Finite State Machines [24] based on graph theory, where each state corresponds to an interaction state and a transition sends or receives a message. AgenTalk [25] and COOL [26] are two examples of formal description techniques based on finite state machines.
2. Petri nets [27] based on finite state machines but allowing multiple flows and synchronization on the same net. [28] and [29] are two examples of interaction protocols represented via a Petri net.
3. UML-based notations [30]. UML and profiles of UML are frequently used to represent interaction protocols. FIPA UAML [31] and Agent UML [32] are the main ones and are both agent specific.

This is some of the most used formal description techniques, we can mention too temporal logic [33] and the Z language [34].

Validation At this stage of the protocol engineering process, designers have a formal description of an interaction protocol. A formal description should remove misunderstanding, but it does not preclude protocols that are ill designed. It is hence important to verify the protocol against the requirements defined in the analysis phase. The validation can be structural (checking for deadlock, termination, etc.) or behavioral (checking whether the protocol achieves its goals). Two techniques exist for the validation of interaction protocols: (1) reachability analysis [21], where a graph of all the reachable states of the protocol is built—validation is based on graph properties; (2) model checking [65], where once again a graph of reachable states is built, but this time the property is expressed as a temporal logic formula. Checking a property via model checking implies the generation of a graph from the temporal logic formula and checking whether this graph is contained within the graph of the protocol. Model checking is the main technique for validating interaction protocols [36].

Another kind of validation is the agent communication language compliance verification, which checks whether an agent correctly implements the protocol and the agent communication language [37–39].

Protocol Synthesis Once the protocol is formalized and verified, it is time to implement it. Communication protocol engineering uses the term "protocol synthesis." The usual way to do that is to first generate the skeleton of the protocol corresponding to the transitions in the protocol, then to add the semantics associated with each transition. The first phase is automatic and the second one is manual. Actually, a program is unable to generate the semantics particularly in cases where it is required to account for standards [35]. We propose to directly execute the protocol in its formalism. The advantage of this approach is that it reduces the effort required for generating a protocol since it is not necessary to rewrite each time the semantics of the protocol if it is modified [40].

Conformance Testing This last phase in interaction protocol engineering checks whether the implemented protocol contains the requirements defined in the analysis phase. The process is to verify whether the output of an interaction state for the implemented protocol corresponds to the one defined for the formally described protocol.

In the remainder of this section, we present a few well-known multi-agent protocols.

4.1.1 The Contract Net Protocol

The Contract Net protocol [41] is certainly the most renowned and widely used protocol in multi-agent systems. The Contract Net protocol describes a protocol in which there are two kinds of agents: (1) a task manager that has to perform a task and does not have the skills for that, and (2) bidders that will bid to realize the task. The Contract Net protocol is composed of four phases. In the first phase, the task manager advertises the task to potential bidders. The message also contains the constraints associated with the task such as the deadline by which the task has to be performed. In the second phase, bidders can bid for the task. In the third phase, the task manager selects one bidder based on its bid and awards it. Finally, the fourth phase corresponds to performing the task.

The first message sent is the *cfp* message, where the task is advertised with its constraints. The bidders can answer either by *propose* denoting that they agree to realize the task subject to the constraints associated with it (as expressed in the message content), or by *refuse* if the bidder refuses to execute the task—the reason refusal is provided by the bidder in the message content field. After the deadline, the manager agent selects a bid based on the constraints. It then sends an *accept-proposal* to the awarded bidder and a *reject-proposal* to all other bidders. When task execution completes, the awarded bidder informs the manager that the task is realized (the *inform-done* message), or sends the result (the *inform-result* message), or sends the *failure* message if it fails performing the task.

The Contract Net protocol is presented in Fig. 6.1.

4.1.2 Auction Protocols

Many auction protocols are implemented in multi-agent systems. Among them, the English auction and the Dutch auction are likely the most widely implemented and used. The English auction is an ascending open cry auction where the price of the item for sale increases as long as at least one auction participant is willing to pay the price. It stops when no participant is willing to raise the price beyond the current bid. The English auction protocol is shown in Fig. 6.2.

The first message *inform(start-auction)* informs auction participants that the auction has begun. The second message is sent by the auctioneer (the *cfp* message). It informs the auction participants of the starting bid price. The participants can

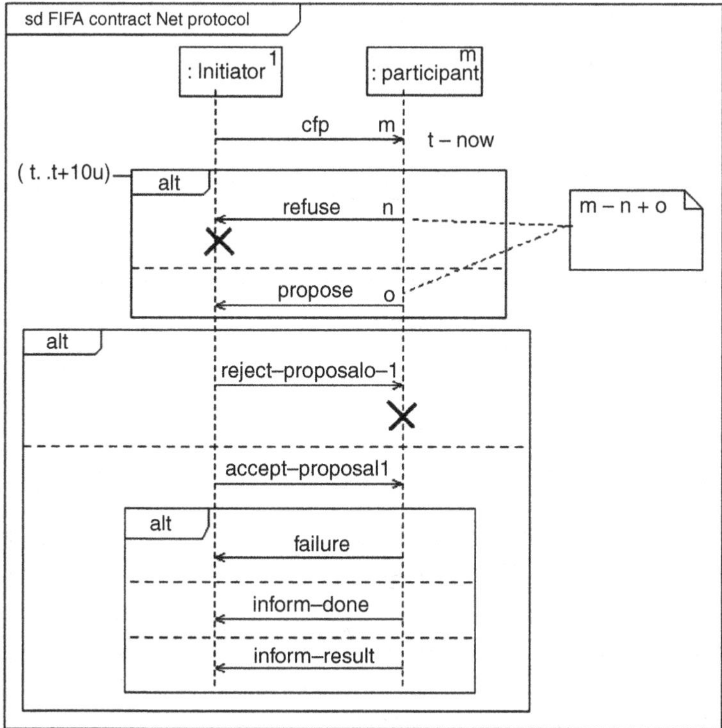

Fig. 6.1 The Contract Net Protocol

respond by a *propose* message including a bid equal to or greater than the current bid. This can continue iteratively until a deadline is reached. After a deadline, the auctioneer selects a bid and informs the winner with the *accept-proposal* message. The other participants who placed bids receive the *reject-proposal* message. The auction continues as long as there are at least two offers.

The auctioneer may close the auction (the *inform(end of auction)*) if there are less than two offers. The protocol allows the auctioneer to check whether the hammer price is greater than the reservation price, and to allocate the sold good to the winner conditioned on this.

The Dutch auction protocol is a descending open cry auction. Unlike the English auction, the price decreases as long as a participant does not inform it accepts to pay the price.

The sequence of messages in the Dutch auction protocol is similar to the sequence in the English auction. Here, however, the price decreases over time.

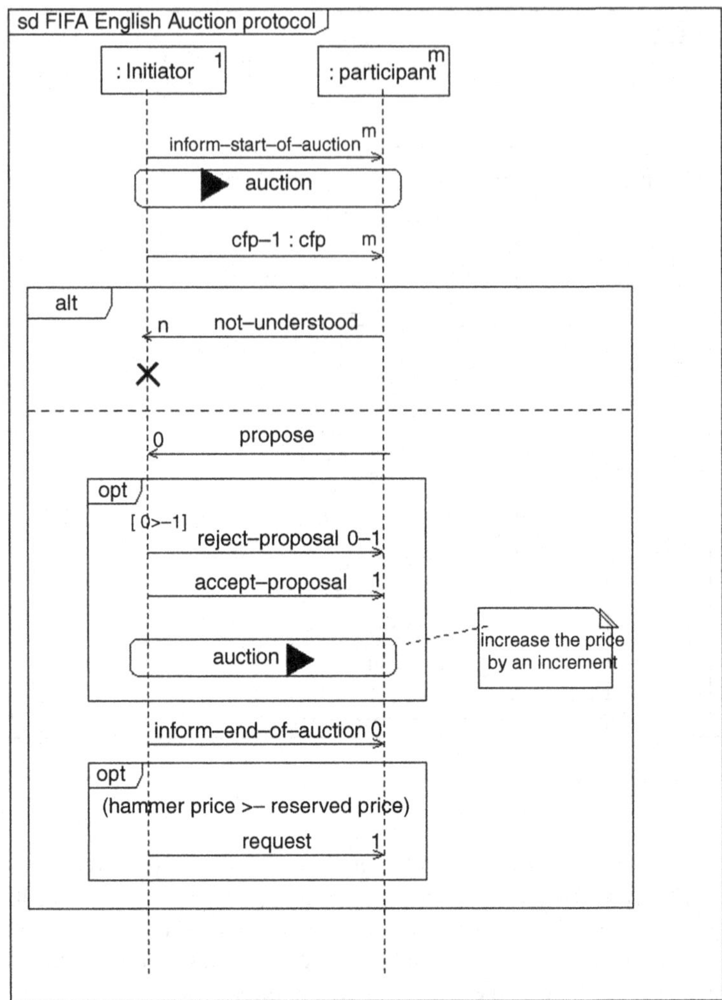

Fig. 6.2 The English auction protocol

4.1.3 Sian's Learning Protocol

Sian's learning protocol [42] is a simple protocol where an agent proposes a hypothesis to other agents. Those agents provide their opinion on whether the hypothesis is correct or incorrect, and whether they want to modify it. Each agent votes on the correctness of the hypothesis. The agent that proposed the hypothesis gathers the votes and, using some heuristics, decides whether the hypothesis is accepted or not. If the hypothesis is accepted, it informs other agents of the acceptance.

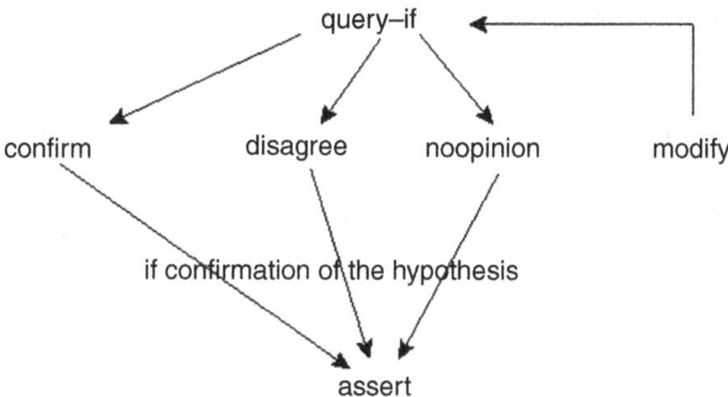

Fig. 6.3 Sian's learning protocol

The first message is a *query-if* message containing the hypothesis to validate. The other agents can answer either by a *confirm* message denoting that the hypothesis is correct, by a *disagree* message denoting that the hypothesis is wrong, by a *noopinion* message denoting that they have no idea about this hypothesis, or by a *modify* message requesting to modify the hypothesis. Based on heuristics and answers from other agents, the initiator decides whether the hypothesis is true. If it decides that the hypothesis is true, it informs the other agents via an *assert* message that the hypothesis is considered true. Figure 6.3 illustrates the Sian protocol.

4.2 Dialogue Games

A prominent property of protocols is the strict definition of messages and message sequences. As a consequence, conforming to a protocol implies conforming to the admissible sequence of messages. While it has many advantages, this approach is rather restricted, particularly regarding agents' autonomy. Dialogue game protocols were conceived with the idea of restoring agents' autonomy. In dialogue game protocols, only pairs of communicative acts are defined, e.g., a request with an answer. It is then easier to create dialogues since the only constraint is the state of the interaction and the last message.

Dialogue games are interactions between two or more players, where each utters according to a defined set of rules given below. Such dialogue games found application in philosophy [43], in computational linguistics [44], and in artificial intelligence [45]. Dialogue games were used in philosophy to study fallacious reasoning and in computational linguistics to study human–machine interaction.

There exist different types of dialogues as proposed by Walton and Krabbe [46]. This categorization is based upon the information the participants have at the beginning of a dialogue, their individual goals for the dialogue, and the goals they share. Here are the different types of dialogues:

Information seeking dialogues are those where one participant seeks the answer to some question(s) from another participant, who is believed by the first to know the answer(s).

Inquiry dialogues are those where the participants collaborate to answer some question or questions where answers are not known to any single participant.

Persuasion dialogues involve one participant seeking to persuade another to accept a proposition he or she does not currently endorse.

Negotiation dialogues are those where the participants bargain over the division of some scarce resource. Here, the goal of the dialogue—a division of the resource acceptable to all—may be in conflict with the individual goals of the participants.

Deliberation dialogues are those where the participants collaborate to decide what action or course of action should be adopted in some situation. Here, participants share a responsibility to decide upon the course of action, or, at least, they share a willingness to discuss whether they have such a shared responsibility. Note that the best course of action for a group may conflict with the preferences or intentions of each individual member of the group; moreover no one participant may have all the information required to decide what is best for the group.

Eristic dialogues are those where participants quarrel verbally as a substitute for physical fighting, aiming to vent perceived grievances.

A dialogue game consists of the following elements (from [47]):

Commencement rules: Rules that define the circumstances under which the dialogue commences.

Locutions: Rules that indicate what utterances are permitted. Typically, admissible locutions permit participants to assert propositions, permit others to question or contest prior assertions, and permit those asserting propositions that are subsequently questioned or contested to justify their assertions. Justifications may involve the presentation of a proof of the proposition or an argument for it. The dialogue game rules may also permit participants to utter propositions to which they assign differing degrees of commitment, for example, one may merely propose a proposition, a speech act that entails less commitment than would an assertion of the same proposition.

Combination rules: Rules that define the dialogical contexts under which particular locutions are permitted or not, or obligatory or not. For instance, it may not be permitted for a participant to assert a proposition p and subsequently the proposition $\neg p$ in the same dialogue, without in the interim having retracted the former assertion.

Commitments: Rules that define the circumstances under which participants express commitment to a proposition. Typically, the assertion of a claim p in the debate is defined as indicating to other participants some level of commitment to, or support for, the claim. Since the work of Hamblin [43], formal dialogue systems typically establish and maintain public sets of commitments, called *commitment stores*, for each participant; these stores are usually non-monotonic, in the sense that participants can also retract committed claims, although possibly only under defined circumstances.

Termination rules: Rules that define the circumstances under which the dialogue ends.

A purchase negotiation dialogue game taken from [48] is illustrated below. The example deals with buying a new car under some specific constraints such as price, quality, number of seats, etc. The different communicative acts (also called locutions) in this dialogue game are:

open_dialogue()
Locution: open_dialogue(P_{Xi},All,θ).

Preconditions: This locution must not already have been uttered by a participant within the dialogue. To utter this locution, an agent P_{Xi} must have a potential need for a purchase of a product in the specified category, or a willingness to sell or to advice on the sale of products in the category.
Meaning: The speaker, participant P_{Xi}, suggests the opening of a purchase dialogue on product category θ. A dialogue can only commence with this move. The second argument, All, indicates that this is a statement broadcast to all participants.
Response: Every other agent P_{Xi} wishing to participate in the dialogue must respond with enter_dialogue(P_{Xi}, All, θ).
Information Store Updates: No effect.
Commitment Store Updates: No effect.

enter_dialogue()

Locution: enter_dialogue(P_{Xj}, All, θ).
Preconditions: Within the dialogue, a participant P_{Xj} with $i \neq j$ must have uttered the locution open_dialogue(P_{Xi}, All, θ). Participant P_{Xj} must have a potential need for the purchase of a product in the specified category, or a willingness to sell or advice on the sale of products in the category.
Meaning: The speaker, participant P_{Xj}, indicates a willingness to join a purchase negotiation dialogue on product category θ. All intending participants other than the mover of the locution open_dialogue(P_{Xi},All, θ) must announce their participation with this move.
Response: No response required.
Information Store Updates: No effect.
Commitment Store Updates: No effect.

seek_info()

Locution: seek_info(P_{Xi}, S, p).
Preconditions: No specific preconditions.
Meaning: The speaker, a consumer or advisor participant P_{Xi} seeks information from one or more participants in the set S about what sale options are available, subject to the constraint expressed by p. For example, the constraint

may be a budgetary one, with p expressing the statement that the price is less than some threshold. The constraint may also be a null statement, i.e., expressing no constraints.

Response: A seller or advisor participant $P_{Yj} \in S$ must subsequently utter a willing_to_sell(P_{Yj}, T, P_{Sj}, V) locution, where the elements of the set V of sales options satisfy the constraint p, and where $P_{Xi} \in T$.

Information Store Updates: No effect.

Commitment Store Updates: No effect.

willing_to_sell()

Locution: willing_to_sell(P_{Yj}, T, P_{Sk}, V).

Preconditions: Some participant P_{Xi} must have previously uttered a locution seek_info(P_{Xi} ,S,p), where $P_{Yj} \in S$, and the set of sales options V in the willing_to_sell() locution must satisfy constraint p.

Meaning: The speaker, a seller or advisor P_{Yj}, indicates to the audience T a willingness by seller participant P_{Sk} to supply a finite and possibly empty set $V = \{a, b, \ldots\}$ of purchase options to any buyer participant in the set T. Each of the sales options tendered in the set V must satisfy constraint p uttered as part of the prior seek_info() locution.

Response: None required.

Information Store Updates: For each $a \in V$, the 3-tuple (T, P_{Sk}, a) is inserted into IS(P_{Yj}), the Information Store for participant P_{Yj}.

Commitment Store Updates: No effect.

desire_to_buy()

Locution: desire_to_buy(P_{Bi},S,T,V).

Preconditions: No specific preconditions. The options included in this utterance need not have been presented in the dialogue before this time.

Meaning: Consumer participant, P_{Bi}, speaking to all the participants in the set S, requests to purchase an option in the set V of options from any seller in the set T, where $T \subseteq S$.

Response: None required.

Information Store Update: For each $a \in V$ and each $P_{Sk} \in T$, the 3-tuple (S, P_{Sk},a) is inserted into IS(P_{Bi}), the Information Store for participant P_{Bi}.

Commitment Store Update: No effect.

prefer()

Locution: prefer(P_{Bi},S,V,W).

Preconditions: Each of the sale or purchase options contained in the sets V and W must previously have been included as an option in a willing_to_sell() locution, for which participant P_{Bi} and every participant in S was in the intended audience, or a desire_to_buy() locution, uttered by P_{Bi} to an audience that included S. Equivalently, we could express this precondition by saying that each of the options contained in V and in W must be elements of an

Information Store tuple, a tuple to which P_{Bi} and every participant in S has viewing access.

Meaning: The speaker, a buyer participant P_{Bi}, indicates to the participants in the S that she prefers each option in the finite set V of options to each option in the finite set W.

Response: No response required.

Information Store Update: No effect.

Commitment Store Update: No effect.

refuse_to_buy()

Locution: refuse_to_buy(P_{Bi} ,S,T,W).

Preconditions: This locution cannot be uttered following a valid utterance of agree_to_buy(P_{Bi},U, P_{Sj},V), for which both $P_{Sj} \in T$ and $V \cap W$ is non-empty.

Meaning: A buyer participant P_{Bi}, speaking to audience S, which includes every participant in the set T, expresses a refusal to purchase any option in the set W of options from any seller in the set T of seller participants.

Response: None required.

Information Store Update: No effect.

Commitment Store Update: No effect.

refuse_to_sell

Locution: refuse_to_sell(P_{Sj},S,T,W).

Preconditions: This locution cannot be uttered following a valid utterance of agree_to_sell(P_{Sj},U, P_{Bi} ,V), for which both $P_{Bi} \in T$ and $V \cap W$ are non-empty.

Meaning: A seller participant P_{Sj}, speaking to audience S, which includes every participant in the set T, expresses a refusal to sell any option in the set W of options to any buyer in the set T of buyer participants.

Response: None required.

Information Store Update: No effect.

Commitment Store Update: No effect.

agree_to_buy

Locution: agree_to_buy(P_{Bi} ,S, P_{Sj},V).

Preconditions: For each option $a \in V$, a locution of the form willing_to_sell (P_{Yk},T, P_{Sj},W) must previously have been uttered such that $a \in W$, and such that $P_{Bi} \in T$. In other words, buyer P_{Bi} can only agree to purchase options that have previously been offered to her for sale.

Meaning: Buyer agent P_{Bi}, speaking to audience S, commits to purchase one of each of the options in the set V from seller agent P_{Sj}. We call P_{Sj} the intended seller of the locution.

Response: If seller P_{Sj} is willing to sell some or all of the options in the set V to buyer P_{Bi}, she may respond with an appropriate agree_to_sell() locution.

Information Store Update: No effect.

Commitment Store Update: For each a ∈ V, the 3-tuple (S, P_{Sj},a) is inserted into CS(P_{Bi}), the Commitment Store for participant P_{Bi}.

agree_to_sell

Locution: agree_to_sell(P_{Sj},S, P_{Bi},V).
Preconditions: For every option a ∈ V, participant P_{Bi} must previously have uttered the locution agree_to_buy(P_{Bi},S, P_{Sj},W) for some set of options W containing a. Note that this condition in turn implies that the options contained in V must previously have been announced to an audience including buyer P_{Bi} through a willing_to_sell() locution.
Meaning: Seller participant P_{Sj}, speaking to audience S, commits to selling each of the options contained in the set V to buyer P_{Bi}. We call P_{Bi} the intended buyer of the locution.
Response: None required.
Information Store Update: No effect.
Commitment Store Update: For each a ∈ V, the 3-tuple (S,P_{Bi},a) is inserted into CS(P_{Sj}), the Commitment Store for participant P_{Sj}.

withdraw_dialogue

Locution: withdraw_dialogue(P_{Xi},All,θ).
Preconditions: No specific precondition.
Meaning: The speaker, participant P_{Xi}, announces to all participants her withdrawal from the dialogue negotiating the potential purchase of products in the category θ. This move may be executed at any time following her entry to the dialogue.
Response: None required.
Information Store Update: No effect.
Commitment Store Update: No effect.

In terms of phase in the dialogue, one can arrange locutions as follows:

Open dialogue stage: open_dialogue and enter_dialogue
Inform stage: seek_info and willing_to_sell
Negotiate stage: desire_to_buy, prefer, refuse_to_buy, refuse_to_sell, seek_info, and willing_to_sell
Confirm stage: agree_to_buy and agree_to_sell
Close dialogue stage: withdraw_dialogue

A trace of use of this dialogue can be found in [48].

4.3 Argumentation Systems

Protocols and even dialogue games assume that information and beliefs from agents do not suffer from contradictions except for cases in which it is requested to (see the example of Sian's learning protocol [42]). Agents say something and it is considered to be true. An alternative is to allow challenging agents on their beliefs. Consequently, agents can support their beliefs by other information. This kind of process is called argumentation.

We first describe how argumentation is represented within an agent and then we describe the process of argumentation between agents. The description given below is an excerpt from [20].

> To define an argumentation system we start with a propositional language which we call Λ. From Λ we then construct formulae such as $B_i(p)$, $D_i(p)$ and $I_i(q)$ for any p and q which are formulae of Λ. This extended propositional language, and the compound formulae that may be built from it using the usual logical connectives, is the base language L of the argumentation-based dialogue system we are describing. $B_i(.)$ denotes a belief of agent i, $D_i(.)$ denotes a desire of agent i, and $I_i(.)$ denotes an intention of agent i, so the overall effect of this language is just to force every formula to be a belief, a desire, or an intention. We will denote formulae of L by $\varphi,\psi,\sigma\ldots$. Since we are only interested in syntactic manipulation of beliefs, desires and intentions here, we will give no semantics for formulae such as $B_i(p)$ and $B_i(p) \rightarrow D_i(p)$-suitable ways of dealing with the semantics are given elsewhere (e.g., [38]). An agent has a knowledge base Σ which is allowed to be inconsistent, and has no deductive closure. The symbol $\vdash$ denotes classical inference and $\equiv$ denotes logical equivalence.

An argument is a formula of L and the set of formulae from which it can be inferred:

Definition 1

An *argument* is a pair $A = (H,h)$ where h is a formula of

L and H a subset of Σ such that:

1. H is consistent
2. $H \vdash h$
3. H is minimal, so no subset of H satisfying both 1 and 2 exists

H is called the *support* of A, written $H = \text{Support}(A)$ and h is the *conclusion* of A written
$h = \text{Conclusion}(A)$.
We talk of h being *supported* by the argument (H,h).
In general, since Σ is inconsistent, arguments in $A(\Sigma)$, the set of all arguments that can be made from Σ, will conflict, and we make this idea precise with the notions of rebutting, undercutting, and attacking.

Definition 2

Let A_1 and A_2 be two distinct arguments of $A(\Sigma)$. A_1 *undercuts* A_2 iff $\exists h \in \text{Support}(A_2)$ such that $\text{Conclusion}(A_1)$ *attacks* h.

Definition 3

Let A_1 and A_2 be two distinct arguments of $A(\Sigma)$. A_1 *rebuts* A_2 iff $\text{Conclusion}(A_1)$ *attacks* $\text{Conclusion}(A_2)$.

Definition 4

Given two distinct formulae h and g of Λ such that h $\equiv\neg$g, then, for any i and j:

- $B_i(h)$ *attacks* $B_j(g)$
- $D_i(h)$ *attacks* $D_j(g)$
- $I_i(h)$ *attacks* $I_j(g)$

With these definitions, an argument is rebutted if it has a conclusion $B_i(p)$ and there is another argument that has as its conclusion $B_j(\neg p)$ or $B_j(q)$ such that $q\equiv\neg p$. An argument with a desire as its conclusion can similarly be rebutted by another argument with a desire as its conclusion, and the same thing holds for intentions. Undercutting occurs in exactly the same situations, except that it holds between the conclusions of one argument and an element of the support of the other.[2]

To capture that some facts are more strongly believed and intended than others, we assume that any set of facts has a preference order over it.[3] We suppose that this ordering derives from the fact that the knowledge base Σ is stratified into non-overlapping sets $\Sigma_1, \ldots, \Sigma_n$ such that facts in Σ_i are all equally preferred and are more preferred than those in Σ_j, where $j > i$. The preference level of a nonempty subset H of Σ, level(H), is the number of the highest numbered layer that has a member in H.

Definition 5

Let A_1 and A_2 be two arguments in A(Σ). A_1 is *preferred* to A_2 according to Pref iff level(Support(A_1)) $\leq$ level(Support(A_2)).

By $>>^{Pref}$ we denote the strict pre-order associated with *Pref*. If A_1 is strictly preferred to A_2, we say that A_1 is *stronger* than A_2. We can now define the argumentation system we will use:

Definition 6

An *argumentation system* (AS) is a triple
< A(Σ), *Undercut/Rebut*, *Pref*>
such that:

- A(Σ) is a set of the arguments built from Σ
- *Undercut/Rebut* is a binary relation capturing the existence of an undercut or rebut holding between arguments, *Undercut/Rebut* $\subseteq$ A(Σ)x A(Σ)
- *Pref* is a (partial or complete) preordering on A(Σ) x A(Σ)

---

[2]Note that attacking and rebutting are symmetric but not reflexive or transitive, while undercutting is neither symmetric, reflexive, nor transitive.

[3]We ignore for now the fact that we might require different preference orders over beliefs and intentions and indeed that different agents will almost certainly have different preference orders, noting that the problem of handling a number of different preference orders was considered in [50] and [64].

The preference order makes it possible to distinguish different types of relation between arguments:

Definition 7

Let A_1, A_2 be two arguments of $A(\Sigma)$.

- If A_2 undercuts or rebuts A_1, then A_1 *defends itself* against A_2 iff $A_1 >>^{Pref} A_2$. Otherwise, A1 *does not defend itself.*
- A set of arguments Σ *defends* A iff ∀ B such that B undercuts or rebuts A and A does not defend itself against B then ∃C ∈ Σ such that C undercuts or rebuts B and B does not defend itself against C.

Henceforth, $C_{Undercut/Rebut,Pref}$ will gather all non-undercut and non-rebut arguments along with arguments defending themselves against all their undercutting and rebutting arguments. [49] showed that the set Σ of acceptable arguments of the argumentation system <A(Σ),*Undercut/Rebut,Pref*> is the least fix point of a function Φ

$$\Phi(\Sigma) = \left\{ (\mathrm{H},\mathrm{h}) \in \mathrm{A}(\Sigma) \,\middle|\, (\mathrm{H},\mathrm{h}) \text{ is defended by } S \right\}$$

where $S \subseteq A(\Sigma)$

Note that while we have given a language L for this system, we have given no language ML. This particular system does not have a meta-language (and the notion of preferences it uses is not expressed in a meta-language). It is, of course, possible to add a meta-language to this system—for example, in [50] we added a meta-language that allowed us to express preferences over elements of L, thus making it possible to exchange (and indeed argue about, though this was not done in [50]) preferences between formulae.

4.3.1 Arguments Between Agents

Now, this system is sufficient for internal argumentation within a single agent, and the agent can use it to, for example, perform nonmonotonic reasoning and to deal with inconsistent information. To allow for dialogues, we have to introduce some more machinery. Clearly part of this will be the communication language, but we need to introduce some additional elements first. These elements are data structures that our system inherits from its dialogue game ancestors as well as previous presentations of this kind of system [51,52].

Dialogues are assumed to take place between two agents, P and C.[4] Each agent has a knowledge base, Σ_P and Σ_C, respectively, containing their beliefs. In addition, following Hamblin [43], each agent has a further knowledge base,

[4]The names stem from the study of persuasion dialogues—P argues "pro" some proposition, and C argues "con."

accessible to both agents, containing commitments made in the dialogue. These commitment stores are denoted *CS(P)* and *CS(C)*, respectively, and in this dialogue system (unlike that of [52], for example) an agent's commitment store is just a subset of its knowledge base. Note that the union of the commitment stores can be viewed as the state of the dialogue at a given time. Each agent has access to their own private knowledge base and to both commitment stores. Thus, P can make use of $<A(\Sigma_P),,\textit{Undercut/Rebut},\textit{Pref}>$ and C can make use of $<A(\Sigma_C),,\textit{Undercut/Rebut},\textit{Pref}>$. All the knowledge bases contain propositional formulae and are not closed under deduction, and all are stratified by a degree of belief as discussed above.

With this background, we can present the set of dialogue moves that we use, the set that comprises the locutions of CL. For each move, we give what we call rationality rules, dialogue rules, and update rules. These locutions are those from [53] and are based on the rules suggested in [54] which, in turn, were based on those in the dialogue game DC introduced by MacKenzie [55]. The rationality rules specify the preconditions for making the move.

The update rules specify how commitment stores are modified by the move.

In the following, player P directs the move to player C. We start with the assertion of facts:

assert(ϕ) where ϕ is a formula of L.

rationality: the usual assertion condition for the agent
update: $CS_i(P) = CS_{i-1}(P) \cup \{\phi\}$ and $CS_i(C) = CS_{i-1}(C)$
Here, ϕ can be any formula of L, as well as the special character Y, discussed in [48].

assert(S) where S is a set of formulae of L representing the support of an argument.

rationality: the usual assertion condition for the agent
update: $CS_i(P) = CS_{i-1} \cup S$ and $CS_i(C) = CS_{i-1}(C)$
The counterpart of these moves are acceptance moves:

accept(ϕ) ϕ is a formula of L.

rationality: The usual acceptance condition for the agent
update: $CS_i(P) = CS_{i-1}(P) \cup \{\phi\}$ and $CS_i(C) = CS_{i-1}(C)$

accept(S) S is a set of formulae of L.

rationality: the usual acceptance condition for every S
update: $CS_i(P) = CS_{i-1}(P) \cup S$ and $CS_i(C) = CS_{i-1}(C)$
There are also moves that allow questions to be posed.

challenge(ϕ) where ϕ is a formula of L.

rationality: ϕ
update: $CS_i(P) = CS_{i-1}(P)$ and $CS_i(C) = CS_{i-1}(C)$

A challenge is a means of making the other player explicitly state the argument supporting a proposition. In contrast, a question can be used to query the other player about any proposition.

question(ϕ) where ϕ is a formula of L.

rationality: ϕ
update: $CS_i(P) = CS_{i-1}(P)$ and $CS_i(C) = CS_{i-1}(C)$

We refer to this set of moves as the set $M^d{}_{DC}$. These locutions are the bare minimum to carry out a dialogue, and, as we will see below, require a fairly rigid protocol with a lot of aspects implicit. Further locutions such as those discussed in [56] would be required to be able to debate the beginning and end of dialogues or to have an explicit representation of movement between embedded dialogues.

Clearly, this set of moves/locutions defines the communication language CL, and hopefully it is reasonably clear from the description so far how argumentation between agents takes place; a prototypical dialogue might be as follows:

1. P has an acceptable argument $(S,B_p(p))$, built from Σ_P, and wants C to accept $B_p(p)$. Thus, P asserts $B_p(p)$.
2. C has an argument $(S', B_c(\neg p))$ and so cannot accept $B_p(p)$. Thus, C asserts $B_c(\neg p)$.
3. P cannot accept $B_c(\neg p)$ and challenges it.
4. C responds by asserting S'.
5. ...

At each stage in the dialogue, agents can build arguments using information from their own private knowledge base, and the propositions made public (by assertion into commitment stores).

5 Multiparty Communication

Early work in agent communication takes roots in distributed system communication and as a consequence favors one-to-one communication (although alternatives are found in the multi-agent art): A speaker communicates with an addressee on a dedicated channel [1]. Even if this mode of communication is efficient when it is unnecessary to have auditors and over hearers, such an approach is rather restrictive and does not support well all aspects of multi-agent communication. Agents are not able to listen in to dialogue moves made by other agents and therefore cannot react upon them. A few studies on multi-party communication do exist, e.g., [57–59]. The focus of [59] is on multi-modal multi-party dialogues where verbal and non-verbal behaviors are used for dialogues, focus of attention, and initiative. The work reported in [57] concentrates on a system for multi-party dialogues based on a blackboard. In [58], multi-dialogism based on the Ethernet protocol is described; that is, agents are on a ring and receive messages serially.

We first describe what the differences between agent communication and multi-agent communication are. Then, we present our proposal for multi-party communication [60]. Alternatives do exist but are not described here.

5.1 Agent Communication Versus Multi-agent Communication

Agent communication (as opposed to multi-agent communication) is a one-to-one communication in which a speaker utters speech acts to a single addressee. One-to-many agent communication, e.g., in the Contract Net protocol [41], is artificial since it corresponds to many one-to-one communications. Bidders cannot hear offers placed by other agents and cannot use such information for planning their proposals. Several features characterize one-to-one communication:

- Communication is between two agents: a speaker and an addressee.
- Communication is privileged between two agents, that is, it is not possible for other agents to hear the communication.
- Entering and leaving communications are subject to agreement from other agents, particularly in dialogue games where there are dedicated speech acts for this purpose [19].
- Terms of termination of communication are necessarily known before beginning the communication.

Note that some of the features above may contrast concepts sought in multi-agent systems. The remainder of this section reviews the above features, their fitness to MAS, and gaps to be bridged to facilitate multi-agent communication. This review sheds light on the structure for multi-agent communication and features it should support.

1. Except for private conversations that should not be disclosed, communication should not be restricted to message passing between two agents only. It is frequently the case in human conversations that humans intervene in conversations where they are neither the speaker nor the addressee. Humans overhear the content of a conversation and express their opinion when they perceive it of importance. Multi-agent communication should allow such overhearing and intervention in others' conversations. Actually, one needs three different kinds of communication: communications with potentially many hearers; private communications, but agents are able to *perceive* that agents are conversing; and finally, secret communications where agents outside of the communicating group are unaware of this communication.
2. Multi-agent communication should allow for *indirect communication*. That is, it should allow agents to listen to messages transmitted in their vicinity (either physical or logical) but not too far-away communication. It is then important to add the notion of earshot. In human communication, earshot can range from

whispering (private communications) to shouting where even further agents can hear. An equivalent earshot for multi-agent communication is needed.

3. Multi-agent systems are open systems; as a consequence, agents can enter and leave at any moment during the conversation. Such openness should be facilitated in multi-agent communication as well. One issue arises from this openness: addressees may disappear before the message arrives to them. Multi-agent communication needs, more than before, to be asynchronous in the sense that agents participating in a protocol should be able to exit if protocol participants with which they communicate are no longer present.
4. Termination of communications is not necessarily decided in advance. Termination can happen if no more communication is needed—there is no more argument against a proposal—or if a certain event appears such as weariness in a long-lasting negotiation or an external event modifies the subject of the communication—the subject of dispute is no longer present.
5. Turn taking introduces another main difference between multi-agent communication and one-to-one communication. In protocols, agents know when they have to speak; however, this is not necessarily the case in multi-agent communication: some agents can interrupt other agents or they can monopolize the conversation. It is therefore required to augment a multi-agent communication framework to address these issues. It is particularly important to allow agents avoiding other agents that clog the conversation (e.g., communicating too frequently) or monopolize it.

5.2 *Multiparty Communication Proposal*

5.2.1 Three Modes of Communication

Agent communication is based on Shannon's ideas [1], that is, a message is sent from a sender to a receiver via a medium also called a communication channel. As a consequence, communication between agents is private to these agents. It is then not possible to send the *same* message to all the agents and to see the answers without using a multicast or a broadcast mechanism. Moreover, *hearing* the message assumes that the agent is recognized as a member of this communication. An agent cannot overhear the communication and intervene if needed. In our proposal, this mode of communication is called the *secret* mode since this thread of communication is only visible to members of the communication group. We also consider two other modes of communication: the *public* mode and the *private* mode. The public mode is similar to the Internet multi-party communication where chats and forums are accessible to everybody and even if a message is addressed to a specific addressee, everybody can read the message, and they can answer the message too. This is essentially a many-to-many communication. The private (but not secret) mode corresponds to private conversations in which other agents can observe that agents are involved in communication but they cannot listen to that communication.

In Internet applications, the more common modes are the public and the secret modes. The secret mode is frequent in chats and forums when two participants want to exchange messages without disclosing them to other participants. We briefly present this mode for completeness; however, its application to agent communication is limited.

The three communication modes are described from a technical point of view in the following sections. They are all supported by a communication server.

5.2.2 Public Communication

As stated above, the public communication mode resembles the Internet multi-party communication, where potentially all agents are able to "hear" a message. The agent communication not only contains the sender and the addressees but auditors and overhearers as well. If we want to allow auditors to hear this message, it is necessary to either "open" this channel to everybody or to send the message to all agents. The latter approach is commonly too resource-consumptive to be used, in particular in large-scale MAS. Chats and forums on the Internet are using a dedicated "area" where everybody can read the messages as they arrive to the chat server. We follow two different approaches for our public mode: (1) a forum-based communication and (2) an environment-based communication. The difference between the two approaches is in the way in which communication is handled. For instance, one can gather a couple of hundred people in the same place—a physical environment—to hold a discussion; gathering thousands of people for this would be more challenging. In an Internet environment, this is resolved via forums and the similar, where there is no difficulty in gathering thousands of people in a shared virtual environment. We follow these two approaches in agent communication too: Public communication via the environment is reserved for small multi-party communication whereas the forum is used for larger-scale multi-party communication.

5.2.3 Forum Communication

Forum communication is used when communication is focused on discussion comprised of messages posted by multiple parties. Argumentation and auctions are examples of communication that can be addressed by a forum. Multi-agent communication forums are equivalent to the ones found on the Internet, that is, a shared zone where one or several threads of conversation run concurrently. For the sake of simplicity, we restrict our discussion to one thread and several subsequent threads derived from the main thread. Subsequent threads are used to clarify some points in the current conversation. Clarifying message content is an example of a subsequent thread since it deserves the main thread. Forums are created on request of agents for a particular need. For instance, an agent may want to open an auction to sell an item.

When an agent begins a new dialogue in forum mode, the communication server creates a forum with one participant and posts the message. Then, the communication server advertises this forum to other agents. The way of advertising can be done along different modes:

1. The sender identifies an agent role to which the advertisement should be sent.
2. The sender gives an advertisement to be sent to all the agents.
3. The sender gives no advertisement, the message is sent to all the agents.

The communication server should update the list of active forums. For each forum, it creates a slot that contains the list of participants and the advertisement if one exists. This list is used by agents to access the forum if they have not received the advertisement. This list contains only details relevant to public and private communication (and not to secret communication). All the messages posted to the forum are stored. One of the reasons for storing the messages is to facilitate agent joining during the conversation. This allows new-comers to find what the current state of the conversation is. Turn taking is not restricted and agents can speak freely whenever they see fit. Termination in multi-party communication is ensured either by the communication server or by the agents. The communication server may remove inactive agents when this is found necessary, according to a removal policy. A common reason for agent removal is communication slowdown agents may be imposing. Removal requests may be made by the participants, but the server has the sole responsibility for such removals.

5.2.4 Environment-Based Communication

In contrast to forum communication, the environment-based communication presented here assumes that agents communicate via the environment. Thus, the sending of a message is not done via a dedicated communication channel but via propagation in the environment. A similar approach was presented in MANTA [2] where the message is a pheromone. One reason for agents to choose this mode of communication is the need to coordinate or to cooperate with multiple agents, many of which are possibly unknown. This mode of communication is also driven by some specific applications such as human-lifelike applications or games. For instance, a war game can use this approach to coordinate platoons or to help soldiers in danger. An excellent example of communication via the environment is found in the software Massive, widely used in movies (e.g., in *Lord of the Rings*, Massive was used for the battle of Helm's Deep). In Massive, attacks are passed via the environment to allow opponents' reaction. This facilitates reduction in agent complexity as there is no need for a complex vision process to recognize opponents and attacks.

In environment-based communication, messages are released in the environment with a specific intensity. The associated intensity of the message is maximal at the

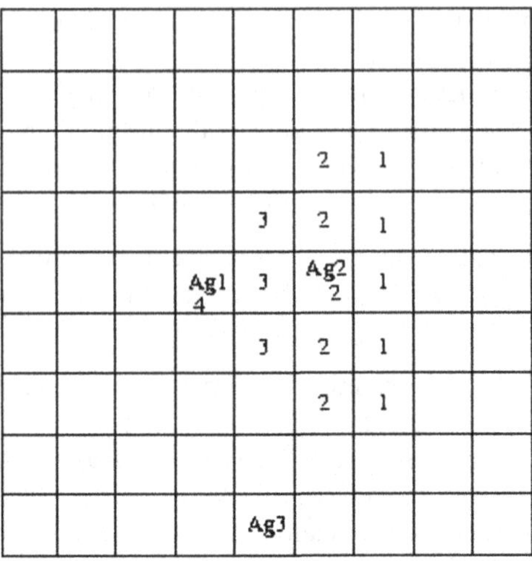

Fig. 6.4 Environment-based communication in public mode

message source location, and it decreases as the distance grows (in Fig. 6.4 the decrement is by 1 unit per cell distance). Thus, the further the message is from its source, the weaker it is. In Fig. 6.4, agent Ag1 sends a message *inform* with an intensity of 4 and a decrement of 1. Agent Ag2 "hears" the message since it is within earshot, but Ag3 does not "hear" it since it is out of earshot.

Contrarily to communication via forums, messages are not stored in environment-based communication. Moreover, messages may be substituted by new ones if the earshot of a new message covers some cells of a previous message. In some cases, physical agents (or simulations thereof) can face different directions. In such cases, agent direction may affect message perception. For instance, a message may be more easily heard if the speaker faces the recipient compared to the case in which the speaker has its back to the recipient. The structure of the environment (e.g., the presence of obstacles) may also affect message propagation and perception. For example, the decay in message intensity when propagating through obstacles such as walls may be of 3 units instead of 1.

When an agent begins a new dialogue in the environment-based mode, the communication server retrieves the intensity of the message and updates the environment with this message. That is, it propagates the message within the environment and decreases the intensity of the message based on the distance between the current location and the source, as shown in Fig. 6.4. Message perception by addressees is performed by perceiving the environment and retrieving the message. This is only possible if the agent is within earshot. An expiration time is associated with messages. When that time passes, the message is removed from the environment. The same approach is used for pheromones in MANTA to avoid considering outdated information [2].

5.2.5 Private Communication

Private communication is certainly the less frequent mode of communication in multi-agent systems. The aim of this mode is to offer some privacy to agents during the conversation. Agents outside the communication group may be aware of this communication but cannot perceive the content. Private communication is similar to secret communication; in the latter, agents outside the communicating group are not aware of the communication. The aim of this mode of communication is to let agents outside the communicating group learn that some agents are acquainted. Agents can infer beliefs about this private conversation. For instance, in games, it can imply that some relationships exist between characters and this can in turn affect agent strategies in the game.

In this mode, communication privacy has to be ensured and agents outside the communication have to be aware of this communication going on. Private communication is enabled via a forum with a restricted accessibility. That is, the communication server controls the access to the forum and only agents approved by the participants can access it. New participants are chosen either by the leader of the communication—if exists—or by a vote of all the participants. If most of the participants agree, new participants can enter the discussion. The communication server saves a list of all the active forums. It is straightforward for agents to retrieve the list and learn about agents involved in forums.

5.2.6 Secret Communication

Our mode of secret communications is similar to current one-to-one communication. That is, it is not possible for agents other than the participants of the communication to be aware of this communication. We adopt the same approach as for private communications, that is, the communication server uses a forum to store the messages exchanged during this communication, but in this case, this forum does not appear in the list of ongoing forums. The use of this forum is as described above.

6 Summary

This chapter describes two different uses of communication in agent systems: (1) direct communication and (2) indirect communication.

Direct communication shares roots from distributed systems and natural language conversations with three different approaches: (a) protocols that have strong similarity with distributed protocols and differ slightly from these to cope with agent-specific features such as autonomy and asynchronous communication to name a few, (b) dialogue games that restore agents' autonomy by providing a more flexible way to communicate, and finally (c) argumentation systems that are more flexible than the two other approaches since agents in an argumentation system may revise their beliefs hence updating their arguments during the conversation.

Recent approaches in agent communication consider multi-party communication where communication is not restricted to two-way channels between senders and receivers. Communication may be enlarged to an audience that can enter in the discussion at every moment.

The notion of communication is central in multi-agent systems since it could help to coordinate [61], cooperate [62], and negotiate [36]. As a consequence, this domain of research remains active even if it shifts from its early subjects. First, research on agent communication just considered how it is possible to efficiently communicate between agents but it seems important now to address the question of *when* it is required to communicate. Agents are more and more frequently used on resource-bounded devices (such as sensors, motes, and mobile phones) and it is preferable to save energy when communicating. It is then essential to find the fastest protocols to reach a goal [63].

References

1. Shannon CE (1948) A mathematical theory of communication. Bell Syst Tech J 27
2. Drogoul A (1993) De la simulation multi-agents à la résolution collective de problème. Une étude de l'émergence de structures d'organisation dans les systèmes multi-agents, PhD thesis. Université Paris 6
3. Smith R, Davis R (1981) Framework for cooperation in distributed problem solving. IEEE Trans Syst Man Cybern 11(1):61–70
4. Austin JL (1962) How to do things with words. Clarendon, Oxford
5. Finin T, Fritzson R (1994) KQML - a language and protocol for knowledge and information exchange. In: Proceedings of the thirteenth international workshop on distributed artificial intelligence, Lake Quinalt, WA, July. pp 126–136
6. FIPA (2000). *Specification.* Foundation for intelligent physical agents, http://www.fipa.org/repository/fipa2000.html
7. Searle J (1969) Speech acts: an essay in the philosophy of language. Cambridge University Press, Cambridge
8. FIPA (2002) FIPA SL Content language specification. Technical Report SC00008l, FIPA
9. Rao A, Georgeff M (1991) Modeling rational agents within a BDI architecture. In: Fikes R, Sandewall E (eds) Proceedings of knowledge representation and reasoning (KR&R 91). Kaufmann, San Mateo, Morgan, pp 473–484
10. Guerin F (2002) Specifying agent communication languages. PhD thesis, Dept. of Electrical and Electronic Engineering, Imperial College
11. Sierra C, Jennings N, Noriega P, Parsons S (1998) A framework for argumentation based negotiation. In: Singh MP, Rao A, Wooldridge MJ (eds) (ATAL97) Intelligent agents IV, number 1365, LNAI. Springer, Berlin, pp 177–192
12. Singh MP (1998) Agent communication languages: rethinking the principles. IEEE Comput 31(12):40–47
13. Cohen PR, Levesque HJ (1990) Rational interaction as the basis for communication. In: Cohen PR, Morgan J, Pollack ME (eds) Intentions in communication. MIT Press, Cambridge, pp 221–256

14. Gomez-Perez A, Corcho O, Fernandez-Lopez M (2003) Ontological engineering: with examples from the areas of knowledge management, E-Commerce and Semantic Web. Springer, Berlin
15. JADE information page. http://sharon.cselt.it/projects/jade
16. Gutknecht O, Ferber J (2000) The MADKIT agent platform architecture. In: Agents workshop on infrastructure for multi-agent systems. pp 48–55
17. Kristina Lerman, Onn Shehory (2000) Coalition formation for large-scale electronic markets. Proc ICMAS 2000, pp 167–174, IEEE
18. Baeijs C, Demazeau Y, Alvares L (1997) Sigma: application of multi-agent systems to cartographic generalization. In: Boman M, de Velde WV (eds) Multi-agent rationality: eighth european workshop on modelling autonomous agents and multi-agent world (MAAMAW-97), volume LNCS/LNAI 1038, Sweden, May. Springer, Heidelberg
19. McBurney P (2002) Rational interaction, PhD thesis. Department of Computer Science, University of Liverpool
20. Parsons S, McBurney P (2003) Argumentation-based communication between agents. In: Huget M-P (ed) Communication in multiagent systems, vol 2650, Lecture notes in artificial intelligence. Springer, Heidelberg, pp 164–178
21. Holzmann GJ (1991) Design and validation of computer protocols. Prentice-Hall, Englewood Cliffs, NJ
22. Huget M-P (2001) Une ingénierie des protocoles d'interaction pour les systèmes multi-agents, PhD thesis. Université Paris 9 Dauphine, June 2001
23. Huget M-P, Koning J-L (2003) Requirement analysis for interaction protocols. In: Marik V, Mueller J, Pechoucek M (eds) Proceedings of the third central and eastern european conference on multi-agents systems (CEEMAS 2003), Prague, Czech Republic, June 2003
24. Salomaa A (1969) Theory of automata. Pergamon, Oxford
25. Kuwabara K, Ishida T, Osato N (1995) AgenTalk: describing multiagent coordination protocols with inheritance. In: Seventh IEEE international conference on tools with artificial intelligence, Herndon, Virginia, November 1995. pp 460–465
26. Barbuceanu M, Fox MS (1995) COOL: a language for describing coordination in multiagent system. In: First international conference on multi-agent systems (ICMAS-95), San Francisco, USA, June 1995. AAAI Press, pp 17–24
27. Jensen K (1991) High-level petri nets, theory and application. Springer, Heidelberg
28. Cost RS, Chen Y, Finin T, Labrou Y, Peng Y (1999) Modeling agent conversation with colored Petri nets. In: Bradshaw J (ed) Autonomous Agents '99, Special workshop on conversation policies, May
29. El Fallah Seghrouchni A, Haddad S, Mazouzi H (1999) A formal study of interaction in multi-agent systems. Modelling autonomous agents in multi-agent Worlds (MAAMAW)
30. Booch G, Rumbaugh J, Jacobson I (1999) The unified modeling language user guide. Addison-Wesley, Reading, Massachusetts
31. Koning J-L, Huget M-P, Wei J, Wang X (2001) Extended modeling languages for interaction protocol design. In: Proceedings of agent-oriented software engineering (AOSE 2001), Montreal, Canada, May 2001
32. Huget M-P, Odell J, Bauer B (2004) The AUML approach. Methodologies and software engineering for agent systems. Kluwer
33. Fisher M, Wooldridge M (1994) Specifying and executing protocols for cooperative action. International working conference on cooperating knowledge-based systems (CKBS-94), Keele
34. Luck M, d'Inverno M (2003) Understanding agent systems. Springer, Berlin
35. Chu P-YM (1989) Towards automating protocol synthesis and analysis, PhD thesis. Ohio State University
36. Lacey T, DeLoach SA (2000) Automatic verification of multiagent conversations. In: Eleventh annual Midwest artificial intelligence and cognitive science conference, University of Arkansas, USA, April, 15–16

37. Huget M-P, Wooldridge M (2003) Model checking for ACL compliance verification. In: Sandholm T, Yokoo M (eds) Proceedings of the second international conference on autonomous agents and multi-agent systems (AAMAS 2003), Melbourne, Australia, July 2003
38. Wooldridge M (1999) Verifying that agents implement a communication language. In: Proceedings of the AAAI, Orlando, July 1999
39. Wooldridge M, Fisher M, Huget M-P, Parsons S (2002) Model checking multi-agent systems with MABLE. In: Proceedings of autonomous agents and multi-agent systems (AAMAS 02), Bologna, Italy, July 2002
40. Huget M-P, Koning J-L (2003) Interaction protocol engineering in multi-agent systems. In: Huget M-P (ed) Communication in multi-agent systems: background, current trends and future, number 2650 in LNCS/LNAI State of the Art Survey. Springer, Heidelberg
41. Davis R, Smith RG (1983) Negotiation as a metaphor for distributed problem-solving. Artificial Intell 20:63–109
42. Sian SS (1991) Adaptation based on cooperative learning in multiagent systems. In: Demazeau Y, Müller JP (eds) Decentralized AI 2, Elsevier
43. Hamblin C (1970) Fallacies. Methuen and Co Ltd, London, UK
44. Levin J, Moore J (1978) Dialogue-games: metacommunications structures for natural language interaction. Cogn Sci 1(4):395–420
45. Bench-Capon T, Gelard T, Leng PH (2000) A method for the computational modelling of dialectical argument with dialogue games. Artific Intell Law 8:233–254
46. Walton D, Krabbe E (1995) Commitment in dialogue: basic concepts of interpersonal reasoning, SUNY series in logic and language. State University of New York Press, Albany, NY
47. McBurney P, Parsons S (2003) Dialogue game protocols. In: Huget M-P (ed) Communication in multiagent systems, vol 2650, Lecture Notes in Computer Science—State of the Art. Springer, Berlin, pp 269–281
48. McBurney P, van Eijk R, Parsons S, Amgoud L (2003) A dialogue-game protocol for agent purchase negotiations. J Autonom Agent Multi-Agent Syst 7(3):235–273
49. Amgoud L, Cayrol C (1998) On the acceptability of arguments in preference-based argumentation framework. In: Proceedings of the 14th conference on uncertainty in artificial intelligence. pp 1–7
50. Amgoud L, Parsons S (2001) Agent dialogues with conflicting preferences. In: Proceedings of the 8th International workshop on agent theories, architectures and languages (ATAL 2001). pp 1–15
51. Amgoud L, Maudet N, Parsons S (2000) Modeling dialogues using argumentation. In: Proceedings of the 4th International conference on multi-agent systems (ICMAS 2000). Boston, MA, IEEE Press. pp 31–38
52. Amgoud L, Parsons S, Maudet N (2000) Arguments, dialogue and negotiation. In: Proceedings of the 15th European conference on artificial intelligence (ECAI 2000). Berlin, Germany, pp 338–342
53. Parsons S, Wooldridge M, Amgoud L (2002) An analysis of formal interagent dialogues. In: Proceedings of the first international conference on autonomous agents and multi-agent systems (AAMAS 2002), Bologna, Italy, pp 394–401
54. Maudet N, Evrard F (1998) A generic framework for dialogue game implementation. In: Proceedings of the 2nd workshop on formal semantics and pragmatics of dialogue
55. Mackenzie J (1979) Question-begging in non-cumulative systems. J Philos Logic 8:117–133
56. McBurney P, Parsons S (2002) Games that agents play: a formal framework for dialogues between autonomous agents. J Logic Lang Inform 11(3):315–334
57. Dignum F, Vreeswijk G (2003) Towards a testbed for multi-party dialogues. In: Huget M-P, Dignum F (eds) AAMAS 2003 Workshop on agent communication language and conversation policies (ACL 2003), Melbourne, July 2003
58. Ricordel P-M, Pesty S, Demazeau Y (1999) About conversations between multiple agents. In: First international conference of central Eastern Europe on multi-agent systems (CEEMAS), St Petersbourg, June 1999

59. Traum D, Rickel J (2002) Embodied agents for multi-party dialogue in immersive virtual worlds. In: Proceedings of the first international conference on autonomous agents and multi-agent systems (AAMAS 2002), Bologna, Italy, July 2002
60. Huget M-P, Demazeau Y (2004) First steps towards multiparty communication. In: Dignum F, van Eijk R, Huget M-P (eds) Proceedings of the AAMAS 2004 workshop on agent communication (AC 2004), New York, USA, July 2004
61. Bocchi L, Ciancarini P (2003) A perspective on multiagent coordination models. In: Huget M-P (eds) Communication in multiagent systems, number 2650. Lecture notes in computer science—State of the Art. Springer, Berlin, pp 146–163
62. Haddadi A (1996) Communication and cooperation in agent systems: a pragmatic theory. In: Lecture Notes in Computer Science, Vol 1056. Springer, Berlin
63. Chopra A, Artikis A, Bentahar J, Colombetti M, Dignum F, Fornara N, Jones AJI, Singh M (2013) Research directions on agent communication. ACM Transact Intell Syst 4(2):1–23
64. Amgoud L, Parsons S, Perussel L (2000) An argumentation framework based on contextual preferences. In: Proceedings of the international conference on pure and applied practical reasoning. London, UK
65. Clarke E, Grumberg O, Peled D (2000) Model checking. MIT Press, Cambridge
66. Wooldridge M (2000) Reasoning about rational agents. MIT Press, Cambridge, MA
67. Yolum P, Singh M (2002) Flexible protocol specification and execution: applying event calculus planning using commitments. In: Proceedings of the 1st international joint conference on autonomous agents and multi-agent systems (AAMAS 2002), Bologna, Italy

Part III
Agent-Oriented Software Engineering Methodologies

Chapter 7
The Landscape of Agent-Oriented Methodologies

Arnon Sturm and Onn Shehory

Abstract Agent-based systems have evolved during the last two decades. To support the development of such systems, agent-oriented methodologies have emerged. In general, most of the methodologies have originated from two major research domains, namely software engineering and artificial intelligence, and were adjusted to address the agent abstraction. It seems that many of the methodologies share a common basis, an observation that calls for unification and for standardization. In this chapter, we survey existing agent-oriented methodologies and describe the support for agent-based concepts required in such methodologies. We then analyze the most influential agent-oriented methodologies in light of the required agent-based concepts as well as other criteria. We also examine alternatives such as methodology integration and the support for developing a tailored agent-oriented methodology. The main concern that arises from the survey and the analysis is the lack of evaluation of agent-based methodologies, which may have negatively affected, at least in part, the adoption of these methodologies for developing agent-based systems. We also discuss the need to further extend the methodologies to support the entire lifecycle.

Keywords Software Development • Agent-Oriented Methodologies • Evaluation • Comparison

A. Sturm (✉)
Department of Information Systems Engineering, Ben-Gurion University of the Negev, Beer-Sheva, Israel
e-mail: sturm@bgu.ac.il

O. Shehory
IBM – Haifa Research Lab, Haifa, Israel
e-mail: onn@il.ibm.com

O. Shehory and A. Sturm (eds.), *Agent-Oriented Software Engineering*,
DOI 10.1007/978-3-642-54432-3_7,

1 Introduction

During the last 15 years, many methodologies for developing agent-based systems have been developed. When referring to a methodology, we follow the definition of [1], according to which a methodology should provide the following: a full lifecycle process; a comprehensive set of concepts and models; a full set of techniques (rules, guidelines, heuristics); a fully delineated set of deliverables; a modeling language; a set of metrics; quality assurance; coding (and other) standards; reuse advice; and guidelines for project management. Naturally, Agent-Oriented Software Engineering (AOSE) methodologies adopt general software engineering concepts. However, their coverage of activities required from a comprehensive methodology is partial, as they mainly focus on technical issues and not on managerial ones.

Agent-oriented methodologies can be classified into two major classes: general-purpose methodologies and domain-specific methodologies. In this chapter we refer to the former. Methodologies of that kind have emerged from several disciplines, but mainly from the classical software engineering, in times influenced by the knowledge engineering stream. When referring to software engineering, these methodologies emphasize the way in which agent-based systems should be constructed following software engineering principles (e.g., expressiveness, accessibility, and reuse). When referring to knowledge engineering, these methodologies emphasize implementation mechanisms of agents within the system (e.g., cooperation, reasoning, negotiation) in terms of the knowledge perspective. Table 7.1 lists most of the agent-oriented methodologies that were developed during the last two decades. In that table, the methodologies are classified according to their domains of origin.

This chapter aims to explore the plethora of AOSE methodologies and the way these were evaluated. This should shed light on research and practice in this area and present challenges in the field of AOSE methodologies.

The chapter is organized as follows. In Sect. 2, we introduce and define a set of evaluation criteria. These are then used in Sect. 3, where we shortly introduce the main methodologies and evaluate them. In Sect. 4, we discuss alternative approaches for AOSE methodologies. Section 5 concludes, presenting major challenges in the area of AOSE methodologies.

2 Criteria for Examining AOSE Methodologies

Several techniques for evaluating a methodology or comparing it to alternatives exist. These include the following:

- Feature analysis, in which a set of features is determined before the evaluation takes place followed by subjective grading of the features for each methodology.
- Survey, in which a methodology is evaluated by an individual, usually following a questionnaire.

Table 7.1 AOSE methodologies

Methodology name	Domain of origin	Methodology name	Domain of origin
AAII [2, 3]	AI-KE	MAS-CommonKADS [4]	SE + AI-KE
ADELFE [5]	SE	MASSIVE [6]	SE
ADEM [7]	SE	MESSAGE [8]	SE
ADEPT [9–11]	AI-KE	Nemo [12]	SE + AI-KE
AO [13]	SE	ODAC [14]	SE
AOR [15]	SE	OPEN for MAS [16]	SE
Cassiopeia [17]	SE	PASSI [18]	SE + AI-KE
CoMoMas [19]	SE + AI-KE	Prometheus [20]	SE + AI-KE
DESIRE [21–23]	AI-KE	Roadmap [24]	SE + AI-KE
FAF [25–29]	SE	SADDE [30]	SE
GAIA [31–33]	SE	SODA [34]	SE
INGENIAS [35]	SE	Styx [36]	SE
MASD [37]	SE + AI-KE	Tropos [38]	SE + AI-KE
MaSE [39]	SE		

SE Software Engineering, *AI-KE* Artificial Intelligence and Knowledge Engineering

- Case study, in which the strengths of the methodology are demonstrated on a case study. Usually, case studies are of limited extent and are within the context of research projects.
- Field experiment, in which a methodology is examined in a real world environment, yet with some kind of control.
- Lab experiment, in which a methodology is examined in an artificial setting.
- Qualitative approach, in which the methodology is examined for understanding phenomena that occur during its use. The approach may use techniques such as observations, interviews, and think aloud techniques.

Many of the aforementioned evaluation techniques are difficult to apply. Therefore, they are rarely used. Thus, in the area of AOSE methodologies, evaluation is performed using case studies for specific methodologies, and comparison is done using the feature analysis approach. The latter is also used in this chapter. Multiple research efforts were allocated to feature-based evaluation frameworks for agent-oriented methodologies. In [40], the authors set a list of questions that a methodology should address. In [41], the authors suggest a framework for evaluating agent-oriented methodologies referring to the expressiveness of the methodologies. In [42], the authors perform an evaluation of the modeling part within a methodology. In [43] and [44], a comparison of several agent-oriented methodologies is presented. In [45], [46], and [47], the authors also present alternative frameworks for evaluating agent-oriented methodologies; the frameworks suggest different sets of criteria with partial overlaps. Due to the proliferation of evaluation frameworks, in [48] the authors performed some meta-analysis and proposed a profile-based approach to examiningAOSE methodologies.

In this chapter, we follow the set of characteristics that was adopted by [48] and explain each of these.

2.1 Concepts and Properties

As mentioned within the first chapter of this book, agent-based systems are unique in several characteristics. These are elaborated in the following:

1. **Autonomy** is the ability of an agent to operate without supervision.
2. **Reactiveness** is the ability of an agent to respond in a timely manner to changes in the environment.
3. **Proactiveness** is the ability of an agent to pursue new goals.
4. **Mental notions** is the ability if an agent to refer to metal attitudes such as a belief (which is a fact about the world), a desire (which is a fact an agent would prefer that it be true), and an intention (which is a fact that represents the way of realizing a desire).
5. **Organization** is a group of agents working together to achieve a common purpose. An organization consists of roles that characterize the agents, which are members of the organization.
6. **Protocol** is an ordered set of messages that together define the admissible patterns of a particular type of interaction between entities.

2.2 Modeling and Notations

When examining a methodology that includes modeling capabilities, one should look at the following issues:

1. **Analyzability** is a capability to check the internal consistency or implications of models.
2. **Complexity management** (abstraction) is an ability to deal with various levels of abstraction (i.e., various levels of detail).
3. **Expressiveness** is a capability of presenting system concepts that refer to: the structure of the system; the knowledge encapsulated within the system; the system's ontology; the data flow within the system; the control flow within the system; the concurrent activities within the system (and the agents); the resource constraints within the system (e.g., time, CPU, and memory); the system's physical architecture; the agents' mobility; the interaction of the system with external systems; and the user interface definitions.
4. **Accessibility** is the ability that refers to the ease, or the simplicity, of understanding and using a method.

2.3 *Process*

A development process is a series of actions, changes, and functions that, when performed, result in a working computerized system. In particular, we refer to the **lifecycle coverage** and the development stages that are supported by the methodology.

2.4 *Pragmatics*

A methodology requires support for using it. Thus, from a pragmatic viewpoint it is beneficial to examine the extent to which the methodology addresses the following.

1. **Resources:** What resources are available in order to support the methodology? Is a textbook available? Are users' groups established? Are training and consulting offered by the vendor and/or third parties? In addition, are automated tools (CASE tools) available in support of the methodology (e.g., graphical editors, code generators, and checkers)? This issue should be examined in order to enable a project/organization aiming at adopting a methodology to check the resources (in terms of training and budget) required and the alternatives for acquiring these.
2. **Domain applicability:** Is the use of the methodology suitable for a particular application domain (e.g., real-time and information systems)?
3. **Scalability:** Can the methodology, or subsets thereof, be used to handle various application sizes? For example, can it provide a lightweight version for simpler problems? This issue should be examined to check whether the methodology is appropriate for handling the intended scale of applications within the project/organization.

3 Analysis of Existing AOSE Methodologies

In this section, we review several methodologies selected from the list above and discuss their evolution and their characteristics. The selection of these methodologies was motivated by the continuous flow of publications as well as their impact on the AOSE methodologies field. As the purpose of this chapter is to provide an overview of the field, we focus on evaluation criteria that are accessible to a wide readership and can be objectively measured.

3.1 *GAIA*

GAIA is an agent-oriented methodology that is not coupled to a specific programming language nor deals with implementation issues. GAIA [31, 33] provides a set of models that are used at the analysis and design stages of the multi-agent system development and evolve over that process. Following the (plain vanilla) GAIA guidelines, the analysis of an agent-based system results in an environmental model, a preliminary role model, a preliminary interaction model, and a set of organizational rules.

- The **environmental** model is intended as an abstract, computational representation of the environment in which the multi-agent system will be situated.
- The **preliminary role** model is used for identifying the basic skills required by the organization and contains only those roles, possibly not completely defined, that can be identified without committing to the imposition of a specific organizational structure. Also, the notion of roles, at this stage, is abstracted from any mapping into agents.
- The **preliminary interaction** model specifies the basic interactions required to accomplish the preliminary roles. This model must abstract away from the organizational structure and can be left incomplete.
- The **organizational rules** that should be respected and enforced. These rules express constraints on the execution activities of roles and protocols of the organization.

In the architectural design stage, there are two main activities:

- The **definition of the system's organizational structure** in terms of its topology and control regime. This activity, which could also exploit catalogue organizational patterns, involves considering: (1) the organizational efficiency, (2) the real-world organization in which the multi-agent system is situated, and (3) the need to enforce the organizational rules.
- The **completion of the preliminary role** and **interaction models**.

Finally, in the detailed design stage the following activities are executed:

- The **definition of the agent model**. This identifies the agent classes that will make up the system and the *agent instances* that will be instantiated from these classes.
- The **definition of the services model**. This identifies the main services intended as coherent blocks of activity, in which agents will engage, that are required to realize the agent's roles, and their properties.

Note that GAIA has many extensions and elaborations such as [24, 49–53]. These include CASE tool development, additional models, moving towards implementation, case studies, etc.

Examining GAIA in light of the evaluation criteria, we found out that it supports well all multi-agent concepts except for the mental notion (i.e., BDI). With respect to the modeling and notation aspect, GAIA requires further attention, mainly in analyzing the specification and in its scalability. As for the development lifecycle coverage, although many extensions have been made to GAIA, further adjustments are still required. From the pragmatic point of view, as there is no coordinating effort of developing GAIA, its resources are limited.

3.2 INGENIAS

INGENIAS is a methodology for the development of multi-agent systems, which is based on the well-known, well-established software development process, the unified process. It is based on a definition of a set of meta-models that describe the elements that form a multi-agent system from several viewpoints, and that allow to define a specification language for MAS. There are five viewpoints within INGENIAS: agent, interactions, organization, environment, and goals/tasks. In the following, we elaborate on these views.

- The **organization** view consists of agents and their groups from the structural point of view and the goals and workflows they should execute from the behavioral point of view.
- The **environment** view consists of the elements that surround the systems and the various stimuli, as well as the system resources.
- The **tasks/goals** view consists of a description of the agent mental states and the way they change over time, the consequence of executing a task with respect to the mental state of an agent, and how to achieve goals.
- The **agent** view consists of the primitives that describe a single agent. It can be used to define the capabilities of an agent or its mental state.
- The **interaction** view consists of the description of two or more agents interacting.

INGENIAS uses the Meta-Object Facility (MOF) standard to describe the five-view metamodels, to enable easy change when required.

As for the development process, INGENIAS adopts the unified process concepts and provides more than 70 activities to be performed during the development process of a multi-agent system. In general, INGENIAS has two main workflows: the analysis and the design. During the analysis workflow, it is expected to generate use cases and identify their actors, sketch system architecture with an organization model, and generate environment models. Next, there is a need to refine use cases and the interactions associated with them, develop agent models that detail elements of the system architecture, describe workflows and tasks in organization models, and refine the environment model. During the design workflow, the first task is to generate a prototype (out of the analysis results); then, refinements of the workflows should be introduced; following, it is necessary to specify the interaction models, to model tasks and goals, and to define the agent models. Finally, the social relationships that regulate organizational behavior should be outlined. According to INGENIAS, the implementation of MAS follows the Model-Driven Engineering (MDE) approach. Also, note that INGENIAS supports an iterative approach in which the workflows and activities are repeated during the development lifecycle.

Similarly to GAIA, INGENIAS supports well all multi-agent concepts except for the mental notion (i.e., BDI). With respect to the modeling and notation aspect, it seems that using INGENIAS requires more training. INGENIAS covers most of the development lifecycle. From a pragmatic point of view, INGENIAS was applied in many contexts and has a supporting IDE. A detailed description of INGENIAS and its evolution is described in Chap. 10.

3.3 *MaSE*

Multi-agent Systems Engineering (MaSE) is a general-purpose methodology for developing heterogeneous multi-agent systems [39, 54]. MaSE uses a number of graphical models to describe system goals, behaviors, agent types, and agent communication interfaces. It uses most of the Unified Modeling Language (UML) diagrams and makes some enhancements to adjust them to the MAS domain. MaSE also supplies a method (process) for developing MAS that consists of two major phases: analysis and design.

The purpose of the analysis phase is to provide a set of roles whose tasks meet the system's requirements, i.e., specifying *what* the system should do. The analysis phase consists of the following stages:

- **Capturing goals**, in which the system goals are elaborated and specified from the system point of view in a hierarchical manner.
- **Applying use cases**, in which the system's use cases are specified along with their elaborating sequence diagrams.
- **Refining roles**, in which system functional decomposition is performed by producing a set of roles and their associated tasks. This stage consists of two sub-stages: building the role diagram and specifying the tasks' behavior.

The purpose of the design phase is to specify the way according to which the system-to-be should behave and be constructed. This means, specifying *how* the system will achieve its goals. The design phase consists of the following stages:

- **Creating agent classes**, in which the overall multi-agent system architecture in terms of agents and the conversations among them is determined
- **Constructing conversations**, in which the designer defines the coordination protocols (i.e., conversations) between agent pairs. In particular, two communication class diagrams are defined for each conversation. One diagram specifies the initiator's behavior during that conversation and the other specifies the responder's behavior during that conversation
- **Assembling agents**, in which the internal architecture of the agents is specified
- **System design**, in which the physical system architecture and the distribution of agent classes' instances within that architecture is specified

MaSE is also supported by a CASE tool and was applied in various contexts [55]. Recently, MaSE has shifted into the area of method engineering in which the development process is further customized according to specific needs [54, 56] (see Chap. 9).

MaSE supports all multi-agent concepts except for the mental notion (i.e., BDI). With respect to the modeling and notation aspect, we found out that MaSE supports well all of the criteria. MaSE also covers most of the development lifecycle. From a pragmatic point of view, MaSE is also equipped with a CASE tool.

3.4 PASSI

PASSI (a Process for Agent Societies Specification and Implementation) is a step-by-step requirement-to-code methodology for designing and developing multi-agent societies, integrating design models and concepts from software engineering approaches and using the UML notation [18].

PASSI consists of five models that should be built sequentially in an iterative manner. In the following, we elaborate on these models and the activities that should be done in order to achieve their purposes.

- The system requirements model aims at describing the system requirements in terms of agents and their goals. It consists of the following:
  - **Domain description**, in which the system functionalities are described using the use case technique
  - **Agent identification**, in which separation of concerns is done by identifying agents using the UML stereotype mechanism. Each agent functionality is represented as a package of use cases
  - **Role identification**, in which each agent is specified by the roles it can play. This is done using class diagram accompanied by the object constraint language
  - **Task specification**, in which the agent behavior is described using the activity diagram of UML
- The agent society model aims at depicting agent interactions and dependencies. It is achieved by performing the following tasks:
  - **Role identification**, in which an elaboration of the previous outcomes is performed by analyzing agent interactions to gather additional understanding on the agent roles
  - **Ontology description**, in which the knowledge that is used within the system is modeled using class diagrams and the stereotype mechanism. In addition, a communication ontology description is achieved within that activity and its purpose is to identify the protocol, the content language, and the ontology mapping
  - **Role description**, in which the roles are described in the context of the agents that play them
  - **Protocol description**, in which protocols that were not defined by FIPA need to be specified using sequence diagrams
- The agent implementation model captures the solution architecture in terms of classes and methods. It is achieved by:

- **Agent structure definition**, in which one class diagram represents the MAS as a whole, whereas attribute compartments can be used to represent the knowledge of the agent and operations' compartments are used to signify the agent's tasks. In addition, for each agent one class diagram is used to specify the agent's internal structure
- **Agent behavior description**, in which one or more activity diagrams are drawn to show the flow of events between and within both the main agents' classes and their inner classes (representing their tasks). In addition, the internal behavior of an agent or a task can be specified using flowcharts, activity diagrams, or statecharts

• The code model aims at describing the solution at the code level and consists of the following activities:

  - **Code reuse library**, in which special design patterns are gathered and applied
  - **Code completion baseline,** in which the designer/programmer completes the generate code

• The deployment model aims at specifying the distribution of the parts of the system across hardware processing units, and their migration between processing units. It is done via a deployment configuration diagram.

PASSI is supported by a CASE tool and continuously evolved over the years. It made its progress through patterns [57], agility [58], and tools [59].

PASSI supports all multi-agent concepts except for the mental notion (i.e., BDI). With respect to the modeling and notation aspect, we found that PASSI—as it uses the common modeling language UML—supports well accessibility, expressiveness, and complexity management; however, little information is provided regarding its support for analysis. PASSI also covers most of the development lifecycle. From a pragmatic point of view, PASSI is equipped with a CASE tool and has set plans for continuous improvements.

3.5 Prometheus

The Prometheus methodology aims to provide a means for designing multi-agent systems [20]. It is specifically aimed at building intelligent agents. The Prometheus methodology consists of three phases: (1) the system specification phase that is focused on identifying the basic functionalities of the system, its inputs, its outputs, and its shared data sources; (2) the architectural design phase that is focused on determining the system agents and their interactions; and (3) the detailed design phase that is focused on the internals of each agent. In the following, we elaborate on the activities required in each of the Prometheus phases:

• During the **system specification** phase, the designer is expected to identify the system goals and assign them to roles. She should also spot the actions to be taken

and the precepts to be considered by the system and assign them to roles as well. Finally, she should specify the system functionality using the use case technique; the latter provides a set of scenarios to be associated with the identified roles.
- During the **architectural design** phase, the designer should identify the agent types within the system. In addition, an analysis of the knowledge and data coupling is done along with the agent acquaintance model. Moreover, the agents' lifecycle and description are determined. Referring to the system behavior (phase 1), the interaction protocols are identified in this phase. Finally, the system overview is determined in terms of agents, protocols, events, actions, and shared data.
- During the **detailed design** phase, the internals of the agents should be specified. This should be done by identifying capabilities, plans, internal events, and data. The capabilities can be defined in a hierarchal manner.

The Prometheus methodology also provides a CASE tool that makes it easy to follow its guidelines [60]. The methodology has been integrated into a MAS platform called JACK [61].

Prometheus supports all multi-agent concepts. It supports the modeling and notation to some extent as it introduces additional concepts into the development process. Prometheus also covers most of the development lifecycle. From a pragmatic point of view, Prometheus is equipped with a CASE tool, is taught in courses, is continuously refined [62] and examines additional software engineering aspects to be supported. In Chap. 8, additional research directions of Prometheus are elaborated.

3.6 Tropos

Tropos is an agent-oriented software development methodology founded on two key features: (1) the notion of agent and the associated mentalistic notions (e.g., goals and tasks), and (2) requirements analysis and specification of the system to-be is analyzed with respect to its intended environment [38, 63]. Tropos consists of five development stages:

1. **Early requirements analysis** focuses on the intentions of stakeholders. These intentions are modeled as goals that, through some form of a goal-oriented analysis, eventually lead to the functional and nonfunctional requirements of the system-to-be. The modeling is performed using the i* modeling language, in which stakeholders are represented as (social) actors who depend on each other for goals to be achieved, tasks to be performed, and resources to be furnished.
2. **Late requirements analysis** results in a requirements specification that describes all functional and non-functional requirements for the system-to-be. In Tropos, the system is represented as one or more actors specified in the early requirement stage.

3. **Architectural design** describes how system components work together. Tropos defines organizational architectural styles for cooperative, dynamic, and distributed applications like multi-agent systems, to guide the design of the system architecture. These styles are used to express assertions on the system organizational structure and help match the MAS architecture to the organizational context in which the system will operate.
4. **Detailed design** introduces additional details for each architectural component of a system. In Tropos, one can define how the goals assigned to each actor are fulfilled by agents with respect to pre-defined design patterns.
5. **Implementation** refers to the actual coding of the system-to-be.

Note that Tropos supports the transformational approach in which the transitions from one stage to the next are done by following certain transformational guidelines.

Tropos supports all multi-agent concepts, yet integration with the mental notions (i.e., BDI) requires further examination. It supports the modeling and notation to some extent as it introduces several concepts into the development process that need to be examined. Also, the transitions among the stages require further attention. Tropos also covers most of the development lifecycle. From a pragmatic point of view, Tropos is equipped with a set of tools that provide a suite for specifying, analyzing, and implementing MAS applications. Also, Tropos is continuously evaluated using various techniques.

3.7 ADEM

The agent-oriented development methodology (ADEM) aims at supporting the development of agent-based systems [64]. In particular, ADEM focuses on modeling aspects of agent-based systems using the Agent-Modeling Language (AML) [7, 65]. Similarly to other newer methodologies, ADEM consists of method fragments, techniques, artifacts, and guidelines for creating MAS models. As it is based on RUP, ADEM mainly addresses the business modeling, requirements, and analysis and design workflows. In the following, we list the method fragments provided by ADEM.

Workflow	Activity
Business modeling	Define the business domain ontology
	Model business goals
	Detail a business actor
	Identify business use case responsibility
	Structure the extended identify business use case model
	Model business organization structure
	Model business interactions
	Model business services

(continued)

Workflow	Activity
	Model business observations and affecting interactions
	Model business deployment
	Detail business architecture
	Define the business domain ontology
Requirements	Define the domain ontology
	Model system goal-based requirements
	Detail an actor
	Identify use case responsibilities
	Structure the extended use case model
Analysis and design	Model society
	Model interactions
	Model interaction ontology
	Model services
	Model observations and effecting interactions
	Detail an entity
	Model mental attitudes
	Structure behavior
	Model deployment
	Detail design

ADEM follows the situational method engineering approach, according to which organizations may adapt their development processes to better fit in. ADEM was developed based on industrial needs within Whitestein Technology, which might position it as better suited for practitioners. However, no evidence is provided of applying the methodology elsewhere. As AML is based on the UML profile, it has several implementations and supporting tools.

It seems that ADEM addresses all multi-agent concepts. It supports the modeling and notation to some extent as it requires the integration of multiple elements and diagram types. Also, the model verification/validation/checking requires more exploration. ADEM also covers most of the development lifecycle. From a pragmatic point of view, ADEM is supported by tools and has been used in various industrial projects.

4 Alternative AOSE Methodologies

With the proliferation of AOSE methodologies, the need to integrate these has emerged. In [66] the authors analyzed the meta-models of six methods for developing agent-based systems and found that there is a wide agreement on the concepts of agent-based systems. Following that finding, the authors proposed a unified (and abstract) metamodel that captures the agent-based notions of the six methods.

The resulting metamodeling has many similarities with the metamodels of AML [64] and OPM/MAS [67] in which various aspects of agent-based systems are captured. Another similar effort results in FAML—a generic metamodel for MAS development [68]. Following [69], in which the authors call for standardization of AOSE methodology concepts that will serve as the basis for the next generation methodology, similar to what has been achieved with UML, FAML is a potential candidate for such an effort.

Nevertheless, there in a common understanding that one solution cannot fit well for all cases. Thus, an alternative approach to handle the diversity in AOSE methodologies has emerged, following the method engineering (ME) notions [70]. The approach refers to each of the AOSE methodologies as a set of method fragments. For setting a specific method, one should select the relevant fragments and glue these together. Note that some of the aforementioned methodologies have already adopted that direction. These include INGENIAS, O-MaSE, and ADEM. Akbari [71] also calls for the adoption of the ME approach. However, the ME-based approaches may result in problems in integrating and gluing fragments into a single coherent method. Thus, further examination of this approach is required.

5 Concluding Remarks

There are more than two dozen agent-oriented methodologies. Although differences exist among them, there are many similarities as well. As a result of diversity with similarities, the selection of a methodology for developing agent-based systems and applications is nontrivial. This problem intensifies when industrial development is sought, where specific requirements and constraints apply. Additionally, in many cases insufficient resources are available for issues other than modeling, notation, and development process. In particular, as suggested in [72], much work is needed to allow the quantitative evaluation of the agent-based paradigm and the associated methodologies. Such quantitative evaluation should facilitate better assessment of the advantages of agent-based methodologies over existing paradigms in software analysis, design, and maintenance. Additionally, it seems that existing agent-oriented methodologies focus on the development of new systems and not on other stages and aspects within the system lifecycle. Even with reference to development process, not all phases are well supported (e.g., the testing phase is hardly supported). An example of a non-supported aspect is system maintenance, which is hardly dealt with in agent-oriented methodologies. Yet, another void is the lack of support for a paradigm shift to agent orientation. We believe that the latter is a grand challenge for agent-oriented methodologies. That is, it is necessary—yet challenging—to justify the paradigm shift from existing paradigms such as object-oriented, service-oriented, and business-process-oriented to the agent-oriented paradigm.

References

1. Graham I, Hederson-Sellers B, Younessi H (1997) The OPEN process specification. Addison-Wesley
2. Kinny D, Georgeff M (1996) Modelling and design of multi-agent systems. In: Proceedings of the third international workshop on agent theories, architectures, and languages (ATAL). Lecture notes in computer science 1193. Springer, pp 1–20
3. Kinny D, Georgeff M, Rao A (1996) A methodology and modelling technique for systems of BDI agents. In: Proceedings of the seventh European workshop on modelling autonomous agents in a multi-agent world. Lecture notes in computer science 1038. Springer, pp 56–71
4. Iglesias CA, Garrijo M, Gonzalez J, Velasco JR (1998) Analysis and design of multiagent systems using MAS-CommonKADS. In: Proceedings of the fourth international workshop on agent Theories, architectures and languages (ATAL). Lecture notes in computer science 1365. Springer, pp 313–328
5. Bernon C, Gleizes MP, Picard G, Glize P (2002) The Adelfe methodology for an intranet system design. In: Proceedings of the fourth international bi-conference workshop on agent-oriented information systems (AOIS)
6. Lind J (2001) Iterative software engineering for multiagent systems - The MASSIVE method. In: Lecture notes in computer science 1994. Springer
7. Trencanský I, Cervenka R (2005) Agent modeling language (AML): a comprehensive approach to modeling MAS. Informatica (Slovenia) 29(4):391–400
8. Caire G, Leal F, Chainho P, Evans R, Garijo F, Gomez J, Pavon J, Kearney P, Stark J, Massonet P (2002) Agent oriented analysis using MESSAGE/UML. In: Proceeding of the second international workshop on agent-oriented software engineering May 2001. Lecture notes in computer science 2222. Springer, pp 119–135
9. Jennings NR, Faratin P, Johnson MJ, O'Brien P, Wiegand ME (1996) Using intelligent agents to manage business processes. In: Proceedings of first international conference and exhibition on the practical application of intelligent agents and multiagents, pp 345–360
10. Jennings NR, Faratin P, Norman TJ, O'Brien P, Odgers B (2000) Autonomous agents for business process management. Int J Appl AI 14(2):145–189
11. Jennings NR, Faratin P, Norman TJ, O'Brien P, Odgers B, Alty JL (2000) Implementing a business process management system using ADEPT: a real-world case study. Int J of Appl AI 14(5):421–465
12. Huget M-P (2002) Nemo: an agent-oriented software engineering methodology. In: Proceedings of the OOPSLA 2002 workshop on agent-oriented methodologies
13. Burmeister B (1996) Models and methodology for agent-oriented analysis and design. In: Fischer K (ed) KI'96 Workshop on agent-oriented programming and distributed artificial intelligence, DFKI document D-96-06, http://www.dfki.uni-kl.de/dfkidok/publications/D/96/06/abstract.html
14. Gervais M-P (2003) ODAC: an agent-oriented methodology based on ODP. J Autonom Agent Multi-Agent Syst 7(3); 199–228
15. Wagner G (2003) The agent-object-relationship metamodel: towards a unified view of state and behaviour. Inform Syst 28(5):475–504
16. Debenham J, Henderson-Sellers B (2002) Full lifecycle methodologies for agent-oriented systems - the extended open process framework. In: Proceedings of the fourth international bi-conference workshop on agent-oriented information systems (AOIS)
17. Collinot A, Drogoul A (1998) Using the Cassiopeia method to design a Robot Soccer Team. Appl Artif Intell 12(2–3):127–147
18. Cossentino M (2005) From requirements to CODE with the PASSI methodology. In: Henderson-Sellers B, Giorgini P (eds) Agent-oriented methodologies. Idea Group Inc., Hershey, PA, USA
19. Glaser N (1996) Contribution to knowledge modelling in a multi-agent framework -the CoMoMAS approach- PhD Thesis, L'Universite Henri Poincare

20. Padgham L, Winikoff M (2005) Prometheus: a practical agent-oriented methodology. In: Henderson-Sellers B, Giorgini P (eds) Agent-oriented methodologies. Idea Group Inc., Hershey, PA
21. Brazier FMT, Dunin-Keplicz B, Jennings NR, Treur J (1997) DESIRE: modelling multi-agent systems in a compositional formal framework. Int J Cooperat Inform Syst 6:67–94
22. Brazier FMT, Dunin-Keplicz B, Treur J, Verbrugge LC (1999) Modeling internal dynamic behaviour of BDI agents. In: Meyer JJCh, Schobbes PY (eds) Formal models of agents. Lecture notes in computer science 1760. Springer, pp 36–56
23. Brazier FMT, Jonker CM, Treur J, Wijngaards NJE (1998) Compositional design of a generic design agent. In: Luger G, Interrante L (eds) Proceedings of AAAI workshop on ai and manufacturing: state of the art and state of practice. AAAI Press, pp 30–39
24. Juan T, Pearce A, Sterling L (2002) ROADMAP: extending the GAIA methodology for complex OPEN systems. In: Proceedings of AAMAS '02. pp 3–10
25. d'Inverno M, Kinny D, Luck M, Wooldridge M (1997) A formal specification of dMARS. In: Proceedings of the fourth international workshop on agent theories, architectures and languages (ATAL). Lecture notes in computer science 1365. Springer, pp 155–176
26. d'Inverno M, Luck M (1997) Development and application of a formal agent framework. In: Proceedings of the first IEEE international conference on formal engineering methods. pp 222–231
27. d'Inverno M, Luck M (2004), Understanding agent systems. Springer
28. Luck M, d'Inverno M (1995) Structuring a Z specification to provide a formal framework for autonomous agent systems. In: Proceedings. of ZUM '95. Lecture notes in computer science 967. Springer, pp 47–62
29. Luck M, Griffiths N, d'Inverno M (1996) From agent theory to agent construction: a case study. In: Proceedings of third international workshop on agent theories, architectures and languages (ATAL). Lecture notes in computer science 1193. Springer, pp 49–63
30. Sierra C, Sabater J, Agustí J, Garcia P (2002) Evolutionary programming in SADDE. In: Proceedings of the first international joint conference on autonomous agents and multi agent systems (AAMAS). pp 1270–1271
31. Wooldridge M, Jennings NR, Kinny D (2000) The Gaia methodology for agent-oriented analysis and design. J Autonom Agent MAS 3(3):285–312
32. Zambonelli F, Jennings N, Wooldridge M (2001) Organizational rules as an abstraction for the analysis and design of multiagent systems. Int J Software Eng Knowledge Eng 11(4):303–328
33. Zambonelli F, Jennings NR, Wooldridge M (2003) Developing multiagent systems: the Gaia methodology. ACM Trans on Software Eng Methodol 12(3):317–370
34. Omicini A (2001) SODA: societies and infrastructures in the analysis and design of agent-based systems. In: Proceedings of the first international workshop on agent-oriented software engineering (AOSE). Lecture notes in computer science 1957. Springer, pp 185–194
35. Pavón JJ, Gómez-Sanz JJ, Fuentes R (2005) The INGENIAS methodology and tools. In: Henderson-Sellers B, Giorgini P (eds) Agent-oriented methodologies. Idea Group Inc., Hershey, PA
36. Bush G, Cranefield S, Purvis M (2001) The Styx agent methodology, The Information Science Discussion Paper Series 2001/02. Department of Information Science, University of Otago, New Zealand
37. Abdelaziz T, Elammari M, Unland R, Branki C (2010) MASD: multi-agent systems development methodology. Multiagent Grid Syst J 6(1):71–101
38. Bresciani P, Giorgini P, Giunchiglia F, Mylopoulos J, Perini A (2004) TROPOS: an agent-oriented software development methodology. J Autonom Agent Multi-Agent Syst 8(3):203–236
39. DeLoach SA, Wood MF, Sparkman CH (2001) Multiagent systems engineering. Int J Software Eng Knowledge Eng 11(3):231–258
40. Yu E, Cysneiros M (2002) Agent-oriented methodologies—towards a challenge Exemplar. In: Proceedings of the 4th Intl. Workshop on agent-oriented information systems (AOIS'02)

41. Cernuzzi L, Rossi G (2002) On the evaluation of agent oriented methodologies. In: Proceedings of the OOPSLA 2002 workshop on agent-oriented methodologies
42. Shehory O, Sturm A (2001) Evaluation of modeling techniques for agent-based systems. Agents 2001:624–631
43. Dam HK, Winikoff M (2004) Comparing agent-oriented methodologies, AOIS 2003. Lect Notes Comput Sci 3030:78–93
44. Sturm A, Shehory O (2003) A framework for evaluating agent-oriented methodologies, AOIS 2003. Lecture notes in computer science 3030. pp 94–109
45. Cuesta P, Gómez A, González JC, Rodríguez FJ (2003) a framework for evaluation of agent oriented methodologies. In: The conference of the Spanish Association for Artificial Intelligence (CAEPIA)
46. Garcia E, Giret A, Botti V (2011) Evaluating software engineering techniques for developing complex systems with multiagent approaches. Inform Software Technol 53(5):494–506
47. Tran QN, Low G (2005) Comparison of ten agent-oriented methodologies. In: Henderson-Sellers B, Giorgini P (eds) Agent-oriented methodologies, vol 12, Idea Group Publishing., pp 341–367
48. Cernuzzi L, Zambonelli F (2011) Improving comparative analysis for the evaluation of AOSE methodologies. IJAOSE 4(4):331–352
49. Cernuzzi L, Molesini A, Omicini A, Zambonelli F (2011) Adaptable multi-agent systems: the case of the Gaia methodology. Int J Software Eng Knowledge Eng 21(4):491–521
50. Cernuzzi L, Zambonelli F (2009) Gaia4E: a tool supporting the design of MAS using Gaia. ICEIS 4:82–88
51. García-Ojeda J, Arenas A, Pérez-Alcázar J (2005) Paving the way for implementing multiagent systems: refining GAIA with AUML. In: Proceedings of the 6th international workshop (AOSE2005). Lecture notes in computer science 3950. Springer, pp 179–189
52. Moraitis P, Spanoudakis N (2006) The GAIA2JADE process for multi-agent systems development. Appl Artif Intell 20(2–4):251–273
53. Spanoudakis N, Moraitis P (2009) Gaia agents implementation through models transformation. In: Proceedings of the 12th international conference on principles of practice in multi-agent systems (PRIMA '09). Springer, pp 127–142
54. DeLoach SA, García-Ojeda JC (2010) O-MaSE: a customisable approach to designing and building complex, adaptive multi-agent systems. IJAOSE 4(3):244–280
55. DeLoach SA, Wood M (2001) Developing multiagent systems with agentTool. In: Proceedings of the seventh international workshop on agent theories, architectures, and languages (ATAL). Lecture notes in computer science 1986. Springer, pp 46–60
56. Juan C. García-Ojeda, DeLoach SA, Robby: agentTool process editor: supporting the design of tailored agent-based processes. In: Proceedings of SAC 2009. pp 707–714
57. Cossentino M, Sabatucci L, Sorace S, Chella A (2003) Patterns reuse in the PASSI methodology. In: Fourth international workshop engineering societies in the agents World (ESAW '03)
58. Chella A, Cossentino M, Sabatucci L, Seidita V (2006) Agile PASSI: an agile process for designing agents. Int J Comput Syst Sci Eng. Special issue on "Software Engineering for Multi-Agent Systems" 21(2)
59. Chella A, Cossentino M, Sabatucci L (2004) Tools and patterns in designing multi-agent systems with PASSI. WSEAS Trans Commun 3(1):352–358
60. Padgham L, Thangarajah J, Winikoff M (2007) The prometheus design tool - a conference management system case study DOI:10.1007/978-3-540-79488-2_15. In: Agent-oriented software engineering VIII DOI:10.1007/978-3-540-79488-2: 8th International Workshop, AOSE 2007. Lecture notes in computer science 4951. Springer, pp 197–211
61. Winikoff M (2005) JACK intelligent agents: an industrial strength platform. In: Multi-agent programming: languages, platforms, and applications. Springer, pp 175–193
62. Khallouf J, Winikoff M (2009) Goal-oriented design of agent systems: a refinement of prometheus and its evaluation. Int J Agent-Oriented Software Eng 3(1):88–112
63. Castro J, Kolp M, Mylopoulos J (2002) Towards requirements-driven information systems engineering: the Tropos Project. Inform Syst 27(6):365–389

64. Cervenka R, Trencansky I (2007). The agent modeling language - AML: a comprehensive approach to modeling multi-agent systems (Whitestein Series in Software Agent Technologies and Autonomic Computing). Birkhäuser
65. Cervenka R (2012) Modeling multi-agent systems with AML. Software Agents, Agent Systems and Their Applications 2012, NATO, pp 9–27
66. Bernon C, Cossentino M, Pavon J (2006) Agent-oriented software engineering. Knowledge Eng Rev 20(2):99–116
67. Sturm A, Dori D, Shehory O, An object-process- based modeling language for multiagent systems. IEEE Trans Syst Man and Cybern—Part C: Appl Rev 40(2);227–24
68. Beydoun G, Low G, Henderson-Sellers B, Mouratidis H, Gomez-Sanz J-J, Pavon J, Gonzalez-Perez C (2009) FAML: a generic metamodel for MAS development. IEEE Trans Software Eng 35(6):841–863
69. Dam HK, Winikoff M (2013) Towards a next-generation AOSE methodology. Sci Comput Program 78(8):684–694
70. Henderson-Sellers B, Ralyte J (2010) Situational method engineering: state-of-the-art review. J Universal Comput Sci 16(3):424–478
71. Akbari OZ (2010) A Survey of agent-oriented software engineering paradigm: towards its industrial acceptance. J Comput Eng Res 1(2):14–28
72. Zambonelli F, Omicini A (2004) Challenges and research directions in agent-oriented software engineering. J Autonom Agent Multi-Agent Syst 9(3):253–287

Chapter 8
Prometheus Research Directions

Lin Padgham, John Thangarajah, and Michael Winikoff

Abstract Prometheus is a well-established and widely used methodology. In this chapter, we briefly review the methodology and then discuss a number of active research directions. The key research directions that we discuss are: automated testing of agent systems, including test coverage; development of agent systems that are structured as *teams*, and of open agent systems that operate within Electronic Institutions; and the design and representation of agent interaction. We also briefly present the Prometheus Design Tool (PDT) and conclude with a brief look at other areas for future work.

Keywords Agent-oriented software engineering • Interaction design • Prometheus • Teams and organizations • Testing

1 Introduction

Prometheus is a well-established methodology for assisting and guiding developers in building agent-based applications. Its development started in the late 1990s as a result of collaboration between academics at RMIT University who were teaching students to develop agent programs and doing research in agent systems, and practitioners who were building and marketing agent development platforms and doing commercial work in building agent based applications. In the early 2000s, work was consolidated into the named methodology, a support tool (PDT) was developed, and in 2004 a book was published [19], which provided detailed

L. Padgham (✉) • J. Thangarajah
RMIT University, Melbourne, Australia
e-mail: lin.padgham@rmit.edu.au; john.thangarajah@rmit.edu.au

M. Winikoff
University of Otago, Dunedin, New Zealand
e-mail: michael.winikoff@otago.ac.nz

O. Shehory and A. Sturm (eds.), *Agent-Oriented Software Engineering*,
DOI 10.1007/978-3-642-54432-3_8,

guidelines and a running example for agent system design. In 2005, PDT was demonstrated at AAMAS and won the award for best demonstration.

Today Prometheus is used quite widely internationally, though primarily for teaching and research purposes with only relatively limited use within industry. Nevertheless, it is used by some industry practitioners, including some customers of Agent-Oriented Software, the producers of the JACK™ development platform, a widely used and comprehensive commercial agent development platform [24].

We now briefly outline the three phases that constitute the core of Prometheus, after which we mention a number of topics that are not part of the core of the methodology, but where we have done some work. The remainder of this chapter focuses on three areas where we have substantial recent or ongoing research relating to Prometheus: automated testing, representation of teams and organizations, and the design of agent interactions. We then discuss the Prometheus Design Tool, before concluding with a look to the future. A more comprehensive overview of the state-of-the-art in Agent-Oriented Software Engineering can be found in [27].

1.1 Prometheus Design Phases

The core of the Prometheus methodology consists of three design phases: System Specification, Architectural design, and Detailed design. Each of these phases includes a number of design artifacts encompassing structural design, dynamic processes and detailed descriptors. Many of the artifacts are highly structured to support automated propagation of information, both between phases and between aspects of a specific phase. The use of structured information also supports a range of consistency checks to ensure the internal coherence of the design. Figure 8.1 shows the key artifacts in each phase and how they relate to other artifacts. The three phases are discussed in a little more detail below. This discussion is intended to give a high-level summary of the methodology. Since the focus of this chapter is not to introduce the methodology in detail, we do not include a detailed example, but instead refer the reader to existing examples of Prometheus designs that have been published [6, 19].

1.1.1 System Specification

During System Specification, the designer develops an overview of how the agent system fits into the context in which it will operate, and what are the interactions it has with external *actors*, which may be humans or other systems/subsystems. This is captured in an analysis overview diagram that shows the core system scenarios or functionalities and their interactions with key external actors (via *percepts* or incoming information, and *actions* where the system provides information to or otherwise influences external entities). This, together with a goal hierarchy of top-level goals and their subgoals, provides a high-level view of the structure of the system. Scenarios, similar to use cases, provide examples of key processes and

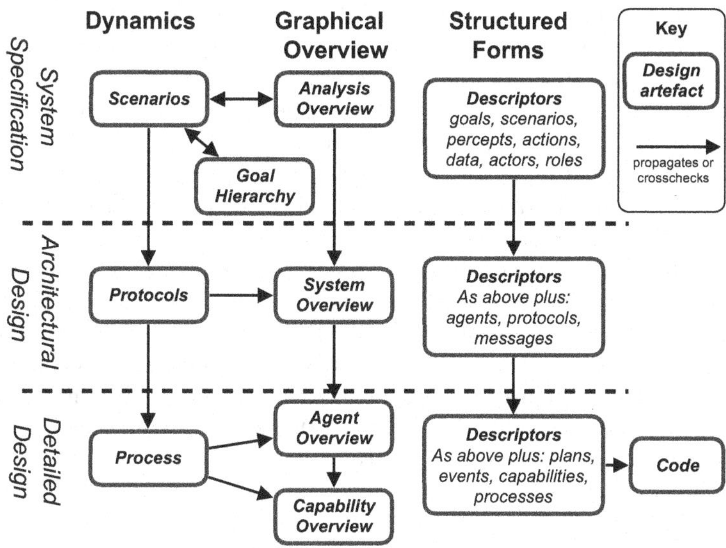

Fig. 8.1 Overview of prometheus

how they execute. These are described using a possible sequence of actions, goals, percepts, and subscenarios. Roles are also specified, and descriptors (structured forms) are developed to describe these as well as all the other entities such as percepts, actions and goals.

1.1.2 Architectural Design

During architectural design, decisions are made as to how to group the roles into agents, and which goals should belong to each agent. The communication protocols are also developed to specify the dynamics of agent interactions required to achieve the various goals. The system overview diagram captures the top-level view of the system architecture, showing which agents (agent types) exist, what communication protocols are defined for interaction between which agent types, and also any data stores within the system with shared access. Various information is also captured in descriptors for each of the entities in the design.

1.1.3 Detailed Design

During detailed design the internals of each agent type are developed to allow the agents to accomplish their specific goals or tasks within the overall system. Information from the architectural design specifies what percepts an agent is expected to respond to, what actions it is expected to take, and what messages it is expected to both receive and send as part of communication protocols. Internally it must then do whatever processing is necessary to make choices and fulfill its role. Detailed design may contain multiple levels of hierarchy using the concept of capabilities to encapsulate modules (or collections of plans and goals), which are related to a specific aspect of the agent's functioning. An agent overview diagram captures the structure of capabilities and the interactions between them, while a capability overview diagram (at least at the lowest level) specifies which plans are designed to accomplish which subgoals, and which subgoals are part of achieving some plan. The capability overview diagram (at least at the lowest level) shows plans and their triggers (e.g., messages, internal events, or (sub-)goals),[1] where each goal has a number of plans, from which one is selected to achieve the goal based on the particular situation. Each plan may have a number of subgoals, the achievement of which is part of executing the plan. A modified version of UML activity diagrams can be used to describe the dynamic process within an agent, as part of a particular protocol, or joint effort to achieve a system goal. Descriptors are again used to provide details of each entity.

1.2 Extensions Beyond the Core

Prometheus is continually being developed and refined as a result of use, feedback, and ongoing research work. There have been a number of areas where work has been done that builds on the core. These include scoping and prioritising [18], maintenance [3], goal oriented protocols [2], testing [23, 29] debugging [20], and model driven architecture [12]. Currently, the key research areas in Prometheus are automated testing using design specifications, design of agent systems using teams and organizations, and a better representation of agent dynamics and interactions. There are also important issues around tool development and support. We will discuss each of these, outlining briefly the current research and state of the art. There are also a range of topics that are an important aspect of future work in refining and developing Prometheus and PDT, including integration with other design paradigms such as object oriented design (UML) and database design. However, many of these have to do more with industry needs than research areas, so we do not cover them in any detail here.

2 Automating Testing

Automated testing is an area where there is tremendous potential for added value within agent-oriented development environments and methodologies. Within Prometheus we have been doing substantial work in this area, with its beginnings

[1]The diagram also shows data, actions, and percepts.

about 10 years ago, but with increased focus over the last 4–5 years. The fact that Prometheus provides structured artifacts—generally produced using PDT—means that these can be used as input to software that can automate (or partially automate) testing processes. The flexible nature of agent systems means that there are very many different ways that tasks can be accomplished [26], making it very difficult to do manual testing sufficiently thoroughly. Consequently, we see automated testing as extremely important. In looking at testing there are three different essential phases to any testing process[2]: specifying the test cases, running the test cases, and checking and reporting on the correctness of the output. Our aim is to automate as much as possible of all three of these phases. There are also different levels at which a system can potentially be tested: unit testing that separately tests the component pieces, integration testing that tests how the components work together, and system testing that tests the system as a whole. We have done some work within Prometheus on each of these levels, and we have also done some initial work on how one might characterize the adequacy of a particular set of tests with respect to a specific program [16]. We describe below the work we have done at each of the testing levels and finish with a description of our work on measuring test coverage.

2.1 Unit Testing

Unit testing is the most well-developed aspect of testing within Prometheus [31], and we have a preliminary version of PDT that integrates automated unit testing, generating a comprehensive test report of issues found. This was the focus of a 2011 PhD thesis [29], and evaluation found that the approach was able to identify some intermittent and difficult-to-reproduce bugs in student written software.

In doing unit testing for an agent system, one of the issues is what are the units, or components that should be tested, as well as what aspects should/could be tested. In Prometheus we identified events (or goals), plans, and beliefs as the core component units that we test. The aspects of these components that we test are developed by considering what information is captured in a Prometheus design, and how this information can be used to test these components. For example, if a number of different plans are specified for achieving a goal, one would expect that, with a comprehensive set of tests, each plan would be used in some situation. If it is not, then, while it is not necessarily an error (it may be that we did not test the right cases, or it may be that the plan is there only as a backup in case a preferred plan fails during execution), a warning is generated to allow the developer to check. If it is the case that a suitable test was not used, the developer can add the appropriate test case, and it will be recorded for future use. If the intention is that no test case should result in the plan being chosen as the first priority, then it can be noted and

[2]An additional, nonessential, phase that we discuss below is assessing the quality of a collection of test cases, that is, coverage analysis.

the system will not notify the warning in future (unless it is requested to ignore such cases).

Another test that is related to a goal/event and a set of plans is whether, in any particular situation there is an applicable plan type. It is not necessarily wrong to have no suitable plan for achieving a goal in some situations. However, having this situation arise unexpectedly is a common cause of errors in agent programs. Developers using Prometheus are prompted to specify both *coverage* (whether there will always be some plan applicable for the event/goal) and *overlap* (whether there are any situations where there will be multiple plan types applicable—and if so how should the choice be made between them). During testing these aspects are checked, and all cases of overlap or lack of coverage are recorded for potential checking. If they are inconsistent with the specification they are flagged as an error.

Nineteen different aspects were identified that could be tested with respect to goals, plans and beliefs. The testing tool developed annotates program code automatically, to provide a test driver for each component that can automatically be executed with a suite of tests, collecting the data for analysis and reporting. Components are tested in an order appropriate to the hierarchical structure of the program, that is, components that are used by another component are tested prior to testing the using component. Cyclical structures are managed separately as a unit.

Generation of test cases is also an important aspect of testing. If these must be specified manually this will inevitably limit the extent of testing. In Prometheus, we require that the developer provide some information about variables, such as type and valid value ranges. On the basis of this information, we automatically generate test cases using equivalence classes of variable values. Where possible we generate test cases with all valid equivalence class combinations of values. However, if desired we can apply pairwise reduction to limit the number of test cases.

In our unit testing work, we assume that the design artifacts form the oracle that identifies correct behavior. It may of course be the case that code is functioning as desired but the design artifact is faulty. Our position here is that such errors are as important to identify and fix as bugs in code, in order to ensure ongoing consistency between design and implementation, as a support for maintenance and ongoing development.

2.2 Integration/Interaction Testing

Integration testing involves ensuring that no errors in behavior are introduced when components that are individually tested are used together within the system. Our approach to unit testing ensures integration testing within an agent, as our approach to testing abstract plans involves execution of all (previously tested) subsidiary plans. An important aspect of testing agent systems is the interaction between agents, and this is an area where errors often arise. In work on debugging [21], we have used the protocol specifications developed during design as an oracle regarding correct interaction behavior. The approach developed converts these to a

Petri net specification that is then executed as the program executes, identifying any mismatches between specification and actual execution. These are then identified as errors.

This work provides an oracle for determining correctness of behavior. However, work on automated generation of test cases for interaction testing, as well as their automated execution, is work in progress as part of a PhD thesis.

2.3 System Testing

In the area of system testing, we have currently focused on use of scenarios as the oracle against which behavior will be measured. In [23], we refined the previous specification of scenarios to provide additional information about percepts and actions, in particular their possible order of occurrence. This then enables us to use this specification to determine whether a particular test case conforms to expectations. We use a simulation system to initialize different configurations of the environment, and then to accept actions and generate percepts, allowing us to systematically test all scenarios. Automated test case generation can in principle follow the same approach as for unit testing—namely creating test cases where relevant variables are initialized to a value within each equivalence class, and combined systematically to create a comprehensive set of situations.

2.4 Test Coverage

One of the key issues in testing is how to know when you have tested sufficiently. The approach we have used in our unit testing is systematic generation of test cases according to equivalence classes of variable values. An alternative approach is to measure to what extent the test suite provides coverage of the code. In [16], we define different levels of coverage for interaction testing. We (loosely) base our coverage criteria on a notion of graph coverage, where the graphs are induced from messages within a protocol, or for more extensive coverage, on plans sending and receiving messages within a protocol, or plans within a decision chain regarding sending of such messages.

The basic idea in this work is that protocol specifications, together with detailed design of plan–event relationships, allows induction of a graph showing all possible paths from the start of a conversation, through plans and messages, to the conclusion of a conversation. Given this graph it is possible to define different levels of coverage, mapping to node, arc and path coverage in the graph. The most basic is message coverage, and requires only that every message is sent at least once. Plan coverage requires that each plan that sends or receives a message in the protocol is executed at least once. However, these are weak criteria, equating only to ensuring that every method in an interface is called, for standard integration testing. Arc coverage is stronger than node coverage, and path coverage—which can include or exclude plan nodes between message receipt and message sending—is stronger again.

The paper [16] explores the nuances of these different coverage criteria and how they can be monitored using the Petri-net representation used for protocol testing as described above and in [21]. Using this kind of coverage criteria it is possible to keep generating test cases (possibly with some "intelligence") until an acceptable level of coverage has been reached.

3 Teams, Organizations, and Social Agents

The Prometheus methodology supports the development of multi-agent systems, where multiple agents may communicate (via message passing as specified in a protocol) to achieve their own goals as well as goals of the system. However, the current Prometheus design does not provide explicit support for specifying team and organizational structures that are specializations of multi-agent systems. Developing methodology support for agent teams is one of our current areas of research and we have developed an approach for designing agents for Electronic Institutions.

3.1 Teams

There are many existing team-based agent programming tools, for example, JACK Team,[3] Machinetta,[4] and GORITE.[5] These approaches incorporate team specific concepts such as team, role, joint-goal, shared-belief, shared-plan, and subteam, which are not found in the common agent design methodologies, including Prometheus.

We are currently investigating, by considering the popular team-based agent frameworks mentioned above, the common and necessary concepts for building agent teams. Whilst some of these concepts such as "team", will be new to the methodology, others such as "role" and "goal" exist but may require different semantics in a team environment. In addition to incorporating these concepts into the different stages of design, we will also develop suitable mechanisms for auto-propagation. For example, a "team-goal" will be propagated into the Agent design of the agents that belong to the team.

---

[3] www.aosgrp.com.

[4] teamcore.usc.edu/doc/Machinetta.

[5] www.intendico.com/gorite.

The result of our current research will be a *Team* plugin to the Eclipse-based (PDT, see Sect. 5) that, when enabled, provides the additional constructs and mechanisms necessary for developing teams, including automatic-code generation.

3.2 Electronic Institutions

Virtual organizations where heterogenous agents can join and interact with other agents to achieve their own individual objectives (e.g., agents in an auction house where buyers and sellers interact) are becoming more commonplace. Electronic Institutions are a way of implementing the interaction conventions for agents to regulate their interactions and establish commitments in such environments.

In [22], we developed an approach for designing agents for Electronic Institutions, by incorporating a *social design* phase developed using ISLANDER—a tool for building e-institutions—into the methodology. The approach is for the initial analysis and requirements to be developed in PDT using the Prometheus System Specification stage with additional concepts, such as *soft goals*, to incorporate the additional needs of an e-institution. This is then exported to the ISLANDER tool for developing the social design, which is the electronic institution component, where the interaction rules, norms and obligations of the various roles are specified. The social design is then imported into PDT, and the Prometheus approach is used to develop those parts of the system that lie outside the actual electronic institution infrastructure, in particular the agents that participate. The social design provides information such as interaction specification and ontology definitions that are incorporated into the architectural design with PDT.

One challenge with Electronic Institutions is that they should allow heterogenous agents to interact in an open environment. We explored some of these issues, proposing a layered architecture for enabling agents to join an e-institution [7].

4 Representing Interactions

A significant outstanding challenge concerns the design of agent interactions, and their representation. Almost any multi-agent system involves interactions between agents, and almost invariably (for the sorts of systems that AOSE methodologies deal with[6]) this interaction is realized using messages sent between agents. Unfortunately, current approaches to designing agent interactions have two significant weaknesses.

[6]There are also certain types of agent systems where interaction is realized not by messages, but through changes to the environment ("stigmergy"), such as depositing pheromones to indicate paths.

The first weakness is that the common approach for designing agent interactions is one that focuses on the messages, by describing explicitly the legal sequences of messages that are permitted in an interaction (i.e., an interaction protocol). Whilst using interaction protocols works fine for non-agent software, it is a poor match for agents [2]. This is because an interaction protocol is *prescriptive*: it prescribes the precise sequences of messages that can occur. Flexibility needs to be explicitly indicated, and is the exception, not the default behavior. On the other hand, agents are designed to be flexible in how they achieve their goals, and this flexibility allows them to be robust: if something goes wrong, a plan-based agent will try an alternative plan to realize the goal at hand. In other words, there is a mismatch between prescriptive interaction protocols based on legal sequences of messages, and flexible and robust agents. One consequence of this mismatch is that interactions designed using the common message-sequence-based approach tend to be brittle, because they do not exploit the flexibility of the agents participating in the protocol.

The solution to this first issue is to develop alternative representations for interactions that allow the flexibility of agents to be exploited, along with appropriate design processes and heuristics for using these alternative representations. A range of approaches have been proposed (e.g. [2, 8, 14, 28]), and they all have in common that they design the interaction not at the level of legal sequences of messages, but at the level of what *drives* the messages to be sent, such as goals or social commitments. By focusing on *why* an interaction is taking place, rather than on the sequence of messages, the interactions tend to be more flexible. For example, using an approach based on commitment machines [28], any sequence of messages that discharges existing commitments is permissible. However, although these approaches are promising, none of them are sufficiently well developed and refined to be currently usable for real applications. More work is needed to further develop and refine these approaches, including both concepts, and also clear and detailed methodologies, including support tools.

The second weakness relating to agent interactions and their representation is that the notations used to capture interaction protocols—such as Finite State Machines (FSMs), Petri nets, and Agent UML—are lacking features to support designers. Specifically, a good notation should provide mechanisms for *abstraction* that make it easy for the designer to decompose a design into loosely coupled aspects, and then consider each aspect in (relative) isolation. For example, in a Holonic manufacturing system [11] a rotating table needs to be locked at various points in the interaction (in order to prevent it moving while a robot is loading, unloading, or joining parts). It would be useful for a designer to be able to specify the sequence of steps involved in manufacturing a part (and associated agent interactions), separately from the details of locking. However, this cannot be specified using existing notations (such as the `ref` region in Agent UML). This is because locking involves three steps (lock, perform a task, and then unlock), and the second step is specific to the context: each time we invoke the lock sub-protocol, the second step will be a different sequence of messages. Agent UML does not have a way to pass a protocol as a parameter to a `ref` region, which means that its abstraction mechanism cannot handle this sort of situation. The lack of a good mechanism for abstraction in interactions leads to

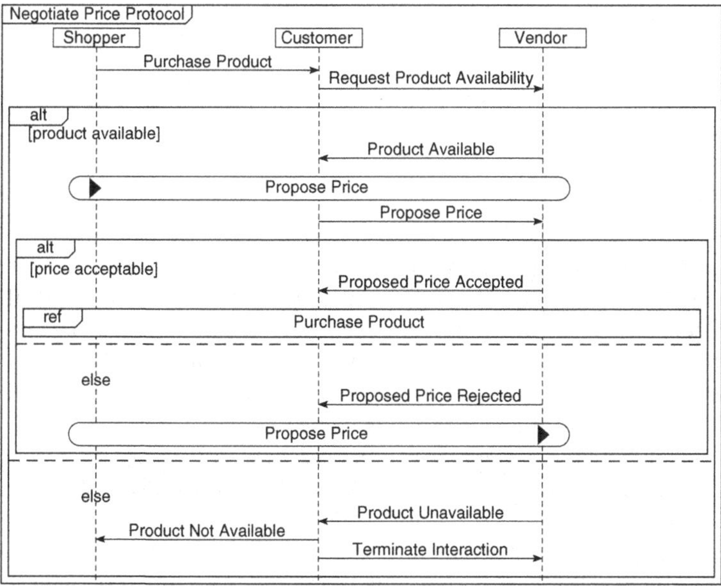

Fig. 8.2 Example interaction protocol in Agent UML

interaction protocols being difficult to specify and to understand (see Fig. 8.2 for a typical interaction protocol).

Other desirable features that are lacking in current notations include: representing agent responsibilities; showing the creation and discharge of social commitments; depicting percepts and actions[7]; clearly indicating the trigger of an interaction; and linking to the processing within each agent (e.g., the goals that it achieves at various points in the interaction [13]). These missing features also have implications for the implementation of interaction protocols. Currently, mapping a protocol into what each individual agent needs to do to play its part in the interaction, is a manual and error-prone process. Extending protocols to include information on triggers and on the agent goals that are involved would allow this process to be better supported.

Unfortunately, this second issue has not been adequately tackled in the literature. What is needed is a new notation (or significant extensions to existing notations) that allow for these various aspects to be represented; along with a revised design process. It is important for the new (or extended) notation to be precisely defined; for the design process to include detailed heuristics and clearly specified steps; and for there to be tool support, especially for the implementation step.

Taken together, these issues imply that the current state of the art in designing multi-agent interactions is adequate (at least for interactions that are not too

[7]It is fairly easy to extend AUML to do this, for instance, by depicting the environment as an additional agent.

complex), but that interaction design is not well supported by existing notations and processes, and that the interactions that are produced tend not to exploit the flexibility and robustness of individual agents.

5 Tool Development

An essential aspect of any software development methodology, is tool support. The Prometheus Design Tool is an integrated development environment (IDE) for agent system designers that offers a graphical interface for designing agent systems following the Prometheus methodology. It includes features such as type safety, entity propagation, automatic code generation, report generation and other features, some of which we describe further in this section.

PDT is developed as a plugin to the Eclipse IDE[8]—a popular open source and extensible IDE for developing software applications. Thus, PDT inherits many of the rich features of Eclipse such as file management, project management, version control, editing, coding and debugging tools that supports a variety of languages.

Figure 8.3 provides a screenshot of the PDT tool within Eclipse with the main views highlighted: *Graphical Editor* (top-center) where each diagram is displayed and edited, *Entity Palette* (top-left) for adding entities to a diagram, *Diagram Outline* (top-right) that lists the diagrams in a Prometheus design and *Entity Properties* (bottom-right) that displays the structured descriptor of a selected entity including its relationships to other entities. The tabs in this view group related attributes. For example, a data entity has a "general properties" tab (for name, description etc.), a "data fields" tab (describing the fields of the data) and an "events posted" tab that describes any events posted when the data is modified.

We highlight some of the features of the PDT tool below:

- **Graphical Editor**: All of the diagrams that are part of a Prometheus design can be graphically edited in PDT. The graphical layouts take advantage of Eclipse features such auto-arrange and a miniature view to easily navigate large diagrams. PDT also provides a drag-and-drop feature for grouping entities in an agent design into new capabilities.
- **Automatic Propagation**: As with type safety, appropriate automatic propagation of entities assists in minimising design errors and is an important support aspect of PDT. Propagation occurs in PDT when entity relations are created or modified. For example, when a role is associated to an agent, all goals achieved by the role are automatically propagated to that agent.
- **AUML Protocols**: PDT supports protocol specification via a textual protocol editor that employs a modified version of Agent UML [25]. The corresponding

[8]www.eclipse.org.

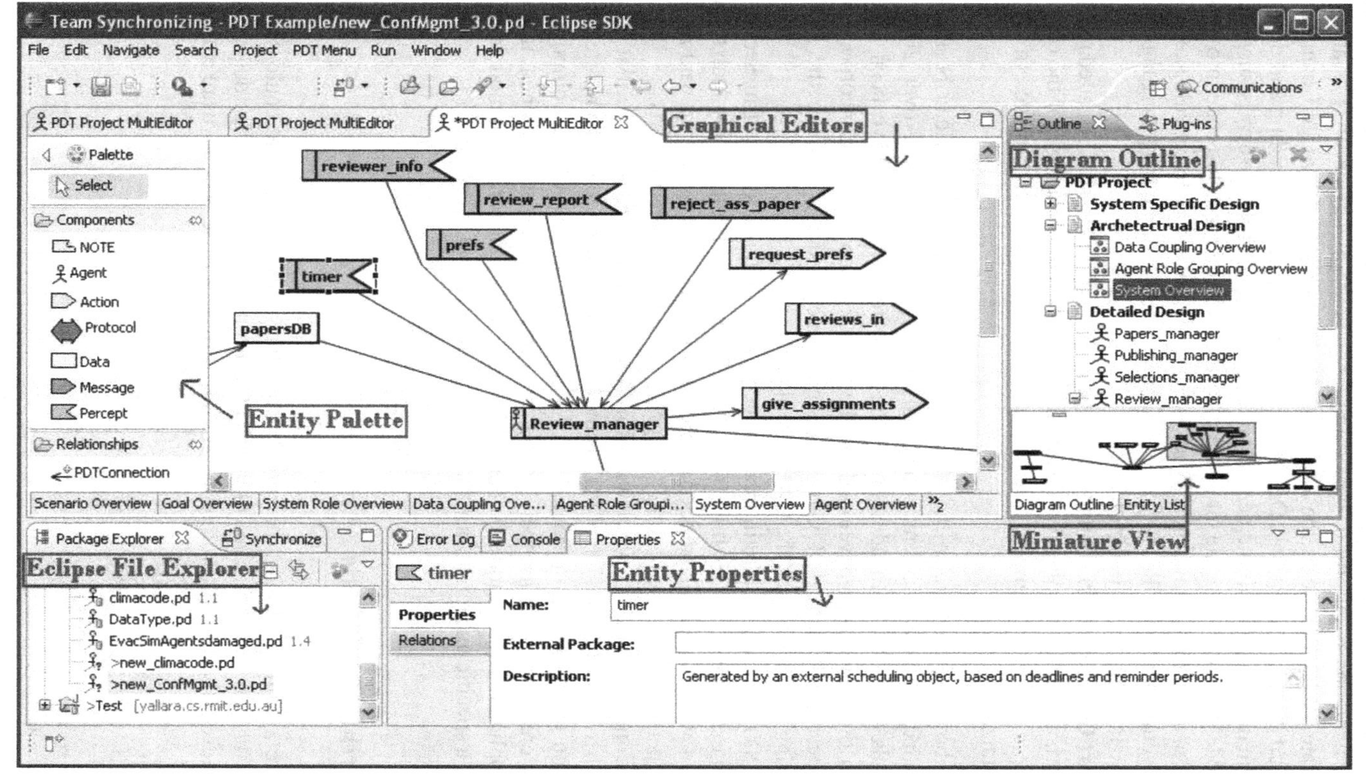

Fig. 8.3 Snapshot of PDT in eclipse

AUML interaction diagram is automatically generated by the tool. The text editor supports syntax highlighting and auto-indentation.

- **Code Generation**: This is an important aspect to assist in ensuring that the implementation is faithful to the design. In the current version, PDT is able to generate skeleton code in the JACK agent programming language,[9] using the detailed design descriptions. Developers may iterate between coding and design with manual updates to the code retained. We note that the design is such that the code generation module may be replaced to generate skeleton code into other agent programming languages. Work is currently underway to provide skeleton code generation to GORITE,[10] an open source agent programming language that we use in a number of our projects.
- **Report Generation**: PDT supports the generation of an HTML formatted report comprising all the graphical and textual information of the design, or the export of the individual diagrams, where the resolution/size of the images may be customized.

The above features are in the mainstream release of PDT that can be freely downloaded from www.cs.rmit.edu.au/pdt. The tool has attracted over 2000+ downloads since 2005. In addition to the main release, there have been other branches that have been developed by the agents group at RMIT incorporating various research aspects. Of particular significance and maturity are the PDT-UnitTesting plugin [30] and the CAFnE tool [12].

The PDT-UnitTesting plugin incorporates the techniques discussed in Sect. 2.1 and is an extension to PDT within the Eclipse framework. It adds a "test" tab to the properties view that elicits additional information necessary for testing, and menu items to perform automated testing that generate and display test reports.

The Component Agent Framework for domain-Experts (CAFnE) toolkit is an extension to an earlier version of PDT (now deprecated) that allowed complete code generation via component modules. CAFnE takes the detailed design components and first creates a domain dependent but platform independent component model of the application. This model is then transformed by a transformation module into code for a specific agent platform that can be compiled and executed.

6 Further Directions

There are a number of other potentially valuable areas of work that could use or refine/extend Prometheus, some of which are currently receiving varying degrees of attention from the AOSE community. We have covered those where we are actively

[9] www.aosgrp.com.

[10] www.intendico.com/gorite.

working, but we now briefly mention a number of additional topics, that could be fruitful areas of endeavor.

Beyond Testing: As discussed earlier, it is particularly challenging to obtain assurance that an agent system will behave appropriately in all situations. Work on formal verification (e.g., [5]) can be an alternative or complement to testing. Currently state-of-the-art model checkers for agent systems are still only applicable to toy programs, not real systems. Potentially, formal verification could be integrated into Prometheus with regard to crucial subparts of the system, or some form of partial formal verification could be done using some of the design artifacts of Prometheus.

Designing Emergent Systems: The bulk of the work on AOSE methodologies has focussed on so-called *cognitive* agents. That is, multi-agent systems where each agent has some form of reasoning capability (such as BDI agents). However, there are also agent systems that consist of very simple agents, where interesting behavior arises from the emergent interaction of many agents [1, 15]. While development environments exist for such systems (e.g. Repast [17]), there are no real methodologies for design of such. There is also potential for a design methodology for systems incorporating both cognitive and simple agents.

Software Maintenance: Once it has been implemented, software is usually subject to ongoing changes ("software evolution" or "software maintenance") to fix bugs, add features, or deal with changes in the deployment environment. Although these changes can account for most of the cost of software, there has been very little work on software maintenance of agent software [3].

Standardization: Although the number of AOSE methodologies in active use and development has shrunk, there are still a number of methodologies. It has been argued that it would be desirable to standardize methodologies, in order to avoid gratuitous differences, and to allow further development to build on a common core [4, 10].

Industrial Adoption: Finally, the industrial adoption of agent-based solutions is being held back by various practical issues [9]. If agents are to be more widely adopted, then we need to ensure that we integrate AOSE methodologies, tools and standards with mainstream approaches. Although this work is arguably best done by industry, the academic community has a role to play.

References

1. Axelrod R (1997) The complexity of cooperation: agent-based models of competition and collaboration. Princeton University Press, New Jersey
2. Cheong C, Winikoff M (2009) Hermes: designing flexible and robust agent interactions. In: Dignum V (ed) Multi-agent systems: semantics and dynamics of organizational models, Chap. 5. IGI, Hershey, pp 105–139
3. Dam HK, Winikoff M (2011) An agent-oriented approach to change propagation in software maintenance. J Auton Agents Multi-Agent Syst 23(3):384–452. doi:10.1007/s10458-010-9163-0

4. Dam HK, Winikoff M (2013) Towards a next-generation AOSE methodology. Sci Comput Program 78:684–694 doi:10.1016/j.scico.2011.12.005
5. Dastani M, Hindriks KV, Meyer JJC (eds) (2010) Specification and verification of multi-agent systems. Springer, Berlin/Heidelberg
6. DeLoach SA, Padgham L, Perini A, Susi A, Thangarajah J (2009) Using three AOSE toolkits to develop a sample design. Int J Agent-Oriented Software Eng 3(4):416–476
7. Dignum F, Dignum V, Thangarajah J, Padgham L, Winikoff M (2008) Open agent systems. In: Agent-oriented software engineering VIII. Lecture notes in computer science, vol 4951. Springer, pp 73–87
8. Flores RA, Kremer RC (2004) A pragmatic approach to build conversation protocols using social commitments. In: Jennings NR, Sierra C, Sonenberg L, Tambe M (eds) Autonomous agents and multi-agent systems (AAMAS). ACM, pp 1242–1243
9. Georgeff M (2009) The gap between software engineering and multi-agent systems: bridging the divide. Int J Agent-Oriented Software Eng 3(4):391–396
10. Henderson-Sellers B (2010) Consolidating diagram types from several agent-oriented methodologies. In: Proceeding of the 2010 conference on new trends in Software Methodologies, Tools and Techniques (SoMeT). IOS, The Netherlands, pp 293–345
11. Jarvis J, Rönnquist R, McFarlane D, Jain L (2006) A team-based holonic approach to robotic assembly cell control. J Netw Comput Appl 29(2–3):160–176. doi:10.1016/j.jnca.2004.10.001
12. Jayatilleke GB, Padgham L, Winikoff M (2005) A model driven component-based development framework for agents. Int J Comput Syst Sci Eng 4(20):273–283
13. Khallouf J, Winikoff M (2009) Goal-oriented design of agent systems: a refinement of prometheus and its evaluation. Int J Agent-Oriented Software Eng 3(1):88–112
14. Kumar S, Huber MJ, Cohen PR (2002) Representing and executing protocols as joint actions. In: Proceedings of the first international joint conference on autonomous agents and multi-agent Systems. ACM, Bologna, pp 543–550
15. Macal CM, North MJ (2008) Agent-based modeling and simulation: ABMS examples. In: Mason SJ, Hill RR, Mönch L, Rose O, Jefferson T, Fowler JW (eds) Winter Simulation Conference, (WSC 2008) Miami, Florida. WSC, pp 101–112, 7–10 December 2008
16. Miller T, Padgham L, Thangarajah J (2010) Test coverage criteria for agent interaction testing. In: Weyns D, Gleizes MP (eds) Proceedings of the 11th International Workshop on Agent Oriented Software Engineering, pp 1–12
17. North MJ, Collier NT, Vos JR (2006) Experiences creating three implementations of the repast agent modeling toolkit. ACM Trans Model Comput Simul 16(1):1–25
18. Padgham L, Perepletchikov M (2007) Prioritisation mechanisms to support incremental development of agent systems. Int J Agent-Oriented Software Eng 1(3/4):477–497
19. Padgham L, Winikoff M (2004) Developing intelligent agent systems: a practical guide. Wiley series in agent technology. Wiley, Chichester
20. Padgham L, Winikoff M, Poutakidis D (2005) Adding debugging support to the prometheus methodology. J Eng Appl Artif Intell 18(2):173–190
21. Poutakidis D, Winikoff M, Padgham L, Zhang Z (2009) Debugging and testing of multi-agent systems using design artefacts. In: Bordini RH, Dastani M, Dix J, El Fallah Seghrouchni A (eds) Multi-agent programming: languages, tools, and applications, Chap 7. Springer, pp 215–258
22. Sierra C, Thangarajah J, Padgham L, Winikoff M (2007) Designing institutional multi-agent systems. In: Padgham L, Zambonelli F (eds) Agent Oriented Software Engineering VII: 7th International Workshop, AOSE 2006. Lecture notes in computer science. Springer, pp 84–103
23. Thangarajah J, Jayatilleke GB, Padgham L (2011) Scenarios for system requirements traceability and testing. In: Sonenberg L, Stone P, Tumer K, Yolum P (eds) 10th International Conference on Autonomous Agents and Multiagent Systems (AAMAS 2011), Taipei, Taiwan, vol 1–3. IFAAMAS, pp 285–292, 2–6 May 2011
24. Winikoff M (2005) JACK^{TM} Intelligent agents: an industrial strength platform. In: Bordini RH, Dastani M, Dix J, Fallah-Seghrouchni AE (eds) Multi-agent programming: languages, platforms and applications. Springer, pp 175–193

25. Winikoff M (2007) Defining syntax and providing tool support for Agent UML using a textual notation. Int J Agent-Oriented Software Eng 1(2):123–144
26. Winikoff M, Cranefield S (2008) On the testability of BDI agent systems. Information Science Discussion Paper Series 2008/03, University of Otago, Dunedin, New Zealand
27. Winikoff M, Padgham L (2013) Agent oriented software engineering. In: Weiß G (ed) Multiagent systems, Chap 15, 2nd edn. MIT Press, Cambridge, MA
28. Yolum P, Singh MP (2002) Flexible protocol specification and execution: applying event calculus planning using commitments. In: Proceedings of the 1st Joint Conference on Autonomous Agents and MultiAgent Systems (AAMAS), pp 527–534
29. Zhang Z (2011) Automated unit testing of agent systems. Ph.D. thesis, RMIT University, Melbourne, Australia
30. Zhang Z, Thangarajah J, Padgham L (2008) Automated unit testing intelligent agents in PDT. In: 7th International Joint Conference on Autonomous Agents and Multiagent Systems (AAMAS 2008), Demo Proceedings, Estoril, Portugal. IFAAMAS, pp 1673–1674, 12–16 May 2008
31. Zhang Z, Thangarajah J, Padgham L (2011) Automated testing for intelligent agent systems. In: Gleizes MP, Gómez-Sanz JJ (eds) Agent-Oriented Software Engineering X - 10th International Workshop, AOSE 2009, Revised Selected Papers. Lecture notes in computer science, vol 6038, Budapest, Hungary. Springer, pp 66–79, 11–12 May 2009

Chapter 9
O-MaSE: An Extensible Methodology for Multi-agent Systems

Scott A. DeLoach

Abstract As the complexity of software systems continues to grow, the multi-agent systems approach has been proposed as an approach to handling this complexity. A key factor to the use of multi-agent systems in real systems is the existence of industrial strength development methodologies. The Organization-based Multi-agent Software Engineering (O-MaSE) methodology was created in response to this realization. O-MaSE integrates a set of concrete technologies aimed at making multi-agent technology available to industry and facilitating widespread acceptance. Specifically, O-MaSE was created as a customizable methodology that can be adapted and extended for a wide variety of uses.

Keywords Agent-oriented methodology • Method engineering • Metamodel • Software analysis • Software design

1 Introduction

One of the discoveries related to software methodologies over the last several decades is that there is not a single methodology that will work for all software development projects. This is true due to the vast number of different software applications as well as the increasingly large number of paradigms used to develop software. To develop complex, distributed, and adaptive software solutions, multi-agent systems (MAS) have been proposed as a promising approach to meet these difficult demands [1]. However, even within a given paradigm such as MAS, a single methodology or approach will never be sufficient given the broad range of applications for which MAS are applicable. Thus, either several unique methodologies must be created to handle a broad range of MAS applications or an approach must

S.A. DeLoach (✉)
Kansas State University, Manhattan, KS, USA
e-mail: sdeloach@k-state.edu

O. Shehory and A. Sturm (eds.), *Agent-Oriented Software Engineering*,
DOI 10.1007/978-3-642-54432-3_9,

be found to tailor methodologies to their proposed applications. One approach to supporting the ability to tailor methodologies to a specific application is *situational method engineering* (SME) [2]. Henderson-Sellers [3] was one of the first to argue that SME is the key to creating flexible, industrial strength methodologies as it allows the development of standard approaches that are widely used and accepted while continuing to allow the methods and processes of those approaches to be modified and extended. SME provides this flexibility by allowing method engineers to construct methods and processes[1] (a.k.a. methodologies) from a set of existing method fragments.

There has been some work at unifying the disparate MAS methodologies. For example, the Agent-Oriented Software Engineering Technical Forum Group (AOSE-TFG) was created to help find a way to allow MAS methodologies to move toward interoperability by creating a common metamodel of MAS concepts [4, 5]. More recently, the IEEE FIPA Design Process Documentation and Fragmentation working group has been working to standardize the definition of existing MAS methodologies [6]. This group held a workshop in 2010 where authors of several MAS methodologies (including ASPECS [7], GORMAS [8], O-MaSE [9], INGENIAS [10], PASSI [11], and SODA [11]) presented their experiences in applying a proposed standard for process documentation. This work resulted in an IEEE FIPA standard [12]. There has even been work done by a group of MAS researchers on developing standard notations [13].

However, Dam and Winikoff [14] argue that while combing existing MAS methodologies may have its utility, it is time to begin working on a new generation of the MAS methodologies. Their first step was to study the strengths, weaknesses, and application domains for existing methodologies followed by identifying the commonalities and differences of the methodology's processes and models. Their next step will be to propose an entirely new methodology that incorporates aspects of these well-established approaches.

This chapter presents an overview of the Organization-based Multi-agent Software Engineering (O-MaSE) methodology, which is a customizable agent-oriented methodology based on consistent, well-defined concepts. O-MaSE was designed from its foundation using SME concepts in order to integrate a set of MAS development methods and techniques into a flexible methodology creation framework. This chapter also shows how O-MaSE can be extended to include new methods and techniques to allow it to handle new applications.

The goal of O-MaSE is to allow method engineers to build custom agent-oriented methods using a set of method fragments, all of which are based on a common metamodel. To achieve this, O-MaSE is defined in terms of a metamodel, a set of method fragments, and a set of method construction guidelines. The O-MaSE *metamodel* defines a set of analysis, design, and implementation concepts and a set

[1] In this chapter, the terms *method* and *methodology* are used synonymously with *process model* while *process* is used to denote an instance of a process model that is enacted to develop a specific system.

of constraints between them. The *method fragments* define a set of work products, a set of activities that produce work products, and the performers of those activities. Finally, *method construction guidelines* define how the method fragments may be combined to create O-MaSE compliant methods. In general, an *O-MaSE compliant method* is an instance of the O-MaSE methodology in which appropriate method fragments are assembled into a method such that the method construction guidelines are satisfied. Critical to the O-MaSE methodology is the agentTool III integrated development environment[2] that supports the creation of custom O-MaSE compliant methods as well as providing the editors, verification tools, and code generators for creating complex, adaptive systems using MAS technology [15, 16]. In addition, agentTool includes the agentTool Process Editor that can be used to create and verify O-MaSE compliant processes.

O-MaSE currently omits many tasks critical for a complete software methodology such as management, product deployment, and testing and evaluation. Management and deployment issues are non-MAS-specific issues, and existing approaches can be applied. While many traditional test and evaluation techniques can be applied to MAS, the need for research into MAS-specific approaches and tools is clear [17, 18].

O-MaSE is introduced in Sect. 2 and described in terms of its metamodel, method fragments, and method guidelines. Then, an extension to O-MaSE is introduced in Sect. 3 in the form of a new type of goal model, a Value-based Goal Model (VGM), with an example showing its use in a custom process in Sect. 4.

2 The O-MaSE Methodology

In *method engineering*, methodologies are created from a set of method fragments, which are typically tasks and techniques taken from existing methods that have been redefined using a common metamodel of concepts. Unfortunately, the application of method engineering for MAS is made more difficult by the lack of consensus on the key MAS elements. While concepts such as agents, roles, and goals appear in many MAS techniques and methodologies, the definitions of those concepts are inconsistent and often unrelated. Thus, it has been suggested that the first order of business in applying SME to MAS is to develop a well-defined metamodel of common agent-oriented concepts agreed upon by the MAS community [5]. While a MAS-specific metamodel has yet to be created, we did base O-MaSE method fragments on a well-defined MAS metamodel so that their relationship to other methods and techniques can at least be made clear.

The O-MaSE methodology is based on two metamodels: SPEM 2.0 and the O-MaSE metamodel. The SPEM metamodel defines methodology-related concepts while the O-MaSE metamodel defines the product-related concepts. O-MaSE

[2]http://agentTool.cis.ksu.edu/

consists of three main components: the O-MaSE metamodel, method fragments, and guidelines. In general, a method engineer creates new O-MaSE compliant methods in agentTool by selecting O-MaSE fragments and combining them into a method that is consistent with the method construction guidelines. O-MaSE fragments are instances of SPEM elements such as *tasks*, *work products*, and *roles*, and are defined in terms of concepts from the O-MaSE metamodel. For example, the O-MaSE Role Model is an instance of the SPEM work product and is defined in terms of roles, goals, and capabilities, each of which are defined in the O-MaSE metamodel. After a brief discussion of the SPEM 2.0, the three O-MaSE components are defined. First, the O-MaSE metamodel is defined. Next, a discussion of O-MaSE phases is given followed by an explanation of the method fragments. Finally, guidelines governing the assembly of O-MaSE compliant methods are given.

2.1 SPEM 2.0

To describe SME-based methodologies, a metamodel defining key concepts is used. While there are several metamodels to choose from (e.g., [19–21], etc.), we have chosen to use the Software and Systems Process Engineering Metamodel (SPEM). SPEM is "a process engineering metamodel as well as conceptual framework, which can provide the necessary concepts for modeling, documenting, presenting, managing, interchanging, and enacting development processes" [21]. SPEM distinguishes between reusable *method content* and the way it is applied in actual *methodologies*. SPEM method content captures and defines the key tasks, roles, and work products[3] that are used in a software methodology. *Tasks* define the work that is performed by *roles* in order to create *work products*, which are used as inputs to other tasks that create new work products. Methodologies are assembled into a set of *activities* that consist of a set of tasks and their associated roles and work products. SPEM defines three types of activities: phases, iterations, and processes. *Phases* are special activities that take a period of time and end with a major milestone or a set of work products. *Iterations* are activities that group other activities that are often repeated. Finally, *processes* are special activities that specify the structure of a software development project.

SPEM has been used to document other MAS methodologies such as ADELFE [22]. While ADELFE was not designed from scratch as a methodology creation framework from which a variety of ADELFE-compliant methods could be created as was O-MaSE, its use of SPEM was instrumental in supporting the extraction of existing ADELFE fragments for use in SME approaches [23].

[3]SPEM 2.0 defines *task definitions*, *role definitions*, and *work product definitions* as method content with *task uses*, *role uses*, and *work product uses* as instances of those methods. This paper refers to both forms as tasks, roles, or work products.

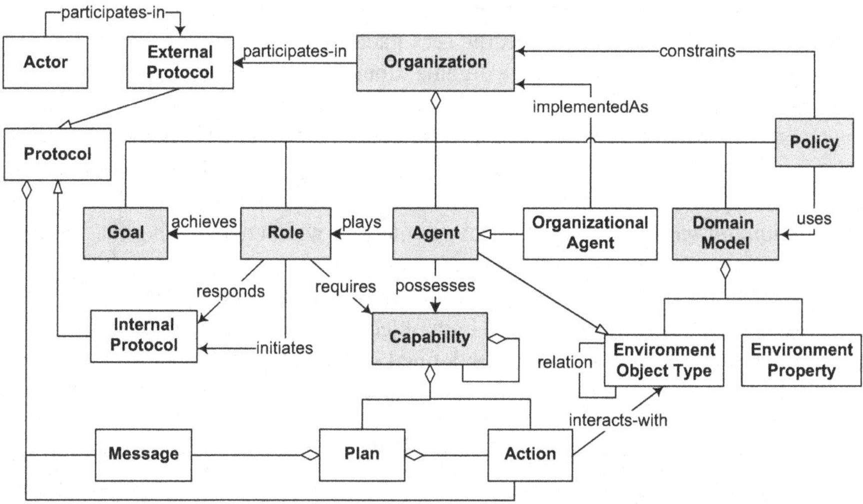

Fig. 9.1 O-MaSE metamodel (multiplicities are omitted for clarity)

2.2 O-MaSE Metamodel

The O-MaSE metamodel, shown in Fig. 9.1, defines the main concepts and relationships used to define MAS. The O-MaSE metamodel is based on an organization-based approach to building MAS [24] and includes notions that allow for hierarchical, holonic, and team-based decomposition of organizations [25]. The O-MaSE metamodel was derived from the Organization Model for Adaptive Computational Systems (OMACS), which captures the knowledge required of a system's structure and capabilities to allow it to organize and reorganize at runtime [24]. The key decision in OMACS-based systems is determining which agent to assign to which role in order to acheve which goal. While O-MaSE does not focus solely on OMACS based systems, it does support the definition of such systems. In O-MaSE, an *Organization* is composed of five entities: goals, roles, agents, a domain model, and policies. In Fig. 9.1, shaded entities correspond to OMACS entities. Each type of entity is discussed below.

O-MaSE uses goals to define the objectives of the organization. As such, a *goal* may represent a desired state [26], the objective of a computational procedure [27], or "a mental attitude representing preferred progressions of a particular multi-agent system" [28]. A *role* defines a position within an organization whose behavior is expected to *achieve* a particular goal or set of goals. *Agents* are autonomous entities that can perceive and act upon their environment [26] using their inherent capabilities. *Capabilities* can be *soft* (i.e., algorithms) or hard capabilities (i.e., physical sensors or effectors). An agent that *possesses* all the capabilities *required* to play a role, may be assigned that role in order to achieve a specific goal. Capabilities can be defined in several ways including as a set of sub-capabilities, as a set of actions, or as a plan that uses a specific set of actions.

Organizational agents (OAs) are organizations that act as agents in a higher-level organization and thus capture the notion of organizational hierarchy. As agents, OAs may possess capabilities, coordinate with other agents, and be assigned to play roles. OAs are similar to the notion of nonatomic holons [29] and can be used to represent a variety of agent groups.

The *domain model* captures the environment in which agents operate. The key elements of the environment are captured as *domain object types* and include agents as well as the *relationships* between object types. The domain model also captures *environment properties* that describe how objects behave and interact. Elements of the domain model, along with entities defined in the O-MaSE model such as goals, roles, agents, can be used to define organizational *policies* to constrain organization behavior.

Protocols define interactions between roles or between the organization and external *actors* in terms of patterns of communication [17]. A protocol can be external or internal. *External protocols* define interactions between external actors and the organization and *internal protocols* define interactions between agents in the organization. Either messages or actions can be used to define protocols. *Messages* are typically used for communications although *actions* that modify the environment may also be used to communicate with other agents [30].

2.3 Method-Roles

As discussed above, SPEM *roles* perform specific tasks in order to create work products, while O-MaSE *roles* refer to positions within an organization. Due to the name conflict between O-MaSE roles and SPEM roles, we use the term *method-role* to refer to SPEM roles in the remainder of this chapter. The current version of O-MaSE has 12 method-roles: Requirements Engineer, Goal Modeler, Domain Modeler, Organization Modeler, Role Modeler, Agent Class Modeler, Protocol Modeler, Policy Modeler, Plan Modeler, Capabilities Modeler, Action Modeler, and Programmer. Each O-MaSE method-role is responsible for carrying out specific tasks to produce the work products shown in Table 9.1.

2.4 Phases

Phases are generally used by methodologists to organize activities. However, since O-MaSE is defined to be customizable, we make no commitments to a specific set of phases. Instead, method engineers may organize activities based on their needs or preferences. We have used O-MaSE in iterative, incremental approaches [31] as well as more traditional waterfall approaches [32].

Table 9.1 O-MaSE method fragments

Activities	Tasks	Work Products Created/Modified	Responsible Method-Roles
Requirements Gathering	Requirements Specification	Requirements Spec	Requirements Engineer
Problem Analysis	Model Goals	Goal Model	Goal Modeler
	Refine Goals		
	Model Domain	Domain Model	Domain Modeler
Solution Analysis	Model Organization Interfaces	Organization Model	Organization Modeler
	Model Roles	Role Model	Role Modeler
	Define Roles	Role Description Document	
	Define Role Goals	Role Goal Model	
Architecture Design	Model Agent Classes	Agent Class Model	Agent Class Modeler
	Model Protocols	Protocol Model	Protocol Modeler
	Model Policies	Policy Model	Policy Modeler
Low Level Design	Model Plans	Agent Plan Model	Plan Modeler
	Model Capabilities	Capabilities Model	Capabilities Modeler
	Model Actions	Action Model	Action Modeler
Code Generation	Generate Code	Source code	Programmer

Figure 9.2 shows how a method engineer might allocate O-MaSE activities in an iterative, incremental approach. The *Inception Phase* establishes what should be part of the product, the *Elaboration Phase* defines an architecture for the system, and the *Construction Phase* completes the implementation of the system. Thus, an O-MaSE compliant method defines the distribution of activities and tasks to a set of phases. While there are no hard and fast rules on what activities should be placed in which phases, the dependencies between the method fragments (captured as method construction guidelines) must be preserved.

2.5 *Activities*

Table 9.1 shows six activities currently covered by O-MaSE: Requirements Gathering, Problem Analysis, Solution Analysis, Architecture Design, Low-Level Design, and Code Generation. Yet, as O-MaSE is flexible and extensible, these activities can only be considered the *current* set since O-MaSE continues to evolve.

Inception		Elaboration		Construction	
Problem Analysis	Problem Analysis Solution Analysis Architecture Design	Solution Analysis Architecture Design	Architecture Design Low Level Design	Low Level Design Code Generation	Low Level Design Code Generation

Fig. 9.2 O-MaSE applied in iterations

Requirements Gathering is used to identify software requirements from a variety of sources. Typically, requirements are classified as functional or non-functional requirements. The goal of the *Problem Analysis* is identifying the overall purpose of the product and documenting the environment in which it will be deployed. O-MaSE captures this information in a Goal Model and a Domain Model. The objective of *Solution Analysis* is to translate the purpose and environment of the project into a description of the required system behavior and interactions with external entities such as users and existing systems. This behavior is captured as roles and interactions in the Organization Model and Role Model.

Once the goals, environment, behavior, and interactions of the system are defined, *Architecture Design* is used to create a high-level description of the main system components and their interactions, which are captured in Agent Class Models, Protocols, and Policies. This Architecture is then used to drive *Low-Level Design*, where the detailed specification of the internal agent behavior is captured in Plan, Capability, and Action models. These low-level specifications are then used to implement agents during *Code Generation*.

While not currently defined in O-MaSE, system creation ends with testing, evaluation, and deployment of the system. Fortunately, the nature of O-MaSE allows it to be easily extended, as will be demonstrated in Sect. 3.

2.6 *Tasks*

Next, the typical tasks, work products, and method-roles used in O-MaSE are presented. Although Table 9.1 shows tasks as being associated with specific activities, in reality, O-MaSE does not require specific tasks to be assigned to specific activities. However, to help organize the tasks, we will present them based on the activities defined in Table 9.1. The only constraints that must be realized are defined in the method construction guidelines discussed in Sect. 2.7. Due to page limitations, only a general description of each task is given. The reader is referred to [33] for a more detailed explanation and examples of the work products produced by each task.

2.6.1 Requirements Gathering

There are several techniques for gathering software requirements. In many cases, traditional techniques for gathering requirements will be sufficient [34] while in other cases newer approaches focused toward multi-agent systems are applicable [35, 36]. O-MaSE assumes that either traditional or multi-agent-focused requirements gathering techniques are sufficient and thus does not stipulate a specific technique.

2.6.2 Problem Analysis

The *Model Goals* task transforms the requirements into a set of system goals in the form of an initial Goal Model, which is shared by many agent-oriented approaches [37–39]. The most common way of modeling goals is via AND/OR decomposition [27], which refines the overall goal of the system into a set of subgoals.

The *Refine Goals* task captures the dynamic aspects using a technique called Attribute-Precede-Trigger Analysis, resulting in a GMoDS (Goal Model for Dynamic Systems) goal model [40]. The Refine Goals task captures sequential constraints among goals, parameters used to define a unique goal state, and the runtime events that cause new goal instances to be created.

The *Model Domain* task captures the object types, relationships, and behaviors that define the domain in which agents will sense and act. The domain model is developed using traditional domain modeling or domain analysis techniques common to many object-oriented methodologies [41].

2.6.3 Solution Analysis

The *Model Organization Interfaces* task identifies the organization's interfaces to external entities, whether they are other agents, organizations, or actors external to the system. Sub-organizations (an OA) of a higher-level organization should consider the interactions between the OA and the roles/agents in the higher-level organization while a top-level organization should consider interactions with users, external systems, or databases to find the appropriate interfaces. The interfaces are defined in an Organization Model, which depicts a single organization interacting with a set of external actors.

The *Model Roles* task identifies and documents the roles in the organization in a Role Model. To ensure consistency, each leaf goal from the Goal Model should be assigned to at least one role. The Role Model also identifies interactions between roles as well as those with external actors; interactions with external actors should be consistent with those defined in the Organization Model.

The *Define Roles* task defines the behavior of a role in terms of a plan, along with the capabilities required to carry out that plan. The designer specifies the capabilities required by each role, the goals the role can achieve, constraints associated with the role, and the plan(s) that implement the role. The plan details are developed later using Model Plan task described below.

The *Define Role Goals* task is an alternative to the Define Roles task as it defines role behavior in terms of a role Goal Model. The starting point for a role Goal Model is the organization leaf goal that the role is designed to achieve; that leaf goal becomes the top goal of the role Goal Model. The semantics of the role Goal Models is the same as for organization Goal Models created except that at the role level, each leaf goal is achieved by a capability instead of a role.

2.6.4 Architecture Design

The *Model Agent Classes* task identifies the types of agents in the organization. Agent classes may be defined to play specific roles or in terms of capabilities, thus implicitly defining the roles that may be played. An Agent Class is a template for a type of agent in the system. In an open system where specific agents are not known a priori, an Agent Class Model may not be used as agents register themselves and their capabilities directly with the system.

The *Model Protocols* task defines the interactions between agents or roles in terms of messages, thus implementing the protocols specified in Organization Models, Role Models or Agent Class Models. The Protocol Model has the same basic semantics as the Agent UML [17] and UML [42] interaction models.

The *Model Capabilities* task defines the internal structure of the capabilities in a Capability Model, where each capability is modeled as an Action or a Plan. An *action* is a piece of atomic functionality that is further defined in the Model Actions task described below. A *plan* is a state-based algorithmic definition that is defined via the Model Plans task discussed below.

2.6.5 Low-Level Design

The *Model Plans* task captures how an agent can achieve a specific goal using either a set of actions to define a soft capability. The result is a Plan Model that is specified in terms of a finite state machine where states contain action sequences and transitions contain inter-agent communications using two special transition actions, send and receive. User-defined actions are carried out sequentially within states and the variables used in actions and messages are globally visible within the Plan.

The *Model Actions* task defines the details of user-defined actions used in the Plan Model. Each action used in a plan must belong to one of the capabilities required by the plan. Actions are typically defined as a function with a signature and a set of pre- and postconditions, but may also be defined via an algorithm, which may be encoded directly in a programming language.

The *Model Policies* task defines a set of rules to which an organization must adhere. In general, policies are used to *restrict* agent behavior and may either be specified informally for use at design time or formally for automated enforcement at runtime. How policies are enforced is a critical decision that affects the way the Policy Model is used during development.

2.6.6 Code Generation

The *Generate Code* task takes all the design models created during the development and converts them into code that correctly implements the models. Obviously, there are several approaches to code generation based on the runtime platform and implementation language chosen. Automated code generation facilities can be used to generate code for specific languages and platforms, while manual code generation can be used to develop systems in virtually any language or runtime platform. The choice of automated versus manually generated code can significantly affect the choice and formality of design models used for development. The agentTool toolkit includes an automatic code generation framework that currently supports the JADE platform [43].

2.7 Method Construction Guidelines

Table 9.2 shows the method construction guidelines, which are defined in terms of preconditions and postconditions for each O-MaSE task. The precondition specifies the set of work products that must be available prior to the task being undertaken while the postconditions specify the work products produced by the task. For example, the Model Goals task requires that either a (1) Requirements Spec or (2) a Goal Model/GMoDS and a Role Model work products must be available. While preconditions specify required/alternative work product inputs for a task, they do not limit the information that can be used during task execution. Although the Model Domain task only requires a Requirements Spec as input, other work products such as Goal Models can also be used; this information is generally documented in the individual task definitions.

3 Extending O-MaSE

While the customization of O-MaSE has been the focus of previous papers (e.g., [33]), one of the main goals of O-MaSE is to allow O-MaSE to be easily extended to capture new types of models and tasks, while not affecting the existing tasks and methods. To ensure backward compatibility, we require that any new extensions

Table 9.2 Method construction guidelines

Task	Pre-condition	Post-condition
Requirements Specification	True	Requirements Spec
Model Goals	Requirements Spec ∨ ((Goal Model ∨ GMoDS) ∧ Role Model)	Goal Model
Refine Goals	Goal Model	GMoDS
Model Domain	Requirements Spec	Domain Model
Model Organization Interfaces	Requirements Spec ∧ GMoDS	Organization Model
Model Roles	GMoDS ∧ Organization Model	Role Model
Define Roles	Role Model	Role Description
Model Agent Classes	GMoDS ∨ Role Model ∨ Organization Model	Agent Class Model
Model Protocols	Role Model ∨ Agent Class Model	Protocol Model
Model Policies	GMoDS ∨ Organization Model ∨ Role Description ∨ Agent Class Model	Policy Model
Model Plans	(GMoDS ∧ Role Model) ∨ (GMoDS ∧ Agent Class Model)	Plan Model
Model Capabilities	(Role Model ∧ Agent Class Model) ∨ Domain Model	Capability Model
Model Actions	Capability Model ∧ Domain Model	Action Model
Code Generation	(Plan Model ∨ Protocol Model) ∧ (Capability Model ∨ Action Model)	Source Code

be just that, true extensions. While not formally defined, a true extension to O-MaSE would require that (1) no new constraints be placed on existing entities and relationships in the O-MaSE metamodel, (2) the method guideline pre-conditions must not become stronger or postconditions made weaker, and (3) no existing metamodel entities, tasks, work products, or method-roles may be eliminated.

To demonstrate extensibility, we add a new type of Goal Model to O-MaSE called the Value-based Goal Model (VGM) [44]. While the current O-MaSE goal model, GMoDS, is good for capturing goals of achievement, it is not always suitable for long-lived systems where the overall objective is to maintain a set of goals and, if necessary, make tradeoffs to ensure continued support of the most important of those goals in the case that limited resources require the system to choose between which goals to support. To integrate the VGM, we define a new work product, a new task to produce that work product, and extensions to the method guidelines to allow existing tasks to use the VGM.

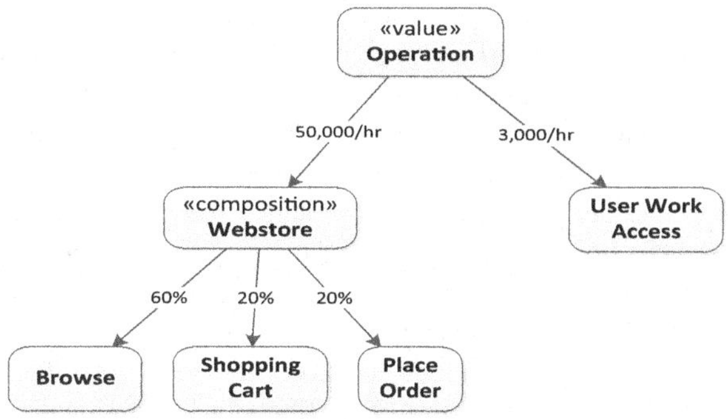

Fig. 9.3 VGM example

3.1 VGM Work Product

A VGM is a tree whose nodes are value-based goals (G) rooted at goal g_0, where g_0 represents the overall mission goal of the system. Value-based goals are defined as a desired state of the world that must be preserved, or *maintained*, by the system. There are five types of value-based goals: Value goals, AND goals, OR goals, composition goals, and leaf goals. All subgoals of a *composition goal* contribute some percentage to its value, which must total 100 %. A composition goal's current value is the sum of its currently maintained subgoal contributions. An *AND goal* denotes the case when all subgoals must be maintained for the parent to be maintained. Thus, the current value of an AND goal is the minimum current value of its subgoals. An *OR goal* is maintained if *any* of its subgoal is maintained. However, each subgoal also has a contribution value. *Leaf goals* are the only goals explicitly maintained by the system. As the system maintains (or fails to maintain) leaf goals, the value of the VGM is aggregated based on parent goal types until an overall VGM value is arrived at.

An example of a VGM for an online web system is shown in Fig. 9.3, which includes a web server that supports online-shopping business and additional computers that are used by employees for their daily work. In our example, the system's goals are decomposed into two main goals: supporting a web store (Webstore) and work access (User Work Access). Since the Webstore goal constitutes the majority of our business income, we have estimated that if this goal is 100 % operational, we will generate approximately $50,000 per hour from it. Likewise, for each hour it is not operational, our business will lose $50,000. The User Work Access goal represents the ability of the employees to access the system in order to maintain it and perform their daily work. The estimated value of this access is approximately $3,000 per hour. The Webstore goal is decomposed into a set of subgoals, where each subgoal is weighted to express its contribution to its parent goal. The Browse goal represents the ability of consumers to browse our website looking for goods to purchase. This constitutes a major aspect of the webstore and thus we have assigned a 60 % value to the overall webstore goal. The next goal, Shopping Cart, is obviously important for customers who actually purchase items from the website. While customers can browse the website, without the ability to add items to their shopping cart, they cannot actually buy those items. Since there is still functionality to the webstore without the shopping cart, we give it a 20 % contribution. Finally, the Place Order goal represents the actual transaction where the customers buy what is in their shopping cart. While customers can shop and add items to their cart, without the ability to check out and purchase their items, the system is not complete. Thus, we assign a 20 % contribution to this goal.

Based on the values assigned to the VGM, the system can now perform computations to determine the effect of maintaining or not maintaining certain goals as it relates to the overall system value.

3.2 Refine Value-Based Goal Model Task

If we assume we can use the existing Model Goals task to identify and decompose the basic system goals as done for the GMoDS goal model, then we simply need to define the techniques and steps required to convert the basic Goal Model into a VGM. Unfortunately, the approach to defining the value of system goals is not necessarily straightforward for all applications. In some cases, the goals can be monetized and their value assigned based on their monetary value. In other cases, valuation is much harder as goal can have both tangible and intangible value. Determination of intangible values tends to require domain-specific approaches and is a research topic in its own right, for an example, see [45].

3.3 Method Guideline Extensions

To incorporate the Refine Value-based Goal Model task into O-MaSE, we need to define a set of new and modified guidelines for O-MaSE that define (1) the appropriate inputs for the Refine Value-based Goal Model task and (2) what tasks may use a VGM as required or optional inputs. Table 9.3 shows the new and modified guidelines. The first row is the new guideline for the Refine Value-based Goal Model task, which states that it requires a basic Goal Model as input and produces a VGM. The remaining six guidelines in Table 9.3 are modified versions of the guidelines listed in Table 9.2. In each case, since a VGM model is used in the same way as a GMoDS model, each time a GMoDS model was mentioned, the choice of a GMoDS or VGM model is given as (GMoDS $\vee$ VGM).

Table 9.3 New and modified method construction guidelines

Task	Pre-condition	Post-condition
Refine Value-based Goal Model	Goal Model	VGM
Model Goals	Requirements Spec ∨ ((Goal Model ∨ GMoDS ∨ VGM) ∧ Role Model)	Goal Model
Model Organization Interfaces	Requirements Spec ∧ (GMoDS ∨ VGM)	Organization Model
Model Roles	(GMoDS ∨ VGM) ∧ Organization Model	Role Model
Model Agent Classes	GMoDS ∨ VGM ∨ Role Model ∨ Organization Model	Agent Class Model
Model Policies	(GMoDS ∨ VGM) ∨ Organization Model ∨ Role Description ∨ Agent Class Model	Policy Model
Model Plans	((GMoDS ∨ VGM) ∧ Role Model) ∨ ((GMoDS ∨ VGM) ∧ Agent Class Model)	Plan Model

4 Example O-MaSE Process

To demonstrate our approach to assembling customized methods using O-MaSE, an example of a custom O-MaSE process is presented for a sensor-based Building Monitoring System (BMS) whose operation relies on relatively simple sensors with little computational overhead. The BMS will have a predefined set of sensor types and each sensor will be deployed to a fixed location. Each sensor will be modeled as an agent that achieves a specific set of goals; the system will not need to reason about its capabilities or reorganize. While other contractors will design the internal operation of the individual agents, each agent will have to conform to system-specific protocols to ensure compatibility between agents.

Given the well-defined nature of the system, a waterfall development approach is chosen. Appropriate models are selected based on the implementation needs. Because there is no need for adaptivity in terms of reassigning agent responsibility, an organizational approach is not required. Therefore, a straightforward agent-centered approach is taken where agents are designed to achieve specific goals. Figure 9.4 shows the process developed for the project. As shown, the Refine Value-based Goal Model task is used to develop a VGM, which is used as both input to the Model Agent Classes task and the Model Domain task.

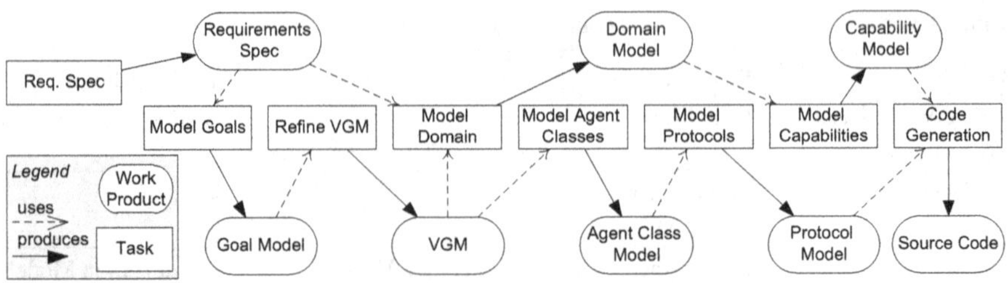

Fig. 9.4 O-MaSE compliant process where *solid arrows denote dashed lines*

5 Conclusions and Future Research

The overall goal of O-MaSE is to provide a suite of technologies aimed at removing impediments to the industrial acceptance of agent technology. O-MaSE provides a customizable agent-oriented methodology based on consistent, well-defined concepts supported by plug-ins to an industrial strength development environment. The O-MaSE methodology allows developers to create custom agent-oriented methods using a set of well-defined method fragments that support a variety of system types and complexities. This is achieved in O-MaSE via the O-MaSE metamodel, a set of method fragments, and a set of method construction guidelines. Each aspect of O-MaSE is supported by the agentTool integrated development environment, which supports method creation and maintenance, model creation and verification, and code generation and maintenance. As shown in this chapter, O-MaSE is easily extensible using a straightforward process. A valid O-MaSE extension has three constraints:

1. No new constraints may be placed on existing entities and relationships in the O-MaSE metamodel.
2. The method guideline preconditions must not become stronger or post-conditions made weaker.
3. No existing metamodel entities, tasks, work products, or method-roles may be eliminated.

When incorporating new tasks, not only must the tasks themselves be defined, but the method guidelines must be modified to allow the new task to be used. These guidelines must define (1) the appropriate set of inputs for the new task and (2) which existing tasks may use the new task as a required or optional input. As the goal of O-MaSE was to build an extensible and customizable methodology, we expect O-MaSE to continue to change and adapt as new models and techniques for building multi-agent systems are created.

O-MaSE has been used to develop several different types of systems including cooperative robotic applications [46], information systems, medical decision support systems [47], and intelligent power distribution systems [48] to name a few. One of the main reasons cited for choosing O-MaSE as the methodology of choice was "easy customization of the analysis and design process" [47], which validates our claims that O-MaSE is both extensible and customizable.

While many pressing issues have been tackled in O-MaSE, at least for the moment, many tasks critical for a complete software methodology such as management, product deployment, and testing and evaluation have been intentionally ignored. Management and deployment issues are generally applicable over a wide variety of software projects and thus existing approaches can and should be applied. Testing and evaluation is not yet included in O-MaSE, as current work has focused strictly on the analysis, design, and implementation of multi-agent systems; while many traditional techniques can be applied to multi-agent systems, the need for unique approaches and tools is recognized. Existing research [18, 49] can be used to extend O-MaSE in this area.

Perhaps, as Dam and Winikoff propose [14], it is time to develop a new generation of MAS methodologies based on the knowledge gained from the first generation of MAS methodologies. If that is the case, then based on our experiences with O-MaSE, we propose that this new generation of methodologies be developed with a method engineering mindset and make use of a common metamodel of MAS concepts. Then, and only then, can true interoperability of MAS methodologies truly be attained.

Acknowledgments This work was supported by grants from the US National Science Foundation and the US Air Force Office of Scientific Research.

References

1. Luck M, McBurney P, Shehory O, Willmott S (2005) Agent technology: computing as interaction (a roadmap for agent based computing). AgentLink, Southampton, UK
2. Brinkkemper S (1996) Method engineering: engineering of information systems development methods and tools. Inf Softw Technol 38:275–280
3. Henderson-Sellers B (2005) Creating a comprehensive agent-oriented methodology: using method engineering and the OPEN metamodel. In: Henderson-Sellers B, Giorgini P (eds) Agent-oriented methodologies. Idea Group, Hershey, PA
4. Bernon C, Cossentino M, Pavon J (2005) Agent-oriented software engineering. Knowl Eng Rev 20:99–116
5. Beydoun G, Gonzalez-Perez C, Low G, Henderson-Sellers B (2005) Synthesis of a generic MAS metamodel. Softw Eng Notes 30:1–5
6. Casare S, Guessoum Z, Brandao Anarosa Sichman, J (2010) Towards a new approach for MAS situational method engineering: a fragment definition. In: Boissier O, El Fallah Seghrouchni A, Hassas S, Maudet S (eds) MALLOW-2010 - the multi-agent logics, languages, and organisations federated workshops 2010, CEUR workshop proceedings, 627, pp 3–16
7. Cossentino M, Galland S, Gaud N, Hilaire V, Koukam A (2010) A glimpse of the ASPECS process documented with the FIPA DPDF template. In: Boissier O, El Fallah Seghrouchni A, Hassas S, Maudet S (eds) MALLOW-2010 - the multi-agent logics, languages, and organisations federated workshops 2010, CEUR Workshop Proceedings, 627, pp 17–28
8. Esparcia S, Argente E, Botti, V (2010) Describing GORMAS using the _pa design process documentation and fragmentation working group template. In: Boissier O, El Fallah

Seghrouchni A, Hassas S, Maudet S (eds) MALLOW-2010 - the multi-agent logics, languages and organisations federated workshops 2010, CEUR workshop proceedings, 627, pp 43–54
9. Garcia-Ojeda JC, DeLoach S (2010) The O-MaSE process: a standard view. In: Boissier O, El Fallah Seghrouchni A, Hassas S, Maudet S (eds) MALLOW-2010 - the multi-agent logics, languages, and organisations federated workshops 2010, CEUR workshop proceedings, 627, pp 22–66
10. Gonzalez-Moreno JC, Gomez-Rodriguez A (2010) Applying process document standardization to INGENIAS. In: Boissier O, El Fallah Seghrouchni A, Hassas S, Maudet S (eds) MALLOW-2010 - the multi-agent logics, languages, and organisations federated workshops 2010, CEUR workshop proceedings, 627, pp 67–78
11. Leonardi C, Sabatucci L, Susi A, Zancanaro, M (2010) Exploring the boundaries: when method fragmentation is not convenient. In: Boissier O, El Fallah Seghrouchni A, Hassas S, Maudet S (eds) MALLOW-2010 - the multi-agent logics, languages, and organisations federated workshops 2010, CEUR workshop proceedings, 627, pp 79–89
12. FIPA (2012) Design process documentation template standard specification. http://fipa.org/specs/fipa00097/
13. Padgham L, Winikoff M, DeLoach S, Cossentino M (2008) A unified graphical notation for AOSE. In: Luck M, Gomez-Sanz JJ (eds) Proceedings of the ninth international workshop on agent oriented software engineering, pp 61–72
14. Dam HK, Winikoff M (2012) Towards a next-generation AOSE methodology. Sci Comp Prog 78:684–694
15. Garcia-Ojeda JC, DeLoach SA, Robby (2009) agentTool III: from process definition to code generation. In: Decker, Sichman, Sierra, Castelfranchi (eds) Proceedings of 8th international conference on autonomous agents and multiagent systems, pp 1393–1394
16. Garcia-Ojeda JC, DeLoach SA, Robby (2009) agentTool process editor: supporting the design of tailored agent-based processes. In: Proceedings of 2009 ACM Symposium on Appl Comput. ACM, New York, pp 707–714
17. Bauer B, Müller J, Odell J (2000) Agent UML: a formalism for specifying multiagent software systems. In: Ciancarini P, Wooldridge M (eds) Proceedings of the First Intern Workshop (AOSE-2000). Springer, Berlin
18. Nguyen DC, Perini A, Tonella P (2008) A goal-oriented software testing methodology 8th International workshop on agent-oriented software engineering. LNCS 4951, Springer, Berlin
19. Firesmith D, Henderson-Sellers B (2002) The OPEN process framework an introduction. Addison-Wesley, Harlow, UK
20. ISO/IEC (2007) ISO/IEC 24744. Software engineering - metamodel for development methodologies. Intern organization for standardization. Intern Electrotechnical Commission
21. OMG (2008) Software and systems process engineering meta-modelmetamodel specification v2.0. http://www.omg.org/docs/formal/08-04-01.pdf. Accessed 30 Mar 2010
22. Bernon C, Gleizes MP, Migeon F, Di Marzo SG (2011) Engineering self-organising systems. In: Bernon C, Gleizes MP, Migeon F, Di Marzo SG (eds) Self-organising software. Springer, Berlin, pp 283–312
23. Puviani M, Di Marzo Serugendo G, Frei R, Cabri G (2009) Methodologies for self-organising systems: a SPEM approach. In: Proceedings of the 2009 international joint conference on web intelligence and intelligent agent technology, vol 2. IEEE Computer Society Press, Washington DC, pp 66–69
24. DeLoach SA, Oyenan W, Matson ET (2008) A capabilities based model for artificial organizations. J Auton Agents Multiagent Syst 16:13–56
25. Horling B, Lesser V (2004) A survey of multi-agent organizational paradigms. Knowl Eng Rev 19:281–316
26. Russell S, Norvig P (2003) Artificial intelligence: a modern approach. Prentice-Hall, Upper Saddle River, NJ
27. van Lamsweerde A, Letier E (2000) Handling obstacles in goal-oriented requirements engineering. IEEE Trans Softw Eng 26:978–1005

28. van Riemsdijk MB, Dastani M, Winikoff M (2008) Goals in agent systems: a unifying framework. In: Proceedings of 7th intern joint conference on autonomous agents and multiagent systems. International foundation for autonomous agents and multiagent systems
29. Cossentino M, Gaud N, Hilaire V, Galland S, Koukam A (2009) ASPECS: an agent-oriented software process for engineering complex systems. J Auton Agents Multiagent Syst 20:260–304
30. Holland O, Melhuish C (1999) Stigmergy, self-organization, and sorting in collective robotics. Art Life 5:173–202
31. Kroll P, Kruchten P (2003) The rational unified process made easy: a practitioners guide to the RUP. Addison-Wesley, Reading, MA
32. Royce W (1970) Managing the development of large software systems. In: Proceedings of IEEE WESCON
33. DeLoach SA, Garcia-Ojeda JC (2010) O-MaSE: a customizable approach to designing and building complex, adaptive multiagent systems. Intern J Agent-Oriented Softw Eng 4:244–280
34. Pressman R (2010) Software engineering: a practitioners approach. McGraw-Hill, Boston
35. Castro J, Kolp M, Mylopoulos J (2002) Towards requirements-driven information systems engineering: the Tropos project. Inf Syst 27:365–389
36. Fuentes-Fernández R, Gómez-Sanz JJ, Pavón J (2009) Requirements elicitation and analysis of multiagent systems using activity theory. IEEE Trans Syst Man Cybernetics 39:282–298
37. DeLoach SA, Wood MF, Sparkman CA (2001) Multiagent systems engineering. Intern J Softw Eng Knowl Eng 11:231–258
38. Giorgini P, Mylopoulos J, Sebastiani R (2005) Goal-oriented requirements analysis and reasoning in the Tropos methodology. Eng Appl Art Intell 18:159–171
39. Padgham L, Winikoff M (2002) Prometheus: a methodology for developing intelligent agents. In: Proceedings of first intern joint conf on autonomous agents and multiagent systems. ACM, NY
40. DeLoach SA, Miller M (2010) A goal model for adaptive complex systems. Intern J Comput Intell Theor Pract 5:83–92
41. Prieto-Diaz R, Arango G (1991) Domain analysis and software systems modeling. IEEE Comput Soc Press, Washington, DC
42. OMG (2011) Unified modeling language (OMG UML), superstructure V2.4.1. http://www.omg.org/spec/UML/2.4.1/Superstructure/PDF. Accessed 10 Dec 2012
43. Bellifemine FL, Caire G, Greenwood D (2007) Developing multiagent systems with JADE. Wiley, England
44. DeLoach SA, Ou X (2011) A value based goal model. multiagent & cooperative reasoning laboratory technical report, MACR-TR-2011-01. Kansas State University
45. Grimaila MR, Fortson LW, Sutton JL (2009) Design considerations for a cyber incident mission impact assessment process. In: Proceedings of international conference on security and management (SAM09)
46. Zhong C, DeLoach SA (2011) Runtime models for automatic reorganization of multi-robot systems. In: Proceedings of the 6th international symposium on soft eng for adaptive and self-managing systems. ACM, New York, 20–29
47. Shirabad JS, Wilk S, Michalowski W, Farion K (2012) Implementing an integrative multi-agent clinical decision support system with open source software. J Med Syst 36:123–137
48. Pahwa A, DeLoach SA, Das S, Natarajan B, Ou X, Andresen D, Schulz N, Singh G (2012) Holonic multi-agent control of power distribution systems of the future. In: CIGRE grid of the future Symposium
49. Poutakidis D, Winikoff M, Padgham L, Zhang Z (2009) Debugging and testing of multi-agent systems using design artefacts. In: El Fallah SA, Dix J, Dastani M, Bordini R (eds) Multi-agent programming. Springer, Berlin

Chapter 10
Ten Years of the INGENIAS Methodology

Jorge J. Gomez-Sanz

Abstract This chapter introduces a review of most of the work done in the INGENIAS methodology along 10 years. Few methodologies have been capable of evolving while keeping their initial premises. The key for INGENIAS survival has been an extreme adoption of Model Driven Development practises since its inception. The needs of its end users, the developers, have been gradually incorporated using those techniques. INGENIAS proposes a modelling language for Multi-agent Systems, recommendations for using it, tool support, and integration with some Software Engineering (SE) development processes. INGENIAS has its own support tools, which concern code generation, documentation, visual edition of the specification, simulation, testing, and installation. This chapter explains how INGENIAS was able to grow while keeping an updated tool support, introduces some important advances, and enumerates some of its challenges in the near future.

Keywords Agent-oriented methodologies • Agent-oriented software • Agent-oriented software engineering • Code generation • INGENIAS • JADE • Metamodel • Model-driven

1 Introduction

In 2012, INGENIAS methodology became 10 years old. The first contribution about INGENIAS was published in the Symposium of Applied Computing held in 2002 [23]. At that time, it was one of the first in presenting complex metamodels applied to Multi-agent Systems, but the methodology was still to be fully developed.

J.J. Gomez-Sanz (✉)
Facultad de Informática, Universidad Complutense de Madrid, Avda. Complutense s/n, 28040 Madrid, Spain
e-mail: jjgomez@fdi.ucm.es

O. Shehory and A. Sturm (eds.), *Agent-Oriented Software Engineering*,
DOI 10.1007/978-3-642-54432-3_10,

Methodology is a term used mainly in the Software Engineering (SE) discipline. It refers to a body of *methods* in the sense of the IEEE Standard Taxonomy of SE Standards [27], *a description of the characteristics of the orderly process or procedure used in the engineering of a product or performing a service*. Similarly, *a process deals with the series of actions or operations used in making or achieving a product*. The SE Book of Knowledge [1], which is a more modern account of SE, remarks that methods come together with tools, and that methods may be heuristic, formal, or prototyping. So, when one talks about a methodology, and for the sake of preventing misunderstandings, one should ask about the process in which this methodology operates, how the method affects the process, which scope it has, what approach (heuristic, formal, or prototyping) it follows, and which tools support the activities.

INGENIAS is an Agent-Oriented SE Methodology created initially to work with the *Rational Unified Process* (RUP) [30], which is different from the *Unified Process*. Other development formulae are possible, though. The INGENIAS-SCRUM variant [10] follows the SCRUM development process [42] and proposes an agile variant to the more rigid RUP. Both SCRUM and RUP are complex development processes to deal with complex problems. When the problem to solve is a small one, usually the kind of problem a single person solves in a matter of a couple of weeks, it is enough by performing a *produce a specification—generate code—execute* cycle.

INGENIAS initially proposed a set of artifacts to be produced during the requirements, design, and implementation basic workflows in the RUP. Artifacts created along the process range from specifications to actual programming code. Specifications are models built according to a meta-model explaining what a Multi-agent System is. Such metamodel is the basis for building a MAS modeling language. This modeling method is semiformal because there are no formal semantics; still, a MAS specification is created using some grammar rules, the metamodel, and converted into programming code, by means of a text to code transformation. In addition, there are tools to assist in the creation of MAS specifications, their documentation, maintenance, and code generation. INGENIAS is supported by the INGENIAS Development Kit (IDK), which is distributed as free software from its main site.[1]

This methodology received the best demo award in AAMAS 2008 [20]. We demonstrated how to quickly create MAS with little effort. The chosen MAS for the demo was a distributed consensus agreement system based on the Delphi method [12]. The video of the demo is still available in the INGENIAS site.

The path to the current INGENIAS has been long. The INGENIAS methodology will be briefly introduced in Sect. 2. Its origin is explained later on in Sect. 3. INGENIAS has gone through changes and it is not the same as in 2002. Evolution happens as a result of trying to apply the methodology to solve problems. Nevertheless, managing the INGENIAS evolution has turned out to be a problem by itself, forcing to devise engineering solutions and take long term decisions, as Sect. 4 shows. INGENIAS has contributed with development experience in several domains listed

[1]http://ingenias.sf.net.

in Sect. 5. As a result of these experiments, INGENIAS has been growing, sometimes incorporating new concepts and sometimes adding new tools to the standard set. Section 6 includes the conclusions and future challenges for INGENIAS.

2 A Gentle Introduction to INGENIAS

Understanding the INGENIAS methodology implies knowing the modeling language it proposes, being aware of the recommendations for applying this language, and being capable of integrating this knowledge into a development process (if needed). These tasks are facilitated by a tool support that will be introduced in Sect. 3.

The notation and vocabulary are embodied into a MAS modeling language. This language is represented through graph-relationship diagrams as in Fig. 10.1. Each element can be represented with an INGENIAS or a UML-like notation and captures a relevant concept in MAS research. In Fig. 10.1, INGENIAS notation is used to represent the agent and its goal, but UML-like is used to represent the fact *GreetTrigger*. It is up to the developer to choose which to use. Each agent has a mental state, whose initial configuration can be included in the specification. In this case, it has a single entity representing a fact about the world. Concepts are related to each other in different ways. An agent pursues a goal (relationship *GTPursues*) and an agent has a mental state (relationship *AHasMS*), for instance. The language identifies several diagram types, each one devised to capture a specific aspect of the system: its organization (organization diagram); an individual description of the agent (agent diagram); a detailed description of its tasks and goals (tasks and goals diagram); a description of the interactions among agents (interaction diagram); the elements in the environment and their relationship with the MAS being defined (environment diagram); the deployment of the MAS (deployment diagram); and a correspondence between elements in the specification with physical elements such as files or pieces of code (component diagram).

The semantics of the modeling language are contained within a reference manual. These semantics are referred to a custom agent framework which is implemented over JADE. The framework is called INGENIAS Agent Framework (IAF), and it will be mentioned again in the next section.

The different tools in INGENIAS are used to support some basic activities. My own PhD [15] reproduced in a stepwise refinement how the INGENIAS modeling language was used to solve the self-organization of virtual communities using the RUP. Further work reinterpreting these results in terms of the Software Process Engineering Modeling Language (SPEM) [34] is available in [14] and [32].

The most basic assumption one can make about the INGENIAS process is the one introduced in Figs. 10.2 and 10.3, a result that was published in [38]. Figure 10.2 refers to the person or persons whose responsibilities attain the support tools mentioned in the previous paragraphs and in Sect. 3. These persons provide assistance to the ones performing the development process. The domain specific

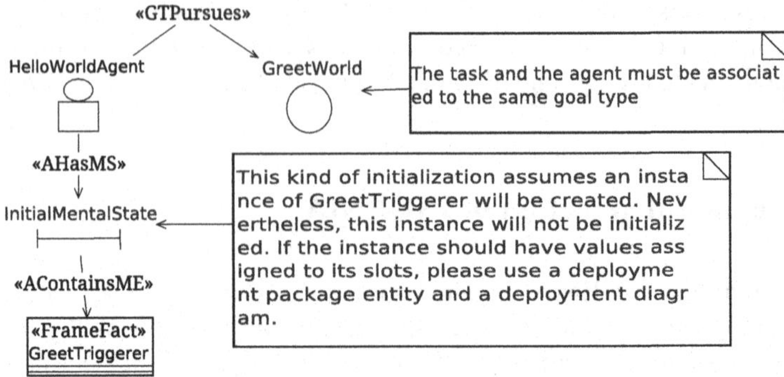

Fig. 10.1 An example of INGENIAS *agent diagram* modeling a hello world agent

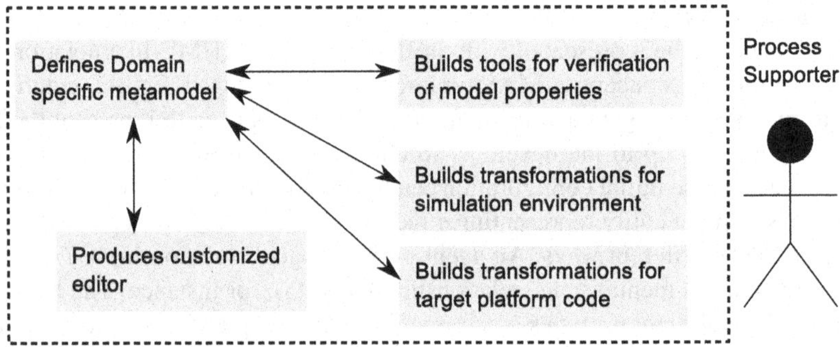

Fig. 10.2 Activities to be performed by supporters of the process

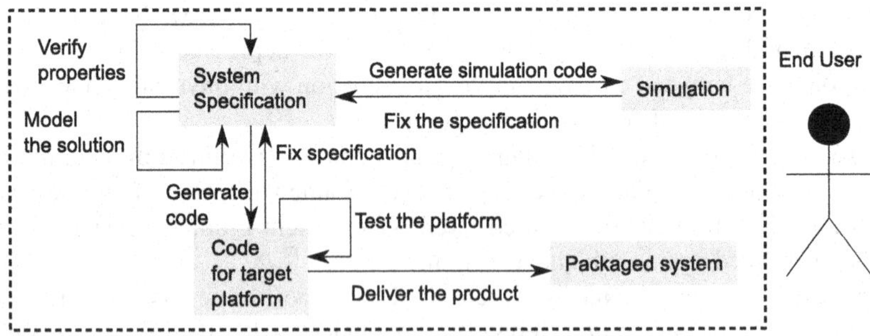

Fig. 10.3 Activities to be performed by the end users of IDK

metamodel activity refers to the customisations one has to make to the original INGENIAS metamodel (see comments about metamodel evolution in Sect. 4). Changes in the metamodel are then to be considered in the other tools, either to ensure some constructions are followed (like those requested by the IAF) or to define new ways to map the specification concepts into code or other models. Figure 10.3

represents a basic cycle design-simulate-deploy-design where developers create the MAS oriented product. It is a very simplified version of what may actually happen, since a longer development ought to refine each one of these activities, perhaps to produce something resembling those activities of [32].

3 The Origins of INGENIAS

INGENIAS stands for *INGENIería de Agentes Software* in Spanish (*Software Agent Engineering*). The seminal work that lead to INGENIAS was our participation in the MESSAGE methodology [3]. MESSAGE was the first full methodology to evidence the potential of Model-Driven practises. It made extensive use of the Meta-Edit tool [44] for producing a customised visual editor to experiment with. Up to MESSAGE, having aids for the specification of MAS was rare. There were remarkable examples at that time, like *agentTool* [5] or *ZEUS* [33]. Both were discontinued, though it should be noted that *agentTool* is being reborn as an Eclipse plugin with the name of agentTool III [13].

The lesson is that having a metaediting facility permitted focusing on the research part. So, the MESSAGE team discussed the best ways to capture MAS concepts and found possible translations of these concepts into a design and an implementation. INGENIAS can be regarded not as a continuation of MESSAGE but as a branch where different modeling concepts are applied and organised. There are links to the original MESSAGE, but it remains fundamentally different, as shows the first version of INGENIAS MAS meta-model [23].

The development of the INGENIAS methodology has been a challenge in several aspects, but I consider the tooling to be the main one. Other methodologies, focused in creating the most adequate MAS modeling language according to some criteria, have seen how the language was unable to evolve due to the costs of modifying the support tool. In this case, where the modeling language support is the bottleneck for the methodology, having technology solving the modeling language evolution issue becomes utterly important. And Model-Driven technology was the key. Perhaps, it is the increasing popularity of the platform, or the need of recognising the benefits of a Model-Driven solution, but all methodologies are slowly converging in the Eclipse platform and applying Model-Driven techniques. They either construct ad hoc plugins that implement the metamodels each methodology is proposing or just use it as it is, taking advantage of existing software for this platform. The Eclipse platform provides many facilities. There are some specially relevant ones for Model-Driven developers: the Plugin Development Environment (support for creating Eclipse extensions), the Eclipse Modeling Framework (support for metamodeling), and the Graphical Modeling Framework (visual editor generation). This migration has happened in the case of Prometheus [35], Tropos [31], the above mentioned agentTool III [13], and GAIA [4]. Nevertheless, Eclipse is not the perfect platform. The long term stability of Eclipse and the difficulties for creating stable plugins are something to take into account [28]. There are alternatives, though. Uhl [45] lists several Model-Driven support tools. Any of them ought to bring the methodology a similar tool independence as INGENIAS has.

In the case of INGENIAS, the development of custom metaediting facilities was motivated by a defect in 2002 Meta-Edit [44] version that could not be fixed. INGENIAS started using Meta-Edit to create prototype editors implementing experimental metamodels, just as in MESSAGE. It turned out the tool did not allow you to alter a hierarchy of concepts once defined. This affected strongly a project like INGENIAS that needed to experiment with different configurations and change whatever is required. Additionally, Meta-Edit commercial nature was a problem if others were to use the editors one produced. So, instead of continuing with this tool, it was studied if some alternative software, preferably free software, existed. Eclipse did not have the facilities it has today, and the best candidate was, and still is, JGraph.[2] It provided very basic diagram support and some simple editors exemplifying trivial modeling languages, though it lacked capabilities to easily change the modeling language those editors supported. Support for complex relationships was also missing, just as multiple diagram management support, persistence services, and others. Anyway, it was a good starting point. So, a proof-of-concept editor was created from this editor that permitted to draw three types of entities and two types of relationship plus basic services enabling to start experimenting in similar conditions as in Meta-Edit. This prototype was analyzed to identify which code sections were associated with each entity or relationship, to establish mappings that permitted to infer, if a new entity type was to be incorporated, what new code should be aggregated. A smart combination of this information with a custom made template management infrastructure, led to a first version of a self-made meta-editor. A file contained the specification of the entities, relationships, and diagrams following a notation inspired by GOPRR [29], which is the metamodeling language of Meta-Edit. This file was interpreted by a program that implied which new code sections were to be added to the basic infrastructure. As a result, there was an editor capable of holding any number of entities and relationships distributed along several diagram types.

This editor was the first component of the IDK, which is the name given to the set of tools that support INGENIAS. Metaediting capabilities were developed separately and conformed the INGENME tool.[3] The resulting editor changed as well to allow the fast development of plugins. These are an extension of its basic capabilities that can be incorporated in runtime, while the editor is open. A plugin can access the specification when plugged to the editor or work in stand alone mode by executing it from command line over a specification file. The specification can be traversed to extract information, and this information can be used to fill in template files, just as it was done to generate new editors. This mechanism constitutes the basic principle for code generation capability.

[2]http://www.jgraph.com.

[3]http://ingenme.sf.net.

The most important plugin for the IDK is the *IAF code generator*, which is coupled with the *INGENIAS Agent Framework* (IAF). IAF is an implementation of an agent architecture over JADE. It allows distributed state protocol implementations, task execution activated by goals, multiple conversation management, and an implementation of the mental-state concept, among others. The *IAF Code Generator* maps the specification elements to chunks of code so that a new agent system can be generated that matches the specification, using the same mechanisms the meta-editing capabilities use.

To complement the IAF, a basic HTML documentation plugin was developed as well. The plugin generated HTML pages with the specification together with hyperlinks interconnecting different sections. The purpose of these was to enable the review of a diagram in a regular Internet browser and define basic navigation: click on an entity to obtain its description and then move to other diagrams where this entity appears.

The experience of using IAF revealed something every developer disliked about code generation: it prevented modifying generated files because they would be overwritten after the code is regenerated. This problem is generally regarded as *round-trip engineering* because one intends to go from the specification to the code, then modify the code, and expect the modification is transferred back to the specification. Trying to reproduce this ideal behavior, two additional plugins were incorporated to the IDK: one to upload pieces of code to the specification, named *Code Uploader*, and another to synchronise APIs between the specification and the code for concrete entities, named *AppLinker*. The first assumes a developer only has to alter concrete parts of some concrete files. These parts were identified and associated with elements of the specification, called *INGENIAS Code Components*. These are responsible of containing pieces of text to be used when generating code for concrete files and concrete parts of these files. This way, a regeneration of the code would take into account these elements and the resulting one would be coherent with the previous state. The *AppLinker* serves to maintain coherence between an API declared in the specification and the API exposed by concrete implementation classes.

The combination of these elements led to a sufficient tool support for a MAS development. This initial set of tools was improved with new features as Sect. 4 discusses. The use of these tools in a development process has been studied to some extent as previous section has introduced.

4 Keeping INGENIAS Healthy

Software Engineering (SE) plays an important role in the INGENIAS methodology. On the one hand, the INGENIAS methodology pursues the practical application of MAS theories to develop Agent-Oriented Software. In such cases, engineering, and not Artificial Intelligence, has to be the driver [16]. Concepts such as planning the development, supporting the software lifecycle, or promoting reusability do belong to this realm. On the other hand, SE also serves to work with INGENIAS as a long term product itself. Needs identified in several developments, like altering the modeling language or including MAS-based simulation features (see Sect. 5), are major changes whose cost-benefit trade-off has to be analysed. Without the resources to realise an exhaustive change management policy, INGENIAS focused on the following requirements:

- The metamodel for MAS specification should improve as development experience increases.
- Support tools do not obstruct the metamodel evolution and keep the same pace.
- Generating releases of IDK must not be an expensive process.
- Any released software artifact must have passed some control tests that ensure a minimum of functionality.

There was not always a clear solution for each requirement. A combination of main stream SE tools and theory was necessary.

Dealing with the MAS specification metamodel evolution has been a most challenging task. Evolution happens as a result of trying to apply the methodology to solve problems (check Sect. 5 for an overview of the problems). In general, a change in the metamodel is needed when:

- You work in a case study and discover some fatal flaw that prevents you from capturing properly the problem and/or the solution.
- Your knowledge on some domain improves in a way that you discover better solutions
- You tried to adapt a current framework or platform to fit the methodology, but the information contained in the model was not enough

The specification language, based on a metamodel for MAS specification, was supported by a custom made metamodeling tool. This tool was introduced in the previous section. It is called INGENME. It is now free software[4] with GPL license. This tool takes as input a XML file containing the modeling language abstract syntax specification, that is, the metamodel, and generates a visual editor supporting it. Concrete syntax, that is, the notation, can be included as well, but it requires extra files containing the images. Even using this tool, there has to be a strict policy for allowed changes in the metamodel. In principle, a change in the metamodel means you cannot reuse a specification conforming with the previous metamodel. INGENME produced backwards compatible visual editors provided that three rules were respected: *extend existing concepts rather than modify existing ones*, *aggregate new attributes rather than eliminate them*, and *never change the name of an existing entity*.

A change in the metamodel was immediately followed by a regeneration of the official editor. Optionally, the IAF was altered to take into account the new elements or just remained the same. Other plugins were usually unaffected. The drawback

[4]http://ingenme.sf.net.

is the size and coherence of the metamodel. After all, having too many concepts may be as bad as having a few. To deal with this issue, the capability of filtering concepts in the editor was included. It is possible to show only those concepts and relationships listed in an external file, which is a very cheap mechanism to customise an already existing editor without altering the underlying meta-model.

The incorporation of metamodeling facilities makes it possible to deliver more versions of the tools. It was decided to follow the *release early and release often* [41] motto, which is an extended philosophy in the free software community. It took time to adopt it because of the inherent risk of releasing buggy versions. Also, releasing a version of the support tools took too much effort despite the meta-editing tools. Metamodeling tools can be buggy too. This reduced the number of releases to one per year until 2008. That year a new release approach was essayed, one simpler to maintain: a Continuous Integration system. These systems, when properly installed, can download snapshots of the software from version control systems, such as SVN or CVS, and generate the releases after some tests are applied. This way, it is easy to know whether a change broke the distribution. We chose the Hudson platform.[5] Hudson is installed in our servers[6] and distributes four flavours of IDK: a jar based self-installer, a zipped full distribution of the IDK (combining IAF, the editor, and all plugins), and the editor only alternative.

Preparing the IDK deliverables with the Hudson framework is a step forward. Being sure the deliverables are the right ones is a different matter. To have guarantees of this, releases now have to go through a testing process that reviews the functionality of the visual editor (this implies simulating user inputs and reproducing actions to generate a new specification from scratch), the code generation features (generating code, e.g., MAS projects), and the functionality of resulting MAS (validating the execution of generated MAS). This is automated using the TestNG[7] platform, which has a good integration with FEST,[8] our favourite GUI testing framework.

Despite the framework and the tests ensuring the quality of the release, developers did not want to have the latest version, a wise decision in some scenarios. So, the Hudson framework did not turn out as successful as expected.

A new step in INGENIAS has been adopting the Maven[9] development scheme. Maven is a software project management tool for building, reporting, and releasing software products. It defines a comprehensive software lifecycle that can be customised. This lifecycle includes managing software dependencies, controlling software heterogeneity when two or more different programming languages are used, or facilitating the installation and release of the developed software, among others. It has required to reorganize the IDK, but now releases can be more stable

[5]http://hudson-ci.org.

[6]http://ingenias.fdi.ucm.es/hudson.

[7]http://testng.org.

[8]http://fest.easytesting.org.

[9]http://maven.apache.org/.

and frequent. Developers can choose which version of the IDK they want. An added value is that INGENIAS is now available to all developers in the world that use Maven without requiring special configurations. Maven has global software repositories where IDK releases are uploaded and downloaded.

5 Results Obtained By INGENIAS

INGENIAS has been tested in a variety of domains. This was useful to validate the expressiveness of INGENIAS metamodel and the viability of developments with the available tools. The list of addressed application domains follows:

- Collaborative Information Filtering [15]. It is the first case study specified in my PhD with INGENIAS. It is about dealing with information overload through collaborative information filtering. There were communities of users where information is distributed according to shared topics of interest and the individual topics of interest of the users. Users are subscribed to communities because of their shared interests. These may change along time, so user subscriptions change as well. Communities and users were represented by agents that learnt what pieces of information were interesting and which ones were not. Users may suggest information to a community. This information would be evaluated by a subset of users through their agents. If found meaningful, the information was forwarded to all users.
- Bookstore management [21, 22]. The Juul Møller BokHandle case study was obtained from Espen Andersen site, which is dedicated to technology and management.[10] It is about a bookstore that sells book mainly to students of one university. This business collaborates with the professors, looking for recommended books, for instance. This bookstore wants to become "electronic," just as Amazon, and needs to define what services may make the bookstore more competitive. The case study solution uses the organization concept and introduces ways in which this concept can be realized during design and implementation.
- eCulture [7]. eCulture is a web-based broker of cultural information developed with Tropos methodology. The case study is the same, but the contribution proposes to use UML-AT to transform the Tropos specification to an INGENIAS one.
- Robocode [8, 36]. Robocode[11] is a Java programming game where the behavior of a tank has to be programmed. The tank has a radar to identify enemies and can shoot bullets. There can be several coordinating tanks, and large battles can be easily deployed.

[10]http://www.espen.com.

[11]http://robocode.sourceforge.net/.

- Delphi process [12]. It studies the application of the Delphi method to build a set of agents that achieve agreements through argumentation based on keyword relevance. The system was designed and implemented using INGENIAS. The Delphi method was created in the fifties by the RAND corporation, in Santa Monica, California. This method was created initially for foresight studies, that is, long-term decisions that guide the policy of a country or a company. Such studies require reaching a consensus in a community of experts, and this is what the method provides. The method was implemented for a document classification problem. The resulting MAS worked better than a common implementation at the expense of dedicating more time to each query. It was demonstrated in AAMAS 2008 [20]. The system contained six expert agents, one referee agent, and one client.
- Social Simulation [39, 40]. The case study is a society of bats that live in roosts. Bats return to them after hunting. In roosts, bats are expected to share food and to groom one another. Assisting other bats gives credits, which are spent when help is returned. The bats have some memory of past grooming and food sharing experiences. In such population, and defining some specific behavior profiles, the simulations intend to investigate the benefits, and drawbacks of altruism. The specification was made with INGENIAS, while coding was made with the REPAST agent based simulation tool.[12]
- Business Intelligence [18]. Technology surveillance is an important activity in Business Intelligence. Elaborating a state-of-the-art report is expensive but necessary if a company wants to evaluate the interest in investing in a concrete technological area. Once there is a basic report, the problem is how to keep this knowledge updated. Such is the challenge technology surveillance addresses. The success of the surveillance depends greatly on which information sources are used. These sources are usually suggested or discovered by individuals, but, again, determining their quality is expensive. To ensure certain quality of the information sources while keeping maintenance costs of such systems, a MAS is proposed that uses a trust & reputation model. Trust & reputation metrics serve to account the quality of individual information sources and decide whether the information source ought to be used or not. The resulting MAS captures the quality evaluation process as well as the intelligence to handle the expected quality.
- Surveillance [37]. Traditionally, the control of a surveillance system has been performed with a centralized configuration. Sensors report to a central controller that makes decisions on what to do and transmits orders to remote devices. The paper studies how a MAS can bring autonomy, coordination, and decentralization to surveillance activities using the INGENIAS methodology. A MAS model is created and an executable system is obtained that simulates a deployment of four mobile platform sensors, ten microphone sensors, two tracking devices, five cameras, and three area coordinators.

[12]http://repast.sourceforge.net/.

- Powergrid [25]. This case study was about modeling coordination for energy distribution in a grid. The scenario considered power faults and how to reconnect the grid so that critical infrastructures, like hospitals, could get energy. The case study synthesizes discussions held in the SOAR'10 workshop.[13]
- Cinema [2,43]. It is one of the testing cases for validating the IAF. There are users that want to go to a cinema, but have very specific interest in the services each cinema provides. This way, some users like giant pop-corn buckets while others prefer comfortable seats. Each cinema offers a price for such services and not all cinemas provide all services. So, first of all, one cinema offering the requested services has to be found. Then, a price has to be arranged and, if it is within the margin provided by the user, a ticket is bought. The problem is captured using INGENIAS and is currently deployed using different sizes, from a few agents to hundreds, reaching the limits of JADE platform. It is interesting as case study, mainly.
- Operation and Maintenance workflows [26]. It introduces several real workflows in a company and studies how INGENIAS provides the concepts to model them. These workflows illustrate the interest in having Tropos-like primitives to express goal positive and negative effects.

As a result of the above-mentioned case studies, INGENIAS has been incorporating techniques and new modeling concepts. A summary of the techniques and associated contributions follows:

- Simulation[18]. This is a major contribution that permits to implement simulations based on a discrete time approach. It required to define new entities to express what a simulation is and how to extract information from a run.
- Testing [17]. This work introduces new testing features in INGENIAS that allow developers to define their own tests, though the test content is not created automatically. Some facilities are given to simplify enquiring about the mental state of agents. Enquiries are the way to check whether the system state is the appropriate one. The new concepts are accompanied with new artifacts in implementation that capture the concrete test.
- Data mining for debugging. Using the cinema test case, it shows how data mining techniques can be used to analyze system traces and deduce what is going on [43]. This work is a continuation of [2]. It uses Aspect-Oriented Programming to obtain a new JADE platform version where communication related methods are intercepted. With this change, accurate information of interchanged information is obtained. This information is stored off-line so that it can be analyzed using different kinds of diagrams. Similar techniques are applied in [24]. This study introduces a crisis management case study elaborated with INGENIAS and proceeds to inspect the involved communication costs.
- Model transformations. Though INGENIAS is strong in modeling support, its solutions for model transformation were not in line with current trends in the

[13] http://distrinet.cs.kuleuven.be/events/soar/2010/papers.php.

Model-Driven community. One of the reasons is that developing a transformation had little support, less than doing it *the old way* using programming constructs. A promising technique in this sense was the generation of transformations by example. The concept was proven with the Model Transformation Generator Tool (MTGenerator). This tool took as input examples of expected input and output models. Using them it deduced what transformation could provide such conversion. Hence, the cost of such transformations can be reduced with the aid of tools like MT Generator [11]. An expanded example of the transformations that can be obtained is available in [9], together with some guidelines for the disciplined use of this tool in the context of an AOSE methodology.

- Model integration [7,40]. It proposed UML-AT as *interlingua* for the translation of models from one methodology to another. It is based on the previous work in UML-AT, where conversion of INGENIAS to UML-AT and vice versa were addressed [6].
- Requirements Elicitation [8]. Creating a specification is always time consuming. Hence, the interest in facilitating the construction of an initial version of the requirements specification. In this research line, it is studied how research in Activity Theory can facilitate the requirement elicitation and analysis of a problem using patterns discovered for human activity. An adequate translation of these concepts for agents can enact a faster identification of relationships and problem entities. The proof of concept is made with INGENIAS and an experiment is conducted with several volunteers.
- Coordination [22]. It introduced the way interactions are handled in INGENIAS. It is a multiparty approach where interactions have an explicit representation, they are a first-class citizen, using UML terms. These interactions are associated with a protocol. The protocol implementation does not uses a global state approach, which is inefficient, but a distributed state one. Each party knows of only the states of the interaction where it has an active role. Besides the implementation, there are several debugging tools.
- Organization modeling [21]. The concept of organization is relevant as well in INGENIAS. Using as example a case study of a book store, it shows possible implementations of the organization. With INGENIAS, subscription and unsubscription services can be costless designed and produced.
- Web applications [19]. It applies INGENIAS to the generation of web applications. The implementation is not agent oriented, but was a proof of concept that, sometimes, an agent-oriented implementation was not the best option.

6 Conclusions

INGENIAS is an Agent-Oriented Methodology with a strong tool support. Its scope includes requirements, design, implementation, and testing related activities. For those activities, there are sets of identified artefacts to be created and guidelines to do so. INGENIAS is a living methodology in the sense that it grows to incorporate new knowledge, something only possible because of the metaediting facilities behind.

INGENIAS is not finished at all. There is a number of problems that need to be addressed:

- Tide-up the metamodel. The INGENIAS metamodel has grown since the 2002 version as a result of dealing with different domain problems. Some concepts were introduced because they were important in some agent theories. Others were introduced trying to cope with some unexpected modeling need. Despite the reasons, the incorporation of concepts has made the current version of the metamodel, in XML format, a file of 446K. Just finding a concrete entity definition, takes time, and existing XML editing facilities do not make the work easier. Besides, from this metamodel, just a few concepts are actually used for code generation . Considered actions to deal with this problem include removing non-used concepts, better structuring the INGENIAS MAS metamodel, or finding better representation mechanisms to deal with modeling languages of that size.
- Information overload. Diagrams tend to be too informative. After some time they are collapsed with all kinds of entities and relationships and it is hard to read anything. As the number of elements grows, the bigger is the need of powerful layout algorithms. Also, new ways of organising the information would be welcome. Ideas like hyperlinks interconnecting parts of the specification may facilitate understanding later the inter-diagram dependencies. By now, this problem is addressed with discipline. Through the use of a folder-like mechanism, diagrams are arranged into groups. Development discipline determines which meaningful groups exist and what kind of content should be expected in each one.
- Improve code generation facilities. Code generation relies in a template-based mechanism. The creation of a template implies certain processing steps which are not fully supported yet. As any other program, a template must be written, executed, and debugged. Specific support for this may motive more developers to create their own code generation module for other target platforms. Support editing tools permit to have different plugins at the same time providing different conversion means. This is a powerful solution to create, from the same specification, different implementations form the same specification.
- Transformation development support. There have been important advances in this direction with the work done with a Model Transformation By Example approach. Nevertheless, more is needed to make this a stable feature. As in the case of templates, creation, execution, and debugging phases need to be experimented further.
- Migration to another standard metamodeling language. At this moment, INGENIAS uses GOPRR that is not as widespread as Ecore, the language the Eclipse Modeling Framework uses. This eliminates for developers the possibility of using the existing software, like ATL Transformations, which is currently developed for Eclipse.
- Multiuser support. This is perhaps the major problem in INGENIAS and other methodologies toward their adoption in big projects. At this moment, having

multiple developers working at the same time in the specification is not possible. Instead of a version control system, Model-Driven community is addressing this problem as a merge of two models coming from the same metamodel. In the case of INGENIAS, merging pieces of the specification, though possible through the "import" feature of the editor tool, does not work well because it requires from developers to be very strict with the way entities are named. Name clash is very easy and have negative effects in the merged specification.

Acknowledgments This chapter has been funded by the project "SOCIAL AMBIENT ASSISTING LIVING - METHODS (SociAAL)", supported by Spanish Ministry for Economy and Competitiveness with grant TIN2011-28335-C02-01, and by the Programa de Creación y Consolidación de Grupos de Investigación UCM-Banco Santander (group number 921354).

References

1. Abran A, Bourque P, Dupuis R, Moore JW, Tripp LL (2004) Guide to the software engineering body of knowledge: SWEBOK. IEEE Press, Piscataway, 2004 version edition
2. Botía JA, Gómez-Sanz JJ, Pavón J (2006) Intelligent data analysis for the verification of multi-agent systems interactions. In: Corchado E, Yin H, Botti VJ, Fyfe C (eds) IDEAL. Lecture notes in computer science, vol 4224. Springer, pp 1207–1214
3. Caire G, Coulier W, Garijo FJ, Gómez-Sanz JJ, Pavón J, Leal F, Chainho P, Kearney PE, Stark J, Evans R, Massonet P (2001) Agent oriented analysis using message/uml. In: Wooldridge M, Weiß G, Ciancarini P (eds) AOSE. Lecture notes in computer science, vol 2222. Springer, pp 119–135
4. Cernuzzi L, Zambonelli F (2009) Gaia4e: a tool supporting the design of mas using gaia. In: Cordeiro J, Filipe J (eds) Proceedings of the 11th Internatinal Conference on Enterprise Information Systems, vol 4, pp 82–88
5. DeLoach SA, Wood MF (2000) Developing multi-agent systems with agenttool. In: Castelfranchi C, Lespérance Y (eds) ATAL. Lecture notes in computer science, vol 1986. Springer, pp 46–60
6. Fuentes R, Gómez-Sanz JJ, Pavón J (2003) Activity theory for the analysis and design of multi-agent systems. In: Giorgini P, Müller JP, Odell J (eds) AOSE. Lecture notes in computer science, vol 2935. Springer, pp 110–122
7. Fuentes R, Gómez-Sanz JJ, Pavón J (2006) Integrating agent-oriented methodologies with uml-at. In:Nakashima H, Wellman MP, Weiss G, Stone P (eds) AAMAS. ACM, pp 1303–1310
8. Fuentes-Fernández R, Gómez-Sanz JJ, Pavón J (2009) Requirements elicitation and analysis of multi-agent systems using activity theory. IEEE T Syst Man Cyb Part A 39(2):282–298
9. García-Magariño I, Fuentes-Fernández R, Gómez-Sanz JJ (2009) Ingenias development process assisted with chains of transformations. In: Cabestany J et al. Bio-inspired systems: computational and ambient intelligence, 10th International Work-Conference on Artificial Neural Networks, IWANN 2009, Salamanca, Spain. Proceedings, Part I. Lecture notes in computer science, vol 5517. Springer, 10–12 June 2009, pp 514–521
10. García-Magariño I, Gómez-Rodríguez A, Gómez-Sanz JJ, González-Moreno JC (2008) Ingenias-scrum development process for multi-agent development. In: Corchado JM, Rodríguez S, Llinas J, Molina JM (eds) DCAI. Advances in soft computing, vol 50. Springer, pp 108–117
11. García-Magariño I, Gómez-Sanz JJ, Fuentes-Fernández R (2009) Model transformations for improving multi-agent system development in ingenias. In: Gleizes MP, Gómez-Sanz JJ (eds) AOSE. Lecture notes in computer science, vol 6038. Springer, pp 51–65

12. García-Magariño I, Gómez-Sanz JJ, Pérez-Agüera JR (2008) A complete-computerised delphi process with a multi-agent system. In: Hindriks KV, Pokahr A, Sardiña S (eds) ProMAS. Lecture notes in computer science, vol 5442. Springer, pp 120–135
13. García-Ojeda JC, DeLoach SA, Robby (2009) Agenttool iii: from process definition to code generation. In: Sierra C, Castelfranchi C, Decker KS, Sichman JS (eds) AAMAS, vol 2. pp 1393–1394
14. Gómez-Rodríguez AM, González-Moreno JC (2010) Application of a modeling standard language on the definition of agent oriented development processes. In: Demazeau Y, Dignum F, Corchado JM, Bajo J, Corchuelo R, Corchado E, Riverola FF, Julián V, Pawlewski P, Campbell A (eds) PAAMS (Special Sessions and Workshops). Advances in soft computing, vol 71. Springer, pp 363–370
15. Gomez-Sanz JJ (2002) Modelado de Sistemas Multi-Agente (Modeling Multi-Agent Systems). Ph.D. thesis, Facultad de Informatica (Universidad Complutense de Madrid)
16. Gómez-Sanz JJ (2006) The construction of multi-agent systems as an engineering discipline. In: O'Hare GMP, Ricci A, O'Grady MJ, Dikenelli O (eds) ESAW. Lecture notes in computer science, vol 4457. Springer, pp 25–37
17. Gómez-Sanz JJ, Botía Blaya JA, Serrano E, Pavón J (2008) Testing and debugging of MAS interactions with ingenias. In: Luck M, Gómez-Sanz JJ (eds) AOSE. Lecture notes in computer science, vol 5386. Springer, pp 199–212
18. Gómez-Sanz JJ, Fernández CR, Arroyo J (2010) Model driven development and simulations with the ingenias agent framework. Simulat Model Pract Theory 18(10):1468–1482
19. Gómez-Sanz JJ, Fuentes R (2004) Agent oriented software engineering with web applications. Int J Web Eng Technol 1(4):471–483
20. Gómez-Sanz JJ, Fuentes R, Pavón J, García-Magariño I (2008) Ingenias development kit: a visual multi-agent system development environment. In: AAMAS (Demos). IFAAMAS, pp 1675–1676
21. Gómez-Sanz JJ, Pavón J (2005) Implementing multi-agent systems organizations with ingenias. In: Bordini RH, Dastani M, Dix J, Fallah-Seghrouchni AE (eds) PROMAS. Lecture notes in computer science, vol 3862. Springer, pp 236–251
22. Gómez-Sanz JJ, Pavón J (2006) Defining coordination in multi-agent systems within an agent oriented software engineering methodology. In: Haddad H (ed) SAC. ACM, pp 424–428
23. Gómez-Sanz JJ, Pavón J, Garijo FJ (2002) Meta-models for building multi-agent systems. In: SAC. ACM, pp 37–41
24. Gutiérrez C, García-Magariño I, Gómez-Sanz JJ (2009) Evaluation of multi-agent system communication in ingenias. In: Cabestany J et al. Bio-inspired systems: computational and ambient intelligence, 10th International Work-Conference on Artificial Neural Networks, IWANN 2009, Salamanca, Spain. Proceedings, Part I. Lecture notes in computer science, vol 5517. Springer, 10–12 June 2009, pp 619–626
25. Hernandez L, Zorita CB, Aguiar J, Carro B, Sánchez-Esguevillas A, Lloret J, Chinarro D, Gómez-Sanz JJ, Cook D (2013) A multi-agent system architecture for smart grid management and forecasting of energy demand in virtual power plants. IEEE Commun Mag 51(1): 106–113
26. Hidalgo AG, Gomez-Sanz JJ, Mestras JP (2007) Workflow modelling with ingenias methodology. In: 5th IEEE international conference on industrial informatics, vol 2, pp 1103–1108, June 2007
27. Standard IEEE (1987) IEEE Standard Taxonomy of software engineering standards. IEEE Std 1002–1987, 1987
28. Kelly S (2004) Comparison of Eclipse EMF/GEF and MetaEdit+ for DSM. In: 19th annual ACM conference on object-oriented programming, systems, languages, and applications, workshop on best practices for model driven software development
29. Kelly S, Lyytinen K, Rossi M (1996) Metaedit+: a fully configurable multi-user and multi-tool case and came environment. In: Constantopoulos P, Mylopoulos J, Vassiliou Y (eds) CAiSE. Lecture notes in computer science, vol 1080. Springer, pp 1–21

30. Kruchten P (2003) The Rational Unified Process: an introduction, Addison-Wesley Longman Publishing Co., Boston, MA, USA, 2003
31. Morandini M, Nguyen DC, Penserini L, Perini A, Susi A (2011) Tropos modeling, code generation and testing with the taom4e tool. In: de Castro JB, Franch X, Mylopoulos J, Yu ESK (eds) iStar, CEUR workshop proceedings, vol 766. CEUR-WS.org, pp 172–174
32. González-Moreno JC, Gómez-Rodríguez A (2010) Applying process document standarization to ingenias. In: Boissier O, Fallah-Seghrouchni AE, Hassas S, Maudet N (eds) MALLOW, CEUR workshop proceedings, vol 627. CEUR-WS.org
33. Nwana HS, Ndumu DT, Lee LC, Collis JC (1999) Zeus: a toolkit and approach for building distributed multi-agent systems. In: Agents, pp 360–361
34. Object Management Group (2008) Software and Systems Process Engineering Metamodel Specification (SPEM) 2.0
35. Padgham L, Thangarajah J, Winikoff M (2008) Prometheus design tool. In: Fox D, Gomes CP (eds) AAAI. AAAI, pp 1882–1883
36. Pavón J, Gómez-Sanz JJ (2003) Agent oriented software engineering with ingenias. In: Marík V, Müller JP, Pechoucek M (eds) CEEMAS. Lecture notes in computer science, vol 2691. Springer, pp 394–403
37. Pavón J, Gómez-Sanz JJ, Fernández-Caballero A, Valencia-Jiménez JJ (2007) Development of intelligent multisensor surveillance systems with agents. Robot Auton Syst 55(12):892–903
38. Pavón J, Gómez-Sanz JJ, Fuentes R (2006) Model driven development of multi-agent systems. In: Rensink A, Warmer J (eds) ECMDA-FA. Lecture notes in computer science, vol 4066. Springer, pp 284–298
39. Pavón J, Sansores C, Gómez-Sanz JJ (2006) Agent based modeling of social systems. In: Dunin-Keplicz B, Omicini A, Padget JA (eds) EUMAS, CEUR workshop proceedings, vol 223. CEUR-WS.org
40. Pavón J, Sansores C, Gómez-Sanz JJ (2008) Modelling and simulation of social systems with ingenias. IJAOSE 2(2):196–221
41. Raymond E (1999) The cathedral and the bazaar. Knowl Technol Policy 12(3):23–49
42. Schwaber K, Sutherland J (2011) The scrum guide. Technical report. www.scrum.org
43. Serrano E, Gómez-Sanz JJ, Botía JA, Pavón J (2009) Intelligent data analysis applied to debug complex software systems. Neurocomputing 72(13–15):2785–2795
44. Smolander K, Lyytinen K, Tahvanainen V-P, Marttiin P (1991) Metaedit: a flexible graphical environment for methodology modelling. In: CAiSE, pp 168–193
45. Uhl A (2008) Model-driven development in the enterprise. IEEE Software 25(1):46–49

Part IV
Agent-Oriented Programming Languages

Chapter 11
A Survey of Multi-agent Programming Languages and Frameworks

Mehdi Dastani

Abstract This chapter surveys the multi-agent programming research field by presenting and discussing some typical multi-agent programming languages and frameworks. It provides an overview of the concepts and abstractions that are used to describe multi-agent systems. It is argued that the existing programming languages and frameworks are designed to support the implementation of high-level abstractions such as individual agents, the organization that controls and regulates the behavior of individual agents, or the environment with which individual agents interact. The distinction between agent, organization, and environment is used to structure the presentation of the programming languages and frameworks.

Keywords Agent-oriented programming languages • Multi-agent development frameworks • Multi-agent programming • Organization-oriented programming languages

1 Introduction

Multi-agent systems can be seen as an advance in software engineering that has resulted in new software development methodologies. Multi-agent systems provide a repertoire of high-level concepts and abstractions to model and develop distributed complex systems. At the highest level of abstraction, multi-agent systems are conceived as consisting of communicating individual agents, an environment with which individual agents interact, and an organization that regulates the behavior of individual agents. These entities are in turn defined in terms of other concepts and abstractions such as beliefs, goals, plans, actions, events, roles, interaction, organizational rules and structures, communication, norms and regulation policies.

M. Dastani (✉)
Institute of Information and Computing Sciences, Utrecht University, Utrecht, The Netherlands
e-mail: m.m.dastani@uu.nl

O. Shehory and A. Sturm (eds.), *Agent-Oriented Software Engineering*,
DOI 10.1007/978-3-642-54432-3_11,

Like other software development methodologies, multi-agent systems cover different phases such as requirement, specification, design, implementation, and testing. In the literature of multi-agent systems there have been various multi-agent software development methodologies proposed, e.g., Gaia [62], Prometheus [43], Tropos [14], INGENIAS [30], and others (see [8]). Each methodology focuses on specific phases of the software development process and assumes that other phases can be used and instantiated from other software development methodologies. For example, Gaia focuses mainly on the analysis and design phases of software development, and assumes that the generated design documents from the design phase can be implemented in some conventional programming language such as Java. Gaia assumes also that conventional requirement engineering and testing approaches can be employed for the development of multi-agent systems.

This chapter focuses on the implementation of multi-agent systems and provides an overview of the multi-agent programming research field. The main aim of the multi-agent programming research field is to propose programming languages and development frameworks that facilitate direct and effective implementations of multi-agent systems. One can consider a multi-agent programming language or a development framework as a computational specification language or a computational framework that can be used to implement a certain class of multi-agent system architectures. After all, a multi-agent programming language or framework provides computational constructs and tools to implement specific concepts and abstractions that are proposed by some multi-agent architectures. Therefore, it is plausible to assert that the existence of various multi-agent development methodologies together with the fact that these methodologies propose different abstractions and architectures have inspired the proposal of various multi-agent programming languages and development frameworks.

In order to present this survey in a systematic way, the existing programming languages and development frameworks will be structured along their foci on individual agents, multi-agent organizations, and multi-agent environments. The proposals that focus on individual agents aim at introducing programming constructs to support the implementation of individual agent issues such as autonomy, reactive behaviors, social awareness, reasoning about norms and organizations, communication with other agents, and capabilities to sense and act in the environment. The proposals focussing on multi-agent organizations aim at facilitating the implementation of social and organizational issues such as norms (obligation, prohibition, permission), norm compliance, norm enforcement mechanisms, sanctions or rewards that should be imposed if norms are violated, roles that agents can or should enact, responsibilities and tasks assigned to agents, delegation of tasks and responsibilities, or the synchronisation of agents' actions. Multi-agent organizations can be implemented either endogenously or exogenously. In endogenous organizations individual agents are internally designed and implemented by means of social and organizational concepts such that their executions generate organized multi-agent system behaviors. On the other hand, exogenous organizations are implemented as computational entities that reside outside the agents' codes and their executions control the concurrent executions of individual agent programs at runtime. Finally, programming languages and development frameworks that are designed to support the implementation of multi-agent environments provide programming constructs to support the interaction between individual agents and their external environments. Such programming constructs should allow a programmer to implement the results of sense and act abilities of individual agents as well as tools, artifacts, services, and resources that can be used by individual agents.

This chapter starts with a brief discussion on concepts and abstractions that are used to describe and model multi-agent systems. It then presents an overview of the existing multi-agent programming languages and development frameworks, and discuss the subset of multi-agent concepts and abstractions that are addressed by them. This overview is by no means complete. The programming languages and frameworks covered in this overview are chosen because they illustrate different ways to program multi-agent concepts and abstractions, have execution platforms, and of course, because of the author's familiarity with them. Other multi-agent programming languages and development frameworks can be found in [10, 11].

2 Multi-agent Concepts and Abstractions

This section presents some key concepts and abstractions that are used to describe multi-agent systems. The concepts and abstractions are structured in three subsections reflecting the highest level of abstraction in multi-agent systems: agents, environments, and organizations.

2.1 Individual Agents

Generally speaking, multi-agent systems comprises a set of individual agents. An essential characteristic of individual agents is autonomy, that is, the ability of an agent to decide and perform actions at each moment of time in order to achieve its goals and objectives [61]. We consider an agent as autonomous if it has a decision making component that determines its decisions based on its informational (e.g., beliefs, distributions, knowledge), motivational (e.g., desires, utilities, preferences), and deliberational (e.g., intention, plans, commitments) attitudes. One can argue that any computational system that interacts with other systems can be seen as autonomous, at least from an external point of view. However, the development of an autonomous software agent requires developing the internals of the agent including an explicit decision making component that can be specified, designed and implemented in terms of informational, motivational and deliberational attitudes. The decision-making component should allow a programmer to implement different decision issues such as decision strategies, resolving decision conflicts, and rationality or realism of decisions. Programming languages that support the implementation of autonomous agents should therefore provide programming constructs to implement their decision components. There are various abstract decision models that can be used to implement an agent's decision component. For example, an agent's decision component can be implemented based on decision models such as POMDP (Partially Observable Markov Decision Process model) [55], BDI (Belief-Desire-Intention) [15, 48], or a combination of both [41].

Another characteristic of an individual agent is its reactive behavior (see, e.g., [40]). The implementation of reactive agents requires an event handling mechanism that generates reactions to the received events. There are many types of events such as messages that are received from other agents, information that are originated from the external environment, and information about the internal working of agents. It should be noted that there is an essential difference between events and goals. In principle, an event causes the generation of a plan and, as soon as the plan is generated, the event is deleted and considered as being processed. Goals are similar to events in the sense that they cause the generation of plans. However, and in contrast to events, goals are not dropped after they have caused plans to be generated. An achieve goal is, for example, dropped if the state denoted by it is achieved, i.e., if the agent believes that the state denoted by the goal is achieved. It should also be noted that autonomy and reactive behavior are two different characteristics such that agents can be both autonomous and reactive, be autonomous without being reactive, or vice versa.

Finally, individual agents should be able to cope with plan execution failures since they generate and execute plans in uncertain environments or because the agents' state may change between the time a plan is generated and the time the plan is executed. The implementation of individual agents with such capability requires programming constructs to implement plan repair mechanisms. This includes constructs to identify failed plans and constructs to indicate how failed plans should be repaired. A particular difficulty for such a mechanism is that the execution of a plan may fail at different execution steps such that the reparation procedure depends on the exact step in the plan execution where failure has occurred. In general, the reparation procedure should be simple and intuitive, but at the same time expressive enough to specify how a plan should be repaired if it fails at different execution steps.

2.2 Multi-agent Environment

In many multi-agent system applications, individual software agents have to interact with an environment consisting of shared resources or services. An environment is often implemented as an external software component. The state of the software component is considered as the state of the environment while the methods that allow the interaction with the software component are used to implement the effect of the actions that agents can perform in the environment. In fact, the repertoire of the actions that an agent can perform in an environment is determined by the methods of the corresponding software component.

The concept of environment was originally used with different meanings [44, 59]. Some researchers considered multi-agent system environments as runtime environments and equivalent to infrastructures such as message transport system and other infrastructural tools, for example, brokers and management tools. Other researchers considered multi-agent system environments as encapsulating resources, services, and objects. It should be emphasized that the concept of multi-agent system environment as used in this chapter is also different from agent-based simulation environment. An agent-based simulation environment can be used to model, execute, and analyse agent-based simulations. An agent-based simulation environment can be compared with an integrated development environment for multi-agent systems. In particular, agent-based simulation environments can be seen as special cases of integrated development environments where the focus is on tools for analyzing simulation behaviors rather than general purpose tools for the development of multi-agent systems.

A multi-agent system environment can also be used for various other purposes, for example to coordinate agents' interactions by means of exchanging information through it (i.e., using environment as a shared space such as in blackboard architectures and tuple spaces),[1] or to provide agents the sense and act abilities in order to observe and modify the state of the environment, respectively (see e.g., [44, 59]). In particular, an environment can provide artifacts or services to allow agents to manage their coordination or to exchange information. An environment can also provide various sense and act modalities such as blocking and non-blocking sense operations, event broadcasting, event subscription mechanisms, and synchronous or asynchronous actions.

The implementation of environments therefore requires dedicated programming languages and development frameworks that allow direct and effective implementations of related concepts and abstractions such as resources, services, and objects. Like the development in agent-oriented programming languages, one may expect typical architectures for multi-agent environments. Such architectures would suggest specific concepts, concerns, or components that often need to be implemented when developing a multi-agent system environment. In particular, a dedicated environment programming language or development framework should provide programming constructs to implement resources, services, artifacts, processes, and several sense and action types. In this sense, one can consider the A&A model (see, e.g., [42]) as a generic approach for modelling environments. In the A&A model, an application is composed of agents and a dynamic set of so-called artifacts each of which encapsulates resources, services, or objects designed by the environment developer.

[1] In contrast to direct communication by means of send and receive messages, a shared environment can be used to communicate indirectly by reading and writing information from/to it.

2.3 Multi-agent Organization

The overall behavior of multi-agent systems depend on the behavior of individual agents, which pursue their own objectives. The overall multi-agent system objectives, which may be different or even conflicting with individual agents' objectives, can be ensured by controlling and coordinating the behaviors and the interactions of individual agents. There have been various proposals for regulating and organising the behaviors of individual agents. Some of these proposals advocate the use of coordination artifacts that are specified in terms of low-level coordination concepts such as synchronization (see, e.g., [2]). Other approaches are motivated by organizational models, normative systems, or electronic institutions (e.g., [19,25,26,31,34,37]). In these approaches, the behaviors of individual agents are regulated by means of norms and organization concepts that are either used by individual agents to decide how to behave, or being enforced or regimented by an exogenous organization component. A plethora of social and organizational concepts (e.g., roles, groups, social structures, organizations, institutions, norms) has been introduced in multi-agent system methodologies such as Gaia [62], models such as OperA [23], specification and modelling languages such as S-MOISE+ [35], platforms such as ISLANDER [25], and computational frameworks such as AMELI [26].

The implementation of organizations requires programming constructs to implement social/organizational concepts and mechanisms such as roles, role enactment/deactment [20], norms, policies, regulations, and enforcement. Such constructs may allow multi-agent programmers to either endogenously or exogenously coordinate the behaviors of individual agents. In an endogenous approach, the programming constructs allow the implementation of agents that make their decisions not only based on their individual goals and beliefs, but also based on the existing interaction protocols, norms, regulations, and other organizational rules. However, in an exogenous approach, an organization is implemented as an external software component that monitors the behaviors of individual agents, evaluate their behaviors, and intervene when needed. As the internals of individual agents are generally assumed not to be externally accessible, their external behaviors (i.e., communication and interaction with the environment) remain the only observable and controllable entities [22]. An exogenous organization component can thus observe agents' external behaviors, evaluate them based on a given organization specification, and take necessary measures as specified by the given organization specification. For example, if the organization specification disallows certain agents to interact, then the organization component should be able to block (or respond to) such interactions. This suggests that the agents' actions (e.g., communication, environment actions including sense actions) should be processed and managed through the organization component, that is, the organization component intermediates the interaction between agents as well as the interaction between agents and environments. This implies that an organization component can access and control environment and the message transport system at runtime.

3 Programming Individual Agents

In this section, we use the term agent-oriented programming language to denote programming languages that are developed to support the implementation of individual agents. One of the earliest agent-oriented programming languages is `AGENT-0` proposed in [53]. In his seminal paper, Shoham proposes to implement agents in terms of mental components such as beliefs, commitments, capabilities and actions. An agent program in `AGENT-0` consists of an initial belief base, a set of capabilities, a set of commitment rules, together with a repertoire of private actions. Agents can perform different types of actions such as communication, private, conditional and unconditional actions. Agents enter into new commitments by means of commitment rules. A commitment rule consists of conditions on an agent's mental state and the incoming messages. The application of a commitment rule generates a commitment consisting of an action together with the agent identifier towards whom the commitment is made. In fact, the commitments define the actions that an agent have to perform. The execution of an agent is a continuous cyclic process. At each cycle, the received messages are processed, commitments are generated, and actions are performed. `AGENT-0` is undoubtedly one of the first attempts to develop an agent programming language that supports the implementation of autonomous agents, i.e., agents that decide actions based on their mental states. However, as indicated in the discussion section of this seminal paper, the state of an `AGENT-0` agent lacks motivational attitudes such as utility, desires, goals, or preferences such that an agent's decisions are based only on events and messages rather than the agent's motivational attitude.

Since the introduction of `AGENT-0` various agent-oriented programming languages have been proposed that extend `AGENT-0` with a larger repertoire of agent concepts and abstractions. The aim of these programming languages is to support the implementation of multi-agent systems, although most of them focus on the implementation of individual agent abstractions. Some of these agent-oriented programming languages have an imperative programming style, some languages have a declarative programming style, and yet others combine both styles.

3.1 Imperative-Style Programming Frameworks

In this subsection, some typical imperative-style agent-oriented programming frameworks are presented. The programming framework Jade (Java Agent DEvelopment framework) [7] is based on Java programming language and extends Java with a set of agent concepts and abstractions. An agent is created by extending the predefined Jade agent class and redefining its `setup` method. After an agent is created, it will receive an identifier and is registered with the agent management system (a Jade built-in service). The agent is then put in the active state and its `setup` method is executed. The `setup` method is therefore the point where any agent activity should start. Jade agents are behavior-based in the sense that they can create and execute behaviors. A behavior can be created by extending the Jade behavior class via a special construct that adds behaviors (initially in the `setup` method). The created behaviors are added to a behavior pool. Behaviors are selected for execution from this pool based on a scheduler that constitutes the execution model of the Jade agents. Agents are executed concurrently as different pre-emptive Java threads. The Jade framework is developed for practical and industrial applications and comes with a development environment providing a set of graphical tools that can be used to monitor and log the execution of multi-agent programs. The Jade execution platform is based on a middleware that facilitates the development of distributed multi-agent applications based on a peer-to-peer communication architecture. The platform is distributed in the sense that it can run over multiple machines while seen as a whole from the outside world. The Jade platform implements the basic services and infrastructure of a distributed multi-agent application. It supports agent life-cycle, agent mobility, and agent security, and provides services such as white and yellow-pages that can be used by the agents to register their services and search for each other.

In contrast to the behavior-based Jade, other imperative-style agent-oriented programming frameworks are based on the BDI abstractions. Jadex [45] builds on Jade and extend it with programming constructs to implement BDI concepts such as beliefs, goals, plans, and events. It uses XML notation to define and declare an agent's BDI ingredients and Java constructs to implement the agent's plans. Yet another imperative-style BDI-based agent-oriented programming framework is JACK [60]. This framework extends Java with programming constructs to implement BDI concepts. In both JACK and Jadex a number of syntactic constructs are added to Java to allow programmers to declare beliefsets, to post events, and to select and execute plans. The execution of agent programs in both languages are motivated by the classical sense-reason-act cycle, i.e., processing events, selecting relevant and applicable plans, and execute applicable plans. Beliefs and goals in JACK and Jadex have no logical semantics such that an agent cannot logically reason about its beliefs and goals. A consequence of this is that JACK or Jadex agents cannot achieve their goals gradually in terms of subgoals. Moreover, the consistency as well as the rational balance of an agent's state in both JACK and Jadex, as far as they are defined, is left to the agent programmer, i.e., the agent programmer is responsible to ensure that state updates preserve the state consistency and that the rational balance (e.g., between beliefs and goals) is maintained. In these programming languages, an agent's goal is not automatically dropped because it is entailed by the agent's beliefs. Finally, Jadex provides a programming construct to implement non-interleaving execution of plans. Jadex and JACK come also with integrated development environments and provide monitoring and logging facilities, similar to those proposed in the Jade framework.

3.2 Declarative-Style Programming Frameworks

There are many proposals for declarative-style agent-oriented programming languages and frameworks. One reason for this is probably the easy modelling of an agent's reasoning. This subsection describes some of these programming languages and frameworks.

KGP (Knowledge, Goals, and Plans) [13, 38, 50] is a declarative-style programming framework characterized by a set of modules. The framework is based on computational logic and logic programming techniques. It has an internal state module consisting of a collection of knowledge bases, the current agent's goals and plans. The knowledge bases represent different types of knowledge such as the agent's knowledge about observed facts, actions, and communication, but also knowledge to be used for planning, goal decision, reactive behavior, and temporal reasoning. KGP includes also a module consisting of a set of capabilities such as planning, reactivity, temporal reasoning, and reasoning about goals. These capabilities are specified by means of abductive logic programming or logic programming with priorities. Another KGP module contains a set of transitions to change the agent's internal state. Each transition performs one or more capabilities, which in turn use different knowledge bases to determine the next state of the agent. Finally, KGP has a module, called cyclic theory, that determines which transition should be performed at each moment of time.

Minerva [39] aims at specifying an agent's state and its dynamics. A Minerva agent consists of a set of specialized sub-agents manipulating a common knowledge base, where subagents (i.e., planner, scheduler, learner, etc.) evaluate and manipulate the knowledge base. These subagents are assumed to be implemented in arbitrary programming languages. Minerva gives both declarative and operational semantics to agents allowing the internal state of the agent, represented by logic programs, to modify. Minerva is based on multidimensional dynamic logic programming and uses explicit rules for modifying its knowledge bases.

The family of Golog languages, as presented in [29, 51], propose high-level program execution as an alternative for controlling the behavior of agents that operate in dynamic environments with partial observation. In fact, the high-level (agent) program consists of a set of actions, including the sense action (e.g., IndiGolog [51]), composed by means of conditionals, iteration, recursion, concurrency and non-deterministic operators. Instead of finding a sequence of actions to achieve a desired state from an initial state, the problem is to find a sequence of actions that constitute a legal execution of the high-level program. When there is no non-determinism in the agent program, then the problem is straightforward as the agent program determines one sequence of actions. However, on the other extreme, when the agent program consists of actions that are merely composed by non-deterministic operators, then the problem becomes identical to the planning problem.

Concurrent MetateM [27] is based on the direct execution of an extension of propositional temporal logic specifications. A multi-agent system in Concurrent

MetateM consists of a set of concurrently executing agents with the ability to communicate asynchronously. Each agent is programmed by means of a temporal logic specification of the behavior that the agent have to generate. In particular, it consists of rules that can be fired when their antecedents are satisfied with respect to the execution history. The consequent of a fired rule, which can be a temporal formula, forms the commitment of the agent that needs to be satisfied. The execution of an agents builds iteratively a logical model for the temporal agent specification. In Concurrent MetateM, the beliefs of agents are propositions extended with modal belief operators (allowing agents to reason about each others' beliefs), goals are temporal eventualities, and plans are primitive actions.

CLAIM [52] is a declarative multi-agent programming language focusing on mobile agents. It comes with a distributed platform called SyMPA that enables the execution of multi-agent programs. A multi-agent system in CLAIM is a set of hierarchies of agents distributed over a network. An agent in CLAIM can be a sub-agent of another one such that the hierarchies determine the parent–child relation between agents. Agents in CLAIM are BDI-based and can be programmed in terms of knowledge, goals, capabilities, messages, parent and children. Agents can migrate within a hierarchy as well as between hierarchies by means of the move-operation. The migration of agents in CLAIM is a strong migration, i.e., the state of the agent just before the migration is saved, encrypted, and transferred to the destination. At the destination, the agent's state is restored and processes are resumed from their interruption point.

3.3 Hybrid-Style Programming Frameworks

While imperative-style programming constructs are powerful means to implement an agent's procedural issues such as an agent's actions and plans, declarative-style programming constructs support the implementation of an agent's reasoning and decision making mechanism. This subsection describes some hybrid agent programming frameworks that combine both imperative and declarative programming styles.

3APL (An Abstract Agent Programming Language), as originally proposed by [33], assumes an agent as having a state consisting of declarative beliefs and plans. Plans comprises belief update, test, and abstract actions composed by sequence and conditional choice and iteration operators. This initial version of 3APL provides only plan revision rules that are applied to revise an agent's plan. The execution of a 3APL agent program is a cyclic process. At each cycle, a plan revision rule is selected and applied after which a plan from the plan base is selected and executed. The execution of a plan modifies the belief base of the agent program. This original version of 3APL was an abstract programming language which lacked a development and execution platform. This version is extended in [21] with declarative goals and a variety of action types and reasoning rules. Also, an execution platform is developed for the extended version of 3APL.

2APL (A Practical Agent Programming Language) [16] is developed to implement multi-agent systems. It provides two sets of programming constructs to implement multi-agent and individual agent concepts. The multi-agent programming constructs are provided to create individual agents, external environments, and to specify the agents' access to the external environments. In 2APL, an environment is implemented as a Java object having a state and providing a set of methods which model the actions that can be performed in the environment. Individual agents that interact with the environment can execute actions (by calling the methods of the Java object) in order to change the state of the environment. At the individual agent level, 2APL agents are implemented in terms of beliefs, goals, actions, plans, events, and three different types of reasoning rules. The beliefs and goals of 2APL agents are implemented in a declarative way, while plans and (interfaces to) external environments are implemented in an imperative style. The declarative part of the programming language supports the implementation of an agent's reasoning task and the update of its mental state. The imperative part of the programming language facilitates the implementation of plans, control flow, and mechanisms such as procedure call, recursion, and interfacing with legacy codes. 2APL agents can perform different types of actions such as belief update actions, belief and goal test actions, external actions (including sense actions), actions to manage the dynamics of goals, and communication actions. Three types of reasoning rules are used to generate plans. The first type of rules is designed to generate plans to achieve goals, the second type of rules generates plans to process (internal and external) events and messages, and the third type of rules generate plans to replace the failed plans. Finally, 2APL comes with a development environment with tools to log and monitor the execution of multi-agent programs. These tools are similar as those provided by the Jade framework.

GOAL [32] is a BDI-based programming language developed to implement individual agents with declarative goals. It provides programming constructs to implement an agent's knowledge, beliefs and goals declaratively. It also provides programming constructs to implement action selection rules that can be used to select actions based on the agent's current knowledge, beliefs and goals. A characteristic feature of GOAL is the distinction between knowledge and beliefs. Knowledge represents an agent's general information that are not the subject of modification, for example the agent's domain knowledge, while beliefs represents an agent's current information that can be modified during the agent execution, for example by sensing the environment or performing mental actions. Another characteristic feature of GOAL is the absence of plans. The action selection rules generate only atomic actions when they are applied. GOAL provides different types of actions such as user defined actions, built-in actions, and the communication actions. The execution of a GOAL agent is a cyclic process where at each cycle the agent senses the environment, applies action selection rules, and performs the generated actions. The development environment of GOAL can be used to log and monitor the execution of multi-agent programs.

Jason [12] is introduced as an interpreter of an extension of AgentSpeak, which is originally proposed by [47]. Jason distinguishes multi-agent system concerns from individual agent concerns, though it does not allow the specification of agents' access to external environments. An individual agent in Jason is characterized by its beliefs, plans and the events that are either received from the environment or generated internally. A plan in Jason is designed for a specific event and belief context. The execution of individual agents in Jason is controlled by means of a cycle of operations encoded in its operational semantics. In each cycle, events from the environment are collected, an event is selected, a plan is generated for the selected event and added to the intention base, and finally a plan is selected from the intention base and executed. A plan rule in Jason indicates that a plan should be generated by an agent if an event is received/generated and the agent has certain beliefs. Jason has no explicit programming construct to implement declarative goals, though goals can indirectly be simulated by means of a pattern of plans. Moreover, the beliefs and plans in Jason can be annotated with additional information that can be used in belief queries and plan selection process. Finally, plan failure in Jason can be modelled by means of plans that react to the so-called deletion events. The development environment of Jason provides tools to log and monitor the execution of multi-agent programs.

IMPACT [24] is a project that aims at developing a multi-agent system platform. This project is based on the idea of agentisation, that is, agents are built around given legacy code. The multi-agent system platform comes with a programming language and its formal semantics. An agent is built around a legacy code by abstracting from the legacy code and describing its main features. In particular, an agent is specified in terms of the set of all datatypes managed by the legacy code, a set of functions over the datatypes allowing external processes to access the datatypes, and a set of composition operators that are defined on the datatypes and generate new composed datatypes. The state of an agent is determined by the state of the data in terms of which the agent is defined. Each agent has a set of actions that it can perform in its environment. An action can have different status such as permitted, obliged, or forbidden. The execution of an agent follows a cycle where messages from other agents are processed (which may in turn change the data and thus its state), the status of each action is determined, the actions that can be executed are determined, and the state is updated accordingly.

4 Programming Multi-agent Organizations

The behavior of individual agents can be controlled and regulated by the so-called multi-agent organizations. There have been many proposals for specification languages and logics to specify and reason about multi-agent organizations (see, e.g., [1, 9, 37, 46]). How to develop, program, and execute such organizations was one of the central themes that were discussed and promoted during the AgentLink technical fora on programming multi-agent systems (see [17, 18] for the general report of these technical fora). In this section, we discuss some proposals for specifying and programming multi-agent organizations.

One of the early frameworks for multi-agent organizations and institutions is ISLANDER [25]. This framework specifies multi-agent organizations and institutions in terms of organizational rules and norms. In order to interpret such specifications and execute them, an execution platform, called AMELI , has been developed by [26]. This platform implements an infrastructure that, on the one hand, facilitates agent participation within the institutional environment and supports their communication and, on the other hand, enforces the institutional rules and norms as specified in the organizational specification. The key aspect of ISLANDER/AMELI is that norms can never be violated by the agents. In other words, systems programmed via ISLANDER/AMELI make only use of regimentation in order to guarantee that norms are actually followed. The norms in [26, 28, 54] are related to actions that the agents should or should not perform. In these approaches the issue of expressing more high-level norms concerning a state of the system that should be brought about is ignored. Such high-level norms can be used to represent *what* the agents should establish—in terms of a declarative description of a system state—rather than specifying *how* they should establish it.

Another approach concerning specification of multi-agent organizations by means of social and organizational concepts is $\mathscr{M}$OISE$^+$ [36]. This modelling language can be used to specify multi-agent systems through three organizational dimensions: structural (e.g., specifying roles, groups, and links within organizations, subgroup relation, number of agents that can play a role), functional (e.g., goals, missions, and social schemes specifying structured sets of goals), and deontic (e.g., norms, obligations, and prohibitions within organizations). In a series of papers, different computational frameworks have been proposed to implement and execute $\mathscr{M}$OISE$^+$ specifications. Examples of such frameworks are $\mathscr{S}$-$\mathscr{M}$OISE$^+$ [35] and its artifact-based version ORG4MAS [34]. These frameworks are concerned with norms that are about declarative descriptions of a state that should be achieved. $\mathscr{S}$-$\mathscr{M}$OISE$^+$ is an organizational middleware that provides agents access to the communication layer and the current state of the organization specified in $\mathscr{M}$OISE$^+$. This middleware allows agents to change the organization and its specification, as long as such changes do not violate organizational constraints. In the artifact version of this framework, ORG4MAS, various organizational artifacts are used to implement specific components of an organization such as group and goal schema. In this framework, a special artifact, called reputation artifact, is introduced to manage the enforcement of the norms.

It should be noted that AMELI and $\mathscr{S}$-$\mathscr{M}$OISE$^+$ lack a complete operational semantics. An explicit formal and operational treatment of organizational concepts and operations such as norm enforcement is essential for a thorough understanding and analysis of computational frameworks of multi-agent systems. Also, the computational frameworks related to $\mathscr{M}$OISE$^+$ are not grounded in a logical system such that the soundness and properties of the programmed systems cannot be analysed through formal verification mechanisms. One of the main contributions of ISLANDER/AMELI and $\mathscr{M}$OISE$^+$/$\mathscr{S}$-$\mathscr{M}$OISE$^+$ is the variety of social and organizational concepts that they have proposed to specify and implement multi-agent organizations.

powerJava [5] and powerJade [1] are developed to implement institutions in terms of roles. While powerJava extends Java with programming constructs to implement institutions, powerJade proposes similar extensions to the Jade framework. In these frameworks, an institution is considered as an exogenous coordination mechanism that manages the interactions between participating computational entities (objects in powerJava and agents in powerJade) by means of roles. A role is defined in the context of an institution (e.g., a student role is defined in the context of a school) and encapsulates capabilities, also called powers, that its players can use to interact with the institution and with other roles in the institution (e.g., a student can participate in an exam). For an object or an agent to play a role in an institution to gain specific abilities, they should satisfy specific requirements. In powerJava roles and organizations are implemented as Java classes. In particular, a role within an institution is implemented as an inner class of the class that implements the organization. Moreover, the powers that a player of a role gains and the requirements that the player of the role should satisfy are implemented as methods of the class that implements the role. In powerJade, organizations, roles and players are implemented as subclasses of the Jade agent class. The powers that the player of a role gains and the requirements that a player of a role should satisfy are implemented as Jade behaviors (associated to the role).

A recent programming language that is developed to support the implementation of multi-agent organizations is 2OPL (Organization Oriented Programming) [19, 58]. This is a rule-based programming language that facilitates the implementation of norm-based organizations. In this approach, an organization is considered as a software entity that exogenously coordinates the interaction between agents and their shared environment. In particular, the organization is a software entity that manages the interaction between the agents themselves and between agents and their environment. 2OPL provides programming constructs to specify (1) the initial state of an organization, (2) the effects of agents' actions in the shared environment, and (3) the applicable norms and regulations. In 2OPL norms can be either enforced by means of regulations or regimented. In the first case, agents are allowed to violate norms after which sanctions or rewards are imposed. In the second case, norms are considered as constraints that cannot be violated. The enforcement of norms by means of regulations (imposing sanctions or rewards) is a way to guarantee higher autonomy for agents and higher flexibility for multi-agent systems. The interpreter of 2OPL is based on a cyclic control process. At each cycle, the observable actions of the individual agents (i.e., communication and environment actions) are monitored, the effects of the actions are determined, and norms are enforced by means regulation policies. An advantage of 2OPL approach is its complete operational semantics such that normative organization programs can be formally analysed by means of verification techniques (see, e.g., [3]). This organization-oriented programming language is extended with programming constructs that support the implementation of concepts such as obligation, permission, prohibition, deadline, norm change, and conditional norm (see [56–58]).

5 Programming Multi-agent Environments

In contrast to the variety of programming languages and frameworks that are proposed to facilitate the implementation of individual agents and their organizations, there are only few programming proposals to support the development of agents' environments.

A framework for the development of multi-agent environments is Cartago (Common artifact infrastructure for agent open environment) [49]. This framework is based on the A&A model which proposes a working environment to be used by agents for supporting their activities. A working environment is considered as consisting of a set of artifacts organized in workspaces (containers of artifacts). The artifacts are meant to encapsulate specific functionalities and can be added, removed, and organized in the workspaces by agents at runtime. Artifacts can be used by agents through their usage interfaces. They allow agents to trigger and control the execution of artifacts' operations and to perceive events from the artifacts. Different operations are supported by artifact interfaces. An agent can for example create, remove, or search for artifacts and workspaces. Agents can also execute operations of artifacts, e.g., sense the events generated by the artifacts or inspect the artifacts by retrieving their descriptions. This framework can be distributed in the sense that a working environment can consist of one or more workspaces that can be mapped onto different nodes of a network. Cartago is implemented in Java and has been connected to various agent executions platforms such as the execution platforms for 2APL and Jason.

Beside this generic framework for the development of multi-agent environments, there have been many interesting environments implemented using existing programming languages such as Java or C++. These environments are initially developed in an ad-hoc manner either for an existing agent platform (e.g., the platforms for 2APL, GOAL, Jadex, and Jason) or as a simulation environment. The availability of these implemented environments raises the question how they can be (re)used and applied to arbitrary agent platforms. In practice, agent developers rebuild similar environments from scratch. Apart from this duplicating works, the interaction between agents and environments are managed in an ad-hoc manner making the reuse of the environments a dedicated task that depends on the specific agent platform and the environment at hand. This problem has lead to an initiative for creating a generic environment interface which provides the required functionalities for connecting agents to environments (see, e.g., [6]). This initiative wants to become a de-facto standard and it is already supported by the 2APL, Jason, and GOAL platforms. If environments were developed using such a standard, they could be exchanged freely between agent platforms that support the standard and thus would make already existing environments widely available. In order to develop a generic environment interface standard various issues should be addressed. An important issue is the right level of abstraction for modelling the interaction between agents and environments. This generic environment interface standard supports the interaction between agents and environment in two ways. On the one hand, agents can perform actions, including sense action, in the environment (the environment is assumed to realize the effect of the actions). On the other hand, the environment can send events to individual agents. This interface provides constructs to establish and manage the relation between agents with entities (agent bodies) in the environment, the registration of agents by the interface, adding and removing entities from the environment, and performing actions and retrieving percepts from the environment.

6 Conclusion

This chapter surveyed the multi-agent programming research field by discussing some existing multi-agent programming languages and frameworks. The presented languages and frameworks differ from each other in the set of abstractions, programming constructs, and principles they convey. Although these programming languages and frameworks are evolving towards a certain level of maturity in the sense that their programming concepts and operations are well motivated and have profound semantics, a majority of them are still not being employed for the development of large-scale industrial applications. Currently, these programming languages and frameworks, in particular those that are based on cognitive and social constructs, are mainly considered as research works that aim at designing and prototyping high-level multi-agent abstractions.

The main focus of multi-agent programming community has been on the development of programming languages and development frameworks for individual agents. Although research on (formal) models for multi-agent organizations and environments has relatively a long history, the emergence of programming languages and development frameworks for supporting their implementations is a recent phenomenon. The evolution of programming languages and development frameworks for individual agents show a convergence in the sense that they propose programming constructs for an established set of concepts and abstractions. These languages and frameworks differ from each other as they use different programming styles (declarative, imperative, or both), support different programming principles such as modularity, abstraction, recursion, exception handling, support for legacy code, and as their corresponding integrated development environments provide different sets of functionalities such as editing, debugging, and automatic generation of codes.

One of the current challenges in multi-agent programming research field is the integration of programming languages and development frameworks for individual agents, multi-agent organizations and multi-agent environments. Although there have been several attempts to integrate specific programming languages, the ultimate goal is a mechanism to facilitate the integration of arbitrary programming languages and development frameworks for individual agents, multi-agent organizations, and multi-agent environments. A possible solution to realize such a goal is to develop standard interfaces that can manage the interactions between individual agent programs, multi-agent organization programs, and multi-agent environment programs. There have already been some initiatives to establish standard interfaces for managing the interaction of individual agent programs and environment programs, but the research in this direction is still in a preliminary phase and needs support and collaboration from the community.

Another issue currently challenging the multi-agent programming community is the debugging and testing of multi-agent programs. There is a need for powerful debugging facilities and testing tools that can cope with the distributed nature of multi-agent systems, the autonomy of individual agents, and the interactions between individual agent, multi-agent organization, and multi-agent environment programs. There have been some initial attempts for enriching debugging tools with expressive specification languages such that tools can be initialized and activated when the execution of multi-agent programs satisfy certain properties, but these approaches are mainly concerned with debugging individual agents and have ignored multi-agent organization and environment programs.

There are still many issues related to multi-agent programming that need to be investigated. Among these issues are mechanisms to deal with plan failure, goal types, reasoning about organizations and environments from an agent's point of view, the integration of concepts such as sensing, planning, acting, learning and emotions in the agent's deliberation process, the adaptivity of organization and environment based on the executions of individual agent programs, and formal verification of multi-agent programs.

The observation that the proposed multi-agent programming languages and development frameworks have not been adopted by the industry may sound disappointing, in particular because technology transfer was identified as a main challenge and a milestone for the multi-agent programming community. There are various reasons for why these programming languages and frameworks fell short of expectations [18]. First of all, the adoption of new technologies by the industry is generally assumed to be a slow process as the industry often tends to be conservative, employing known and proven technologies. Moreover, industry adopts new technologies when they can be integrated in their existing technologies, and more importantly, when they reduce their production costs, which is in this case the costs of the software development process. Finally, the industry tends to see the contribution of multi-agent programming community as AI technology. Main problems with such technologies are thought to be their theoretical purpose, scalability, and performance.

One possible approach to stimulate technology transfer is by integrating the contribution of multi-agent programming community in the technologies that are already adopted by the industry. The fact that object-oriented programming languages and development frameworks have already found their ways to the industry together with the claim that multi-agent systems provide solutions to reoccurring problems in large-scale distributed applications make it plausible to propose multi-agent programming techniques and technologies as design patterns in object-oriented technologies. The starting point for this approach is to identify high-level multi-agent concepts and abstractions for which programming constructs have been developed. The identified concepts and abstractions together with their developed programming proposals can then be used to introduce corresponding design patterns in the standard object-oriented technology.

As explained earlier in this chapter, multi-agent concepts and abstractions are defined with respect to individual agents, multi-agent organizations and multi-agent environments. For example, individual agents are conceived as being pro-active (i.e., agents behave to achieve their objectives), reactive (i.e., agents behave to respond to their received events), or autonomic (i.e., agents behave to recover their failures). These characteristic behaviors of individual agents, which are introduced to meet reoccurring challenges in the design and development of software systems, can be presented as behavioral patterns in object-oriented technology. This vision suggests having objects which can be fed with various plan libraries to achieve objectives, to respond to events, or to repair failures. At the level of multi-agent organization, the provided concepts and abstractions can be used to introduce design patterns to cope with coordination and regulation challenges involved in distributed software systems. These software systems often require mechanisms to monitor and regulate the execution behavior of software components. Such mechanisms can be introduced using existing technologies such as aspect-oriented programming, which allows monitoring specific aspects or crosscutting concerns in software components, and intervening by means of advices when irregularities are observed. The monitor and regulation mechanisms can be presented as design patterns in object-oriented technology too. The introduction of aspects and advices may suggest to separate the organization concerns from individual agent concerns. Finally, concepts and abstraction that are related to multi-agent environments can also be used to introduce design patterns for modelling multi-agent environments in object-oriented frameworks. Examples of such concepts and abstractions are various types of actions (including sense actions), resources, and services. It should be emphasized that the existing practice to design an agent's environment as an object having a state and methods to change the state (as described earlier in this chapter) can be considered as a design pattern. Such a design pattern can be refined to accommodate related concepts such as various types of actions, resources, and services.

References

1. Ågotnes T, van der Hoek W, Wooldridge M (2008) Robust normative systems. In: Padgham P, Muller P (eds) Proceedings of the seventh international conference on autonomous agents and multiagent systems (AAMAS 2008). IFAMAAS/ACM DL, Estoril, pp 747–754
2. Arbab F, Astefanoaei L, de Boer F, Dastani M, Meyer JJ, Tinnermeier N (2009) Reo connectors as coordination artifacts in 2APL systems. In: Proceedings of the 11th pacific rim international conference on multi-agents (PRIMA 2008). Lecture notes in computer science, vol 5357. Springer, New York, pp 42–53
3. Astefanoaei L, Dastani M, Meyer JJC, Boer F (2009) On the semantics and verification of normative multi-agent systems. Int J Universal Comput Sci 15(13):2629–2652

4. Baldoni M, Boella G, Dorni M, Grenna R, Mugnaini A (2008) PowerJADE: organizations and roles as primitives in the JADE framework. In: WOA 2008: Dagli oggetti agli agenti, Evoluzione dell'agent development: metodologie, tool, piattaforme e linguaggi, pp 84–92
5. Baldoni M, Boella G, Torre LVD (2005) Roles as a coordination construct: introducing powerJava. In: Proceedings of 1st international workshop on methods and tools for coordinating concurrent, distributed and mobile systems, Namur, 23 April 2005. Electron Notes Theor Comp Sci 150(1):9–29
6. Behrens T, Dix J, Hindriks K, Dastani M, Bordini R, Hubner J, Pokahr A, Braubach L (2012) An interface for agent-environment interaction. In: Proceedings of the eighth international workshop on programming multi-agent systems (ProMAS'10). Springer, Berlin, pp 139–158
7. Bellifemine F, Bergenti F, Caire G, Poggi A (2005) JADE - a java agent development framework. In: Multi-agent programming: languages, platforms and applications. Springer, Berlin, pp 125–148
8. Bergenti F, Gleizes MP, Zambonelli F (eds) (2004) Methodologies and software engineering for agent systems. In: Multiagent systems, artificial societies, and simulated organizations, vol 11. Kluwer Academic, Dordrecht
9. Boella G, van der Torre L (2008) Substantive and procedural norms in normative multiagent systems. J Appl Logic 6:152–171
10. Bordini RH, Dastani M, Dix J, Fallah-Seghrouchni AE (eds) (2005) Multi-agent programming: languages, platforms and applications, multiagent systems, artificial societies, and simulated organizations, vol 15. Springer, Berlin
11. Bordini RH, Dastani M, Dix J, Fallah-Seghrouchni AE (eds) (2009) Multi-agent programming: languages, tools and applications. Springer, Heidelberg
12. Bordini R, Hübner J, Wooldridge M (2007) Programming multi-agent systems in AgentSpeak using Jason. Wiley series in agent technology. Wiley, Hoboken
13. Bracciali A, Demetriou N, Endriss U, Kakas A, Lu W, Sadri PMF, Stathis K, Terreni G, Toni F (2004) The KGP model of agency for global computing: computational model and prototype implementation. In: Global computing. Lecture notes in computer science, vol 3267. Springer, New York, pp 340–367
14. Bresciani P, Giorgini P, Giunchiglia F, Mylopoulos J, Perini A (2003) TROPOS: an agent-oriented software development methodology. Int J Auton Agents Multi-Agent Syst 8(3):203–236
15. Cohen P, Levesque H (1990) Intention is choice with commitment. Artif Intell 42:213–261
16. Dastani M (2008) 2APL: a practical agent programming language. Int J Auton Agents Multi-Agent Syst 16(3):214–248
17. Dastani M, Gomez-Sanz J (2004). AgentLink III technical forum group, programming multiagent systems. http://people.cs.uu.nl/mehdi/al3promas.html
18. Dastani M, Gomez-Sanz J (2006) Programming multi-agent systems. Knowl Eng Rev 20(2):151–164
19. Dastani M, Grossi D, Meyer JJC, Tinnemeier N (2009) Normative multi-agent programs and their logics. In: Post proceedings of the international workshop on knowledge representation for agents and multi-agent systems (KRAMAS'08). Lecture notes in artificial intelligence, vol 5605. Springer, Berlin, pp 16–31
20. Dastani M, van Riemsdijk B, Hulstijn J, Dignum F, Meyer JJC (2004) Enacting and deacting roles in agent programming. In: Proceedings of the agent-oriented software engineering (AOSE'04), pp 189–204
21. Dastani M, van Riemsdijk M, Meyer JJC (2005) Programming multi-agent systems in 3APL. In: Multi-agent programming: languages, platforms and applications. Springer, Berlin, pp 39–67
22. Dastani M, van der Torre L, Yorke-Smith N (2013) Monitoring interaction in organisations. In: Post-Proceedings of the fourteenth international workshop on coordination, organization, institutions and norms (COIN'12), Springer, Berlin, pp 17–34
23. Dignum V (2004) A model for organizational interaction. Ph.D. thesis, Utrecht University, SIKS

24. Dix J, Zhang Y (2005) IMPACT: a multi-agent framework with declarative semantics. In: Multi-agent programming: languages, platforms and applications. Springer, Berlin, pp 69–94
25. Esteva M, de la Cruz D, Sierra C (2002) ISLANDER: an electronic institutions editor. In: Proceedings of the first international joint conference on autonomous agents and multiagent systems (AAMAS 2002), Bologna, pp 1045–1052
26. Esteva M, Rodríguez-Aguilar J, Rosell B, Arcos J (2004) AMELI: an agent-based middleware for electronic institutions. In: Proceedings of the third international joint conference on autonomous agents and multiagent systems (AAMAS 2004), New York, pp 236–243
27. Fisher M (2006) METATEM: the story so far. In: Proceedings of the third international workshop on programming multi-agent systems (ProMAS'05). Lecture notes in artificial intelligence, vol 3862. Springer, Berlin, pp 3–22
28. Garcia-Camino A, Noriega P, Rodriguez-Aguilar JA (2005) Implementing norms in electronic institutions. In: Proceedings of the fourth international joint conference on Autonomous Agents and MultiAgent Systems (AAMAS'05), New York, pp 667–673
29. Giacomo GD, Lesperance Y, Levesque H (2000) Congolog, a concurrent programming language based on the situation calculus. Artif Intell 121(1–2):109–169
30. Gomez-Sanz J, Pavon J (2003) Agent oriented software engineering with ingenias. In: CEEMAS'03. Lecture notes in computer science, vol 2691. Springer, Berlin, pp 394–403
31. Grossi D (2007) Designing invisible handcuffs. Ph.D. thesis, Utrecht University, SIKS
32. Hindriks K (2009) Programming rational agents in GOAL. In: Multi-agent programming: languages and tools and applications. Springer, New York, pp 119–157
33. Hindriks K, Boer FD, der Hoek WV, Meyer JJ (1999) Agent programming in 3APL. Int J Auton Agents Multi-Agent Syst 2(4):357–401
34. Hübner J, Boissier O, Kitio R, Ricci A (2010) Instrumenting multi-agent organisations with organisational artifacts and agents: giving the organisational power back to the agents. Int J Auton Agents Multi-Agent Syst 20:369–400
35. Hübner J, Sichman J, Boissier O (2006) $\mathscr{S}-\mathscr{M}$OISE$^+$: a middleware for developing organised multi-agent systems. In: Proceedings of the international workshop on coordination, organizations, institutions, and norms in multi-agent systems. Lecture notes in computer science, vol 3913. Springer, Berlin, pp 64–78
36. Hübner J, Sichman J, Boissier O (2007) Developing organised multiagent systems using the $\mathscr{M}$OISE$^+$ model: programming issues at the system and agent levels. Int J Agent-Oriented Software Eng 1(3/4):370–395
37. Jones AJI, Sergot M (1993) On the characterization of law and computer systems. In: Meyer JJC, Wieringa R (eds) Deontic logic in computer science: normative system specification. Wiley, Chichester, pp 275–307
38. Kakas A, Mancarella P, Sadri F, Stathis K, Toni F (2004) The KGP model of agency. In: The 16th European Conference on Artificial Intelligence (ECAI'04), pp 33–37
39. Leite J, Alferes J, Pereira L (2001) Minerva: a dynamic logic programming agent architecture. In: Meyer JJ, Tambe M (eds) Pre-proceedings of the eighth international workshop on Agent Theories, Architectures, and Languages (ATAL-2001), pp 133–145
40. Müller J (1996) The design of autonomous agents: a layered approach. Lecture notes in artificial intelligence, vol 1177. Springer, New York
41. Nair R, Tambe M (2005) Hybrid BDI-POMDP framework for multiagent teaming. J Artif Intell Res 23:367–420
42. Omicini A (2007) Formal ReSpecT in the A&A perspective. Electronic Notes Theor Comput Sci 175(2):97–117
43. Padgham L, Winikoff M (2003) Prometheus: a methodology for developing intelligent agents. In: AOSE'02. Lecture notes in artificial intelligence, vol 2585. Springer, Berlin, pp 174–185
44. Parunak HVD, Weyns D (2007) Guest editors' introduction, special issue on environments for multi-agent systems. Int J Auton Agents Multi-Agent Syst 14(1):1–4
45. Pokahr A, Braubach L, Lamersdorf W (2005) Jadex: a BDI reasoning engine. In: Multi-agent programming: languages, platforms and applications. Springer, Berlin, pp 149–174
46. Prakken H, Sergot M (1996) Contrary-to-duty obligations. Studia Logica 57:91–115

47. Rao A (1996) AgentSpeak(L): BDI agents speak out in a logical computable language. In: van Hoe R (ed) Proceedings of the seventh European workshop on Modelling Autonomous Agents in a Multi-Agent World (MAAMAW'96), Eindhoven, pp 42–55
48. Rao A, Georgeff M (1991) Modeling rational agents within a BDI-architecture. In: Allen J, Fikes R, Sandewall E (eds) Proceedings of the second international conference on principles of knowledge representation and reasoning (KR'91), Morgan Kaufmann, San Francisco, pp 473–484
49. Ricci A, Viroli M, Omicini A (2006) Cartago: a framework for prototyping artifact-based environments in mas. In: E4MAS, pp 67–86
50. Sadri F (2006) Using the KGP model of agency to design applications. In: Proceedings of the 6th international conference on Computational Logic in Multi-Agent Systems (CLIMA'05), vol 3900. Springer, Berlin, pp 165–185
51. Sardina S, Giacomo GD, Lespérance Y, Levesque H (2004) On the semantics of deliberation in IndiGolog - from theory to implementation. Ann Math Artif Intell 41(2–4):259–299
52. Seghrouchni AEF, Suna A (2005) CLAIM and SyMPA: a programming environment for intelligent and mobile agents. In: Multi-agent programming: languages, platforms and applications. Springer, Berlin, pp 95–122
53. Shoham Y (1993) Agent-oriented programming. Artif Intell 60:51–92
54. Silva VT (2008) From the specification to the implementation of norms: an automatic approach to generate rules from norms to govern the behavior of agents. Int J Auton Agents Multiagent Syst 17 (1):113–155
55. Tasaki M, Yabu Y, Iwanari Y, Yokoo M, Tambe M, Marecki J, Varakantham P (2008) Introducing communication in Dis-POMDPs with locality of interaction. International conference on web intelligence and intelligent agent technology, IEEE/WIC/ACM, vol 2, pp 169–175
56. Tinnemeier N, Dastani M, Meyer JJC (2009) Roles and norms for programming agent organizations. In: Decker S, Sichman J, Sierra C, Castelfranchi C (eds) Proceedings of the eight international conference on autonomous agents and multiagent systems (AAMAS'09). IFAMAAS/ACM DL, pp 121–128
57. Tinnemeier N, Dastani M, Meyer JJC (2010) Programming norm change. In: van der Hoek W, Kaminka GA, Lespérance Y, Luck M, Sen S (eds) Proceedings of the ninth international conference on autonomous agents and multiagent systems (AAMAS'10). IFAAMAS, Richland, pp 957–964
58. Tinnemeier N, Dastani M, Meyer JJC, van der Torre L (2009) Programming normative artifacts with declarative obligations and prohibitions. In: Proceedings of IEEE/WIC/ACM international joint conference on web intelligence and intelligent agent technology. IEEE Computer Society, Los Alamitos, pp 145–152
59. Weyns D, Parunak HVD, Michel F, Holvoet T, Ferber J (eds) (2005) Environments for multiagent systems state-of-the-art and research challenges. Lecture notes in computer science, vol 3374. Springer, New York
60. Winikoff M (2005) JACK™ intelligent agents: an industrial strength platform. In: Multi-agent programming: languages, platforms and applications. Springer, Berlin, pp 175–196
61. Woolridge M (2002) Introduction to multiagent systems. Wiley, New york
62. Zambonelli F, Jennings N, Wooldridge M (2003) Developing multiagent systems: the Gaia methodology. ACM T Softw Eng Meth 12(3):317–370

Chapter 12
GOAL: A Multi-agent Programming Language Applied to an Exploration Game

Koen V. Hindriks and Jügen Dix

Abstract GOAL is a multi-agent programming language based on the BDI paradigm. It is a logic-based language that supports modular agent design based on established software engineering principles and interaction with environments using an environment interface standard (EIS). GOAL recently won the multi-agent programming contest (MAPC), where two teams consisting of ten agents play against each other in order to explore and defend occupied territory on a distant planet. The MAPC game is a complex and dynamic environment that supports EIS and thus facilitates easy connection of a multi-agent system (MAS) to an environment that is remotely run. We describe the design of the multi-agent solution that won the competition, the EIS interface that was used, and the MAPC scenario.

Keywords Agent programming • Environment interface • Multi-agent programming contest • Testing

1 Introduction

The aim of this chapter is not to describe *yet-another* agent programming language and claim that it is the best on the market. Developing good software for non-trivial applications using the agent paradigm is a highly complex task depending not only on the chosen programming language.

We strongly believe that documenting and discussing projects that use existing agent platforms for software development is useful for a number of reasons. Only

K.V. Hindriks
Delft University of Technology, Mekelweg 4, Delft, The Netherlands
e-mail: k.v.hindriks@tudelft.nl

J. Dix (✉)
Clausthal University of Technology, Julius-Albert-Str. 4, Clausthal-Zellerfeld, Germany
e-mail: dix@tu-clausthal.de

O. Shehory and A. Sturm (eds.), *Agent-Oriented Software Engineering*,
DOI 10.1007/978-3-642-54432-3_12,

by actually using such platforms can we learn about the effectiveness and usability of them as well as about the issues we are facing during such projects. Based upon findings related to the development process itself, comments by software developers, and facts derived from inspection of the agent software developed, insights may be gained in how agent technology is best applied and how the application of agent technology can be made more effective. We can learn new lessons from how software developers or programmers actually used the tools and technology at hand and the choices they made while doing so. We also gain more insight into the needs of agent programmers.

In this chapter, we present an example project that, given the current state of the art, represents one of the larger coding projects that used a *logic-based agent programming language* for developing multiple software agents that control non-player characters in a dynamic and real-time gaming environment. The language that was used is the agent programming language GOAL [8, 9, 16]. This agent platform supports an environment interface standard (EIS) [2]. The gaming environment that was used is the multi-agent programming contest (MAPC) made available for the 2011 contest. The MAPC game is what we call here an *exploration game* that requires multiple vehicles to explore an unknown map, and compete with opponent vehicles for resources. We discuss and analyse how the winning team of MAPC 2011 developed their code base, their approach and most important design decisions and strategies, and discuss the testing strategies that were used by the team.

The chapter is organized as follows. Section 2 introduces the GOAL agent programming language and provides the background necessary for understanding the project that we discuss. In Sect. 3, the MAPC is introduced. This section also discusses the EIS that is supplied with the MAPC software to support easy interaction between a multi-agent system (MAS) and the simulation environment. Section 4 discusses the design and strategy for the MAS implemented in GOAL. Finally, Sect. 5 presents lessons learned and concludes the chapter.

2 The Agent Programming Language GOAL

In this chapter, we present a project that has used the GOAL agent programming language for programming a MAS. It is one of the many agent programming languages that support the agent-oriented programming paradigm [3]. These languages explicitly aim for the construction of autonomous software agents. Most agent programming languages are based on the concept of a *cognitive agent*, derived from the belief–desire–intention (BDI) model of agency [7]. Such cognitive agents maintain a mental state that typically consists of one or more variants of the BDI components, including knowledge, beliefs, desires, goals, and/or intentions. These mental states are used for representing an agent's environment and for decision making or planning. In rule-based agent programming languages, rule libraries that are provided by a programmer are used by the agent to decide what to do next. Agents typically execute a *deliberation or reasoning cycle* similar to the sense-plan-act cycle. Agent programming languages also provide support for agent interaction by means of communication at the knowledge level [11], that is, in terms of what they believe and desire to achieve.

We briefly introduce the main concepts of the agent programming language GOAL that was used by the team to program their MAS for the MAPC 2011. Some code snippets are provided in Sect. 4. We refer the reader to [8, 9, 16] for more detailed information about the language.

GOAL is a *logic-based* agent programming language for programming *cognitive agents*. GOAL agents maintain a mental state that consists of *beliefs* and *goals* and derive their choice of action from their beliefs and goals. GOAL agents also use a *knowledge base* to represent conceptual and domain knowledge. The current version of GOAL uses Prolog to represent the knowledge, beliefs, and goals of an agent.[1] Prolog is a declarative programming language. A Prolog program consists of *Horn clauses*, which are logical rules and simple facts [15]. These clauses represent *what* is the case and *what* is desired; computation in Prolog is performed by evaluating queries by means of an inferencing process. GOAL agents use Prolog for deriving new conclusions from their beliefs about the environment and the goals they want to achieve in combination with the knowledge that they have.

One of the main strengths of the language is that it facilitates the development of *high-level strategies* for agents. GOAL is a *rule-based* language. The philosophy of GOAL is that writing agent programs essentially means writing rules that determine for each situation that the agent finds itself in what it should do in that situation. Rules are ordered, which allows for imposing a priority on what needs to be done first by an agent. On top of this design philosophy GOAL mainly adds two things: a basic *reasoning cycle* and *modular programming*.

GOAL supports a basic reasoning cycle that consists of *two phases*. The purpose of the first phase is to process all *events* such as percepts and messages and make sure that the agent's mental state is up-to-date. In this phase, the GOAL agent retrieves and processes all *perceptual information* available from the environment. Percepts received can be used to update the beliefs and goals of the agent. The idea is that an agent should first make sure its mental state is up-to-date before it decides on a choice of action. The second phase of the cycle is about decision making: Agents decide what to do next. Typically, in this phase one *environment action* is selected and sent to an environment (it is also possible to perform more than one environment action in one cycle if needed). After completing the second phase, the cycle is repeated.

The concept of a *module* is a key programming construct in GOAL for structuring and writing larger agent programs. A GOAL agent *is* a set of modules. With each of the phases of the reasoning cycle corresponds a built-in module. The `event` module corresponds to the first phase and is designed to support event processing

[1]The GOAL agent programming language does not commit to Prolog or any other computational logic in particular (cf. [8]). In principle, other languages such as Answer Set Programming or ontology languages such as OWL might also be used.

whereas the main module corresponds to the second phase and is designed to support decision making. In addition, a special init module is available for initialising the mental state and other components of an agent. More importantly, however, a programmer can add and write its own set of modules for structuring and organizing code. A module provides a container for a set of rules and thus provides an abstraction mechanism: A module can be used for coding more abstract actions as well as for programming roles of agents.

GOAL is a multi-agent programming language and supports *communication* between agents. Both communication from agent-to-agent as well as broadcasting information to all other or a selected set of agents is available. GOAL also supports the distributed running of agents in a MAS on multiple machines.

The GOAL language is distributed with an Integrated Development Environment for coding, testing, and debugging. It provides the usual program editing tools as well as tools to analyse the code (e.g., creating an overview of predicates used in a program). It also provides extensive debugging tools including introspectors for inspecting agent states, stepping functionality, (conditional) breakpoints, runtime querying and modification of agent states, tracing and logging functionality at different levels of granularity, and basic performance measurements of Prolog queries.

The GOAL platform, moreover, fully supports the EIS [2]. EIS provides an elegant interface for interacting with environments. It facilitates the exchange of actions from agents to an environment and the exchange of percepts from an environment to agents. As we will discuss below in more detail, this allowed the team to focus completely on the strategic aspects of the MAPC scenario and no time needed to be spent on low-level details related to, for example, communicating with the simulation server.

3 The MAPC

The MAPC has been annually organized by the CIG-group from Clausthal University of Technology since 2005 [1]. The contest has been initiated with the aim of putting agent programming frameworks to the test, gaining new insights and detecting problems with these platforms that may stimulate research in the area of MAS development and programming [18]. The focus of the contest has shifted more and more toward *coordinated action*, which is perceived as a key issue associated with MAS design and, therefore, should be an essential ingredient in any scenario for evaluating multi-agent programming languages, platforms, and tools. More pragmatically, the contest is also expected to be useful for debugging existing agent platforms and tools and for identifying the strengths and weaknesses of various platforms.

Since 2005 various scenarios have been used in the contest, including *food gathering* (2005), *gold mining* (2006–2007), *cows and cowboys* (2008–2010), and a *Mars* scenario (2011). Scenarios have been changed to focus the contest more and more on coordinated action. All of the scenarios, however, have required agents to *explore* an *unknown map*. The maps used have been *grids with obstacles* except for the Mars scenario which uses a *graph* as a map. In essence, therefore, all of the contest environments can be classified as *exploration games*. In addition, all scenarios are *competitive* and require two agent systems to compete for scarce resources.

The performance of a system developed by a participating team is determined in a series of matches where the systems contributed by various teams compete against all other agent systems. A single match between two competing agent systems consists of several simulations. Winning a simulation yields three points for a team, a draw is worth one point and a loss zero points. The winner of the whole contest is evaluated on the basis of the overall number of collected points in all the matches. HactarV2, the MAS discussed in the next section, scored the highest possible score of 72 points whereas the runner-up scored 60 points.

Technically, the contest is realized by means of a test-bed environment specifically designed for the MAPC called the *MASSim* (multi-agent systems simulation) platform that provides the server infrastructure for running the contest. The contest scenario is realized as a plug-in for the MASSim platform. Participating agent systems connect via TCP/IP to and exchange plain XML messages with the simulation server. In other words, agents receive percepts encoded as XML messages from the server and can act in the gaming environment by encoding their actions as XML messages and transmitting them to the server. The MASSim test-bed supports round-based game simulations where all agents are allowed to perform one action in each round. Agents need to act in real time because the window for transmitting a valid action to the server for each agent is fixed. In the 2011 scenario this time window has been reduced from the 4 s it used to be to 2 s. Taking into account that participating teams are located all over the world and connect via the Internet, which introduces latency, this means that agents need to act well under 2 s to ensure they submit an action to the server in time. After a finite number of steps the simulation server stops and the agents that participated in a simulation receive a notification about the end of that simulation.

3.1 The 2011 Mars Scenario

The Mars scenario used in the 2011 contest concerns an exploration game on the planet Mars [19]. The game requires a set of vehicles to explore, locate and occupy valuable zones on the planet Mars. At the start of a game, vehicles are placed randomly on an unknown map. At first vehicles therefore need to individually explore the map and exchange information. Vehicles need to coordinate their actions to occupy a zone of the planet that is as large as possible.

Story The story of the scenario is that water wells have been discovered on planet Mars. The objective of a team of vehicles is to identify locations with large water wells and to occupy those places. Because multiple companies want to profit from this discovery, a team will have to compete for the possession of water wells. A graph is used to represent Mars, where nodes denote locations and have a value indicating the amount of water that is present in a well. The graph is mirrored to provide a fair symmetric map on which ten vehicles from each team can move around.

Roles Vehicles are each assigned one out of five different roles: *explorer*, *sentinel*, *inspector*, *saboteur*, and *repairer*. Given that ten vehicles are available, each role is evenly distributed and assigned exactly twice. Explorers can determine the amount of water at nodes. Sentinels have a better vision to provide more information about what happens on the planet. Inspectors can determine the roles and status of opponent vehicles. Saboteurs have the ability to attack and disable opponent vehicles. Repairers are able to restore disabled vehicles back to a working state.

Scoring Scheme Two teams play a match over three games each with a duration of 750 steps. The final score of a game is the total of all the step scores in that game. Each team starts the game with ten achievement points which can be spent on upgrades. A team can collect more points by gaining achievement points for actions like attacking enemies and exploring the map. A zone score is determined each step by the nodes that are controlled/guarded by the agents of a team and is computed as the sum of the values of all the nodes in the controlled area. This means that a zone with higher valued nodes will provide a better score. The step score then is determined by adding the number of unspent achievement points to the zone score of that step. This scoring mechanism thus requires a team to weigh and balance scoring achievement points by performing particular actions such as exploring a node or maximizing the value of the occupied zone on the map. Typically, at the start of a game vehicles are not "connected" yet and therefore do not occupy a zone.

3.2 Support for the Environment Interface Standard

The MAPC software provides an implementation of the EIS interface [2] to facilitate easy connection to the MAPC server. This interface automatically establishes and maintains connections to the MASSim-server. It provides support for configuring some parameters of the simulation, registering agents, associating agents with the vehicles in the game, starting a simulation, perceiving the simulation environment, and acting in it. Because the GOAL platform fully supports EIS, a programmer does not need to concern himself with low-level details of connecting to an environment and the functionality that MAPC provides is made available without requiring any effort from a programmer. In addition, the support for the EIS interface by GOAL also ensures that a programmer does not need to concern himself with the low-level details of the XML-format for percepts and actions that is used by the MASSim-server. Instead, a programmer can concentrate completely on how to handle these percepts. Similarly, a programmer can focus on coding a strategy for selecting actions without any need to consider how the environment is able to process actions.

Actions and Percepts We briefly describe some of the more important actions and percepts out of the ten actions that can be performed and out of the 33 percepts that may be received from the simulation environment. For more details, refer to [19].

Actions have a name and some of them have a parameter which identifies a MAPC entity by its name. A saboteur can perform an attack on any vehicle that is in the same location by `attack(<Identifier>)` and the vehicle can use the action `parry` to defend against an attack. Upgrades can be bought by performing `buy(<Identifier>)`. A vehicle moves to a neighbour vertex by performing `goto(<Identifier>)`, which has an energy cost equal to the weight associated with the traversed edge. The actions `probe` and `survey` yield, respectively, the amount of water present on the current vertex and the weights of visible edges.

An action may cost energy, health, and achievement points (money). These costs vary depending on the success or failure of the action, and on whether the agent is in a normal or disabled state. Actions may fail at random with a certain probability and may yield achievement points for six different types of achievements that can be realized. Achievement points can be scored by probing a specific number of nodes, surveying a specific number of edges, inspecting a specific number of opponent vehicles, performing a specific number of successful attacks, performing a specific number of successful parries, and by obtaining points for a zone that is occupied.

Just like an action a percept consists of a name followed by a (possibly empty) list of parameters. Besides names represented by `<Identifier>` a percept may also provide numerical information represented by `<Numeral>`. Percepts differ per individual vehicle and depend on the location and range of sight of the vehicle. Percepts are omitted with a certain probability by the server. The Mars simulation environment provides a large number of different percepts to inform agents about what is going on during the game. Agents are informed about their role, the actual and maximal amounts of energy, health, and strength they can have, their visibility range, whether an action was performed successfully or not, the amount of money (achievement points) available to the team, the total number of vertices and edges present in a simulation, the current round number, and the current (zone) score. The percept `achievement(<Identifier>)` indicates an achievement that has been realized. `position(<Identifier>)` provides the name of the vertex the vehicle is on. `probedVertex(<Identifier>,<Numeral>)` and `surveyedEdge(<Identifier>,<Identifier>,<Numeral>)` yield, respectively, the result of a probing and survey action. Several percepts such as `simStart`, which indicates the start of a simulation, are available that inform agents about the current state of the simulation and the server.

4 Developing a Multi-agent Program for MAPC

This section provides a detailed overview of the code development process of the MAS *HactarV2*. HactarV2 performed exceptionally well during the contest and won every single one of the 24 simulation games against eight other teams. The MAS has been programmed completely in the agent programming languageGOAL. One of the strengths of GOAL is that it facilitates the development of high-level strategies for agents by providing a declarative way to represent and reason about an agent's beliefs and goals.

We provide some information and statistics about the project to indicate the project's size and effort that went into developing the MAS. The agent system has been developed by a team of six students at the Delft University of Technology (henceforth referred to as *the team*). All team members were familiar with GOAL because it is being taught as a first year bachelor course in the Computer Science curriculum at Delft University of Technology. The agile software development approach *Scrum* [14], supported by the open-source platform *iceScrum*[17], has been used to manage the project. The team decided not to use an agent-based development methodology such as Prometheus[13] because of a lack of experience with these methodologies. In total, the team spent roughly 500 man hours on the project. About 60 % of the time was spent on implementing and debugging the multi-agent strategy and the remaining 40 % was spent on system performance and other problems. The final code base consists of 1,758 lines of code spread over 18 files.

The MAS has been run on a single high-end desktop computer consisting of an Intel core i7-870 quad-core CPU running at 3.53 GHz, and 8 GB of DDR3 RAM running at 1,600 MHz. The option of distributing the MAS on multiple machines was considered as a possibility, mainly for performance reasons, but because the MAS turned out to be efficient enough to run on a single machine this option was not investigated any further. The team considered the development on a single machine to be easier. This poses a challenge because the MAS needs to control ten nonplayer characters that each individually need to act within a two second time frame. As explained, because communication with the server over the Internet takes time as well, in fact this means that each agent needs to decide on an action within about a 100 ms (given that agents take turns on a single machine).

In the remainder of this section, we discuss the design of the MAS (Sect. 4.1), the overall flow of control (Sect. 4.2), the ontology that was developed (Sect. 4.3), the testing strategies of the team (Sect. 4.4), and briefly assess the code base against a set of proposed design guidelines (Sect. 4.5).

4.1 Design of the HactarV2 MAS

The design of the HactarV2 MAS has been based on several observations related to the game. Most importantly, two phases may be distinguished within the game: a first phase in which agents do not yet act as a team (initially agents are randomly placed on the map) and a second phase in which agents act as a team in order to occupy valuable zones on the map. The 2011 MAPC map generator produces maps that have a single cluster of higher valued nodes more or less at the center of the map. Because of this, the two phases can be clearly distinguished from each other based upon the fact whether or not this zone has been identified. The main strategy therefore consists of finding these nodes of highest value by means of explorer vehicles and, when such a node (called the *optimum* by the team) is found, informing all other agents about this node so they will start moving toward this node as well. The second phase is called the *swarming* phase because agents are perceived as being part of a swarm that aims at occupying a zone of valuable nodes that is as large as possible.

Because the MAS identifies a single node as the "center" of the *optimum zone* at most one swarm will be created. Agents that are part of this swarm identify the highest valued node directly outside the zone occupied by the swarm and move toward that node. By using this tactic the swarm will always expand in the direction of the highest valued nodes that are not yet owned by the MAS.

Finally, in games where it is difficult to occupy a large, valuable zone, the points that are obtained by achievements can determine the difference between winning and losing. Based on the observation that attack and parry actions yield the most achievement points it was decided to focus on these achievements. Of course, inspections of opponent vehicles and probing nodes, for example, also need to be performed to do well in the game.

It is clear that this general design of the MAS strategy completely depends on a proper *understanding of the MAPC simulation environment*. Such an understanding comes about only after running a MAS in the environment. This suggests that initial experimentation with and testing of a MAS in an environment is a very important aspect of designing a MAS.

Decentralized Coordination and Communication Strategy One of the main challenges of the Agent Contest is to design a *decentralized* MAS that is able to strategically compete with other agent teams. This excludes, for example, the design of a MAS with a central manager that has access to all information available in the MAS and sends instructions to individual agents what to do. The team decided to address this challenge by designing a strategy of HactarV2 that is based on *implicit coordination* between agents.

Another reason for choosing a decentralized design over a centralized design that uses a managing agent is that a decentralized design may reduce the need for communication if properly designed. A managing agent that coordinates the activities of all other agents creates overhead because all information needs to be made available to this manager agent and instructions need to be send back to these agents, which can significantly impact performance.

In order to minimize the communication between agents, agents were designed to base their decisions mainly on the information that is perceived by the agent itself. The main exception concerns the information that is obtained by different agents about the map. Map information is shared by communication between agents because more knowledge about the map can be used to optimize the exploration process and allows agents to prevent doing probe and survey actions twice. Sharing this information may require each agent to process up to 90 messages that are received from the other nine agents per round. Because all agents have to process received map information, special attention has been paid to optimizing the updating of an agent's beliefs with this information. Although in a centralized design only the central manager would maintain a map and need to perform such updates, this single agent would still have to process all information received from all other agents.

In addition to messages about the map, messages with requests for repairs are exchanged between disabled agents and repairer agents and messages with information about the location of opponent agents are exchanged between non-saboteur agents and saboteur agents. Communication has been optimized by making sure that an agent will only send a message if it knows that the receiving agent does not perceive this information itself (which can be deduced from local information and previous messages).

One of the key issues that needs to be addressed in the design of a decentralized MAS concerns the question *how to avoid that agents perform the same action*. Decisions of agents on the action it will perform need to be coordinated to avoid doing the same thing twice. To this end, agents in the HactarV2 MAS have been equipped with the capability to *predict* what other agents will do. Using a simple *agent ranking principle* each agent then can decide by itself which action to perform and rule out conflicts. For example, this principle is used to decide which out of multiple agents on the same edge of the occupied zone will perform a move to another node to expand the zone. The basic idea is simple: Agents that are located on the same node are ranked and assigned a unique number called the *agent's rank*.[2] This rank is used to arbitrate between multiple agents that are about to perform the same action. This mechanism allows agents to divide tasks without having to communicate and ensures that each agent performs a unique action whenever possible.

The design choice to develop a decentralized MAS for the MAPC environment has raised some interesting issues that need to be taken into account. Two issues stand out: The design needs to explicitly deal with *minimizing communication overhead* and the *prevention of the duplication of effort* by agents. One mechanism for dealing with the latter issue used in the HactarV2 team is *prediction* of what other agents may do. An interesting topic for future research is the question whether, and if so, which, alternative mechanisms may be employed to the same end.

Agent Roles and Strategies Apart from the overall MAS strategy discussed above, various goals and strategies were designed and identified at the agent level including strategies for specific *agent roles*, for *defence*, and for *buying* upgrades.

The main goal of *explorer* agents at the start of the game is to locate the highest valued node on the map, called the *optimum*. Once this node has been found, it is the task of the explorer agent to communicate the name of this node to the other agents and start forming a swarm that occupies the zone around this node. The strategy for finding the optimum consists of performing `probe`, `survey` and `goto` actions according to a set of specific rules: Always probe a node if it has not been probed

[2]This can be done, for example, by using the fact that GOAL attaches numbers to names in order to create unique names for each agent.

yet and survey any edges that have not been surveyed yet. The agent then will go to a node that has not been probed yet only if (a) this node is connected to the current and last visited node and (b) the current node has a lower value then the last visited one. If there is a neighboring node that has a higher value than the current one, the agent will go there. The agent will also try to go to a neighbouring node that is not close to a (potentially) dangerous opponent but the agent will take a chance in case there is no such node. Otherwise, the agent will go back to the last visited node, if unexplored options are available at that node. The agent will conclude that the optimum has been found if no move can be made any more. This conclusion may not always be right but turned out to work well in practice. Once the "optimum" has been found, an explorer agent will team up with the other agents and start swarming around this node. It will continue to probe nodes as doing so allows for finding even higher valued nodes than the currently believed optimum.

The defensive strategy of an explorer is to move away from nodes it considers unsafe. A node is considered to be unsafe if an opponent agent is located on that node that is either a saboteur or its role is unknown.

A *sentinel* agent basically uses the same exploration strategy as explorer agents. The defensive strategy of a sentinel is to parry opponent saboteurs. If successful, parry achievements are gained. If the opponent's role is unknown, a repairer will also initially parry. However, if no attack was performed, with a 50 % chance, a sentinel agent will ignore opponents with unknown roles on the same node.

An *inspector* agent also uses the same exploration strategy as explorer agents. The difference is that an inspector agent gives priority to inspecting opponents in order to identify saboteurs, to keeping track of the status of these agents (by repeating inspection of these agents every 50 rounds), and to sharing this information with all other agents. The defensive strategy of an inspector is to move away only from known opponent saboteurs.

The main goal of *repairer* agents is to repair friendly disabled agents. Priority is given to repairing a disabled repairer agent and repairs of other agents are interrupted when a repairer is itself disabled or upon receiving a request from another repairer agent. Disabled agents request a repairer agent for help and will start moving toward the closest repairer. They send a path to the repairer they are moving to which prevents the repairer from having to calculate the same path. Repairers use the same defensive strategy as sentinels.

The main goal of *saboteur* agents is to disable opponent agents. These agents move toward a nearest and last known location of an opponent agent to attack that agent. Tests showed that this strategy reduced the effectiveness of opponent teams. Saboteurs do not have a defensive strategy but are designed to be superior to any opponent agent by means of HactarV2's buying strategy to which we now turn.

Buying is an important aspect of the game but the team considered achievement points (money) more important and they decided to try to spend less money than the opponent does. The reason is that the amount of money available each round has a high impact on the score for that round. Although the team experimented with sentinels that buy sensors to increase visibility range, this performance gain was considered insufficient compared to the costs and the team decided to only upgrade

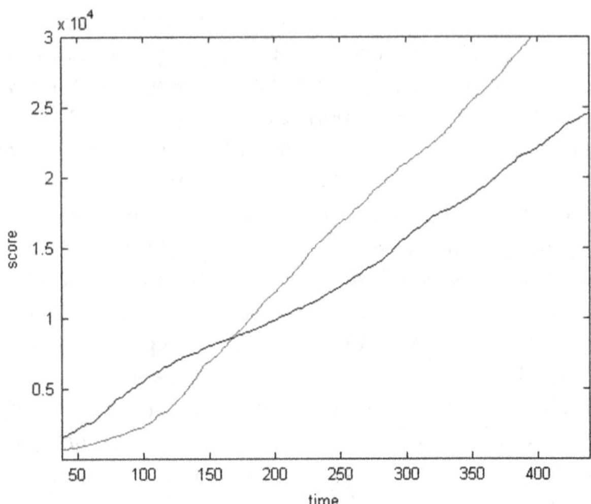

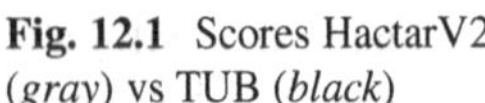
Fig. 12.1 Scores HactarV2 (*gray*) vs TUB (*black*)

saboteur agents. Upgrades are bought right at the start of the game and throughout when it is discovered that upgrades are needed to match opponent health or strength. Upgrading is aimed at two things: (a) saboteurs have one health point more then the maximal strength of opponent saboteurs and (b) the strength of saboteurs is at least equal to the maximal health of opponent saboteurs. If both these goals are realized, saboteur agents will survive opponent attacks while disabling opponents by a single attack. The initial investment at the start of the game means that the score often is lower than that of opponents in the first 100 or so steps but it starts to pay off in the remainder of the match. See Fig. 12.1 for an example game illustrating this.

The fact that the exploration strategy is among the most complex strategies matches the fact that the MAPC environment is what we have called an *exploration game*. It is obvious that in a game of competition that has entities with different roles agent specific role and defensive strategies need to be designed. More interestingly, however, is the fact that the design of the buying strategy is derived from the results of extensive testing, which highlights again the importance of this activity.

4.2 Control Flow of the MAS

GOAL agents execute an Observe–Orient–Decide–Act (OODA) loop [5].[3] At the start of a reasoning cycle of an agent, events including percepts and messages are collected (Observe) and processed by means of so-called *event rules* (Orient). This

[3]In many areas of competitive activity, the theory is that if you can cycle through the OODA loop faster than your opponent, you have the advantage.

ensures that an agent can make a decision based on the most up-to-date information available. A decision on what to do next (Decide) is made using so-called *action rules*. Upon making a choice, the action selected is sent to the environment (Act).

The control flow of this cycle matches the general structure of a GOAL agent program. More specifically, the `event` module of a GOAL agent corresponds to the Observe–Orient part of the loop and its `main` module with the Decide–Act part of the loop. A programmer can add additional structure to the agent's cycle by adding as many user-defined modules as needed. For example, code related to percept handling, communication, navigation, and roles can be placed in separate modules.

A more detailed overview of the structure and flow of control of the event module is provided by the diagrams in Fig. 12.2a, b. Horizontal rectangular boxes in the figures refer to particular modules and submodules, whereas vertical rectangular boxes indicate the flow of control. The notation **LA** in the latter boxes indicates that the order of rule evaluation in the corresponding module is **L**inear and that **A**ll applicable rules need to be applied (in order). This linear-all style of rule evaluation is the default mode for the **init** and **event** modules. In all other modules, the default mode is a linear style mode of evaluation where *only the first* applicable rule is applied. Using the **order** option the rule evaluation style of a module can be changed. This explains the fact that the submodules such as `selectPercepts`, etc. are also indicated in Fig. 12.2 to use linear-all style evaluation.

An agent starts a new cycle upon receiving information from the simulation server that a new round has started. The `commonPercepts` module handles the percepts that every agent uses. The `surveyVertices` module processes vertex-related percepts and broadcasts this information to the other agents if a successful `survey` action just was performed. Next role specific modules handle any role specific percepts. The `selectReceive` module then processes messages, which in a similar fashion uses various sub-modules. For example, a disabled agent uses module `disabledReceiveMail` to handle messages specific to disabled agents. The `clearMailbox` module finally cleans the mailbox of an agent by deleting all received and sent messages.

After all events are processed and the mental state of the agent is made up-to-date again, the agent decides what to do next in the **main** module. Instead of providing a flow diagram for this module, we list the code in Fig. 12.3. As explained above, the rule evaluation in this and user-defined modules is linear style. This means that the action rules in these modules are evaluated one by one from top to bottom and only the first applicable rule is actually applied. If no decision has been made yet (**not**(`doneAction`)), first it is checked whether the agent is disabled and the `disabled` module is entered in that case to ensure the agent gets itself fixed as soon as possible. A special case where the MAS is in control of the entire map (`allMapAreBelongToUs`[4]) because all opponent agents are disabled is checked next which is handled by the `superioritySelect` module. Only if none of

[4]See http://nl.wikipedia.org/wiki/All_your_base_are_belong_to_us.

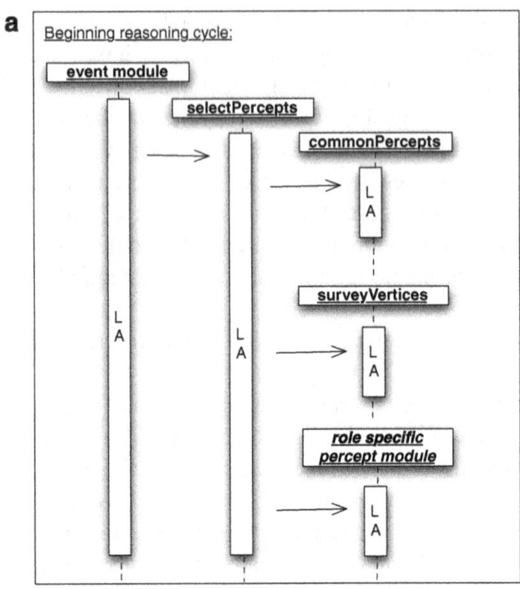

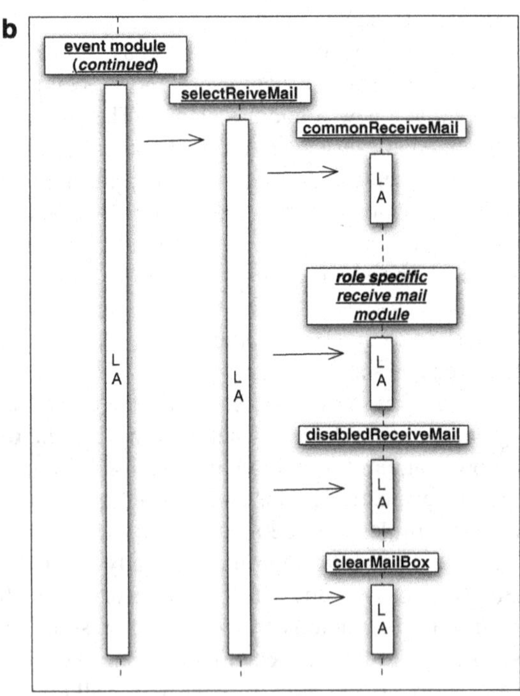

Fig. 12.2 Control flow of the event module. (**a**) First part; (**b**) second part

```
main module{
  program{
    if bel(not(doneAction)) then {
      if bel(disabled, not(role('Repairer'))) then disabled.

      if bel(allMapAreBelongToUs) then superioritySelect.

      if bel(role('Repairer')) then repairerAction.
      if bel(role('Inspector')) then inspectorAction.
      if bel(role('Explorer')) then explorerAction.
      if bel(role('Saboteur')) then saboteurAction.
      if bel(role('Sentinel')) then sentinelAction.

      if bel(true) then explore.
    }
  }
}
```

Fig. 12.3 Main module code

these cases apply enter agents their role specific modules. Finally, if there are no role specific tasks that need to be performed these modules are exited and an agent will try to swarm, or, if that is not an option explore the map.
The use of modules has several benefits. It facilitates programmers that are part of a team to each focus on a specific part of code while at the same time maintaining a clear structural overview of the MAS. It also reduces the chance of code duplication. And last but not least, it facilitates structuring code of roles by means of a pattern similar to the Strategy design pattern [6]. The agent program of every agent in our MAS uses the same structure while still being able to handle agent specific roles due to code that allows an agent to adapt to the particular role associated with a vehicle.

4.3 Ontology

Besides the 33 percept predicates that agents may receive from the environment, in the HactarV2 MAS an additional 60+ Prolog predicates were defined that are used throughout the agent program. In a team of programmers where each programmer codes part of the MAS it is important to have easy access to such large numbers of predicates and their intuitive meaning. Code in a sub-module of the **main** module, for example, may depend on predicates in the belief base that are updated in a sub-module of the **event** module. One lesson learned from a first year bachelor project where student teams have to program a MAS for controlling bots in the real-time, first-person shooter game UNREAL TOURNAMENT 2004 [10] is that the teams that did a better job at maintaining an *ontology* outperformed other teams and obtained better results in the final competition. For this reason, the team also maintained an ontology for the HactarV2 MAS.

Ontology Structure An ontology for a GOAL MAS documents all predicates that are used in the MAS code base. As Prolog is used, the ontology documents in the usual Prolog format `name/nr` a predicate named `name` that has `nr` of arguments. For example, `enabledEnemy/2` means a predicate `enabledEnemy` with two arguments is used. The ontology maintained by the HactarV2 team in the form of a table also indicates the *type* of a predicate label, that is, whether it is used for representing a belief, goal, percept, or knowledge of an agent. It also briefly explains the intuitive meaning of each predicate, how its parameters should be instantiated, and the code base location where the predicate is defined (i.e., the file where it is used).

Example Predicate Definitions In the remainder of this section, we briefly discuss and illustrate two of the predicates used and their definitions. Important other predicates that were defined were used, for example, for implementing the agent ranking principle discussed above (Sect. 4.1), path planning,[5] and for keeping track of which vehicles that are part of the team can be relied upon.

The concept of an agent being connected to others is used in the swarming phase, that is, the second phase of the game. It is an important concept for establishing that nodes are owned by a group of agents. The nodes that connected agents are located on are also called *swarm positions*. Informally, an agent is said to be *connected* if that agent has links with at least two other agents it can depend on. A link between two agents is said to exist if there are at most two edges that connect the nodes on which these agents are located and these nodes are owned by the agent team. The concept is implemented by the predicate `connectedAgent/2`; see Fig. 12.4). Figure 12.4 also lists the most important predicates related to swarming.
Code explanation: the predicate `connectedAgent/2` indicates whether the second agent is connected to the first agent. This means the second agent must be one or two edges apart from the first agent, and must not be considered an independent agent (see below for the concept of independency); `connectedPos/2` does the same as `connectedAgent` but instead of reasoning from the position of the first agent it reasons from any node position; `edgeDest/1`: finds a list of probed nodes (and their corresponding values) that are not in the optimum zone but have a direct edge to a node in the optimum zone; `swarmPos/1`: a vertex that is a swarm position is a vertex that makes sure the agent is still connected to two other agents; `expandPos/1`: checks if a node is neutral (has no vertex owner) and is a swarming position; `expandDest/2`: finds all expanding destination (using expandPos) from the agents current position; `bestExpandDest/3`: finds the highest value expanding position to expand the swarm to from a certain node.

Recall that the map generator produces maps that have one cluster of higher valued nodes at the center of the map. It is the goal of explorers to locate these high valued nodes and identify the *optimum* node. Occupying a zone around this node is very important during the game. Such a zone is called the *optimum zone*. In order

[5]It is often argued that path planning is better delegated to another software component that is not programmed using a logic-based agent programming language. The HactarV2 agents, however, use Prolog for path planning and implement variants of Dijkstra's shortest path algorithm.

```
connectedAgent(Agent1, Agent2) :- team(Team),
  visibleEntity(Agent1, Pos1, Team, normal),
  visibleEntity(Agent2, Pos2, Team, normal),
  visibleEdge(Pos1, Pos2), not(independableAgent(Agent2)),
  vertexOwner(Pos1, Team), vertexOwner(Pos2, Team).
connectedAgent(Agent1, Agent2) :- team(Team),
  visibleEntity(Agent1, Pos1, Team, normal),
  visibleEntity(Agent2, Pos2, Team, normal),
  visibleEdge(Pos1, Pos3), visibleEdge(Pos3, Pos2),
  not(Pos1 == Pos2), not(independableAgent(Agent2)),
  vertexOwner(Pos1, Team), vertexOwner(Pos2, Team),
  vertexOwner(Pos3, Team).

connectedPos(X, Agent) :- currentPos(Agent, Y),
  not(independableAgent(Agent)), visibleEdge(X, Y).
connectedPos(X, Agent) :- currentPos(Agent, Z),
  not(independableAgent(Agent)), not(X == Z), visibleEdge(Z, Y),
  team(Team), vertexOwner(Y, Team), visibleEdge(Y, X).

edgeDest(List3) :- neighboursOfOptimumZone(F), !,
  findall([Value, Vertex], (member(Vertex, F), vertexValue(Vertex, Value),
     not(Value == unknown)), List),
  not(List == []), sort(List, List2), reverse(List2, List3).

swarmPos(X) :- connectedPos(X, Agent1), connectedPos(X, Agent2),
  not(Agent1 == Agent2), !.

expandPos(ID) :- vertexOwner(ID, none), swarmPos(ID).

expandDest(List3, Pos):-
  findall([Value,Neighbour],(neighbour(Pos,Neighbour), expandPos(Neighbour),
    vertexValue(Neighbour,Value), not(Value==unknown)),List),
  not(List == []), sort(List, List2), reverse(List2, List3).

bestExpandDest(ID, Value, Pos):- expandDest(List,Pos), List=[[Value,ID]|_].
```

Fig. 12.4 Related predicates and predicate definition for `connectedAgent/2`

```
allInformationOptimumZone([], [], []) :- not(optimum(_)), !.
allInformationOptimumZone(Agents, Nodes, Neighbours) :-
  optimum(Opt), team(Team),
  allInformationOptimumZone([Opt], [], Nodes, Agents, Neighbours, Team),!.

allInformationOptimumZone([], _, [], [], [], _).
allInformationOptimumZone
 ([First|ToConsider], Visited, [First|Nodes], Agents, Neighbours, Team) :-
  vertexOwner(First,Team),
  findall([Agent, First], visibleEntity(Agent, First, Team, normal), Agts),
  findall(Node,(e4(First, Node, _), not(member(Node, Visited))), TempNodes),
  list_to_set(TempNodes, FoundNodes),
    union(FoundNodes, ToConsider, NewToConsider),
  allInformationOptimumZone(NewToConsider,[First|Visited], Nodes,
        NewAgents, Neighbours, Team),
  union(NewAgents, Agts, Agents).
allInformationOptimumZone([First|ToConsider], Visited, Nodes, Agents,
 [First|Neighbours], Team) :- not(vertexOwner(First, Team)),
  allInformationOptimumZone(ToConsider, [First|Visited], Nodes,
  Agents, Neighbours, Team).

inOptimumZone :- me(Id), agentsInOptimumZone(A), member([Id,_], A).
```

Fig. 12.5 Related predicates and predicate definition for `allInformationOptimumZone/3`

to be able to reason about this important zone, various predicates related to this concept have been defined; see Fig. 12.5.

Code explanation: `allInformationOptimumZone/3`: finds all nodes and agents that are currently in the optimum zone. The definition uses the helper predicate `allInformationOptimumZone/6`. Using a breadth first search this latter predicate finds all nodes owned by the team that have a path to the optimum node, using only nodes that are owned by the team. It also finds all the agents that are currently on these nodes as well as all neutral and enemy owned nodes that have an edge to these nodes; `inOptimumZone/0` checks if the agent is currently in the zone that contains the optimum.

Maintaining an ontology facilitates keeping track of what programmers that are part of a team are doing. The HactarV2 team has reported that using an ontology has saved them a lot of time. They found that it is important to pay special attention to the predicates that are used for representing the environment. An ontology also provides support for understanding the program code and communication between team members. The GOAL platform provides some functionality for automatically identifying the predicates that are used and warns if redundant predicates are present in a MAS. Given the usefulness of an ontology it is worth while to consider extending this functionality and provide more automated support for maintaining an ontology.

4.4 Testing

The team has put a lot of effort into testing and analysing the results while developing the MAPC MAS and reported that extensive testing was very important for becoming familiar with the gaming environment. We briefly discuss the various testing strategies that were used by the team.

The Use of Dummy Agents It is important to test whether the MAS has bugs without other agents disturbing the environment. In order to do so, dummy agents that do nothing were used as opponents. Problems such as agents getting stuck at a certain point, or performing no operations at all are more easily detected and solved this way. For example, if a vehicle controlled by an agent does not perform an action, by stepping through the code of the agent in debugging mode it is often relatively easy to determine what goes wrong in a set-up with dummy agents (other options such as that an agent has been disabled cannot occur in this case).

Strategy Testing Testing is not only suitable for detecting and solving errors but also needed for measuring the performance of a MAS. In a competitive setting, an adequate and readily available way of measuring performance is by testing a current version of the MAS against older versions. This yields insight into whether recent code changes have improved performance. During these tests the team observed suboptimal behavior that they believe could only have been found because the strategy of the opposing MAS of an older version is still quite similar (assuming testing is regularly performed). For the same reason why it is a good idea to test against earlier versions it is also necessary to test against MAS written by other teams, whenever the possibility is available. Only by doing so are issues detected that occur only against MAS that have a very different strategy.

Fig. 12.6 Example debug module for the MAPC

```
module debug[exit=noaction]{
  program{
    if bel(debug(attack(X))) then attack(X).
    if bel(debug(survey)) then survey.
    if bel(debug(probe)) then probe.
    ...
    bel(debug(moving(X)), currentPos(X))
       then delete(debug(moving(X))) + explore.
  }
}
```

Debug Modules In order to properly test agent behavior, it is necessary to create particular situations in an environment to be able to observe the behavior that a program produces in those situations. In order to create such situations, it can be useful to "manually" assign each agent a new task at runtime. For example, it is often quite useful in the MAPC environment to direct an agent to go to a particular location and stay there.

It is useful to have support for setting up particular situations. In GOAL, the team came up with the idea of using a combination of a what they called a *debug module* and so-called *debug facts*. An example of such a module is provided in Fig. 12.6. A debug module is a module like any other module with the name `debug`. The module includes a set of simple action rules that are executed when a corresponding `debug` fact is part of the agent's belief base. A debug module is used in combination with a feature in GOAL that allows to insert new beliefs in the belief base of a particular agent while the MAS is running. Once an agent believes a "debug fact," it will deviate from its normal behavior and will immediately give full priority to the rules in the corresponding debug module. The team reported that this proved to be a very useful debugging tool. All agents can, for example, be instructed to line up in a particular way to make it easy to test a strategy or situation in a controlled manner.

Real-Time Debugging An important problem with testing a MAS is that the environment upon which the system acts is highly dynamic. Many different agents perform actions in real time and continuously affect the state of the environment.

A more specific testing tactic that was used while debugging the MAPC MAS involved the use of an edited XML configuration file for a simulation which granted the agent team two million seconds for sending actions. According to official game settings, all agents have only 2 s to submit their actions. While stepping agents in debugging mode, however, such a time limit is too strict and action would not be submitted in time. In the MAPC environment, this would mean that agents that are being debugged perform skip actions, while the opponent MAS is sending valid actions. By raising the time limit for submitting an action, the server would "pause" during that time and it is possible to complete debugging a simulation step. As a result, bugs were found more easily.

Testing was performed at all levels distinguished in [12], including unit, agent, integration, system, and acceptance testing. Acceptance testing in this context meant testing the system in the environment provided by the MAPC organizers. This required some creativity, as discussed above, from the team. Testing of MASs may be differentiated from other types of software systems and is particularly challenging due to the many interactions that need to be taken into account. Agents run concurrently and interact with other agents, both by means of communication as well as by interacting in a shared environment, and need to take into account how to coordinate their actions or compete with other agents for resources. The metrics that needed to be considered for the MAPC competition in particular were related to real-time performance and the performance of the MAS in terms of the scoring scheme of the competition. Other metrics related to code quality are discussed in the next section.

Generally speaking, the lesson learned from this project is that the more a MAS is being tested the better it is. As noted above, testing is very important to gain a proper understanding of the environment a MAS needs to be programmed for. Interestingly, some techniques were used by the team that can be reused in other cases. The idea of putting an agent in "debug mode" by means of debug modules in order to create specific testing conditions provides only one example. An issue that often arises while debugging MAS for complex environments concerns real-time. Whereas for the MAPC environment the real-time pace of the game could be controlled, parameters for doing so are not available for all environments. It is therefore clear that more effort is needed to improve the tooling for effective debugging and for developing effective testing approaches for multi-agent programs [1].

4.5 A Look at the HactarV2 Code Base

Due to space limitations, we only discuss and illustrate a small but important part of the code base related to the swarming behavior of agents that occupy a zone.

The swarming module shown in Fig. 12.7 is a key module during the second phase of a game, when the objective of the MAS is to occupy a zone that is as large as possible. To be more precise, the objective is to obtain a higher zone score than the opponent team. In order to do so, the swarming agents sometimes will even reduce the occupied zone in order to maintain a steady flow of score instead of aiming for occupied territory that is easily disrupted by the opponent. Agents will only enter this module when they do not have any more important role specific tasks to perform, such as repairing a broken agent or destroying an enemy saboteur that is disrupting one of the repairers.

The module heavily depends on several defined predicates, such as the `swarmPos` predicate defined in Fig. 12.4. The module also uses the agent rank system to efficiently distribute possible moves between agents. Two main cases are distinguished in the module: the agent is (a) inside the occupied zone (dealt with by the first rule) and (b) on a boundary node and has options available for expanding the zone. Using the `expandDest/1` predicate these options are retrieved, the agent's rank is determined, and using the `expandDest/2` predicate options of connected agents are retrieved. In case the agent is allowed to expand (it has more options than other agents), it does so using the `moveSplit/2` module.

```
program{
  if bel(insideZone, edgeDest(List), agentRankHere(Rank))
    then moveSplit(Rank, List).
  if bel(expandDest(List),List=[[Value,Vertex]|_],me(Id),agentRankHere(Rank))
    then {
      if bel(not((connectedAgent(Id, Agent), currentPos(Agent, Pos),
                bestExpandDest(_, Value2, Pos), Value2 >= Value)))
        then gotoSplit(Rank, List).
      if bel(not(kingOfTheHill), Rank2 is Rank-1)
        then gotoSplit(Rank2, List).
      if bel(currentPos(Pos), not(swarmPos(Pos)), optimum(Opt),
                path(Pos, Opt, [Here,Next|Path], _))
        then advancedGoto(Next).
    }

  if true then recharge.
}
```

Fig. 12.7 Program section of the swarming module

The code fragments discussed provide some indication of the quality of the code produced but do not provide an overall perspective. More generally, we can assess the code quality produced by the HactarV2 team by means of a set of design guidelines that have been proposed for GOAL agent programs [16]. Part of these guidelines also concern the earlier discussed topics of ontology and testing. Table 12.1 provides an overview of these guidelines and indicates to what extent they were followed.

It turns out that the HactarV2 team followed most of the design guidelines for producing quality code but not all. Overall, rules were grouped according to purpose (e.g., communication rules were grouped together) and a declarative style of programming has been used. Percepts are not all handled in the event module, however, and the deletion of facts was not always handled by the **delete** action. The team explained that they did not follow these guidelines for reasons of performance and preferred less expensive queries here instead of relatively expensive update actions. Other items that stand out concern the high level of testing and the fact that a project management tool was used at the start of the project but not used actively any more later on.

5 Conclusion

The design and development of a MAS for an exploration game such as the MAPC involves all challenges that will typically be encountered when developing a MAS for controlling a complex and dynamic environment. We think that the Mars contest scenario poses some interesting challenges with respect to coordinating agents. We discussed the programming project and results of a team of six bachelor students that coded a MAS they called *HactarV2* that won the 2011 contest. The team had to *design a winning strategy* for ten agents in a competitive environment facing ten opponent agents, *design a coordination strategy* for coordinating the activities of

Table 12.1 Which design guidelines and best practices were followed?

Code quality and style	
Predicate labels are declarative	✓
Beliefs represent current state	✓
Program does not contain redundant predicates	✓
Knowledge represents conceptual and domain logic	✓
Agent program uses goals	✓
Goals are declarative	✓
Goals are concrete	✓
Only action specifications for environment actions are present	✓
All environment actions are declared in the `init` module	✓
Specified action preconditions match environment constraints	✓
`insert` is used to add and `delete` is used to remove beliefs	✗
Action rules are only used in the `main` module or linked modules	✓
Percepts are only used in the event module	✗
Percepts are handled by `forall` rules	✗
Communication rules are located in the event module after percept handling code	✓
Rules for goal management are located at the end of the event module	✗
Unrelated modules are placed in separate files	✓
Comments (documentation)	
% predicates in knowledge base that are explained in comments	100 %
% action specifications that are explained in comments	50 %
% of modules the use of which are explained in comments	90 %
% of program rule groups that are explained in comments	100 %
Ontology (documentation)	
The ontology was kept up to date throughout the project	✓
Items in the ontology are properly explained	✓
The ontology was used by team members during the project	✓
Testing	
Level of testing during project	High
Team performed module tests	✓
Team performed full MAS system tests	✓
Team performed systematic tests on domain configurations	✓
Project management	
A project management tool was used during the project	✓
The project management tool was kept up to date throughout the project	✗

these agents, *develop a relatively large code base* as a team, and *perform extensive tests* to validate the performance and strategy of the MAS that was developed.

The code for the MAS that was developed has been completely written in the logic-based agent programming language GOAL. This made the coding project a useful object for our study to learn more about the actual use of such a language in a relatively larger project. We discussed key aspects of the project including program and strategy design, the use of modules in a team programming effort, the ontology used for reasoning and representing the gaming environment, strategies for testing a MAS, and we briefly discussed whether code followed proposed design guidelines.

According to the team, the concept of a *module* for structuring code turned out to be of great value. Modules were used to write code for specific roles that were used by only some agents, as well as for shared functions such as navigating the map, for communication, etc. The team reported that being able to structure code by means of modules facilitated the division of coding tasks among team members. Furthermore, writing code in a logic-based agent programming language as a team requires that all team members are aware of the logical predicates that are used throughout the code. We have called this the *ontology* used by the MAS. The team reported that documenting and updating the ontology while developing code facilitated team coordination and saved time. The team followed most but deviated also from some of the proposed guidelines for quality code mainly for reasons of efficiency.

In conclusion, we have found that developing a MAS is far from trivial. In particular, testing a MAS remains one of the key challenges that seems to set development of such a system apart from other software systems. The key differences are the potentially large number of agents that may have different roles and the fact that the MAS is developed for controlling entities in and is connected to an external environment that cannot be fully controlled. A development team needs to become familiar with the external environment at the start of a project. This means that different testing strategies may be useful at the beginning than toward the end of a project. The team used some interesting techniques for debugging some of which can be applied more generally to the development of other MASs as well. In particular, in a *gaming* environment where bots *compete* for resources, at the start of a project it may be more effective to use dummy opponents that pose little or no challenge while testing initial versions of a MAS. A testing approach to evaluate whether subsequent versions of the MAS improve the system's performance is *self-play*, that is, have a newer version play an older version.

In this chapter, we have made an attempt to gain insights from a coding project that uses a logic-based agent programming language. We believe that we have been able to identify and illustrate some useful strategies for making such a project a success. Much, however, remains to be done and we believe it would be useful to draw more lessons learned from other agent-oriented software engineering projects. Analysis of such projects is useful for identifying coding (design) patterns, best practices, improving agent-based development tools, and developing automated testing tools, as well as evolve agent programming languages in a way that enhances their use in real-world applications [20].

Acknowledgments We would like to recognize the effort the students put into developing the HactarV2 MAS and their help in explaining their code while writing this chapter. The chapter is partly based on the MAPC paper for the HactarV2 MAS [4].

References

1. Behrens T, Dastani M, Dix J, Köster M, Novák P (2010) The multi-agent programming contest from 2005–2010. Ann Math Artif Intell 59(3):277–311
2. Behrens TM, Hindriks KV, Dix J (2011) Towards an environment interface standard for agent platforms. Ann Math Artif Intell 61(4):261–295
3. Bordini R, Braubach L, Dastani M, Seghrouchni AEF, Gomez-Sanz J, Leite J, O'Hare G, Pokahr A, Ricci A (2006) A survey of programming languages and platforms for multi-agent systems. Informatica 30(1):33–44
4. Dekker M, Hameete P, Hegemans M, Leysen S, van den Oever J, Smits J, Hindriks KV (2012) Hactarv2: an agent team strategy based on implicit coordination. In: Dennis L, Boissier O, Bordini RH (eds) 9th International Workshop, ProMAS 2011, Taipei, Taiwan, 3 May 2011, Revised Selected Papers. LNAI, vol 7217, pp 173–184
5. Eaton J, Redmayne J, Thordsen M (2007) Joint analysis handbook, 3rd edn. Joint Analysis and Lessons Learned Centre, Lisbon. www.jallc.nato.int
6. Freeman E, Freeman E, Sierra K, Bates B (2004) Head first design patterns, 1st edn. O'Reilly Media, Inc., Sebastopol
7. Georgeff MP, Pell B, Pollack ME, Tambe M, Wooldridge M (1999) The belief-desire-intention model of agency. In: Proceedings of the 5th international workshop on intelligent agents, vol V. Agent theories, architectures, and languages (ATAL '98). Springer, Berlin, pp 1–10
8. Hindriks K (2009) Programming rational agents in goal. In: Multi-agent programming: languages, tools and applications. Springer, Heidelberg, pp 119–157
9. Hindriks K, de Boer FS, van der Hoek W, Meyer J (2001) Agent programming with declarative goals. In: Intelligent agents VII agent theories architectures and languages. Springer, Berlin, pp 248–257
10. Hindriks K, van Riemsdijk B, Behrens T, Korstanje R, Kraayenbrink N, Pasman W, de Rijk L (2011) UNREAL GOAL bots. In: Dignum F (ed) Agents for games and simulations, vol II. Lecture notes in computer science, vol 6525. Springer, Berlin, pp 1–18. http://dx.doi.org/10.1007/978-3-642-18181-8_1
11. Newell A (1981) The knowledge level. AI Mag 2(2):1–20
12. Nguyen C, Perini A, Bernon C, Pavn J, Thangarajah J (2011) Testing in multi-agent systems. In: Gleizes MP, Gomez-Sanz J (eds) Agent-oriented software engineering, vol X. Lecture notes in computer science, vol 6038. Springer, Berlin, pp 180–190
13. Padgham L, Winikoff M (2003) Prometheus: a methodology for developing intelligent agents. In: Proceedings of the 3rd international conference on agent-oriented software engineering, vol III (AOSE'02). Springer, Berlin, pp 174–185
14. Schwaber K (1995) Scrum development process. In: Proceedings of the 10th annual ACM conference on object oriented programming systems, languages, and applications (OOPSLA), pp 117–134
15. Shapiro L, Sterling E (1994) The art of prolog: advanced programming techniques. MIT Press, Cambridge
16. The GOAL website (2012). http://ii.tudelft.nl/trac/goal
17. The iceScrum website (2012). http://www.icescrum.org/en/
18. The Multi-Agent Programming Contest website (2012). http://www.multi-agentcontest.org/
19. The Multi-Agent Programming Contest 2011 website (2012). http://www.multi-agentcontest.org/2011
20. van Riemsdijk MB, Hindriks KV, Jonker CM (2012) An empirical study of cognitive agent programs. Multiagent Grid Syst 8(2):187–222

Chapter 13
Unravelling Multi-agent-Oriented Programming

Olivier Boissier, Rafael H. Bordini, Jomi F. Hübner, and Alessandro Ricci

Abstract A fully-fledged programming paradigm based on ideas from multi-agent systems requires a lot more than early agent-oriented programming languages envisaged. More than interaction between autonomous entities, the social level of multi-agent systems as well as the shared environment where the agents are situated also need to be suitably designed. In fact, the abstractions used at each of those three levels are all equally important and interrelated. In this chapter, we discuss JaCaMo, a platform for multi-agent-oriented programming that covers abstractions such as: beliefs, goals, and plans at the agent level; groups, roles, functional schemes (i.e., social plans), and norms at the organizational level; and artifacts and workspaces at the environment level. The chapter also includes a simple multi-agent system example to illustrate the approach.

Keywords Abstraction • JaCaMo • Multi-agent programming • Multi-agent systems • Programming dimensions

O. Boissier
EMSE, St. Etienne, France
e-mail: Olivier.Boissier@emse.fr

R.H. Bordini (✉)
FACIN–PUCRS, Porto Alegre – RS, Brazil
e-mail: R.Bordini@pucrs.br

J.F. Hübner
DAS–UFSC, Florianópolis – SC, Brazil
e-mail: jomi@das.ufsc.br

A. Ricci
University of Bologna, Cesena, Italy
e-mail: a.ricci@unibo.it

O. Shehory and A. Sturm (eds.), *Agent-Oriented Software Engineering*,
DOI 10.1007/978-3-642-54432-3_13,

1 Introduction

This chapter aims to present the JaCaMo multi-agent-oriented programming platform [3].[1] What we mean by a multi-agent-oriented programming platform is a multi-agent system development platform that provides programming constructs that match the abstractions used at the various levels of a multi-agent system. In particular, JaCaMo allows the use of abstractions such as groups, roles, and norms at the *social/organizational* level; of abstractions such as beliefs, goals, and plans at the *agent* level; and of artifacts and workspaces at the *environment* level.

JaCaMo was developed by solving various issues that arose when trying to put together the $\mathcal{M}$OISE [11, 12][2] organization-oriented programming platform, the JASON [4, 5][3] agent-oriented programming platform, and the CARTAGO [14, 15][4] environment-oriented programming platform. By carefully allowing all those platforms to work together in a unified way, not only did we have a platform for multi-agent-oriented programming, but we could also actually allow users to use all the expressive power originally available in each of the platforms that were being developed for many years before we realized the potential of integrating them. As such, there are many features at each level that would be impossible to present in a single book chapter. So in this chapter we have chosen to present JaCaMo as the unified platform it is, without references to the individual platforms that originated it, and concentrating on those essential features of JaCaMo that were required in modeling a particular scenario we have selected as a running example for this chapter.

Although there are other approaches to multi-agent programming that consider more than one level of abstraction, for example [7, 8, 18], to our knowledge JaCaMo is the only fully operational programming platform that provides first class abstractions for the organization, agent, and environment levels of multi-agent systems. Of course, there is much related literature on programming languages for multi-agent systems and in agent-oriented software engineering; this book covers much of the relevant work in the latter area, but we can also mention [2,9,16,17,20].

Throughout this chapter, we will use a running example to illustrate some the programming constructs available in JaCaMo. The section structure follows the three levels of such abstractions: organization, agent, and environment; that is, we will present the relevant abstractions in a "top-down" fashion from social, to agent, and then the environment shared by the agents. The language constructs or design diagrams related to those abstractions are all introduced through examples from the following scenario. A small metal manufacturing company is modeled as a multi-agent system; this is not industrial production but rather like a workshop where

[1] http://jacamo.sourceforge.net.

[2] http://moise.sourceforge.net.

[3] http://jason.sourceforge.net.

[4] http://cartago.sourceforge.net.

metal products are crafted manually. Employees of the company are, of course, the *agents* who play particular *roles* in that *organization*. The *environment* is the workshop itself, where a variety of *artifacts* available in that environment are used by the agents to help individual labor as well as to coordinate their work. One of the various products produced at that workshop is a pan, so the company has a *scheme* for producing that particular type of pan, which will depend on a number of agents playing particular roles and consequently performing specific tasks (i.e., *goals* the agents have to achieve) so that the pan piece can be produced.

The computational system resulting from the JaCaMo specification could be used for simulation of work practices in an attempt to optimise the work of humans, or indeed for developing a system that would support the work of humans, or even with a view to fully automate the work with robots and so forth. However, the above scenario can also just be thought of as metaphor for various coordination relations, autonomous behavior, and resource sharing that occur in any (large-scale) multi-agent system.

After the next three sections, each covering one of the levels of programming abstractions in JaCaMo, we discuss some issues of multi-agent-oriented programming and finish with conclusions and future work.

2 Organization Level

In this section, we will look into social-level programming in JaCaMo. One of the essential aspects of the social level of a multi-agent system is the *structure* of the agent society. The main abstractions related to the structure of a society of agents are those of *groups* and *roles*. Agents play particular roles within groups. Groups can relate to each other, and form more complex groups. In its simplest form, a group is a functional unit that will need a number of agents playing particular roles in order to accomplish a particular task within the multi-agent system. All these aspects related to social structure are programmed in JaCaMo through a *structural specification*, which is usually first modeled as a diagram using a graphical notation.[5] In Fig. 13.1, we show the structural specification diagram for our running example.

As we can see in the diagram, roles can inherit characteristics from more general roles. For example, a *smith* is a type of *metal worker*, which is represented with a role inheritance arrow. In our scenario, there are *forger* agents who operate the furnace and can cast individual parts from liquid metal. The *smiths* then mould and finish the parts with hammers. The last type of metal worker is the *finisher* who only polishes the assembled pieces and packages the final products. Forgers are highly skilled, as they need to operate the furnace, requiring significant training according to safety regulations. Smiths and finishers need less training so in fact the same

[5]At runtime, the organization program is available to agents and the organization infrastructure as an XML file.

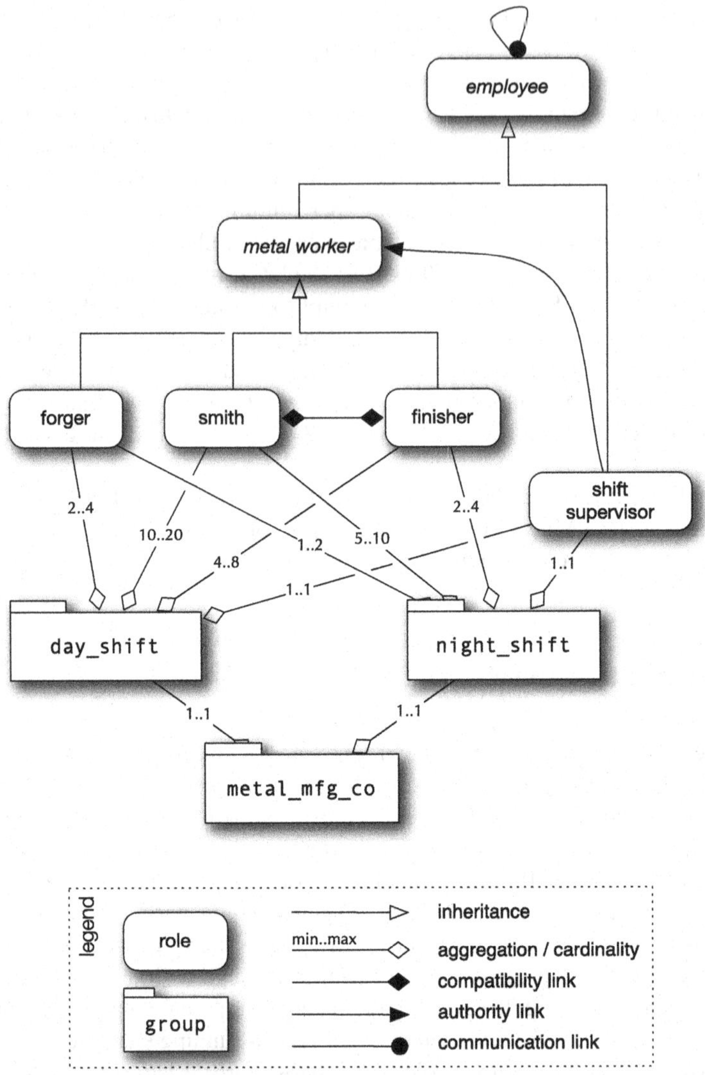

Fig. 13.1 A structural specification showing roles, groups, and some possible links between them

person can act both as a smith and as a finisher (normally in the production of two separate products), hence the compatibility relation between the smith and finisher roles. At any moment in time, there is one *shift supervisor* present in the workshop, who manages all the metal workers. The shift supervisor is in a relation of power over all metal workers and, of course, all employees can communicate with each other.

Although normally groups should be detailed down to the level where the group operates together toward specific tasks (such as producing a particular metal piece), in this example we have purposely left the groups fairly underspecified. We have only stated that the group of agents representing the whole community of interest (the employees of the metal manufacturing company's) has two main (sub)groups, one for the day shift and the other for the night shift. We can also note that the night shift has only half of the workers required in the day shift. When we aggregate roles into groups or groups into other groups, we can state a cardinality. For example, the day shift group requires that at least 2 and up to 4 agents playing role forger have been scheduled to work on that shift.

In this scenario, the workers at the workshop spontaneously engage in the required work to complete incoming orders of handcrafted pieces. In case of dispute or orders that require urgent attention, the shift supervisor intervenes and ask particular workers to take up roles in the ad hoc groups formed to complete the orders. Note again that this is not the usual approach. We could have included in the structural specification specific groups for each type of product, and we could later specify that agents of relevant roles have the obligation to commit to tasks that require the participation of agents playing that role. The obligation ceases to exist if enough agents playing the necessary roles have already committed themselves to a given task. This would be a much more rigid organization, one that is often required in computational systems. Other JaCaMo examples available in the references given at the beginning of the chapter are like that. We chose a different approach in this chapter precisely to emphasize that the degree of freedom left to agents really is a designer choice.

Besides the social structure, another fundamental aspect of the social level are the *schemes*, which provide a practical way for a group to work on particular tasks. A scheme is much like a social plan: it decomposes a social goal into simpler goals, and assigns subsets of those goals, called *missions*, to agents playing particular roles within the group that will be responsible for a particular instance of such scheme. The task decomposition structure makes it explicit whether the goals can be achieved in parallel or only sequentially. The organization infrastructure automatically takes care of informing the agents when they are required to achieve individual goals, based on the dependencies between goals resulting from the partial order specified in the scheme. The *functional specification* of the organization is given by scheme diagrams as the one shown in Fig. 13.2.

The figure shows a scheme used when a new pan of a certain kind needs to be produced. The scheme gives a "recipe" for how a group of agents can efficiently produce a pan. Note that work on the pan would only start if enough agents commit to work on the specific roles required by that scheme; this is also ensured by the organizational infrastructure. As can be seen in the diagram, the agents (playing role *forger* as we see later) responsible for missions *forging1* and *forging2* work in parallel and the smith agent responsible for mission *smithing* will assemble the layers of the pan base while the agent responsible for mission *forging2* finishes forging the other parts of the pan. Note how *smithing* is also annotated as the mission that goal assemble parts belongs to. This means that the agent responsible for

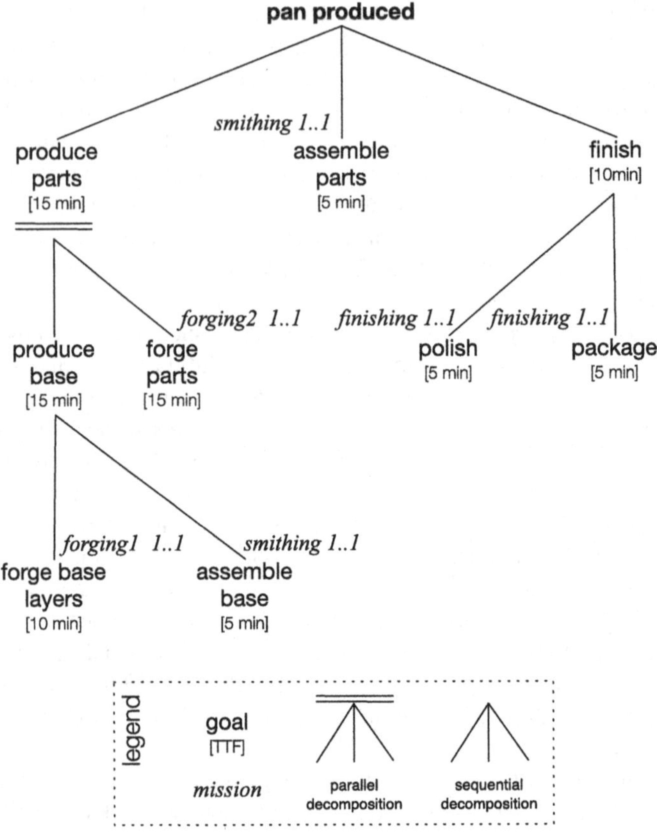

Fig. 13.2 A functional specification showing a scheme containing goals, deadlines, and missions; goals can be achieved either sequentially or in parallel

the mission will have to achieve both goals, and will do so when the organization informs the agent that it can go ahead and try to achieve the next goal in the agent's mission. After the parts are assembled, the agent responsible for mission *finishing* will achieve the goals to polish the piece and then to pack it. Note that, like roles and groups, missions also can have a cardinality specification. In this example, we need exactly one agent (of the appropriate role, as stated later) to commit to each mission before the scheme is considered "well formed" by the organization infrastructure, and only then the work on the scheme can be started. The acronym "TTF" used in Fig. 13.2 stands for "Time to Fulfil" and denotes the specification of a deadline for the achievement of the corresponding goal.

Finally, we need to say which roles are *permitted* or *obliged* to which missions. This is done through a *normative specification*. Table 13.1 shows the normative specification for our running example.

Table 13.1 A normative specification for the running example

Norm	Role	Deontic relation	Mission/goals
n1	Forger	Permission	*Forger1*
n2	Forger	Permission	*Forger2*
n3	Smith	Permission	*Smithing*
n4	Finisher	Permission	*Finishing*

Interestingly, the organization infrastructure, which ensures the organization works according to the specification, is implemented by means of *organizational artifacts*. That is, the same mechanism that agents use to interact with the environment is also used for agents, for example, to request adopting a role in a particular group, or to check which schemes currently instantiated are in need of particular roles to be taken up, and so forth. We do not discuss in details the organization infrastructure here, but refer the interested reader to [12] instead.

3 Agent Level

At the agent level, we need to program the autonomous behavior of individual agents within the system. This time, we will not be using diagrams but we will stick to a logic-based programming language. While there are many trends toward visual programming, most computer scientists still enjoy having an actual language in which to program. The particular language used for JaCaMo agents has constructs that directly map to the main abstractions we associate with autonomous agents: beliefs, goals, and plans in particular. Of course, we could have avoided explaining the language here; for example, we could have used Prometheus [13] *overview diagrams* to give some ideas of the kinds of beliefs, goals, and plans our agents would need in the running example. It would not be difficult to then generate the main code skeleton from such diagrams, if we later wanted to have a fully working code for our JaCaMo agents. However, we have preferred to introduce the actual programming language, as many users find the language quite appealing.

The first abstraction at this level is that of a *belief*. Beliefs are used to represent information available to the agent, and any such information will have one of three main possible sources of information in a multi-agent system: sensing (i.e., perception of the environment), other agents, or the agent itself (in which case we call the belief a "mental note"). For example, in our running example, an agent might need to know the time when the work shift is expected to finish. The agent would then hold a belief:

```
shift_end(1700)[source(percept), artifact_name("shift_time"), ...].
```

This could be used to represent that the agent believes that the shift ends at 17:00 h. In square brackets we have *annotations* that are used to keep in the belief base the relevant meta-level information about the belief itself. The *source* of the information is always present, for all beliefs in the belief base. In this case, we see that this information (about the scheduled end time for the current shift) was acquired via perception of the environment, in particular, in this case, it was obtained from an *artifact* available in the workshop called "shift time", perhaps an electronic sign displaying the shift times and visible to all workers.

Agents also typically need domain knowledge (i.e., theoretical knowledge as opposed to practical knowledge that is given to agents in the form of plans, as discussed below). For this, users can write prolog-like reasoning rules. For example,

```
compatible(R1) :- .my_name(Me) &
                  not ( commitment(Me,G2,_) &
                     goal_for(R1,G1) & ttf(G1,T1) & ttf(G2,T2) &
                     time_todo(G1,T3) & T2+T3 > T1 ).
```

could be used for agents to reason about whether role R1 is compatible with its current commitments toward goals related to other roles the agent is currently playing. In particular, the rule says that there cannot be any goal G2 in any of the missions to which the agent is currently committed that will be finished at a time T2 at which it will be too late to achieve goal G1 (related to role R1) that takes T3 units of time to achieve and for which the deadline is T1. Recall that a TTF is how deadlines for goals to be achieved are specified in the functional specification (see Fig. 13.2). Furthermore, it must be emphasised that some of the predicates used above (such as ttf, goal_for, and time_todo) would have to be defined as rules themselves to facilitate accessing that information that is available in the belief base as originating from organizational artifacts, although represented in more complex structures than used above for illustration purposes. The reader may have guessed that the *internal action* .my_name is how one gets the agent's own name (i.e., the name used to identify that agent within the multi-agent system).

We now turn to the *practical reasoning*, that is, reasoning about actions, which determines the behavior of autonomous agents. This is programmed as a set of *plans*, which are *courses of action* that agents use to achieve goals, or to react to changes in beliefs (e.g., perceived changes in the environment, or acceptable information received from other agents). A plan starts with a *triggering event* that tells for what sort of event (i.e., changes in beliefs or goals) the plan is meant to be used. As a first example, consider de following plan:

```
+alarm(fire)
   : not drill(fire) & using(Equip)
  <- shut_down(Equip);
     !at(assembly_point).
```

which says that whenever the agent comes to believe that the fire alarm has been set off, in case the agent does not believe at that moment that this is just a fire drill exercise (unfortunately, people have different behavior in drill and actual events), the agent should shut down any equipment being used and then have a new goal to be at the assembly point (i.e., this plan prescribes that some action be taken and then a new goal pursued). The agent's plan library will typically have various alternative plans to achieve new instances of the goal to be at a particular place. For example, the plan to use the lift should not be *applicable* in case the building is on fire (that is what the context part of the plan, between : and <-, is for). The behavior of the agent is determined by the choices of such alternative plans, which are made as late as possible so that they can be based on the most up to date information available to the agent. The *goal* to be at a particular place only succeeds when the agent *believes* that it is at that place; a *test goal* (e.g., ?at(SomePlace) can be used to ensure that a plan only finishes successfully under the condition that the agent believes the goal has been achieved. Consider now the following plan:

```
+!forge(Part)[scheme(SchemeName)]
    : .my_name(Me) & not ( commitment(Me,forge(_),AnotherScheme) &
      SchemeName \== AnotherScheme )
   <- pick_mould(Part);   // select the right mould
      fill_mould(Part);   // fill it up with liquid metal
      !cool_down(Part).   // finally have a new goal to use the
                          // appropriate cooling method
```

which is used when the agent has a new goal to achieve (*achievement goals* are preceded by "!") rather than a new belief. However, from the annotation we can see that this achievement goal is a *social goal*: it has been assigned to the agent as part of its work on a particular *scheme* of the agent organization. From the plan context, we can see that agents are not supposed to forge parts for more than one scheme at the same time. The course of action to take if the agent's current believed circumstances are that it is not committed to forging as part of another scheme is as described in the comments of the code above. As a last example, we show a plan that is of generic use and therefore made available with JaCaMo. It could be used in any agent that is meant to always respect its obligations within the organization:

```
+obligation(Ag,achieved(Scheme,Goal),Deadline)
    : .my_name(Ag) // the obligation is for me
   <- // adds the organisational goal
      !Goal[scheme(Scheme)];
      // inform that the goal has been achieved
      goalAchieved(Goal)[artifact_name(Scheme)].
```

The plan says that whenever the agent gets to know (through the organization infrastructure) that it has a new obligation toward achieving a particular goal, the agent should adopt that new goal. That goal has the organization scheme where it comes from as an annotation so that the agent can check whether each particular goal is an individual goal the agent has decided to adopt by itself or whether the goal has been adopted as part of the agent's commitment toward an organization. After achieving that goal, the agent should report back to the organization (through an operation on the respective organizational artifact) that the job has been done.[6] Observe the use of a higher-order variable in the plan above. Variable Goal is

[6]There is further ongoing work on *normative programming* in the context of JaCaMo that removes the burden of reporting back when goals have been achieved, as with that work it is possible to specify which environment changes *count as* the achievement of organizational goals [6].

unified with a particular term occurring in the actual event that took place and later, in the plan body, used to stand for the predicate representing a new goal to be achieved. Adding social goal instances this way works whenever the names of goals in the functional diagrams are the same as used in triggering events of the plans the agent has in order to achieve those social goals.

It should be noted that, if an agent chooses to adopt a role within an organization, and in particular takes part on a particular scheme under that role, it will have *obligations* to achieve the goals related to the missions assigned to that role in that scheme. Organizations therefore restrict the freedom of autonomous agents, and this is precisely what is needed in designing some complex multi-agent systems. Furthermore, there are many features of the JaCaMo platform that facilitate the development of complex, adaptable, distributed systems. For example, the organization can be dynamically changed at runtime, given that the organizational infrastructure follows the specification provided in an XML file. Equally, agent behavior can be adapted at run time, as the plan library can be changed at runtime, even through high-level communication.[7] However, it is not our intention in this chapter to provide the reader with an understanding of how the interpreter for this language works, which of course is necessary for advanced programming in JaCaMo, nor with the various language and platform features at any of the three levels. The literature referenced in Sect. 1 can be used to that intent by the interested reader.

4 Environment Level

Even though JaCaMo was developed in Java, an object in an object-oriented programming language is at a completely different level of abstraction than the multi-agent systems abstractions. We require a first-class high-level abstraction that can be used to model the non-autonomous components of the system environment. The abstractions used here are that of an *artifact*, which can represent tools and other objects available in the environment, and that of a *workspace*, similar to a particular location where agents can share the same artifacts.

One of the most important consequences of the use of an artifact as opposed to a Java object is that *observable properties* of the artifact are automatically observed by agents that focus their attention on those artifacts. In other words, that means that those properties will appear in the agent belief base with annotations stating that the belief originated from perception of the environment and in particular from the artifact it is associated with. Similarly, the *operations* available in the artifact in a particular workspace automatically become *actions* that can appear

[7]As usual in multi-agent systems, communication in JaCaMo is based on speech acts, therefore making explicit to the receiver the intentions of the sender of a *message* (i.e., agents use asynchronous communication); for formal details, see [19].

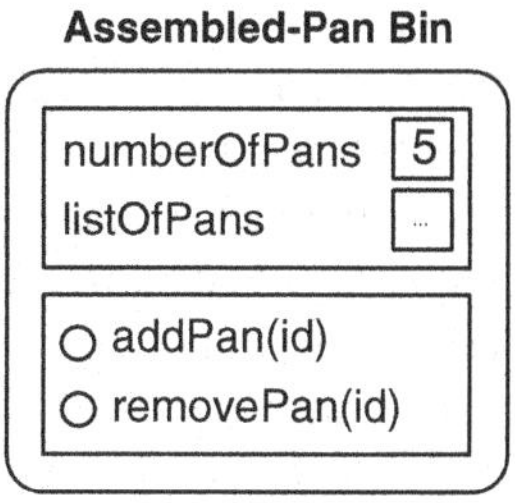

Fig. 13.3 An artifact serving as a bin where assembled pans are left for finishing; a finisher agent can remove any particular pan, so the order in which the pans appear in the bin is not relevant

in the plan body of the plans in an agent's plan library (i.e., agents can perform those operations if they so choose). Interestingly, here again the set of artifact instances in an environment can be changed at runtime, with the consequences that the actions/properties that agents can perform/observe also change accordingly.

As a final note, it is worth mentioning that artifacts do not necessarily represent real-world objects. They can be software entities created exclusively to aid the coordination of agents. Also, as artifacts automatically handle concurrent access problems, they often facilitate the operation of fully asynchronous agent systems, hence somewhat facilitating the development of concurrent/distributed systems.

It should be clear that, in our running example, there could be plenty of artifacts, for example, all the tools used by the smiths, the pieces being produced, and so forth. There could be also an artifact created to help the metal workers coordinate their use of tools that need to be shared between several workers. In Fig. 13.3, to illustrate an artifact (although its Java code is omitted here), we show a bin where smiths leave the pans they have finished assembling, so that the finishers can pick them up for polishing and packaging.

The artifact has two observable properties: one that can be used to check the total number of pans currently in the bin (the shift supervisor, e.g., might be interested in that) and another with a complete list of all the pans (presuming each pan is identified by a serial number of some sort). The operations available on the artifact are those to add or remove individual pans. Of course, any concurrency issues of multiple agents acting simultaneously on the artifact are dealt with intrinsically by the way artifacts are managed in the platform.

5 Discussion

It should be clear by now how the synergies between the abstractions of the three different levels of a multi-agent system provides rich mechanisms for programming complex systems. It is a case where the result of the JaCaMo combination is much more than the sum of the three separate platforms that originally formed it.

Consider, for example, if the social level of the programming platform was not available. A lot of programming would have to be done at the agent level to compensate for that. That code would not be strictly describing agent behavior so to start with that code would make the agent program less elegant and less readable. Furthermore, the social knowledge would have to be replicated in each individual agent. More than that, a lot of inter-agent communication, and possibly deliberation, agent interaction through the environment, etc. would be required each time a social task needed to be accomplished. While inter-agent communication is often useful and important, many social mechanisms require inefficient communication load, which can be avoided by the social-level abstractions. Equally, without the environment level, many extra cumbersome agent plans would be required to ensure agents could coordinate for example in accessing shared resources.

There are also many important aspects of the platform, for example, the fact that changes at all levels of the agent society can take place during runtime. That is, all the mechanisms for agents that are able to reason about social re-organization, to adapt agent behavior, to increase agent capacities through environment (artifact) changes, etc. are all in place. Another aspect not mentioned so far is that none of the platform engines at the three levels cause problems with bottlenecks and single points of failure (of course, designers and programmers can always create systems that display such problems). For example, the organization infrastructure, in its artifact-based implementation, can be fully distributed whereas other platforms require some form of centralization at the social level. Finally, the direct integration with legacy Java code and the many customization mechanisms can be useful in various types of projects.

6 Conclusions

We have described the JaCaMo platform recently put together that allows the programming of multi-agent systems with constructs that match the abstractions used in multi-agent systems at the organizational, agent, as well as environment levels. For this to be possible, various engines, APIs, interfaces, etc. built over many years had to be put together in ways that were by no means trivial and using techniques that we reported in the literature over the years. While other approaches have been reported in the literature, to our knowledge there is no other platform where practical programming at all three levels is readily available in a unified way.

We believe the achievement of such a practical programming platform will open the possibility for finally being able to show that a programming paradigm based on multi-agent systems effectively facilitate software development for certain classes of software. In particular, most visions of the future of computer science point to increasing need for large-scale complex autonomous geographically distributed systems, clearly a type of system for which we will need more appropriate ways to develop than traditional software engineering and programming language approaches can offer. It is also interesting to note the increasing commercial interest in actor-based programming languages [1] and other techniques such as those reported in [10], precisely because, like agent-based, they favor a natural way to design and program concurrent and distributed systems, specially with the current wide availability of multicore architectures.

Of course, much work remains on this front toward full-fledged multi-agent-oriented programming. While work on agent programming has been going on for a couple of decades, because the paradigm lacked the other equally important levels of abstractions of multi-agent systems, the experience with those systems will contribute but are not sufficient for establishing the required best practices for multi-agent-oriented programming. We hope to work both on formalization of our approach as well as in using it in industrial applications where the challenges require significant research effort (including telecommunication, healthcare, and smart grids, to name just a few).

Acknowledgments Thanks to Rafael Cauê Cardoso for proofreading and to Ismael Jabes da Silva Santos for suggesting the metal workshop example used in this chapter. Rafael Bordini and Jomi Hübner are grateful for the support given by CNPq grant numbers 307924/2009-2 and 307350/2009-6.

References

1. Agha G (1986) Actors: a model of concurrent computation in distributed systems. MIT Press, Cambridge
2. Beydoun G, Low G, Henderson-Sellers B, Mouratidis H, Gomez-Sanz JJ, Pavon J, Gonzalez-Perez C (2009) FAML: a generic metamodel for MAS development. IEEE Trans Softw Eng 35:841–863
3. Boissier O, Bordini RH, Hübner JF, Ricci A, Santi A (2013) Multi-agent oriented programming with JaCaMo. Sci Comput Program 78(6):747–761. doi:http://dx.doi.org/10.1016/j.scico.2011.10.004. http://www.sciencedirect.com/science/article/pii/S016764231100181X
4. Bordini RH, Hübner JF, Vieira R (2005) ***Jason*** and the golden fleece of agent-oriented programming. In: Bordini RH, Dastani M, Dix J, Fallah-Seghrouchni AE (eds) Multi-agent programming, multiagent systems, artificial societies, and simulated organizations, vol 15. Springer, Berlin, pp 3–37
5. Bordini RH, Hübner JF, Wooldridge M (2007) Programming multi-agent systems in AgentSpeak using ***Jason***. Wiley Series in Agent Technology. Wiley, New York
6. Brito M, Hübner JF, Bordini RH (2013) Programming institutional facts in multi-agent systems. In: Aldewereld H, Sichman J (eds) Coordination, organizations, institutions, and norms in agent systems, vol VIII. Lecture notes in computer science, vol 7756. Springer, Berlin, pp 158–173. doi:10.1007/978-3-642-37756-3_10. http://dx.doi.org/10.1007/978-3-642-37756-3_10
7. Bromuri S, Stathis K (2008) Situating cognitive agents in GOLEM. In: Weyns D, Brueckner S, Demazeau Y (eds) Engineering environment-mediated multi-agent systems. Lecture notes in computer science, vol 5049. Springer, Berlin, pp 115–134
8. Dastani M, Grossi D, Meyer JJ, Tinnemeier N (2008) Normative multi-agent programs and their logics. In: Proceedings of the KRAMAS-08
9. Dignum V, Sichman J (2010) Agent organizations; models, architectures and applications. Springer, Berlin
10. Harel D, Marron A, Weiss G (2012) Behavioral programming. Commun ACM 55(7):90–100. doi:10.1145/2209249.2209270. http://doi.acm.org/10.1145/2209249.2209270
11. Hübner JF, Sichman JS, Boissier O (2007) Developing organised multiagent systems using the MOISE. IJAOSE 1(3/4):370–395

12. Hübner JF, Boissier O, Kitio R, Ricci A (2010) Instrumenting multi-agent organisations with organisational artifacts and agents. Auton Agent Multi Agent Syst 20(3):369–400
13. Padgham L, Winikoff M (2004) Developing intelligent agent systems: a practical guide. Wiley, New York
14. Ricci A, Piunti M, Viroli M, Omicini A (2009) Environment programming in CArtAgO. In: Bordini RH, Dastani M, Dix J, El Fallah Seghrouchni A (eds) Multi-agent programming, Chap 8. Springer, Berlin, pp 259–288. doi:10.1007/978-0-387-89299-3_8. http://www.springerlink.com/content/p36v9l7446j75828/
15. Ricci A, Piunti M, Viroli M (2011) Environment programming in multi-agent systems: an artifact-based perspective. Auton Agent Multi Agent Syst 23(2):158–192
16. Sterling L, Taveter K (2009) The art of agent-oriented modeling. The MIT Press, Cambridge
17. Stratulat T, Ferber J, Tranier J (2009) MASQ: towards an integral approach to interaction. In: AAMAS (2009), pp 813–820
18. Urovi V, Bromuri S, Stathis K, Artikis A (2010) Initial steps towards run-time support for norm-governed systems. In: Coordination, organizations, institutions, and norms in agent systems, vol VI. Lecture notes in computer science, vol 6541. Springer, Berlin, pp 268–284
19. Vieira R, Moreira ÁF, Wooldridge M, Bordini RH (2007) On the formal semantics of speech-act based communication in an agent-oriented programming language. J Artif Intell Res (JAIR) 29:221–267
20. Weyns D, Parunak HVD (eds) (2007) Special issue on environments for multi-agent systems. Autonomous agents and multi-agent systems, vol 14(1). Springer, The Netherlands

Part V
Multi-Agent Systems Implementation

Chapter 14
The Evolution of MAS Tools

Arnon Sturm and Onn Shehory

Abstract During the evolution of the agent-oriented software engineering area, many tools were developed. These range from application programming interfaces (APIs) for developing agent and multi-agent applications, to platforms that provide the infrastructure for the development, testing, execution, monitoring, and maintaining agent-based applications. In early days there was a proliferation of such tools; however, nowadays, only a limited number of tools have kept on evolving and are being used. Moreover, it seems that most development of such tools occurred in the academia and only a few were devised and are being used within the industry. The challenges in developing such tools include the provisioning of a comprehensive suite to address both the development and the deployment of multi-agent systems.

Keywords Multi-agent framework • Multi-agent platform • Multi-agent infrastructure • Multi-agent middleware

1 Introduction

The evolution of the agent-oriented paradigm has triggered a need for platforms, middleware, frameworks, and tools to support agents and MAS development lifecycle, to validate the paradigm, and to utilize it. Indeed, a large, diverse set of frameworks, platforms, and tools was developed during the years, alongside diversity in terminology, semantics, and functionality. In this chapter we focus

A. Sturm (✉)
Department of Information Systems Engineering, Ben-Gurion University of the Negev, Beer-Sheva, Israel
e-mail: sturm@bgu.ac.il

O. Shehory
IBM – Haifa Research Lab, Haifa, Israel
e-mail: onn@il.ibm.com

O. Shehory and A. Sturm (eds.), *Agent-Oriented Software Engineering*,
DOI 10.1007/978-3-642-54432-3_14,

on frameworks and platforms. Therefore, to facilitate better understanding of the differences among the terminologies of frameworks, platforms, and tools, we first provide a set of definitions of means for implementing Multi-Agent Systems (MAS) applications.

Definition 1 *Software Architecture* refers to the high-level structures of a software system. It can be defined as the set of structures needed to reason about the software system, which comprise the software elements, the relations between them, and the properties of both elements and relations [1].

Definition 2 An *Agent Platform* is a technological architecture providing the environment in which agents can operate to achieve their goals [2].

Definition 3 A *Framework* is a software providing generic functionality that can be selectively changed by additional user-written code, thus providing application-specific software. A software framework is a universal, reusable software platform used to develop applications, products, and solutions. Software frameworks include support programs, compilers, code libraries, tool sets, and application programming interfaces (APIs) that bring together all the different components to enable development of a project or a solution [3].

Definition 4 An *Agent tool* is a term used to include all software technologies that implement (some of the) agent notions, including platforms, frameworks, goal-specific software, and tailored solutions.

Agent and multi-agent architectures are discussed in Chap. 4 of this book. In this chapter we aim at providing an overview of MAS frameworks (including MAS platforms) from the requirements, design, standardization, usage, and future development aspects. In the next section we provide a detailed set of requirements for MAS frameworks. Next, we describe the standardization efforts made by FIPA in terms of agent infrastructure. We then elaborate on MAS frameworks and tools. The following two sections are devoted to describing specific frameworks which are widely used, namely JADE/WADE [4, 5] from the object-oriented stream and JACK [6] from the BDI stream. We conclude the chapter with an overview of future evolution of MAS frameworks and possible research direction.

2 Requirements for MAS Frameworks

As the MAS technology evolved, there was a need to capture the requirements for infrastructure needs. Gasser [7] sets a comprehensive list of criteria while classifying their importance. In the following we describe the requirements originated from [7] and add upon these other requirements which were added later on. The requirements are divided into *components*, which refer to the elements that comprise a MAS framework, desired *properties* of such a framework, *general criteria* which are essentially non-functional requirements, and *usage capabilities*, which are tools and process support.

2.1 Required Components

- *Execution Engine (EE):* A MAS framework should have a mechanism to execute and control the MAS operation.
- *Communication Languages (CL):* A MAS framework should provide support for Agent Communication Languages (ACLs) and their underlying support bases (e.g., belief knowledge bases for MAS based on KQML, FIPA, etc.).
- *Mobility (MO):* A MAS framework should facilitate the mobility of MAS design and execution across environments.
- *Security (SEC):* A MAS framework should provide an inherent support for MAS security.
- *Resource Description and Discovery (RDD) Services (RDDS):* A MAS framework should provide services for resources (such as agent, services, teams, markets, and capabilities) description, offering, and discovery.
- *Simulator and Experimenter (SE):* A MAS framework should provide means for testing and exploring MAS applications' behavior before they are deployed.
- *Data Collector and Monitoring (DCM):* A MAS framework should provide means for collecting data regarding applications' execution, to facilitate analysis of their performance.

2.2 Required Properties

- *Openness (OPEN): A MAS framework should be able to accommodate* agents that are heterogeneous across dimensions (e.g., architecture, resources used, interactivity, and scale).
- *Scalability (SCL):* A MAS framework should support the scalability of MAS in terms of execution and design.

2.3 General Criteria Required

- *Usability (USA):* A MAS framework should provide means to easily learn its usage and limitations.
- *Support (SUP):* A MAS framework should continuously be developed and evolved.
- *Use:* To gain further confidence in adopting a MAS framework, it is preferable that it would have a large number of developed applications. The variety of

implemented applications can also indicate the suitability of the framework for a specific use.

- *Standardization (STD):* It is preferable that a MAS framework would comply with a standard as adhering to a standard will benefit from many components, architectures, languages, interfaces, and would facilitate interoperability of the MASs.

2.4 Required Usage Capabilities

- *Design Methodologies (DM):* It is preferable that a MAS framework would be accompanied with systematic engineering methods for the design and construction of MAS.
- *Integrated Development Environments (IDEs):* It is preferable that a MAS framework would be provided along with an IDE which is specialized for the construction, operation, and use of MAS. The IDE may consist of a debugger, a testing environment, simulation, etc.
- *Templates (TEMP):* It is preferable that a MAS framework would be provided along with a set of templates that better facilitate the development of the appropriate agent types.

3 The FIPA Standardization

With the emergence of agent and MAS tools, standardization efforts also took place. Although these efforts have diminished in recent years, they have set the infrastructure for agent frameworks and platforms. The most prominent standardization effort was undertaken by the Foundation for Intelligent Physical Agent (FIPA).[1] That effort aimed, in part, to address some of the requirements set in the previous section. The results delivered by FIPA consist of various standards related to MAS infrastructure. In particular, it provides a specification of a generic reference model for MAS infrastructure as depicted in Fig. 14.1.

According to FIPA, an agent platform should include the following components:

- Agents, which are computational processes implementing agent characteristics such as autonomy and proactiveness.
- A directory facilitator (DF), which provides yellow pages services. These services include registration, deregistration, modification, and search.
- An agent management system (AMS), which should manage and monitor all agents' lifecycles and provide the control (e.g., scheduling and messaging) for

[1] http://www.fipa.org/

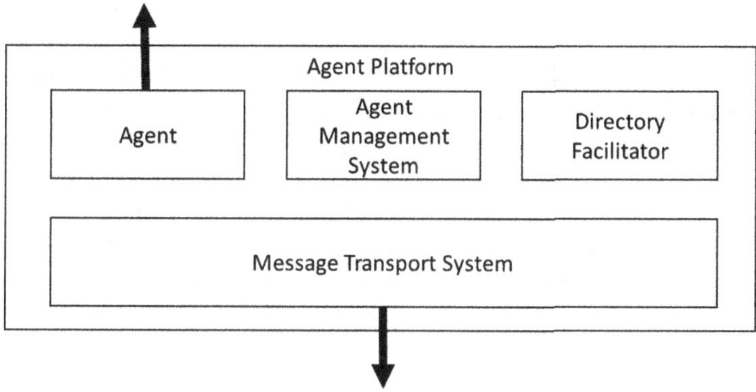

Fig. 14.1 FIPA reference model

the entire platform. The AMS should have the following capabilities: suspend agents, terminate agents, create agents, resume agents' execution, invoke agents, execute agents, and handle resource management.

- A message transport system (MTS), which is responsible for communication between agents that reside on different platforms.

4 A Survey of MAS Frameworks and Platforms

As stated before, many MAS frameworks and platforms were developed over the years. Most of these were developed for research purposes and originated within universities or research institutions. Nevertheless, several initiations from the industry also exist. Despite the proliferation of MAS framework and platforms, only a few of these have lasted and are continually developed and used. In this chapter we intend to expose the reader to the variety of frameworks and platforms. This variety of tools can be found within the agentLink website [8]. In particular, we refer the readers to MAS platforms such as Grasshopper [9], ZEUS [10], JATLite [11], FIPA-OS [12], JAFMAS [13], OAA [14], Ara [15], AgentScape [16], and Bond [17]. In this chapter we put an emphasis on the most recent frameworks and further elaborate on these.

4.1 Cougaar

The Cognitive Agent Architecture—Cougaar [18–20] is an open-source Java-based agent platform which was developed in projects funded by DARPA. It is aimed at problems with the following nature: hierarchical decomposition of complex tasks, integration of distributed separate applications and data sources, generation of dynamic plans in face of execution, and highly parallel applications. The main idea of Cougaar is the imitation of human cognitive processes that includes decomposing, delegating, consolidating, monitoring, gathering, and reporting. In order to support these mini-processes Cougaar adopts the notion of Plugin that implements various behaviors that together work to achieve a task which is composed of plans. Based on these, Cougaar supports both static and dynamic planning.

Cougaar has the major required components of MAS framework, yet it does not have simulation and experimentation facilities. Although Cougaar does not provide a tailored IDE, it is supported by a proprietary methodology for developing MAS.

4.2 Cybele

Cybele is in continuous development by Intelligent Automation Inc. It is a platform for the development and deployment of large-scale distributed systems [21]. The Cybele platform is built on top of Java and provides infrastructure for the kernel, agents, activities and services. Developers use the Activity Oriented Programming Interface (AOPI) for developing MAS. Following Cybele, the main components required for MAS development are containers that consist of agents, which in turn consist of activities, which are essentially the agent behaviors. Cybele was used in the areas of air traffic management, scheduling and planning, and simulation.

Cybele has the major required components of a MAS framework, yet it does not have simulation and experimentation facilities. It is also supported by a proprietary methodology for developing MAS.

4.3 MadKit

MadKit is a modular and scalable platform written in Java and built upon the AGR (Agent/Group/Role) organizational model: agents are situated in groups and play roles [22]. Although written in Java, agents in MadKit can be programmed in Scheme, Jess, Java, Python, or BeanShell. In fact, in order to avoid the need for compilation it is recommended that agents in MadKit would be developed in one of the supported scripting languages.

An agent, in MadKit consists of four parts: (1) *activation*, which is essentially the setup, (2) *live*, which include the agent behavior, (3) *end*, which is the termination procedure, and (4) *initGUI*, which deals with the graphic interface of the agent.

Each agent has access to relevant organizations (groups and roles) and may use various ways of communication.

MadKit is equipped with its own IDE and methodology and provides the infrastructure for executing MAS applications. It also provides system agents, which allow the monitoring of agents and their interactions.

4.4 JIAC

JIAC is a framework aiming at easing the development of complex, distributed applications, supporting system development in heterogeneous environments, and deepening the knowledge in management of multi-agent systems [23]. JIAC was developed by following the component-based development approach, which is being used for developing MAS applications as well. A JIAC application consists of AgentNodes each of which provides facilities for discovery and yellow pages services. Each AgentNode can run many Agents that may have AgentBeans representing behaviors. An AgentBean has two parts: memory and execution.

JIAC provides a comprehensive set of developing tools that facilitate MAS development. These include a design tool (using BPMN), JIAC agent description language editor, and a monitoring tool for the MAS behavior.

4.5 Agent Factory

The Agent Factory Framework is an open source collection of tools, platforms, and languages that support the development and deployment of multi-agent systems [2]. The framework consists of a run-time environment that is compliant with FIPA, thus allowing the use of well-established platform principles, a common language framework, which enables the design and implementation of agent programming languages (these currently include AgentSpeak [24] and TeleoReactive [25]).

5 JADE/WADE

JADE is a Java-based framework that is mostly used within the research community [27]. It is a comprehensive framework for MAS development that complies with the FIPA standards [4]. It provides a platform (or a middleware) for agent execution, a complete set of Java code libraries that facilitate the development of MAS, and can be used and extended for specific applications. Furthermore, JADE provides the developers with facilities supporting the development process that include the following:

- Monitoring console, which enables agent execution, suspension, resumption, and termination, as well as migrating agents to other platforms or cloning them. In addition, it allows the generation of messages to agents
- Sniffer, which monitors the communication among agents and enables filtering and recording of messages
- Debugger, which monitors the internal behavior of agents, including incoming and outgoing messages, the agent status, and its behavior. The debugger also has the capabilities of controlling the agents in terms of breakpoints and states

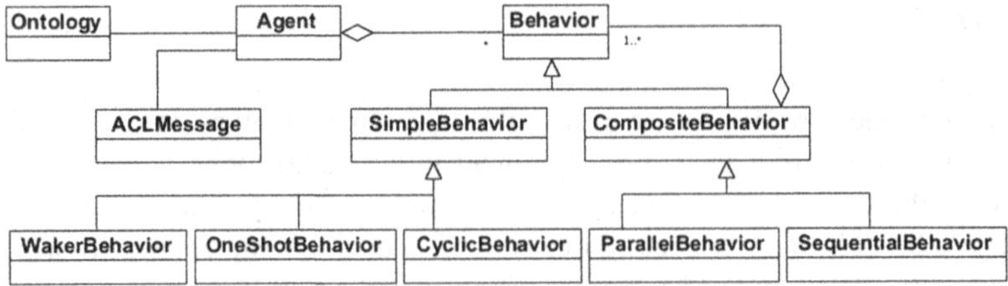

Fig. 14.2 Partial meta-model of JADE

The concepts used within JADE are pretty simple; this contributes to its popularity. In the following we elaborate on these concepts as appear in Fig. 14.2. Note that the meta-model presented in this figure is partial and is meant for describing the notion of the agent structure.

As depicted in Fig. 14.2, the agent class is the main building block that facilitates the MAS application, an agent can be associated with an ontology that can be used while communicating with other agents via ACL messages. The core functionality of agents within JADE is encapsulated in behaviors, which are considered as virtual threads (i.e., these are not real threads over the CPU, rather, the JADE platform manages them). JADE provides various behaviors, including those that appear in the meta-model. The behaviors also enable the specification of various protocols usually via the adoption and extension of the FSM behavior.

In Listing 14.1 we show a fragment of JADE code that demonstrates its use. In that example (adopted from the JADE examples code) a simple Ping Agent registers itself with the Directory Facilitator (DF) and then waits for ACLMessages. In case a REQUEST message is received containing the string "ping" it replies with an INFORM message with the string "pong". Otherwise the agent replies with the proper reply of unexpected content or act.

JADE is in continuous development and has been extended to deal with business processes and workflows. This is done by utilizing JADE architecture and devising new concepts of workflows as reflected in the Workflows and Agents Development Environment (WADE) [5].

Another important extension of JADE resides within the BDI area. As JADE mainly deals with the traditional object-oriented and software engineering aspects of MAS development, Pokahr et al. [26] suggest to extend it to support the mental aspect of MAS. In particular, they introduce the notion of beliefs, which construct the agent knowledge, goals which agents are required to achieve, maintain, or perform, and plans which are predefined and the agents are required to select from those is order to achieve their goals. The implementation is based on the extension of the JADE agent class with additional required specifications.

```
public class PingAgent extends Agent {
  //Inner class of the main behavior
  private class WaitPingAndReplyBehaviour extends CyclicBehaviour{
    public WaitPingAndReplyBehaviour(Agent a) {
      super(a);
    }
    //The behavior functionality
    public void action() {
      ACLMessage  msg = myAgent.receive();
      if(msg != null){
        ACLMessage reply = msg.createReply();
        if(msg.getPerformative()== ACLMessage.REQUEST){
          String content = msg.getContent();
          if((content != null)&&(content.indexOf("ping") != -1)){
            reply.setPerformative(ACLMessage.INFORM);
            reply.setContent("pong");
          }
          else{
            reply.setPerformative(ACLMessage.REFUSE);
            reply.setContent("( UnexpectedContent )");
          }
        }
        else {
          reply.setPerformative(ACLMessage.NOT_UNDERSTOOD);
          reply.setContent("(Unexpected-act )");
        }
        send(reply);
      }
      else {
        block();
      }
    }
  } // END of inner class WaitPingAndReplyBehaviour
//configuring the agent
  protected void setup() {
    // Registration with the DF
    DFAgentDescription dfd = new DFAgentDescription();
    ServiceDescription sd = new ServiceDescription();
    sd.setType("PingAgent");
    sd.setName(getName());
    dfd.setName(getAID());
    dfd.addServices(sd);
    DFService.register(this,dfd);
    // adding the behavior
    WaitPingAndReplyBehaviour PingBehaviour = new  WaitPingAndRe
plyBehaviour(this);
    addBehaviour(PingBehaviour);
  }
}
```

Listing 14.1 The Ping agent (adopted from the JADE examples)

6 JACK

JACK is a mature commercial multi-agent framework that facilitates the development of MAS through the adoption of BDI notions [6]. Similarly to JADE, it consists

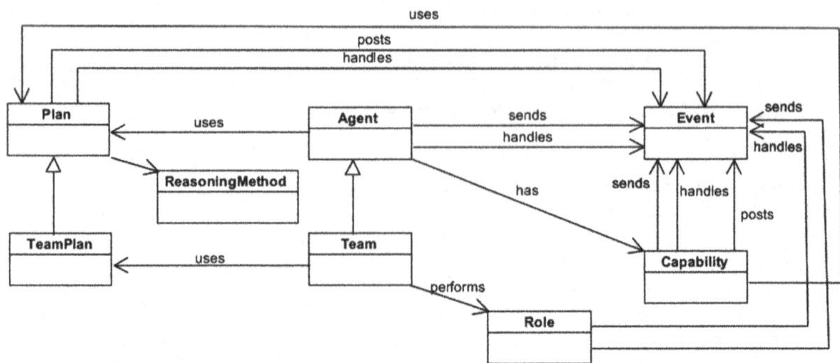

Fig. 14.3 Partial meta-model of JACK

of an execution environment, a framework that provides support for developing MAS applications, and supporting tools. In the following we present an abstract and partial meta-model of the JACK framework (Fig. 14.3).

An agent has capabilities that use plans for their facilitation. The plans are associated with reasoning methods, which can be executed as part of specific plans (see the JACK manual for elaboration [6]). Also, plans and capabilities can send and handle external events (messages) as well as internal events (posts) whereas roles and agents can only send and handle external events. Teams within JACK are special agents that perform roles and use team plans.

To enable readers a more tangible sense of what JACK program consists of, in Listing 14.2 we show an example of JACK sources from a ping application in which multiple messages are sent between two agents.

Having defined and demonstrated the concepts on which JACK is based, in the following we describe the tools provided with JACK.

- Integrated Development Environment (IDE), which is provided to support the new concept. In particular, the IDE provides means for organizing an entire project with the artifacts of agents, plans, teams, capabilities, etc. It also allows the editing of these concepts, as well as compiling these into an executable code. As the entire framework of JACK is implemented in Java, the results of compiling the JACK artifacts are Java source code that can be later on compiled and executed with a regular virtual machine
- Design tool, which is a graphical editor that enables the specification of the various JACK concepts
- Tracing and logging facilities, which address the complexity of testing and monitoring MAS applications. In particular, these facilities enable tracking

```
public agent Pinger extends Agent {
#handles event Ping;
#sends event Ping ping;
#uses plan React;
  public Pinger(String n, String to, String cnt)
  {
   super(n);
send(to,ping.ping(Integer.parseInt(cnt),0,System.currentTimeMillis())
);
  }
  public Pinger(String n)
  { super(n); }
}
```

```
event Ping extends MessageEvent {
  public int   count;
  public long  start;
  public int   hops = 0;
  public int   buffer[] = new int[7000];
  #posted as ping(int cnt, int h, long time) {
    count = cnt;
    start = time;
    hops = h;
    for (int i = 0; i < buffer.length; i++) {
        buffer[i] = i;
    }
  }
}
```

```
plan React extends Plan {
#handles event Ping event;
#sends event Ping ev1;
  body()
  {
      System.err.print("Got Ping-Event "+event.hops+": ");
      for (int i = 6; i < event.buffer.length && i < 9000; i+= 997)
     {System.err.print(i+"="+event.buffer[i]+";");}
      System.err.println("");
      event.hops++;
     @send(event.from,       ev1.ping(event.count,       event.hops,
event.start));
      if (event.hops >= event.count) {
          long ed = System.currentTimeMillis();
          System.err.println("Took " + Long.toString(ed -
          event.start)+ "ms to send the message and get it back)"
                 + Integer.toString(event.count)
                 + " times");
          System.exit(1);
      }
  }
}
```

Listing 14.2 An example of JACK sources (adopted from the JACK examples)

selected agent execution. The traces can be presented graphically over the design specification. In addition, interactions can be monitored, and debugging can be used as well

- Simulation tool, which enables the specification and execution of various scenarios
- Agent run-time engine, which manages the execution of the system, including message passing, reasoning, and meta-reasoning

7 Concluding Remarks

This chapter discusses frameworks and platforms for developing agents and multi-agent systems. Table 14.1 presents the platforms and frameworks we have reviewed and indicates the degree to which each supports the desired properties defined earlier in this chapter. As also seen in the table, all of the tools surveyed provide the developer with an execution engine, and most of them have some kind of a development methodology, they have special IDEs, and they provide templates to ease usage. Most of the tools support system scalability too. However, the tools do not provide openness, and cannot accommodate agents implemented using other platforms, and they lack in providing experimentation and simulation environments. That is, no tool fully addresses the set of requirements presented earlier in this chapter. This void is of course a challenge for future research.

It is evident that many agent and MAS tools have been developed over the years. Based on the review made in this chapter, it seems that many of them use similar concepts though using different terminology. Future research should likely look into this uniformity and check whether it is justified, or other concepts should be introduced. Most of the tools were developed as part of research efforts within research institutes, yet the ones that are continuously being developed and supported are those that are maintained by the industry. From this we can learn that academic tools, regardless of their initial quality, have a difficulty to survive for longer periods. We presume that this may result from lack of resources, or from lack of interest (or both), however this may need the community attention as well.

The comparative analysis we have performed suggests that future extensions of the tools should provide support for simulation and evaluation. Furthermore, there is a need to add mechanisms for incorporating external agents in the frameworks. Although standardization efforts were already made (though have been suspended for a while), it may be necessary to revisit the standards, update, and extend them. This may be reinforced by the prominent divergence of tools from recommendations and standards: many of the tools adopt their own way of implementation, negatively affecting openness and interoperability. New standardization efforts could address the needs of tool developers and may in turn allow interoperability among the agent tools.

The variety of tools available for agent and MAS development calls for means for comparison among them, and in particular for a comprehensive benchmark. Such a benchmark should examine functional properties as well as non-functional properties (such as performance, scalability, security, accessibility, etc.). One facet of the benchmark is to select a common application, which will be implemented

Table 14.1 Summarizing the reviewed frameworks' characterizations

	JADE	JACK	Cougaar	Cybele	Madkit	JIAC	Agent factory
Components							
EE	+	+	+	+	+	+	+
CL	+	–	–	–	+	–	+
MO	+	–	+	+	+	+	–
SEC	+	–	+	+	–	+	+
RDDS	+	–	+	+	–	+	+
SE	–	–	–	–	#	–	–
DCM	#	–	+	–	#	+	+
Properties							
OPEN	–	–	–	–	–	–	–
SCL	#	+	+	+	+	+	+
General criteria							
USA	+	+	#	#	+	+	+
SUP	+	+	#	+	#	+	#
USE	+	+	–	–	–	–	#
STD	+	–	–	–	–	–	+
Usage capabilities							
DM	#	+	#	+	#	+	#
IDE	#	+	–	–	#	+	+
TEMP	+	+	+	+	+	+	#

[a]The comparison is done based on the tools' publication and refers to the author's subjective judgment
+: full support, #: partial support, –: limited support

(using the compared tools) in a controlled manner, along with the measurement of various indicators (e.g., time, coverage, scalability, performance). Also, purpose based or domain-specific tools should be considered and explored.

In summary, while many agent and MAS tools exist, there are several voids, which hamper their usability and usefulness. There are clear needs to further extend the tools to several directions as indicated in this chapter.

References

1. Clements P, Bachmann F, Bass L, Garlan D, Ivers J, Little R, Merson P, Nord R, Stafford J (2010) Documenting software architectures: views and beyond, 2nd edn. Addison-Wesley, Boston
2. Agent Factory (2013) http://www.agentfactory.com/. Accessed June 2013.
3. Fayad M, Schmidt DC, Johnson R (1999) Implementing application frameworks: object-oriented frameworks at work, 1st edn. Wiley, New York
4. Tilab (2013), Jave Agent Development Environment. http://jade.tilab.com/. Accessed June 2013
5. Tilab (2013), Workflows and Agent Development Environment. http://jade.tilab.com/wade/index.html. Accessed June 2013

6. AOS (2013) JACK. http://www.aosgrp.com//products/jack/documentation_and_instructi/#. Uaj62UDrxmw. Accessed June 2013
7. Gasser L (2000) MAS infrastructure definitions, needs, prospects. In: Infrastructure for agents, MAS and scalable MAS, Lecture notes in artificial intelligence, 1887. Springer, Berlin, pp 1–11
8. Agent Link (2013) http://www.agentlink.org/. Accessed June 2013
9. Bäumer C, Magedanz T (1999) Grasshopper—a mobile agent platform for active telecommunication networks, Intelligent agents for telecommunication applications. Lect Notes Comput Sci 1699:19–32
10. Collis JC, Ndumu DT, Nwana HS, Lee LC (1998) The ZEUS Agent Building Tool-kit. BT Technol J 16(3):60–68
11. Jeon H, Petrie C, Cutkosky MR (2000) JATLite: a Java Agent infrastructure with message routing. IEEE Internet Comput 4(2):87–96
12. Poslad S, Buckle P, Hadingham R (2000) The FIPA-OS agent platform: open source for open standards. In: Proceedings of the 5th international conference and exhibition on the practical application of intelligent agents and multi-agents. Manchester, UK
13. Chauhan D, Baker AD (1998) JAFMAS: a multiagent application development system. In: Sycara KP, Wooldridge M (eds) Proceedings of the second international conference on Autonomous agents (AGENTS '98). ACM, New York, NY, pp 100–10
14. Cheyer A, Martin D (2001) The open agent architecture. J Autonomous Agent Multi-Agent Syst 4(1–2):143–148
15. Peine H (2002) Application and programming experience with the Ara mobile agent system. Software-Pract Exp 32(6):515–541
16. AgentScape (2013). http://www.agentscape.org/. Accessed June 2013
17. Bölöni L, Jun K, Palacz SR, Marinescu DC (2000) The bond agent system and applications. ASA/MA 2000:99–112
18. Cougaar (2013) http://www.cougaar.org/. Accessed June 2013
19. Helsinger A, Thome M, Wright T (2004) Cougaar: a scalable, distributed multi-agent architecture. In: Proceedings of the International Conference on Systems, Man and Cybernetics (IEEE SMC 2004). SMC, The Hague, The Netherlands, pp 1910–1917
20. Helsinger A, Wright T (2005) Cougaar: a robust configurable multi agent platform. In: Proceedings of IEEE Conference Aerospace. pp 1–10
21. IAI (2006), CybelePro™ Agent Infrastructure, Users' Guide
22. Madkit (2013) http://www.madkit.org/. Accessed June 2013
23. JIAC (2013) http://www.jiac.de/. Accessed June 2013
24. Bordini RH, Hübner JF, Wooldridge M (2007) Programming multi-agent systems in AgentSpeak using Jason. Wiley, UK
25. Nilsson N (1994) Teleo-reactive programs for agent control. J Artif Intell Res 1:139–158
26. Pokahr A, Braubach L, Lamersdorf W (2003) JADEx: implementing a BDI-Infrastructure for JADE agents, In: EXP - In search of innovation (Special Issue on JADE), Vol 3, Nr. 3, Telecom Italia Lab, Turin, Italy, pp. 76–85.
27. Bellifemine FL, Caire G, Greenwood D (2007) Developing multi-agent systems with JADE. Wiley Series in Agent Technology, Wiley

Chapter 15
Design and Implementation of Very Large Agent-Based Systems

Renato Levy and Goutam Satapathy

Abstract One of the primary reasons to use an agent paradigm to develop a system is that it allows developing systems that can be distributed and scaled to include a large number of participants without the common pitfalls of traditional systems. In this sense, certain key design considerations must be identified and addressed while developing a very large agent system. In this chapter, we will explore these design considerations as applied to the study of an energy distribution use case. We will also explore the nuances of the implementation of this use case in an agent infrastructure such as CybelePro™, which has been used to deploy systems of this magnitude. We finalize by stressing the importance of verifying the system properties of very large agent-based systems with a small demonstration of how to do it.

Keywords Very large agent-based systems design • Requirements traceability • Market-oriented agent interaction • Protocol validation • Distributed system behavior validation • Distributed energy market • Activity-centric design • Agent design methods • PASSI • Cybele

1 Introduction

Very large agent-based systems are usually defined as being composed of at least 100,000 agents. These agents are normally heterogeneous and may use diverse modeling techniques in their knowledge representation and reasoning systems (e.g., Beliefs, Desires, Intentions (BDI), rule-base, programmatic). Even though the ability to scale is one of the key reasons why the agent-based design paradigm is used in software, most agent systems developed to date are relatively small in size (tens to hundreds of agents).

R. Levy (✉) • G. Satapathy
Intelligent Automation, Inc., Rockville, MD, USA
e-mail: rlevy@i-a-i.com; goutam@i-a-i.com

O. Shehory and A. Sturm (eds.), *Agent-Oriented Software Engineering*, DOI 10.1007/978-3-642-54432-3_15, © Springer-Verlag Berlin Heidelberg 2014

In the development of practical systems, the design of very large multi-agent systems has unique considerations that must be addressed. Small agent systems can be analyzed within a limited scope. It is entirely within the capacity of the designer to verify the completeness and correctness of a small system. In very large agent systems, the number of runtime associations is exponentially large, and the number of possible use cases and combinations of actions are beyond what standard software testing procedures are able to handle.

1.1 How Very Large Systems Differ from Small Agent Systems

Some of the assumptions taken for granted in small agent systems are no longer valid in very large systems. Most agent methodologies, including PASSI Agent Oriented Software [1], which is loosely applied in this chapter, analyze the requirements of a system from an agent society model of the system and identify the agents and roles, in order to describe their roles in the society model [2]. In designing very large systems, it is important to invert this attribution, where agents and roles are identified before the system requirement is analyzed using those agents and roles. However, the order of complexity in analyzing such society prevents the application of this approach to very large systems [3].

The solution is to analyze the society by the roles that the actors can perform, and let the agents decide which roles they are capable to implement [4]. In addition, for such a large society, especially for an open system, it is reasonable to expect that not all agents will be implemented at once, using the same technique, or even by the same developers [5]. Even the basic assumption in the design of collaborative agents, which states that all agents work in the best interest of the society, is not sustainable in the presence of selfish or ill-intended agents.

Another feature of very large systems is the natural deployment across a wide or global area network. Common requirements such as persistent connectivity, high degree of reliability and synchronicity in modern communication can no longer be assumed when the area of application and the number of agent hosts grows to large numbers. Most agent infrastructures cannot handle a large number of hosts or intermittent connectivity problems inherent in very large deployments.

Finally, very large systems are extremely hard to test and debug in any manner with coverage and completeness that gives confidence on the system correctness [6]. Such systems must be proven correct, which raises another level of complexity. Despite its importance, very little work has been done in proving agent-based systems correctness as indicated in [7]. The few related studies available are often agent focused rather than proving the whole system's behavior [8].

This chapter will explore the design considerations of very large agent systems as applied to the study of an energy distribution case study. In the next section, the use case is presented, followed by an analysis of system requirements and properties as well as a basic system design. The following sections introduce the infrastructure used for implementation and some final design aspects. The chapter concludes by demonstrating how system properties can be proven even when the behavior of a single agent cannot be bound.

2 Case Study Description

The energy business is divided into three separate markets: generation, transmission, and distribution. The generation market segment focuses on megawatt power plants, long-term contracts, and synchronization of phases. The transmission market segment focuses on power routing, load balancing, and power loss mitigation. Both markets are very stable and new technologies such as wind farms and superconductor lines are not likely to promote significant changes to the way in which these markets operate.

At the consumer end of the energy market is the distribution market. Distribution markets use transmission agreements for the transport of the energy from the power plants to the entry point of the market. This market coordinates the distribution of the energy for every home and business in its area of responsibility. There are thousands of these distribution centers in the USA alone.

The energy distribution market is most likely to be significantly impacted by newer trends in technology: micro-generation and electric cars. Micro-generation is the ability to generate modest amounts of energy at low cost [9,10]. This includes green energy (solar or wind) generated in the homes and office buildings where it is often consumed. The increased affordability of the micro-generation systems and the concerns with global warming along with the high cost of electricity has spawned a new awareness and a wave of deployment of these systems. In fact, it is mandatory for new homes or communities in some counties in the USA to provide such micro-generation. Electric cars have the potential of altering the manner in which energy is procured and stored. Each electric car is an energy demand and a large potential regulatory storage at the same time.

With the ability to generate and store energy, consumers have for the first time the chance to influence the distribution market. Consumers can plan their energy usage profile and offer excess energy from generation in periods of high demand. Since transmission losses are so high, reducing the energy demand for each distribution market would greatly increase the overall efficiency of the system, but creating an infrastructure capable of supporting this market would require a complete overhaul of the way energy is routed in the city neighborhoods.

Such a market would be a perfect candidate for the application of an agent-based system; it is naturally distributed, connected, and each actor in the market pursues a different strategy [11,12]. This is the test case we will use in this chapter to demonstrate the complexities of designing a very large agent system.

2.1 *Energy Distribution Case Study Analysis*

Our approach to system design calls for nine steps, namely: definition of system requirements, extraction of system properties, identification of the actors, description of the roles, market definition, definition of implementation model (i.e., agent infrastructure), adaptation from concept to implementation, protocol and system verification, and finally, validation of system properties and resilience.

The first step in the design methodology is determining the domain requirements and defining the problem. We limit the scope of the case study with a few simplifications to the requirements.

For example, since the current distribution system is capable of powering all consumers in a distribution area, we will assume that routing of the energy is not a problem to be addressed within the scope of this case study. However, in a realistic system, this assumption does not hold true, since energy could be stored and discharged at once, possibly overloading distribution lines.

2.1.1 System Requirements

- At any moment, actors in the market can be either in the Consumer state (buying energy) or in Provider state (selling energy). An actor in this market cannot do both at the same time.
- All consumers should be able to acquire the energy they require, provided they are willing to pay the market price for it.
- Distribution centers have local responsibilities and are organized hierarchically in a manner to aggregate the total demand of a region from the network topology such as street sections feeding into local mains, local main feeding into neighborhood centers, and so forth. This is required in order to evaluate local distribution line capacity to meet the demand. Hence, even though we are not considering the energy routing aspects, topology is still of concern since not everyone can sell to everyone without the agreement of middle actors.
- Consumers and providers in the same street section are connected in a parallel-like circuit configuration with local transmission that can support the energy flow.
- All distribution centers know the price of acquiring energy from the main distribution entry point over the transmission lines, and add a marginal cost to make it available to local consumers.
- Distribution centers do not store energy, but are able to sell unlimited amounts of energy using the energy procured at the distribution entry point without previous agreement.
- Distribution centers are strictly providers, but are able to sell distribution services to connect providers and consumers.
- Both consumers' demand and providers' ability to generate energy fluctuate over any period.
- Consumers pay for the energy contracted (even if not consumed).

- Providers pay a contractual penalty if they do not provide the energy contracted.
- Energy that is generated but not sold or stored is lost.
- Every energy contract has a duration and start time, which could also be set to the time when contract is agreed.

2.1.2 System Properties

The analysis of the use case must start from stating the system requirements. The combination of the systems requirements emerges system properties, which must be satisfied and can be used to verify the system correctness. From the system requirements described in the previous section, the following properties can be deduced:

- The highest price of energy will be the cost at the entry point plus the cost of distribution.
- An actor can only work as an energy broker (i.e., buys energy to sell with a profit) to the extent of its storage capacity.
- Distribution centers work as a team, whereas all the other actors work individually.
- The objective of consumers is to pay the least for the energy they need. They do not run the risk of being without energy because they can always buy energy at the distribution center without contract.
- The objective of providers is to maximize their profit within the limits of their generation capability by managing the risk of overselling.
- Providers that are also consuming energy must negotiate only their net energy availability, since they can be either provider or consumer to the system at any given period.
- Street sections do not need to manage local contracts, but individuals only provide the differential energy as needed.
- Since distribution centers charge fees to transfer energy between providers and consumers in different street sections, it is more efficient to buy energy locally.

2.1.3 Actors and Tasks

The next step in the design process is the identification of the actors and the tasks that they can perform in this system. Observe that we are not defining the agents yet. In our simplified use case, the following types of actors performing the listed tasks are identified:

Consumer: The actor that (i) negotiates energy purchase contracts, (ii) guarantees that the energy required has been procured (either by contract or from spot market), (iii) estimates future energy requirements in order to avoid the spot market, and (iv) has the objective to minimize the cost of the energy it consumes.

Provider: The actor that (i) negotiates energy seller contracts, (ii) estimates the power to be generated to avoid losing energy or paying penalty for overselling, and (iii) has the objective to maximize the revenue obtained by selling the energy.

Storage: The actor that (i) manages the capacity of the storage unit and (ii) works as provider or consumer to the extent of its storage capability.

Energy provider: The actor that supplies energy demands that cannot be fulfilled locally. A local distribution center that provides energy for the spot market is an example.

Other types of actors can be seen as roles of the local distribution center in this use case.

Broker: This role enforces contracts and billing amongst actors. Brokers apply fees on consumers for distribution and providers for failing on their contracts.

Distributer: This role guarantees a contract can be executed by verifying connectivity between a provider and a consumer under maximum load constraints in power lines. The actors with this role may need to team with others to verify contract execution.

The tasks of each of these actors may be viewed as tasks performed by a role such that many instances of the roles can be executed at any time by the actors. For example, many contracts could be undergoing negotiation process at the same time. It may also be noted that while some of the actors with a required role may not be capable of having full functionality, others may be able to perform sophisticated algorithms. In other words, the quality of service provided by each role may be different based on how an individual agent executes this role. In our case study, a consumer actor can be associated with the following roles performing the tasks identified above.

Buyer: A role that fulfills the task of negotiating the purchase of energy contracts.

Consumption estimator: A role that fulfills the task of estimating the current and future needs of the consumer.

Planner: A role that fulfills the task of matching the purchase opportunities with the future needs of the consumer.

A similar analysis will present the following tasks for the provider: *Seller*, *Generation estimator*, and *Planner*.

While performing their roles, the actors of the system are not free to perform at will. There is an expected behavior necessary for the entities in the system to reach an agreement during their interactions. The structure that underlines the accepted behavior during interacting roles is called a protocol. The details of the process in which these roles interact are fundamental for the development of the system dynamics. The set of protocols used, and the details of the object of negotiation, in our case an energy contract, will provide for the emergency of the market we hope to achieve, the energy distribution market.

Table 15.1 Microgeneration energy contract fields

Field name	Definition	M/O
Provider ID	Identifies the provider	M
Consumer ID	Identifies the consumer	M
Energy amount	Amount of energy in trade units	M
Start date/time	When this contract goes in effect	M
Duration	How long this contract will last	M
Price	How much the consumer will pay the provider	M
Provider cancelation deadline	Until when the provider can renege on the contract without paying a penalty	O
Fixed penalty	Fixed fee if provider fails to deliver	O
Proportional penalty	Fee per trade unit that the provider fails to deliver	O
Consumer cancelation deadline (t_c)	Until when the consumer can renege on the contract without paying for the contract	M

3 Market Definition

All the actors are interacting in a market in which energy contracts are traded [13,14]. The flexibility or brittleness of the market is largely mandated by the contract clauses. In this section, we will define the object of negotiation—the contract. The energy contract in our case study can be defined as an agreement by a provider to provide a consumer with a predetermined amount of energy for a given period. Although a contract could include multiple time periods with different levels of demand—a demand profile—we exclude such contract definition in our case study. Before this contract can be validated, distribution nodes must verify that the power lines involved can support the load by solving a coordinated routing problem. Note that roles associated with such tasks are not listed here as per the scope of the case study.

Under this definition, some fields of the contract become mandatory (M) while others are optional (O) such that the contract as a whole can be the product of negotiation. Table 15.1 lists some of these fields with their definitions. More sophisticated contract variations would allow for more complex contract rules and more sophisticated energy markets. A nice real-life market that could serve as a model for this new system is the commodities and options markets.

One must observe that the actual agents in the system may implement one or more of these actors such that the varying actor roles remain active during different times of the day. For example, a normal home with solar generation consumes very little during the day while its occupants are away. During this period, the agent behaves as a provider actor. When the occupants arrive, it starts to transition from provider to the consumer actor role. If an electric car is in the garage, it can play as a storage actor as well. The dynamics of the environment makes the actors, associated roles and their interaction, rather than the agents, to be the focus of the design. The full UML diagram for our agent-based system can be seen in Fig. 15.1.

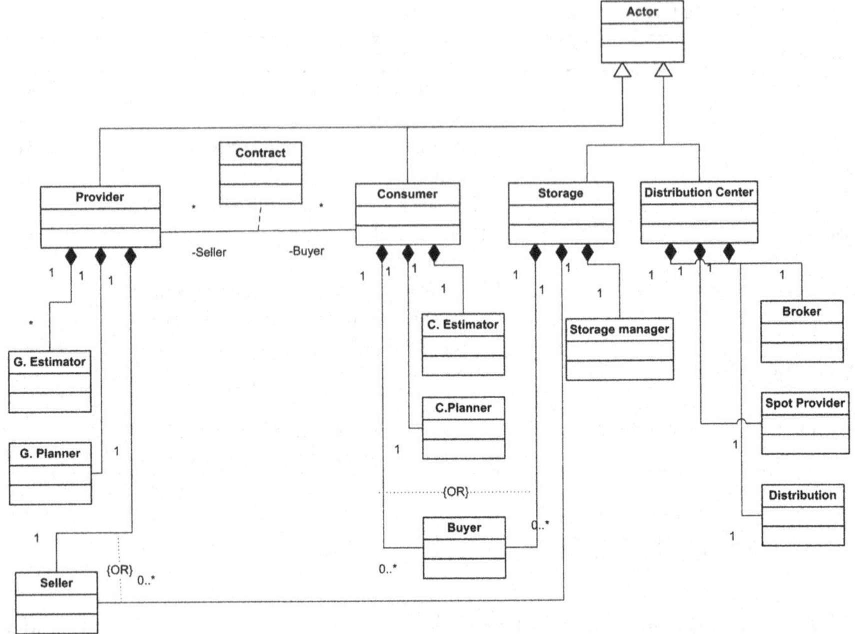

Fig. 15.1 UML diagram of actors and tasks in the energy system

3.1 Energy Distribution Application Implementation

An agent infrastructure to support the implementation of such a system must be able to handle a very large system, and yet since most of these agents will be embedded on energy meters or switch panels [15], it must have a small footprint and be as platform independent as possible. In this section, we describe the infrastructure selected for implementation, its programming model, and the optional development methodology.

3.1.1 The Infrastructure: CybelePro

The CybelePro agent infrastructure is well suited for the energy distribution use case because it presents key features to address these requirements. It is a Java-based distributed environment, which lends platform independence and device-embedded service. It provides only essential agent services (e.g., communication, timing and event management), which lends the required small footprint. It uses an asynchronous publish–subscribe communication paradigm, which is ideal for large-scale systems built on modern communication infrastructure that could have intermittent connectivity and unreliable service.

Over the last decade, several agent-based architectures, infrastructures, frameworks, libraries, and toolkits were developed by academia, industries, and government labs, but very few are actively maintained and used in building complex systems.

Table 15.2 demonstrates a small comparison between popular agent infrastructures in relation to their applicability to our case study. This table is complete, as far the authors know, at the time of publication.

Our selected infrastructure, CybelePro, also provides a programming model called activity-centric programming that includes the above notion of actors, actor roles, agents, and contracts. Finally and most importantly, it follows a design methodology called 3-tier design architecture, which separates the role interactions in performing a task from its algorithmic behavior and makes it easier to maintain and verify completeness and correctness of a very large system.

3.1.2 Activity-Centric Programming

In Cybele, activities are the active components of agents. Activities subscribe to events and indicate the object and method that will handle the event processing. Events that are handled by the same activity cannot be executed concurrently. The environment is responsible for collecting and distributing events, which are generated during the event processing itself. CybelePro supports three types of events (i) message events: events with serializable data exchanged between agents, (ii) internal events: events with reference to data exchanged between activities of the same agent, (iii) timer events: notification events delivered to agents at certain scheduled times. In this model, the developer delegates the object code and data to be managed by the event-driven runtime environment, which ensures that the object and data declared for an agent are not shared with other agents [17]. The developer provides all the hooks and listeners in the handling objects for the environment to deliver events directly to the processing code.

Multiple activities of an agent can hold complex concurrency relationships amongst each other [17]. The activity-centric programming model allows developers to abstract the operating systems' multiprocessing mechanism and focus on the execution requirements of the system. The Cybele infrastructure will automatically map activities to threads or processes according to the deployment platform and the current workload. The activity-centric programming model provides APIs for the developer to declare object code and data for an agent and its activities. The developer makes use of these declarative APIs to manage creation of new activities. As an example, our consumer agent may initialize an activity that will implement its planner role at initialization, while the buyer role can be divided into two different parts: the first activity, initialized at startup, reacts to offers by spawning a secondary activity, which actually performs the negotiation in relation to that specific offer. In this manner, the agent remains aware of other offers during negotiation and can engage in many concurrent negotiations.

Table 15.2 Agent infrastructure comparison

	CybelePro agent infrastructure	JADE: Java agent development framework	JACK intelligent agents	Cougaar: cognitive agent architecture
Source, availability, support	http://www.i-a-i.com/cybelepro; Proprietary; open source version available, support available	jade.tilab.com; Open source/LGPL, third party support	http://www.aosgrp.com; Proprietary, support available	http://www.cougaar.org; Open source/BSD, third party support
Language	Java	Java	Java	Java
Embedded/mobile	Yes/Android	No/PDA	No/PDA	No/No
Agent modeling	Delegate class pattern, UML state achine, FIPA, BDI and rule-based extensions available	Java class, rule based (Jess)	Java class, declarative (JACK agent language), BDI reasoning and planning model	Java class, cognitive model for planning
Agent architecture	Agent composed of activities, activity composed of event handlers	Agent composed of (event handling) behaviors	Agent composed of capabilities (plans and event handlers) and belief set	Agent composed of (behavior) plugins and blackboard
Agent communication	Topic-based publish-subscribe	One-to-one, one-to-many, FIPA-ACL	Peer-to-peer	Blackboard based publish-subscribe
Development environment	Any Java IDE and DIVA—a UML-based agent modeling tool with protocol verification	Workflows and agents development environment	JACK agent development environment (JDE)	Any Java IDE
Example of large scale agent-based system	NASA's ACES [16]—180 K (flight) agent simulation	100 s of agents	100 s of agents	1,000 s of agents for military logistics planning

CybelePro provides a publish-subscribe mechanism for both messages and internal events. CybelePro lets the object code capture user events through Java provided MVC patterns and transforms them into messages or internal events for distribution.

3.1.3 Publish-Subscribe Paradigm

CybelePro agent-based system provides location-independent agent communication using a publish-subscribe paradigm. The activities subscribe to message and internal events by registering an array of objects such as Java String objects representing a topic of interest. Such subscription mechanism allows developing a topic hierarchy where activities can subscribe to messages at different topic levels. The message and internal events are generated when published topics match with subscribed topics. In order to support scalability, the subscribed topics are stored in the nodes where they are subscribed. This decentralized directory mechanism removes the single point of failure pertinent to a centralized or blackboard type of message delivery systems. To reduce the high network traffic of message events, certain topics that can attract high message volume are also registered at each node to limit the number of events introduced in the network.

A publish-subscribe message paradigm along with CybelePro event delivery service lends asynchronous event processing between agents. It also allows asynchronous event processing between activities depending on the user-specified concurrency structure.

3.1.4 Three-Tier Architecture

Although the activity-centric programming model is well suited for agent-based market system with independent agent software vendors, and a publish-subscribe paradigm facilitates scalability, an important consideration must be given to code reusability. A key aspect in open systems is the guarantee that agents developed by other vendors are compatible and able to execute the protocols accordingly. To address this key consideration, we advocate the adoption of a 3-tier architecture of agents based on the adapter design pattern: (i) the interaction or client tier responsible for publishing and subscribing events (including timer events), which provides target interfaces whose methods are used for event processing and generation; reuse of this layer assures that the agent is able to comply with the protocol; and (ii) an adapter tier with a set of wrappers, which implements target interfaces by supporting the adapted class (iii) an adapted tier with domain objects, which provides customer-specific behaviors such as contract cost comparisons. This architecture allows the adopters of this agent development technique to publish interaction tier objects and establish standards of logical behavior of agents and activities. It also encourages vendors to provide various adapters compliant with these logical behaviors and corresponding adapted classes designed to offer different customer-specific behavior or features increasing interoperability.

The 3-tier agent architecture along with the CybelePro agent infrastructure allows easy implementation of an agent-based market system, where an agent software vendor develops a deployable system for customers, e.g., homeowner, building management, and distribution centers with needed domain features without the knowledge of the internals of systems developed by other vendors.

3.2 Adapting Analysis to the Implementation Model

Before we can determine details of the market interactions, we have to map the notional tasks to the conceptual system to the architectural constructs provided by the infrastructure.

All infrastructures have programming constraints that will impact the implementation details. For example, some impose Beliefs, Desires, Intentions (BDI) architectures; some receive all events in a single-entry method responsible for keeping the context on the multiple conversations; some infrastructures restrict the agent to perform one role at a time. Hence, adapting the concept to the selected infrastructure or selecting an infrastructure to facilitate concept implementation is a necessary step in the system development.

3.2.1 Agents and Roles Versus Activities

As we have seen from the above section, Cybele does not place restrictions on the technique used to implement the agent (procedural, BDI, rule-base), but it contains an intrinsic architecture to the agent construction. An agent in Cybele executes tasks by creating and executing activities.

Some of the tasks are singleton (e.g., consume estimator role performing demand estimation); in other words, only one instance of such role can exist per agent. Other tasks may require concurrent execution of several contexts, such as a buyer role negotiating many contracts at any moment. Mapping each task of a role to multiple concurrent and coordinated activities allows the agent to create one activity instance for each contract being negotiated, which will automatically keep the context of each contract within the activity state (encapsulation).

3.2.2 Defining the Protocols

While some roles are performed internally to the agent based on the current state of the agent (e.g., planner), others require the agent to interact with other agents (e.g., agents with buyer role). This interaction cannot be free form; it must be framed into a sequence of events, decisions, actions, and responses. This expected

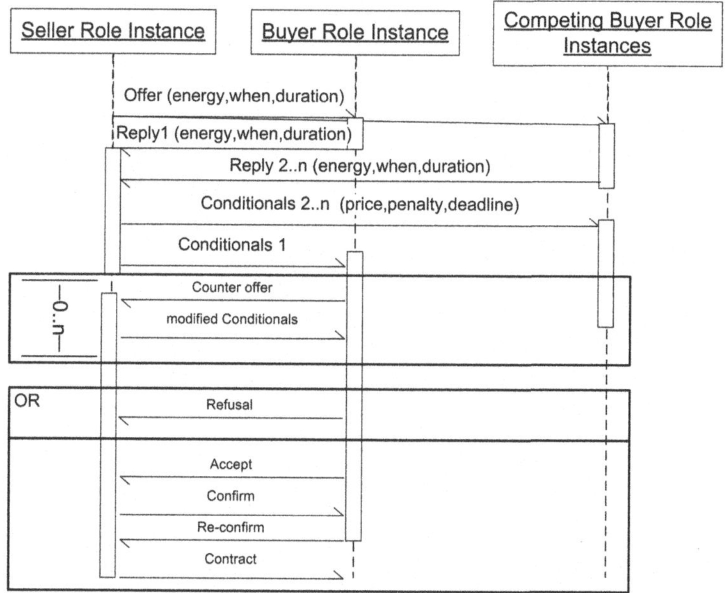

Fig. 15.2 Seller-driven protocol

sequence of events along with their counterpart in other roles of the interaction constitutes a protocol. Figure 15.2 shows a possible sequence diagram of a seller-driven protocol of our energy contract negotiation. Note that this protocol has more optional negotiating steps than standard contracting protocol defined by FIPA [18].

In the seller-driven protocol shown in Fig. 15.2, the negotiation is started by the seller, which requests procurement proposals from potential buyers by presenting the energy available for sale during a time period. Potential buyers interested in that energy offered or part of it reply stating the amount of energy requested and the time period in which it is needed. The seller selects the subset of potential buyers of which requests match the offered energy supply in an acceptable manner (this decision is based on the internal reasoning of the seller). To these buyers, the seller proposes conditions such as price, penalties, and response and commitment deadlines. At this point in the diagram, the negotiations of the buyers are independent and the sequence diagram focuses on a specific buyer. From the point of view of a single buyer, the protocol has three possible outcomes: (i) the buyer can refuse and end the negotiation, (ii) it can present a counter offer for the seller to consider (as many times as needed), or (iii) it can accept.

It is important to note that the seller may have several such negotiations occurring concurrently. The same also occurs with the buyer role responding to multiple requests. Hence a dual-step confirmation is required for the commitment, and the contract is not valid until the reconfirmation is received.

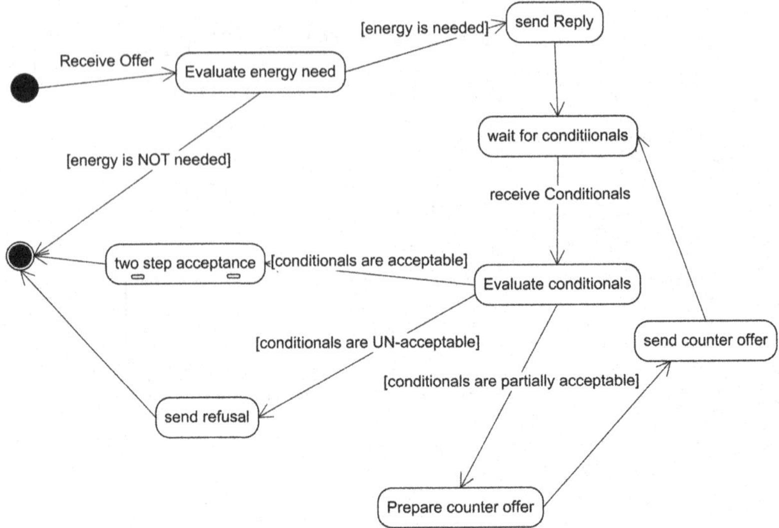

Fig. 15.3 Buyer's state diagram

Since the task implementation of the protocol must encapsulate all the activity space of the agent for this interaction, it must comprise not only the ideal path of the negotiation, but also all possible paths in which the agent may be engaged. Failure to anticipate all possible paths of execution will result in runtime errors that are difficult to track in the case of very large systems. Figure 15.3 shows a Buyer task that executes the sequence diagram above in the form of a state diagram. An agent that plays a consumer actor may instantiate several of these buyer roles at any moment, in order to negotiate with potential producers.

Along with the buyer–seller relationship, which can also include buyer-driven negotiation protocols, other protocols will be required for the execution of the system. For example, since the broker will be responsible for enforcing the contract, the contract must be registered with the broker. The broker must then contact both provider and consumer and collect their acquiescence before the contract is declared valid.

The negotiation and registration protocols allow local providers and consumers to execute contracts and to have those enforced by the broker. But in order to fulfill the system requirements, distribution nodes must charge consumers with fees based on the number of hops made between providers and consumers located in different local centers. This can be accomplished by allowing local distribution centers to propagate the local offers from providers to other local markets. This propagated offer includes the distribution fee. The offer is only propagated forward if distribution node can control the flow of energy within its transmission capacity.

3.2.3 Protocol Verification

Even the simplified protocol discussed above has several pitfalls hidden in the nuances. While in small systems one can assume a known environment and adjust the behavior based on results from the test cases, this approach is not scalable to very large systems. In order to guarantee the correct execution of the protocol, it has to be verified for failures and inconsistencies that would create unanticipated results in the execution of the agent. In other words, the protocol must always end in a designed end state and the agents that implement it on a predictable state regardless of variations in the environment.

System designers tend to underestimate the need of a rigorous design by assuming persistent network connectivity and events synchronicity. In the buyer diagram above, we have included a few common discrete errors that could potentially bring the agent to a halt by breaking the required system property that all consumers can obtain the needed energy at all times, even in the presence of a spot market. For example, since messages can be lost, a timeout and recovery procedure must be added for every state in which the buyer/seller is waiting for a message from the seller/buyer. Another example can be seen at the renegotiation loop. As it is originally designed, there is no guarantee that the cycle would ever end; one must introduce a limit, either time or trials, to guarantee that the protocol eventually ends.

The critical point in protocol verification is that even when the state diagrams appear correct and deterministic independently, the exchange of information through the network makes it necessarily a compound nondeterministic machine. Hence, the order of execution across boundaries cannot be guaranteed. As a result, precedence, reachability, and other simplifying assumptions are no longer valid. There are already developed languages and tools to conduct formal analysis of such systems [19], which should be applied before the protocol can be considered ready for implementation.

3.3 Agent Implementation in CybelePro

An agent in Cybele is a composition of its activities operating on their private and shared data. The agent handler class is initialized by the system upon agent creation and it must, at construction, either create activities or subscribe to events. The handler class is a serializable Java class that implements an interface named *Handler*. Cybele creates an instance of this object to guide the execution of the agent. Once the initial activities of the agent are created, they are capable of launching and requesting the termination of other activities. Agent creation in CybelePro is achieved with the simple API described below. Other more complex options are also available.

```
Cybele.createAgent(java.lang.String agentName,
                   java.lang.String agentHandlerClass,
                   java.io.Serializable[] initialParameters)
```

In our system, an agent can be started by evaluating the capabilities of the entity it represents (provider, consumer, etc.). Based on these capabilities, it starts its planner activity, which creates other required activities such as the consumption or generation estimators.

Estimators typically execute anytime prediction algorithms, which periodically refine the consumption or generation estimates for the predictive horizon. These estimates are used by the planner to compute the shortage energy demand or excess of energy supply that needs to be procured or offered for sale.

With the notion of its needs, the agent or planner can start buyer or seller activities to achieve its objective through contract negotiation protocols discussed earlier. Similar to the agent itself, activities are also created by the similar API described below. The key difference between the APIs is that the Activity creation API allows objects to be shared between activities.

```
createActivity(java.lang.String activityId,
               java.lang.String activityHandlerClass,
               java.lang.Object[] initialParameters)
```

3.3.1 Validation of System Properties

Having the protocols verified and implemented correctly is a big step toward creating a valid agent-based system, but this is just not sufficient for very large agent-based systems. Even with profiling tools such as the IntelliTrace [20] that allows identification of a specific protocol instance and its messages from a large corpus of message traffic, it is extremely difficult to fully analyze and debug a large system. This is possibly the key difference between very large agent-based systems and their smaller versions, and the key point this chapter wants to emphasize on is: conditions for system correctness must be proven, not hoped nor guessed.

There are no simple tools and technologies available to generate and validate enough use cases to state that the system is correct. In this case, correctness of the system must be proven by identifying the boundaries in which the system requirements and the system properties can be guaranteed to operate.

As an example, we will identify the conditions where the first system property stated as follows holds true:

The highest price of energy will be the cost at the entry point plus the cost of distribution.

This property was derived from the fact that at any moment a consumer can buy spot energy from the local distribution node without a contract and hence the consumer would not buy it elsewhere for a higher price. However, there are occasions when a consumer buys energy at a price higher than the cost of spot energy as explained below.

Let S be the cost of buying spot energy from the distribution node, and P be the cost of buying the same amount of energy from a provider. But the cost S is not constant. Two components contribute to the spot energy valuation: (i) a cyclical component, which changes predictably during the time of the day t_s and (ii) a noncyclical component attributed to demand d, which gets updated at different times of the day t_d. Also, from the contract clauses, there is a time t_c after which a consumer can no longer cancel a contract to receive power at time t_s. Then, the cost of energy C for a consumer can be determined by $\min(S(t_s, d), P)$, since the consumer will always try to minimize its cost.

At the time of contract, we know that a consumer accepts P, the cost of buying from the provider when P is less than the consumer's predicted cost of spot energy, i.e., $P < S(t_s, d)$. If the consumer agrees to a cost of buying, P higher than $S(t_s)$, it is because he expects a premium demand d, and does not have a demand update scheduled before the time for cancellation ($t_s > t_d > t_c$); hence, he does not have the correct value expected for $S(t_s, d)$ before he commits. In this case, it is possible that the consumer will overestimate the cost of S and pay a higher price.

Based on this result, we can conclude that the first system property is only guaranteed if the buyer does not accept a contract in which the time for cancelation is earlier than the time for a demand cost update. In this case, $t_d < t_c$ becomes one of the boundary conditions that defines the system.

The example given is quite intuitive, similar analytical proofs have to be defined for each requirement and property. There is no generic methodology to accomplish such proof. Some properties are very complicated to prove, an involve creating composed state machines of the roles involved in a protocol to prove a property holds over a period of time [21]. Extending the property proof over the scope of the system is often a challenge. The need of such proofs in very large systems, due to the impossibility to have a large enough test coverage, opens the research area for such a methodology and tool support to assist its execution.

3.3.2 Validating a New Agent

Another key aspect of large systems is the fact that not all agents will be implemented by the same vendor, or have the same altruistic objectives. In other words, collaboration is only guaranteed if it is in the best interest of the agent in the true sense of game theory. In very large and practical systems, this inherent property needs to be proven rather than stated. Some examples of this situation in our use case are:

- Distribution nodes and brokers are supposedly nonprofit (they add cost, but do not explore the system's faults to make money). In the system proposed, we must prove that distribution nodes cannot undermine the provider's ability to sell, in order to guarantee its spot market. This can only be done by showing that the distributor node would lose if it acts in this fashion. This does not hold true in the system proposed; we leave it for future research to make necessary modifications to demonstrate under which conditions it holds true.

- An agent that can be a provider and a consumer cannot work as intermediary in a transaction, at least not for energy amounts that are beyond its storage capability. This property holds true for this system within a boundary condition, i.e., there is a minimum time requirement for an agent to remain as consumer or as a provider before it can switch functions.

4 Conclusion

In this chapter, we have presented a simple use case explaining why designing very large agent-based systems differs from implementing small systems. Adaptive systems such as model-driven, agent-based, or machine-learning systems greatly expand the complexity of software. Traditional testing techniques are not able to provide enough coverage to provide satisfactory verification and validation. At the same time, standard logical proofers that use algebra style language [22] or logical model checkers, such as LTSA [23], quickly explode in complexity and become unmanageable.

We demonstrated the steps for designing such a system for a simplified case study following a modified popular agent design methodology. The simple modification proposed already increases the chances of capturing required system properties by changing the focus of the design.

We finalize the chapter by presenting the implementation of the proposed design using a popular agent infrastructure applied to very large systems. Following the implementation, we demonstrate how the validation of system requirements can be used to extract critical relationships between parameters in the system.

Some of the areas that we discuss in this chapter, such as protocol verification and validation of system properties, are areas of most needed research and are beyond the scope of this chapter. In this work, we have limited ourselves to emphasize the need of doing so in the development of very large agent-based systems.

References

1. Cossentino M (2005) From requirements to code with the PASSI methodology. In: B. Henderson-Sellers, P. Giorgini (eds) Agent-oriented methodologies. Idea Group Inc., pp 79–101, Chapter 4
2. Parunak HVD, Odell J (2002) Representing social structure in UML. In: Wooldridge M, Weiss G, Ciancarini P (eds) Agent-oriented software engineering II, Montreal, Canada. Springer, Heidelberg, pp 1–16

3. Cao L, ZhangC, Zhou MC (2008) Engineering open complex agent systems: a case study. IEEE transactions on systems, man, and cybernetics, part C: applications and reviews, vol 38(4)
4. Cabri G, Ferrari L, Zambonelli F (2004) Role-based approaches for engineering interactions in large-scale multi-agent systems. In: Software engineering for multi-agent systems II, Lecture Notes in Computer Science, vol 2940, pp 243–263
5. Odell J, Parunak HVD (2003) The role of roles in designing effective agent organizations. In: Software engineering for large-scale multi-agent systems. Springer, Heidelberg
6. Cysneiros LM, Yu E (2003) Requirements engineering for large-scale multi-agent systems. In: Software engineering for large-scale multi-agent systems, Lecture Notes in Computer Science, vol 2603, pp 39–56
7. Dhavacheivan P (2005) Complexity measures for software systems: towards multi-agent based software testing. In: Proceedings of the international conference on intelligent sensing and information processing, January 2005
8. Zheng M, Alagear VS (2005) Conformance testing of BDI properties in agent-based systems. In: 12th Asia-Pacific Software Engineering Conference (ASPEC), December 2005
9. Roche R, Blunier B, Miraoui A, Hilaire V, Koukam A (2010) Multi-agent systems for grid energy management: a short review. In: IECON 2010-36th annual conference on IEEE Industrial Electronics Society, November, pp 3341–3346
10. Zeman A, Prokopenko M, Guo Y, Li R (2008) Adaptive control of distributed energy management: a comparative study. In: Second IEEE international conference on self-adaptive and self-organizing systems, SASO'08, October 2008, pp 84–93
11. Koster M (2011) Reliable multi-agent system for a large scale distributed energy trading network. Doctoral dissertation, Master's thesis, University of Groningen
12. Li J, Poulton G, James G (2007) Agent-based distributed energy management. In: AI 2007: advances in artificial intelligence. Springer, Berlin, pp 569–578
13. Badawy R, Hirsch B, Albayrak S (2010) Agent-based coordination techniques for matching supply and demand in energy networks. Integr Comput Aided Eng 17(4):373–382
14. Li J, Poulton G, James G (2010) Coordination of distributed energy resource agents. Appl Artif Intell 24(5):351–380
15. Capodieci N, Pagani GA, Cabri G, Aiello M (2011) Smart meter aware domestic energy trading agents. In: Proceedings of the 2011 workshop on E-energy market challenge, June 2011, pp 1–10
16. George S, Satapathy G, Manikonda V, Wieland F, Refai MS, Dupee R (2011) Build 8 of the Airspace Concept Evaluation System. In: AIAA Modeling and Simulation Technologies Conference, August 2011
17. CybelePro User manual, http://www.i-a-i.com/products/doc/cybelepro/UsersGuide-CybelePro.pdf
18. http://www.fipa.org/specs/fipa00029/SC00029H.pdf
19. Bell Labs, Basic Spin manual. http://cm.bell-labs.com/cm/cs/what/spin/Man/Manual.html
20. Peng W, et al (2009) Graph-based methods for the analysis of large-scale multiagent systems. In: Proceedings of the 8th international conference on autonomous agents and multiagent systems, pp 545–552
21. Giannakopoulou D, Magee J (2003) Fluent model checking for event-based systems. In: ESEC/FSE'03, Helsinki, Finland, September 1–5
22. Magee J, Kramer J (1999) Concurrency—state models and java programs. Wiley, Chichester
23. Magee J, Kramer J, Giannakopoulou D (1999) Behaviour analysis of software architectures. In: 1st working IFIP conference on software architecture (WICSAI), San Antonio, TX, February 22–24, 1999

Chapter 16
AgentZero: A Framework for Simulating and Evaluating Multi-agent Algorithms

Benny Lutati, Inna Gontmakher, Michael Lando, Arnon Netzer, Amnon Meisels, and Alon Grubshtein

Abstract Applications of multi-agent system (MAS) are versatile. In this chapter we focus on a specific application domain—agent-oriented programming for distributed constraint reasoning (DCR). The field of DCR deals with constraints-based problems that are distributed among multiple agents. The agents need to arrive at an optimal solution to the global combinatorial problem, and in order to do so, they run a distributed search algorithm. Another important aspect of MAS software development is MAS simulation. In this regard, this chapter introduces a new agent-based research tool for designing and testing DCR algorithms. The new tool—AgentZero—is specifically designed for the specification, implementation, and evaluation of DCR search algorithms. AgentZero provides full support to researchers of distributed constraints algorithms in the form of an extensive agent-based environment for algorithmic research that includes a distributed run-time environment, built-in performance measures that are automatically used by all algorithms, and visualization tools that help design and understand the behavior of complex distributed search algorithms. The API of the AgentZero simulator is described in detail and important architectural decisions that enable analysis and smooth implementation of a variety of algorithms are explained and described. In the context of AOSE, this chapter exemplifies two aspects: agent-based simulation environment and tools, and a variety of development and runtime aids for agent-based systems.

Keywords Multi-agent system simulator • Distributed algorithms • Multi-agent visualization • Multi-agent algorithm development • Multi-agent algorithm evaluation environment

---

B. Lutati (✉) • I. Gontmakher • M. Lando • A. Netzer • A. Meisels • A. Grubshtein
Department of Computer Science, Ben-Gurion University of the Negev, Beer-Sheva, Israel
e-mail: benny.lutati@gmail.com; netzerar@cs.bgu.ac.il; am@cs.bgu.ac.il; alon.grubshtein@gmail.com

O. Shehory and A. Sturm (eds.), *Agent-Oriented Software Engineering*,
DOI 10.1007/978-3-642-54432-3_16, © Springer-Verlag Berlin Heidelberg 2014

1 Introduction

A multi-agent system (MAS) is a distributed system composed of multiple autonomous agents. An agent is an independent software entity, which strives to reach a goal; the goal can be either private or shared by several agents. To reach its goal, an agent can communicate with other agents by using message passing. An agent has its own local memory, and in most cases the information that an agent holds can be classified into the following categories: *public data*—which the agent is willing to share with other agents; *private data*—which the agent would like to keep for itself; and *tradable data*—which is kept private but can be traded with other agents with the purpose of influencing them to perform a desired action.

Agent-oriented systems have many applications; in the robotics field, for example, the agent-oriented approach is used to coordinate robots performing different actions without interfering with one another. In the navigation field—applications like Waze [1] are a MAS designed to help drivers navigate by sharing information available to different agents. Managing and working with big data is also a field where the agent-oriented approach plays a crucial role. The Map Reduce paradigm where different agents process different parts of the data in order to extract needed information is becoming the de facto framework for storing and processing massive data. Another good example is the distributed search field where several agents attempt to optimize a solution to a common problem, such as meeting, scheduling, and resource allocation.

As an example of the latter, consider multiple departments at a university, each constructing its weekly schedule for the semester. The schedules of many departments are constrained because the curricula of groups of students include courses from these "constrained departments." The agents constructing their departmental schedules need to arrive at an optimal solution to the global schedule problem, and in order to do so, they run a distributed search algorithm. The family of such distributed search algorithms for solving distributed constraints problems is termed distributed constraint reasoning (DCR) algorithms and is the focus of the present chapter.

MAS applications deployment and testing are inherently complicated. Distributed programming is a resource-consuming task in terms of time and cost. For this reason, simulation tools form a very important measure to be used when developing MAS applications. This chapter presents an innovative multi-agent simulation environment that is tailored specifically for designing, implementing, and testing DCR search algorithms.

The outline of the rest of this chapter is as follows. The next section covers several common settings and properties of different MASs, as well as the AgentZero MAS simulator and research tool. Afterwards, the DCR framework is shortly introduced and an application of distributed search is explained. An implementation of a DCR algorithm using AgentZero will follow together with a short explanation of the simulation behind the scenes. The user front-end is then briefly reviewed and the chapter concludes with a comparison of AgentZero to different tools that are available in the MAS domain.

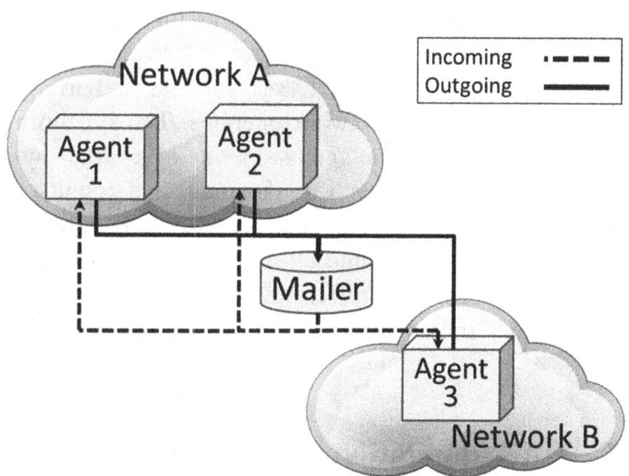

Fig. 16.1 Illustration of a simple MAS system

2 Common MAS Settings and Properties

A common MAS architecture (Fig. 16.1) entails implementing every agent as a process on a different computer. Another alternative suggests implementing a group of agent processes executing on the same machine or several groups on multiple machines. In such cases, the agents communicate with one another via message passing. Indeed, architectures for MASs commonly include a message passing mechanism in support of agent communication.

2.1 Agents Cooperation and Privacy

A typical distributed multi-agent setting assumes that the knowledge of agents about their environment is limited in scope. Agents can influence the actions of one another using message passing by exposing information, performing negotiation, etc. The cooperation level of the agents varies. On one end there are cooperative agents that can be generally described as agents that agree to follow a common protocol for the sake of a shared goal, while on another end, self-interested agents can be thought of as agents that try to maximize their own goal solely.

2.2 Execution Modes

An important attribute of any MAS is its mode of synchronization. There are two primary modes of execution: asynchronous, and synchronous. The asynchronous mode is the more general case. In this mode, there is no assumption of synchronization between the agents. The sent messages will get to their destination eventually.

As in TCP, there are no assumptions on the message ordering between different agents, but in case that an agent sends two messages one after the other to the same recipient—the message that was sent first will arrive first. This mode is similar to the way the Internet network operates. The synchronous mode is an iterative-like mode; in this mode the agents operate in a round-by-round fashion. Any message sent at round i will reach its destination at round $i + 1$. Agents are aware of the round at which they operate and are assumed to process and respond to all messages from round i before round $i + 1$ starts. In a real network, a synchronous execution can be achieved using different synchronization techniques. This type of execution is applicable in many cases, including computer games and online bidding.

3 MAS Simulation via AgentZero

AgentZero is a java-based easy to use, extendible MAS simulator and research tool. It provides a simulated agent execution environment and application analysis support for distributed problem solving. The framework specializes in DCR algorithms design and evaluation but can be used to simulate many other MAS applications too. AgentZero provides an intuitive programming API. It has the capabilities to simulate a multi-agent environment on a single computer and to attach many types of statistical profilers and debug assisting tools into the simulated environment. Another important aspect incorporated into the framework is the AgentZero web laboratory—a collaboration area for researchers, which is designed to provide a simple location for sharing experimental results, algorithms, and modules in order to enhance the ease and productivity of research efforts. In this respect, AgentZero is a good example of practical MAS development and engineering aids.

3.1 AgentZero Modularity

In order for a simulator to be useful for a wide range of applications, it must be capable of supplying generic services, which can be applied to any agent-oriented application implemented on top of it. AgentZero's design goal was to define the widest possible range of generic services that can be automatically used by all implemented applications and especially DCR algorithms, which will be covered in the next section. These services, applied to a wide range of applications with different inherent structures, are the basis for the usability of the simulator as a research tool for investigating and performing comparative evaluation of agent-oriented driven applications. The principles according to which AgentZero was designed are listed below:

- Simple agent design—following simple API, the agent has access to a set of comprehensive tools and can be implemented in a way that is indifferent to the execution mode. Agents have the ability to expose properties that are later to be set in the experiment designing process, fundamental actions of the agents are automatically monitored by the system in order to provide useful statistics—this reduces to minimum the need to write code that is unrelated to the actual agent behavior.

- Powerful message passing mechanism—messages are passed by value and not by reference and are conveniently handled in an RPC fashion; statistical message delays can be applied in order to measure the application's behavior under different network conditions without slowing down the actual execution.
- Both asynchronous and synchronous executions are supported out of the box.
- Generic performance measurements—Measuring performance of a distributed application is a crucial and challenging task. For example, the total execution time of a distributed algorithm in a simulated environment provides little information when the number of agents exceeds the number of concurrent computational cores in the system. Providing a measure of all nonconcurrent actions is both technically challenging and prone to mistakes. Providing standard, application-independent measurements, the implementation architecture must be designed so that aggregating this information is hidden from the application implementation and can easily be extended for gathering additional information.
- Incomplete information—A typical distributed multi-agent setting assumes that the knowledge of agents about their environment is limited in scope. In simulated agent-based environments (such as AgentZero), this limitation is enforced by the framework, leading to realistic implementation of algorithms and applications.
- General purpose tools and modules—As more algorithms and applications are introduced, the number of reoccurring parts used as building blocks increases. These can include a set of preprocessing procedures, common data structures, and benchmark problem structures. Providing such services as tools and pluggable modules do more than just simplifying the work of application and algorithm designers; it also generates a common ground for the reference research community to facilitate comparison among implementations.

4 Distributed Constraint Reasoning

DCR is a specific field of research of MASs [2, 3].Consider, for example, a large hospital that is composed of many wards. Each ward constructs a weekly timetable assigning its nurses to shifts. The construction of a weekly timetable involves solving a constraint satisfaction or optimization problem for each ward. Some of the nurses in every ward are qualified to work in the Emergency Room. Hospital regulations require a certain number of qualified nurses (e.g., for Emergency Room) in each shift. This imposes constraints among the timetables of different wards. Assigning an unqualified nurse to some shift is acceptable only if there are enough qualified nurses assigned to that shift in the other wards. A natural model for this multi-agent combinatorial problem is a distributed constraint satisfaction problem

(DCSP) [14, 17] or distributed constraint optimization problem (DCOP) [15, 16], in which the agents represent the different wards, the value assignments of agents are schedules and the requirement to have at least one qualified nurse per shift among all wards is an example of a constraint between agents.

Formally, DCR problems are composed of a set of agents. Agents contain variables with finite domains of values and are connected by constraints among their variables. A solution to a DCOP is a global assignment for variables that minimizes the costs of all constraints in the system. DCR algorithms are usually distributed search algorithms in which all agents cooperate in the search for a globally consistent or optimal solution. The solving procedure involves assignments of all agents to all their variables and exchange of information among all agents, to check the consistency of assignments with constraints among agents [4–6]. The DCR model assumes that the data held by agents cannot be centralized. Most studies of DCR search algorithms consider the motivation for this assumption to be privacy: consider the hospital example again, in which head nurses of different wards are assigning nurses to shifts while considering the personal constraints of the nurses in each ward. Head nurses would not want to reveal the personal data of nurses in their ward and their own personal preferences and considerations. The only information that a head nurse needs to reveal regarding her ward is the time slots in which she is assigning an Emergency Room qualified nurse, while keeping all other information private.

4.1 Example of a DCR Algorithm

Let us now step through an example of a (very) simple DCR algorithm and see how it proceeds. The simple algorithm is called: synchronous back tracking (SBT) [7]. The algorithm assumes that constraints map joint assignments to either "satisfiable" or "inconsistent" constraints, which makes the problem a DCSP. The SBT approach for solving this type of problem is the simplest possible, but for simplicity, we also introduce several common assumptions:

- Every agent handles only one variable (which means that in this simple example an agent and a variable can be treated as the same thing).
- The domain of the variables is represented as a set of natural numbers.
- Only binary constraints are available in the given problem.
- The agents are lexicographically ordered. That is, agent i precedes agent j in the total ordering if $i < j$.

Given the previous assumptions, the following is the SBT pseudocode:

The algorithm's starting point can be seen in the initialize method. This method is the first to be called by each agent; any other operations that the agent may perform will be in response to receiving a message. The first agent initializes a variable called CPA, which carries a consistent tuple of the assignments of the agents it passed so far. The first agent initializes the search by creating a CPA, assigning its variable on the CPA and sending the CPA to the next agent. Every agent that receives the CPA tries to assign its variable without violating constraints with the assignments on the CPA. If the agent succeeds to find such an assignment to its variable, it appends the assignment to the tuple on the CPA and sends it to the next agent. If it cannot find a consistent assignment, it sends the CPA back to the previous agent to change its assignment, thus performing a chronological backtrack. An agent that receives a backtrack message removes the assignment of its variable and tries to reassign it with a consistent value. The algorithm ends successfully if the last agent manages to find a consistent assignment for its variable. The algorithm ends unsuccessfully if the first agent encounters an empty domain. [8]

5 Agent Implementation Example

Accessibility and ease of use is a fundamental requirement of any application framework. Algorithm designers often require a simple and clean API, which abstract away information on the execution environment. This enables the designer to focus on the algorithms' logic and not on the environment.

The AgentZero programming API is designed to match these clear requirements. Written in Java, Fig. 16.3 presents an SBT implementation corresponding to the pseudocode shown in Fig. 16.2.The previously mentioned pseudo code assumptions still apply and most of the algorithm's pseudocode can be directly translated into the programming API.

6 Agent Implementation

The following covers the part of the API related to agent implementation as can be seen in Fig. 16.3. Agents in AgentZero extend the SimpleAgent abstract class—this class provides an extensive domain-specific language for agents and the following features:

- **Single initialization point**—every agent defines a start method, which will get automatically called as soon as the agent is started.
- **Message sending**—using the API: send(<message-name>, <message-args>).to*(...). This send method is a variadic method, which returns a mediation object that is initialized with the message name and a package of the message arguments. The mediation object has many useful "to*" methods like toNextAgent, toNeighbores, etc. By calling these methods, the actual message is passed to the mailer.
- **Message to method binding**—in the above example, one may notice the usage of the @WhenReceived(<message-name>) annotation. This syntax will cause the agent to automatically call the annotated method when a message with name

```
initialize:
  if first agent:
    create new CPA
    assignCPA()

assignCPA:
   if exists v such that CPA ∪ {< i,v >} is consistent:
     if is-full(CPA)
       send ["TERMINATE", "Solution-found", CPA] to all agents
     else
       send ["CPA", CPA] to next agent
   else
     backtrack()

backtrack:
  if first agent:
    send ["TERMINATE", "No-Solution"] to all agents
  else
    send ["BACKTRACK"] to previous agent

when-received["CPA"](cpa):
  CPA ← cpa
  assignCPA()

when-received["BACKTRACK"]():
  CPA ← CPA - {< i,v >}
  backtrack()

when-received["TERMINATE"](reason):
   end execution
```

Fig. 16.2 The pseudocode of SBT

equals to the name specified in the annotation arrives. The message arguments are unpackaged into the annotated method while invoking it—this behavior resembles RPC behavior, which makes it very easy to manage messages.

- **Termination signaling**—instead of handling the termination of the agent itself, the SimpleAgent includes many useful "finish*" methods, which automatically broadcast a termination signal. Due to the fact that AgentZero is a simulated MAS environment, several of the "finish*" methods also support submitting the algorithm's results, which can then be tested for correctness or aggregated into a final report.

```
public class SBTAgent extends SimpleAgent {
  Assignment cpa;
  public void start() {
    if (this.isFirstAgent()) {
      cpa = new Assignment();
       assignCPA();
    }
  }

  void assignCPA() {
    for (Integer v : getDomain()) {
      if (cpa.isConsistentWith(getId(), v, getProblem())) {
        cpa.assign(getId(), v);
        if (cpa.isFull()) finish(cpa);
        else send("CPA" , cpa).toNextAgent();
        return;
      }
    }
     backtrack();
  }

  void backtrack() {
    if (isFirstAgent()) finishWithNoSolution();
    else send("BACKTRACK").toPreviousAgent ();
  }

   @WhenReceived("CPA" )
   void handleCPA(Assignment cpa) {
    this .cpa = cpa;
    assignCPA();
  }

  @WhenReceived ("BACKTRACK")
  void handleBacktrack() {
    cpa.unassign(getId());
    backtrack();
  }
}
```

Fig. 16.3 SBT implementation with AgentZero programming API

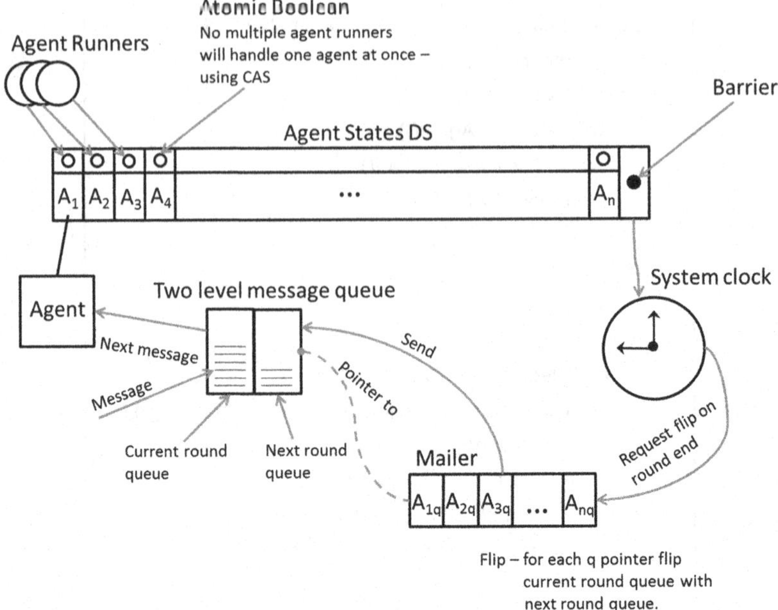

Fig. 16.4 Schematic diagram of the synchronous execution

6.1 Technical Aspects of Simulated Execution

AgentZero simulates a complex MAS network using threads. In the following section, a technical overview of the synchronous execution simulation is described. To build a local agent memory, all messages that are passed between threads are automatically deep-copied. The first step of an AgentZero execution is to configure the environment requested according to a specific configuration file; this enables and configures modules in the environment. This first step entails initializing all the requested modules and generating databases according to the statistic collectors (if this was not already done by previous executions). The next AgentZero step is creating agent runners; there are worker threads that are each responsible for the execution of one or more agents. In synchronous execution, the number of worker threads is the same as the number of CPU cores that the executing computer has. This setup was tested to produce the most efficient and fast execution. After the agent runner threads are up, a structure called agent-states is initialized. This is a shared structure between all the agent runners. This data structure coordinates the agent runners during the execution. Figure 16.4 shows a schematic diagram of the synchronous execution.

As shown in Fig. 16.4, at each round (a.k.a. iteration), the agent runners iterate on the agent states data-structure. By performing the atomic CPU instruction—CAS (Compare and Swap)—on the atomic Boolean, which guards each agent state, the agent runner insures that it is the only thread that currently manages the specific agent state. While managing the agent state, the agent runner will drive the agent to handle all of the requests that are in its current round queue. The agent's queue is a two-layer queue. One belongs to the current round, and the other to the next round. When the agent takes the next message, it will retrieve it from the current round queue, and when the agent sends a message, the mailer will put it in the next round queue of the recipient agent. When the agent is done handling all of its current round messages, the agent runner will continue to iterate and try to drive the next unhandled agent. At the end of the agent states data-structure, there is a barrier. Every agent runner will eventually reach the barrier and when the last runner will enter the barrier, the system clock will be triggered. The system clock will notify its listeners of the end of the round. One of these listeners is the mailer, which has a pointer to all of the agent queues. At the end of the round, the mailer will flip each agent's current round queue with the next round queue and release the barrier, after which this whole process will start over again and continue to do so until the algorithm is done.

6.2 Execution Environment Modules

In AgentZero, agent implementation is decoupled from the execution environment it is running in; thus, every algorithm can be executed on each of these modes. In every environment, one can associate a set of modules, which can generate special problem types, test the solution or the way to the solution, collect wanted statistics, visualize the algorithm progress and many more module types. Although AgentZero comes bundled with many module implementations, the module implementations themselves are not closely coupled with the system and can be contributed via third-party implementers. Every module has its own simple API for creating your own variant of the module. In fact, many of the modules that AgentZero comes bundled with were contributed by the BGU DCR group members while working with the tool. AgentZero has an extensive documentation where you can find all the standard module names. From the AgentZero lab website,[1] one can download and contribute more modules. The modules, similar to the agent definition, are decoupled from the execution environment. The combination of all these modules and algorithms assembles an experiment. This makes the creation of the modules and algorithms very easy, as one needs not care about the execution environment's internal architecture and its comprising components.

---

[1]The complete AgentZero software package is available to DCR researchers and students at our DCR homepage http://www.cs.bgu.ac.il/~dcr. It is routinely used by all members of the DCR research group at BGU. In addition, it is the main tool by which graduate students studying distributed constraints algorithms implement their final projects.

7 Simulation Front End

An important aspect that is often missed or neglected by other research tools and MAS frameworks is the front end and the ease of use both for new and advanced users. AgentZero walks the extra mile by providing simple and powerful front end for developers and researchers.

7.1 Simulation Results Analysis

During the development phase of a problem-solving MAS, the developer has certain needs that cannot be fully satisfied without a proper user interface. For example, to optimize the algorithm, the developer has a need to watch statistical data immediately after each execution. To debug the algorithm, it can be helpful to be able to see the problem, view run-time logs, and even sometimes look at visualizations to better understand the way in which the algorithm works. AgentZero attempts at addressing all these needs via an interactive Eclipse plugin. Using the plugin, it is easy to set up an AgentZero project, creating agents and modules, and viewing the execution data. The plugin also gives the opportunity to use a better debugging mode by automatically saving failed scenarios and providing the possibility to reexecute them with a debugger attached.

7.2 Simulated Environment Visualization

One of the best ways for understanding how an algorithm (or an application) works is to observe visualizations that represent different points of view on the algorithm's execution. An important feature of AgentZero is its ability to visualize the simulated environment. Visualizing an application execution is a two-step process—analysis step and visualization step. The first step includes monitoring an execution by watching the side-effects it induces on the environment and marking important events. The second step focuses on organizing these events on a timeline and presenting these events to the user. As a large simulated environment that is executed on a single core machine will incorrectly translate simulation time into real world time, special measures are taken to produce visualizations that are close to the way the application will operate on a real distributed MAS. Figure 16.5 shows one of the available visualizations that comes with AgentZero—the network traffic visualization that allows the user to understand the impact each agent has on the simulated network.

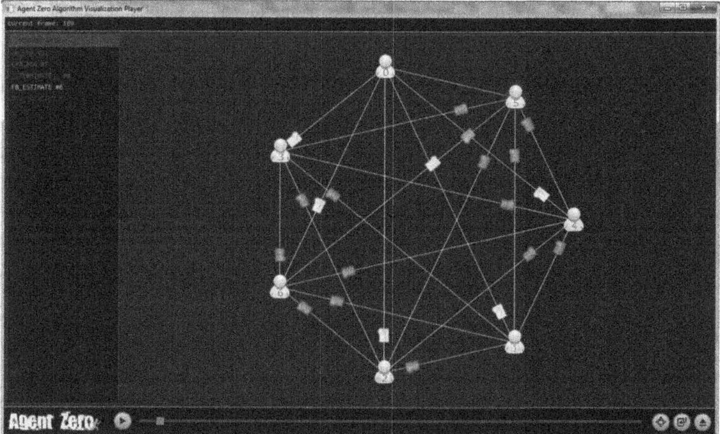

Fig. 16.5 Network traffic—shows the message passing between agents and the responses to these messages

8 Comparison to Related MAS Simulators

AgentZero is a new addition to the DCR research field. Two different DCR specialized MAS simulators already exist, DisChoco and FRODO. In the following, we briefly describe these tools and then compare them to AgentZero and MASS, which is a general MAS simulation tool.

8.1 DisChoco

DisChoco [9] is a Java platform for solving DCR problems developed by Redouane Ezzahir and Mohamed Wahbi—it came with relatively extensive library of problem generators and uses an internal communication simulator. It also has the ability to deploy the agents in a real distributed system.

8.2 FRODO

FRODO [10] is a Java open-source framework for distributed combinatorial optimization, initially developed at the Artificial Intelligence Laboratory (LIA) of École Polytechnique Fédérale de Lausanne (EPFL), Switzerland. FRODO comes with several built-in algorithms and a suite of problem generators for benchmarking. It also support out-of-the-box small number of statistics relevant to DCR.

8.3 MASS

The multi-agent simulation suite (MASS) [15] is a software package intended to enable modelers to utilize the tools of agent-based simulation in various fields, without having to develop heavy programming skills. In the context of this chapter, MASS is a generic MAS simulation that provides a new programming language and IDE that is used to define the behavior of the agent. It than allows relatively easy implementation of an environment for the agent to execute on top and contains several tools to configure this environment and to examine execution results and statistics.

In Table 16.1, we compare the different multi-agent simulation tools along various functionality, usability, and practical criteria. Our observations indicate that AgentZero, although generic and applicable to many domains, specifically introduces benefits for the DCR simulation domain. Note that AgentZero supports most of the features provided by existing simulation tools and also provides a simple, extensive, and better streamlined user experience and research facilities.

9 Summary

This chapter refers to multi-agents systems that support DCR and its search algorithms. In particular, it presents a new simulation tool—AgentZero—for distributed search algorithms for DCOPs. The complexity of DCR algorithmic simulation and its consequent importance is briefly discussed and an example of an agent implementing distributed optimization search was presented. The DCR field is an important example for agent-oriented programming that includes a complex algorithmic component.

In order to alleviate the burden of design and testing of DCR algorithms, a simulation tool like AgentZero is a necessity. In its core, AgentZero is an agent-based simulator that specializes in simulating a DCR-oriented environment. It exposes a relatively simple and intuitive API for implementing agents and has the ability to measure the efficiency of the behavior of agents following the algorithmic protocol in the simulated environment. AgentZero provides a solution for researchers investigating the behavior of different algorithms as it enables comparative simulated studies without the need to set up a large costly and complicated network of agents. For this reason, it serves as one of the main research tools at the BGU DCR group and it is used by students in several DCR-related courses. One can say that MAS simulators are an essential tool for every MAS development and testing environment and not only specific to the DCR area. One may also comment on the need for them to be adjustable and extensible, as suggested by AgentZero. A lot has been learned while developing and applying AgentZero. On the technical side, we have learned about different models for simulation of MAS

Table 16.1 Comparison of different MAS simulation tools

	DisChoco	FRODO	MASS	AgentZero
Functionality	Automatic statistic collection			
	Yes, but limited	No	No	Yes, by using hooks
	Execution modes—supported out of the box			
	Asynchronous	Asynchronous and Synchronous	Synchronous	Asynchronous and Synchronous
	Extendibility of the system (without changing the actual framework code)			
	No	Possible, but complicated	Very extendiblevia programming and in some cases via wizards	Very extendible, many module types available
	Out-of-the box statistics, execution visualizations and tools			
	Single primitive visualization, several statistics	No visualizations, several statistics	Contains a suite for defining statistics and visualizations	Several visualizations, many statistics. More statistics can be added as modules, currently there is no API for adding more visualizations
	Possibility to write non-DCR-related agents			
	Based on Choco, which is a general MAS	Yes	Yes	Yes
	Simulation of local memory on local execution			
	No, sharing pointers to messages	No, sharing pointers to messages	No	Achieved by deep-copying the messages automatically
	Support for execution timeouts			
	Unknown	Yes—only in local mode	Yes	Yes
	Tools for analyzing results			
	The UI shows some options but they are not implemented	No	Yes	Yes

(continued)

Table 16.1 (continued)

	DisChoco	FRODO	MASS	AgentZero
Usability	Agent Programming Language			
	Java	Java and XML	FABLES (dedicated language)	Java
	Documentation			
	No	Yes, including online tutorial	Complete, also offers courses for paying customers	Yes, including online tutorial
	Learning curve			
	Without documentation—very steep	Steep	Moderate-steep, requires learning a new programming language and for some operations Java knowledge is still required	Moderate
	Open source			
	Yes	Yes	The source is available for paying customers	Yes
	Requires modifying the source in order to add algorithms or applications			
	Yes	Yes	No	No
	User interface installation and overall usage			
	Desktop application—mostly non-functional, frequently crushes	Desktop application—many important features missing, not developer friendly	Eclipse integration for development and desktop application for working with the execution itself. Overall, the UI looks complete	Eclipse plug-in worked well. The desktop user interface s helpful for new users
Domain specific	Ability to reproduce an experiment			
	Yes	Yes	Yes	Yes

Ability to run large experiments			
Agent per thread only, thus limited size problems	Agent per thread only, thus limited size problems	Yes, supports execution locally, on local cluster and grid middleware	Support for agent per thread and multi-agents per thread. Support for using cloud computing
Automatic problem and scenario generation—built-in and external			
Built-in and support receiving problems in a dedicated format	Only built-in or by DisChoco	This tool does not specialize in DCR, thus no built-in problem generators are available	Yes
Does coding an agent with the framework resemble the pseudocode			
Partially	No	Yes, with FABLES, the code highly resembles the pseudocode	Yes
Ease of creating an experiment			
Not complicated, contains UI for building the experiment	Very easy, simple XML structure	Very easy, contains relatively easy to use UI	Very easy, simple XML structure
Portable problem format			
Yes	Yes	No	With dedicated problem generator module
Support for simulation of message delays, message corruption, or message loss			
All of the above	No	FABLES does not have fixed communication scheme, one would have to implement those features by himself as part of the model that can be rather difficult	Only message delays

environments. The design and development process has started from the simple but resource wasteful—agent per thread model and ended up by developing our own "reaction model" where threads can help one another in driving several agents together.

From the software engineering viewpoint, the goal was to develop a framework that is modular enough so that it will be able to simulate any environment and agents. Several ways to modularize the execution environment were investigated (e.g., OSGi—Alliance, OSGi. OSGi service platform, release 3. IOS Press, Inc., 2003.) But found too complex for our target audience, the final decision was to design a new module system, such that will be easily understandable for our users. From our users, we learned that the most difficult task related to writing applications on top of a MAS (a.k.a. agents) is the debugging process. Having a locally simulated environment makes it possible to use general-purpose debugging tools. Still, this task remains difficult.

AgentZero was already used in research setting [12–13]. AgentZero is continuously maintained, and we intend to keep extending it. One example is the addition of support for a dynamic execution environment, where agents and agent properties can be dynamically changed over time. Another example includes the addition of built-in support for scenario logging and reconstruction—a feature that we hope will reduce the complexity of debugging the agents' execution.

References

1. Waze. http://www.waze.com.
2. Meisels A (2011) Distributed search by constrained agents. IDC 2011: 5–9
3. Silaghi M, Yokoo M (2009) Distributed constraint reasoning. Encyclopedia of Artificial Intelligence, Information Science Reference (2008) [ISBN 978-1-59904-849-9]
4. Gershman A, Meisels A, Zivan R (2009) Asynchronous forward bounding. J Artif Intell Res 25–46(34)
5. Yeoh W, Felner A, Koenig S (2010) BnB-ADOPT: an asynchronous branch-and-bound DCOP algorithm. J Artif Intell Res 38:85–133
6. Yokoo M, Durfee HE, Ishida T, Kuwabara K (1998) The distributed constraint satisfaction problem: formalization and algorithms. IEEE Trans Knowl Data Eng 10:673–685
7. Meisels A (2007) Distributed search by constrained agents: algorithms, performance, communication. Springer, London
8. Zivan R, Meisels A (2003) Synchronous vs asynchronous search on discsps. Proceedings of the 1st European workshop on multiagent system, EUMAS
9. Ezzahir R, Bessiere C, Belaissaoui M, Bouyakhf EH (2007) DisChoco: a platform for distributed constraint programming. Retrieved from http://www2.lirmm.fr/coconut/dischoco/
10. Léauté T, Ottens B, Szymanek R (2012) FRODO: a FRamework for Open/Distributed Optimization. Retrieved from http://frodo2.sourceforge.net/index.php/research
11. Iványi M, Gulyás L, Bocsi R, Kozma V, Legendi R (2007) The multi-agent simulation suite. In: Emergent Agents and Socialities: Social and Organizational Aspects of Intelligence, pp 57–64
12. Grubshtein A, Meisels A (2012) Finding a nash equilibrium by asynchronous backtracking. CP 2012: 925–940
13. Peri O, Meisels A (2013) Synchronizing for performance-DCOP algorithms. In: Proceedings of the 5th International Conference on Agents and Artificial Intelligence (ICAART-2013), pp 5–14, Barcelona, February 2013

14. Bessiere C, Maestre A, Meseguer P (2001) Distributed dynamic backtracking. In: Proceedings of the 7th international conference on principles and practice of constraint programming. Springer, London, pp 772–
15. Jay Modi P, Shen W-M, Tambe M, Yokoo M (2005) ADOPT: asynchronous distributed constraints optimization with quality guarantees. Artif Intell 161(2):149–180
16. Petcu A, Faltings B (2005) A scalable method for multiagent constraint optimization, Proceedings of the 19th international joint conference on artificial intelligence. Edinburgh, Scotland, pp 266–271
17. Zivan R, Meisels A (2006) Concurrent search for distributed CSPs. Artif Intell 170(4–5):440–461

Index

Printed in the United States
By Bookmasters